BEYOND THE PASSION

BEYOND THE PASSION

Rethinking the Death and Life of Jesus

Stephen J. Patterson

Fortress Press
Minneapolis

Cover and book design: Zan Ceeley

Library of Congress Cataloging-in-Publication Data
Patterson, Stephen J.
  Beyond the Passion : rethinking the death and life of Jesus / Stephen J.
Patterson.
    p. cm.
  ISBN 0-8006-3674-0 (pbk. : alk. paper)—ISBN 0-8006-6091-9 (hardcover
with jacket : alk. paper)
  1. Jesus Christ—Biography. I. Title.
  BT301.3.P38 2004
  232.9'01—dc22
                                    2004011584

Manufactured in the U.S.A.
08   07   06   05   04   1   2   3   4   5   6   7   8   9   10

For
John Warren Patterson
1931–2004

Contents

Abbreviations

AB	Anchor Bible
ABD	*Anchor Bible Dictionary.* Ed. D. N. Freedman. 6 vols. New York: Doubleday, 1992
alt.	altered translation
ANF	*Ante-Nicene Fathers*
Ant.	Josephus, *Antiquities of the Jews*
BHT	Beiträge zur historischen Theologie
CBQ	*Catholic Biblical Quarterly*
CIL	*Corpus Inscriptiones Latinarum.* Berlin: Reimer, 1893–
FCBS	Fortress Classics in Biblical Studies
FRLANT	Forschungen zur Religion und Literatur des Alten und Neuen Testaments
HDR	Harvard Dissertations in Religion
HNT	Handbuch zum Neuen Testament
HR	*History of Religions*
HTR	*Harvard Theological Review*
HTS	Harvard Theological Studies
JSNTSup	Journal for the Study of the New Testament Supplement Series
LCL	Loeb Classical Library
LSJ	H. G. Liddell, Robert Scott, H. Stuart Jones, and Roderick McKenzie, *Greek-English Lexicon,* 9th edition, with supplement. Oxford: Clarendon, 1968
MT	Masoretic text
NRSV	New Revised Standard Version
NTAbh	Neutestamentliche Abhandlungen
NTS	*New Testament Studies*
NTTS	New Testament Tools and Studies
OGIS	*Orientis Graeci Inscriptiones Selectae.* Ed. W. Dittenberger. 2 vols. Reprint. Hildesheim: Olms, 1960
OTP	*The Old Testament Pseudepigrapha.* Ed. James H. Charlesworth. 2 vols. Garden City, N.Y.: Doubleday, 1983–1985
PNTC	Pelican New Testament Commentaries
RB	*Revue biblique*
SBLDS	Society of Biblical Literature Dissertation Series

SBS	Stuttgarter Bibelstudien
SHR	Studies in the History of Religions
SIG	*Sylloge inscriptionum graecarum.* Ed. W. Dittenberger. 3d ed. 4 vols. Leipzig: Olms, 1915–24
SJ	Studia Judaica
SJLA	Studies in Judaism in Late Antiquity
SNTSMS	Society for New Testament Studies Monograph Series
ThQ	*Theologische Quartalschrift*
TRE	*Theologische Realenzyklopädie.* Ed. G. Krause and G. Müller. Berlin: de Gruyter, 1977–
War	Josephus, *The Jewish War*
ZNW	*Zeitschrift für die neutestamentliche Wissenschaft und die Kunde der älteren Kirche*

Introduction

Is Jesus Dead?

I s Jesus dead? It ought to have been a simple question. Jesus lived—
and died—almost two thousand years ago. He was executed by the
Roman governor of Palestine in about the year 35 C.E. Of course
he is dead. He is not alive somewhere today, living incognito in the
south of France. We will not be spotting Jesus ordering a hamburger
in a McDonald's restaurant in Nairobi. He is a figure of the past. He is
dead.

Yet if someone were to ask this simple question today, many would
find it difficult to answer with a simple yes or no. One might not even
have to be a Christian for the question to sound slightly odd. Christian or not, just about everyone associates the name of Jesus with
claims of resurrection. For believers, merely to entertain the thought
"Is Jesus dead?" will be more than a little discomfiting—a flirtation,
even, with blasphemy. Could he be dead? Certainly not! "Jesus is
alive!" we Christians say. "God raised him from the dead!" Then he is
alive? With a little thought, questions arise. If we say Jesus is alive, in
what sense precisely do we imagine this to be true? *Might* we expect to
spot him ordering a hamburger in a McDonald's? A silly thought;
Jesus is not Elvis. Many believers might say that Jesus is alive, but in

1

heaven with God. If one believes in heaven as a place where people go when they die, this may seem sensible. If heaven awaits the dead, then we might well say that Jesus ended up there too. But we would not consider all of those dearly departed saints of heaven to be *alive*. They are dead, or, more delicately, "They have passed away." Has Jesus passed away? This too sounds odd, I suspect.

The question, "Is Jesus dead?" certainly sounded odd to me. It came at the end of a talk I was giving on the life of Jesus, posed by someone who, as it turned out, was troubled by the fact that my discussion had not included a single word about the resurrection. What Jesus said, the things that he did—these historical matters were quite interesting, but ultimately not very important. The life of Jesus, after all, ended in death. For most Christian believers, what is truly remarkable and important about Jesus is not his life, but his resurrection from the dead. Jesus' death is significant not as the end of Jesus' life, but as the first half of the saving event that comprises the Christian gospel: the death and resurrection of Jesus. This great divine cosmic event, around which all of human history pivots, is what saves us from our sins. Apart from this, the death of Jesus would simply be the meaningless end to an interesting but insignificant life. I soon came to understand that "Is Jesus dead?" really meant "So what?"

In this book I intend to challenge this "So what?" One of the great mistakes of Christian theology has been our attempt to understand the death and resurrection of Jesus apart from his life. The first followers of Jesus generally did not do this. All four of the New Testament Gospels tell of Jesus' death as part of the story of his life. His death and resurrection are directly related to his life; they issue from it. In the Gospels, Jesus is put to death for the things he says and does. God then raises him from the dead to undo the injustice done to Jesus, and to place a divine stamp of approval on the words and deeds of Jesus as the words and deeds of a genuine Son of God. This pattern of thinking belongs to the ancient tradition of martyrdom. In this tradition, death and resurrection do not stand alone. Indeed, apart from the life of the martyr, in which comes to expression all that he or she stands for, the cause for which the martyr was willing to die, the death of the martyr has no meaning. Left to itself, the martyr's violent death becomes nothing more than a focus for sadomasochistic passions, or perhaps a tableau to satisfy our prurient fascinations with human violence and death.

Imagine, if you will, celebrating the annual Martin Luther King Jr. holiday simply by fixing our gaze once again on King's death. Over and over again we would replay the film footage of his assassination at the Lorraine Hotel in Memphis. Scholars and preachers might focus on his final twelve hours, his last meal, what he wore, his dying words. They might reflect on the significance of the weapon that killed him, his time of death, or the sort of casket in which he was laid out. Perhaps the actual moment of his death could be re-created and filmed. Imagine spending the holiday like this, all the while saying nothing about King's life. No interest in his great manifesto, "I Have a Dream." No concern for such great prophecies as the "Letter from a Birmingham Jail." Not a word about civil rights, desegregation, the Vietnam War, or King's vision of peace and justice in a world torn by violence and hatred. To celebrate his death apart from the cause for which he lived would be ridiculous and meaningless.

Yet this is what we have done for the most part with Jesus. For most Christians the Apostles' Creed is quite sufficient: Jesus was born of the Virgin Mary, suffered under Pontius Pilate, was crucified, dead, and buried. After the Virgin Birth we leap over Jesus' life to take in his death in all its significance, as if it could be significant without a life to make it so. But so it has become to us: his death is the sacrifice that ensures our forgiveness before a God torn between anger and compassion. What need do we have of his life if it is his death that ensures our salvation? But this was not so for the earliest friends and followers of Jesus. They were profoundly devoted to his way of life, and they used his death to call attention to his life. They did not see his death or his resurrection as events significant in themselves. They were the fitting end of a life of extraordinary power and vision, a life to be embraced and remembered as epiphanic. Virtually every word spoken about the death of Jesus among his first followers was calculated to resurrect the significance of Jesus' life for those who loved him, and would come to love him in the years ahead. They spoke of the movement he began as "the way"—his way of life.

I have arranged the material that follows into three basic sections, each with a focus on a distinct early Christian understanding of Jesus' death: Jesus as "Victim," as "Martyr," and as "Sacrifice." I will treat these categories separately, but they are interrelated. Each overlaps with and is woven into the others to create a loose, if complex, web of meaning surrounding Jesus' death. These strands are nonetheless worth pulling apart so that one may see them for themselves and so understand their distinctive contributions more clearly. In many ways these strands represent familiar territory for us, and into them are woven some of our most cherished ideas about Jesus' death, such as the atonement. But as I revisited these ancient Christian ideas for myself, and examined them in their ancient context, I encountered many surprising things long forgotten and lost under the great pile of medieval atonement theology with which most Christians are burdened today. In the end, I hope to show that these three strands, though distinct, work together to point the would-be follower of Jesus back to his life—to his words, his deeds, and his fate—as a life to be embraced as *the* life, and a fate to call one's own.

Is Jesus dead? It is not a simple question. The earliest friends and followers of Jesus did not answer it with a simple yes or no. They pondered the question, as they pondered the fate of the one they had come to love. They thought about who killed him and why. They thought about the God they had come to know through him, and through the Jewish traditions of their ancestors, and they considered how such a God would react to this tragic, brutal event. They also thought about the fact that even though Jesus was dead, he was not dead *to them*. His spirit was still coursing through their veins. How was this so? What did it mean?

Prologue

The Crucifixion of a Nobody

Hope is not always history, and neither is hyperbole.
In this case, as so often before and after, horror is history.
—John Dominic Crossan, *Who Killed Jesus?*

What Happened to Jesus?

Before we can begin to understand and appreciate the early Christian response to the death of Jesus, we must first have some realistic idea of what happened to him. This is difficult for Christians. From the time we are old enough to understand the stories of the Christian faith, read to us from the pulpit Bible in the tiniest of churches to the great cathedrals, we have seen the events of Jesus' final days unfold before us like a great pageant. Jesus comes to Jerusalem to challenge his enemies, the chief priests, the scribes, and the Pharisees. They have plotted all along to gain his demise. Now he plays right into their hands. He does so deliberately. He knows his fate ahead of time—how he is to be betrayed by one of his own, arrested, tortured, crucified, and after three days rise from the dead. It is all part of God's plan to save us from our sins, which the old religion of the Jews, the religion of law and legalism, could not do.

Thus rendered in this mixture of text and tradition, the death of Jesus is not a calamity, or even a surprise. It is the result of a well-executed, successful plan to create what we know today as the Christian religion. It is a great triumph, not a tragedy. In the end, it is not just Christ's triumph we celebrate in this story, but our own as well. The story of Jesus' death and resurrection has been central to Christians' understanding of themselves over against Jews. His death symbolizes their rejection of the Messiah; his resurrection signals that we are right, they were/are wrong.[1]

But this was not how Jesus' first followers actually experienced his death. This story comes from writers and theologians a generation removed from the actual events surrounding Jesus' death. It was created during a time of great animosity between Jews and those who followed Jesus (by then a group comprising both Jews and Gentiles). It presupposes a great deal of theological reflection on the ultimate significance of Jesus and his fate. Told in context, it can become a powerful and moving story. But it is seldom told in this way—as a story in context. It is usually presented as history, that is, *what really happened*. In fact, I have never heard the story of Good Friday presented to a congregation in a way that did not at least imply its utter historicity. The worst consequence of this has been the legacy of Christian anti-Semitism that has grown from the mistaken notion that "the Jews" were responsible for the death of Jesus. This is one of the great lies of Western civilization, and the origin of unfathomable evil. But a second consequence has had to do more with Christians themselves and their understanding of Jesus and his meaning for our lives. As a story whose content is supplied by theological reflection, it does not turn out to be a very realistic story from a human point of view. It is the story of the death of a god, not of a human being. As such, it can be difficult to connect with as a real human experience.

I can recall seeing cracks in the historical facade placed on this story already as a child hearing it again and again. Why, for example, if Jesus' death was part of God's greater plan, is Judas not worshiped as a saint rather than vilified as a traitor? Or why, if Jesus knew what was happening all the time, did he cry out from the cross with his last breath, "My God, my God, why have you forsaken me?" (Mark 15:34). Or how shall we view the dramatic scene in Gethsemane, in which Jesus prays that he might be delivered from what must soon take place (Mark 14:32-42)? Is this reported history? How would the author have known what Jesus said on that occasion? From the story we learn that the only witnesses, the disciples, were asleep. And what of the trial scenes? In Mark, the only witnesses present—the Jewish leadership of Jerusalem—are hostile (14:55-65; 15:1-5). How did Mark come by so many details that would impugn their role in the matter? Or who could have reported on the private conversation between Pilate and Jesus in the Johannine account of the trial (John 18:33-38)? And what reconnaissance produced the communiqué between Pilate and his wife concerning her dreams (Matt 27:19)?

In due course we shall return to the biblical stories and other traditions attached to Jesus' death, to read them in context as early Christian attempts to give meaning to the dramatic end of his life. They are not history but interpretations of a history, told from the vantage point of an omniscient narrator. But in order to appreciate all that these stories are trying to accomplish, we must begin somewhere else—with the event they are trying to interpret: the death of Jesus. What do we really know about what happened to him? We have but a few facts with which to work, but they can tell us quite a lot.

Crucifixion

We know that Jesus was crucified, probably around Passover, in Jerusalem, by order of the Roman prefect of Judea, Pontius Pilate. This is not much information, but it tells us something significant about Jesus and why he was killed.

Crucifixion was in Jesus' day Rome's trademark means of executing peasants involved in seditious activity against the empire.[2] The Romans did not invent it—the Persians and Carthaginians used it before them to punish errant generals and governors. But one might say the Romans perfected it as the ultimate weapon of terror and intimidation. They did not use it against errant leaders, but against slaves and peasants. They used it against common criminals to deter crime. They used it in laying siege to cities, crucifying enemy captives in plain sight of those inside the city walls in an attempt to demoralize and break the will of the enemy by this gruesome display. But most importantly, they used it to punish peasant rebels in outlying districts. Sometimes leaders were crucified individually; sometimes whole groups were crucified en masse. For example, when Jesus would still have been a small child, a peasant insurrection broke out across Palestine when Herod died and the Jews feared that his much-loathed sons would be given to rule over Palestine. Varus, the Roman general in charge of quashing the rebellion, burned to the ground the towns of Sepphoris, Sappho, and Emmaus, and sold their inhabitants into slavery. Afterward his army searched the countryside for those who had escaped and had them crucified—about two thousand in all—their writhing, tortured bodies providing the necessary message.[3] At the start of the Jewish War (66 C.E.) the Roman governor of Judea, Florus, crucified 3,600 people, including children and infants.[4] Jesus was not the only person to die on a Roman cross. Thousands of peasants suffered this same fate in his day. Crucifixion was highly organized, massive state terrorism,[5] intended to intimidate the vast peasant and slave populations of the empire into passivity. Its record of success is rather impressive. The Roman *Pax* was seldom interrupted by insurrection during the period of the empire, and when unrest did break out, it was usually short-lived.

What does this tell us about the death of Jesus? It tells us that his executioners were Roman, not Jewish. To be sure, Rome could not control a province like Judea without high-level local collaboration. In Jesus' day the high priesthood would have been co-opted entirely by Rome. But this does not get Pilate off the hook. The cross of Jesus was a Roman cross. History cannot get any plainer than this. One of the great ironies of history, it turns out, is that for centuries Gentile Christians have blamed Jews for the death of Jesus, when in fact it was a Gentile official of a Gentile state who had Jesus, a Jew, executed like so many other Jews of his day.

It also tells us that his crime was sedition against the Roman state. This implication is often dismissed on the grounds that Jesus' message was a "religious" one, not "political." But in the ancient world there was no such distinction between religion and politics. The empire was divinely ordained, the emperor God's Son. Worship was to the gods Roma and Augustus. In Judea, Roman tribute may even have been collected in collaboration with the high priest.[6] Jesus could not speak of a new kingdom, an empire of God, without implicating the religious *and* political structures that dominated his life. The preaching of Jesus undermined these structures completely. The suspicion that his ideas were seditious to the Roman Empire was not mistaken.

It tells us also that he was regarded by his executioners as nothing, a peasant nobody who had the unmitigated temerity to challenge the great Roman *Pax*. But this nobody could be used. The manner of his death could intimidate others who might be inspired by what he did. He was crucified as a warning to others: this is what happens to people who might be tempted to think as he dared to think.

What was so intimidating about crucifixion? Quite simply, it was a very slow, agonizing, public way to die. If the victim was flogged, or otherwise tortured prior to the actual crucifixion, death might come more quickly. But victims of the cross might also survive for days, as exposure to the elements, animals, and unkind passersby gradually wore them down. The fear, delirium, loss of control over bodily function all would have contributed to the shame of the peasant victim. Death might come by shock, exposure, or sometimes suffocation, as the weight of the victim's body forced it to collapse in upon itself, making it more and more difficult to take air into the lungs. Loved ones and others could watch—that was the point, after all—but they could not help the victim. Guards were posted to prevent rescue. In the end, not much was left of the victim of crucifixion. The remains would have been disposed of in summary fashion, piled with other corpses nearby, so that the dogs and ravens might finish the work already begun on the cross. This, too, was the point of crucifixion. The victim was not properly buried; his or her soul was not laid to rest. This was, to ancient sensibilities, the curse of eternal shame.

Imagining Jesus' Death

How shall we imagine the death of Jesus, taking all of this into account? It begins with a Passover pilgrim from a remote place, a nobody in the expansive Roman imperial east. But this peasant does not believe that he is a nobody. Nor will he accept this for his companions: lepers, prostitutes, outcasts, tanners, weavers, fishers. He goes to the Temple, as all others do.[7] But he is moved to anger by the scene there. What combination of emotions might have stirred him is impossible to know. As a Jew it was the center of his piety, the locus of God's sojourning with his people. Yet its keepers were also closely allied with Roman power, appointed by the Roman prefect in Caesarea, co-opted. Here is where his expendability to the larger Roman world began. So he is angry. Perhaps he does something to disrupt activity around the Temple. Perhaps he just says the wrong thing in the wrong place at the wrong time. It *is* during Passover, after all. Any small thing would be enough. If there is a trial, it does not last long. He is a peasant, a nobody. The whole world is not watching. How many would even have noticed his disappearance? If Jesus speaks, as he has done on many occasions before, of another kingdom, another empire, God's empire, the charge of sedition is secured. Why, after all, speak of another empire, an empire as God would have it, if there is not something wrong with *the* empire. And so he is crucified, not alone, but with others—probably more than two. In truth, he was crucified with thousands. If he died quickly, we should imagine him being tortured severely before he ever gets crucified. On the cross he dies of shock, or perhaps suffocation. In the end, it would not be customary for friends to take away the body. John Dominic Crossan has suggested that his body likely ended up on a pile of corpses, carrion for the dogs and the birds.[8]

I must admit that when I first read this in Crossan's book I was shocked. But in his description of the death of Jesus he had done something that all the tradition and piety of my religious training had rendered impossible through the years: he had made the death of Jesus real for me. Death—violent death—*is* a shocking thing. The image of Jesus' body lying on a pile of corpses, festering, swarmed by flies, and torn at by ravenous dogs knocked the wind out of me. It stunned me. Then I knew, for the first time, something of how those who followed him must have experienced this event. It was violent and terrifying, filled with agony and grief.

How does one find meaning in a death so violent and repulsive, so wrenching and depressing? This was the challenge faced by Jesus' first followers. No doubt, many of those who were with him disappeared back into the crowd after this. The terror of the cross had done its work. But some did not disappear. They did not give up. They got through the tragedy and horror of the moment, and then began to consider it. They considered it in light of all Jesus had meant to them, in light of the Jewish tradition, and in light of what they were beginning to experience again. Jesus had been killed, but his spirit was not dead yet. The tragedy of Jesus' death was not the final word. Words began to transform it into something else altogether: something definitive for who they would become; something that would give purpose to their lives; something that would redeem them from despair. The death of a nobody was not nothing after all.

Victim

*Whatever the personal aspirations and hopes of Jesus were,
his message of the coming of God's kingdom did not leave him
as the victor, but as the victim.*
—Helmut Koester, "Jesus the Victim" (1992)

Jesus, the Victim of Empire

Jesus was born into an age of peace and security such as the world had never known. It was the age of Augustus—the Augustan renaissance. The hoped-for time of peace and prosperity had finally arrived. Horace, the best-known poet of this age, proclaimed its arrival in idyllic verse:

> In safety range the cattle o'er the mead:
> Sweet Peace, soft Plenty, swell the golden grain:
> O'er unvex'd seas the sailors blithely speed:
> Fair Honour shrinks from stain:
>
> No guilty lusts the shrine of home defile:
> Cleansed is the hand without, the heart within:
> The father's features in his children smile
> Swift vengeance follows sin.
>
> Who fears the Parthian or the Scythian horde,
> Or the rank growth that German forests yield,
> While Caesar lives, who trembles at the sword
> The fierce Iberians wield?

In his own hills each labours down the day,
Teaching the vine to clasp the widow'd tree:
Then to his cups again, where, feasting gay,
He hails his god in thee. (*Odes* 4.5; LCL)

Peace, prosperity, purity, law and order—these were the watchwords of the Augustan renaissance. Jesus was born into this time. But he did not thrive in it. To the contrary, he ran afoul of this pure and virtuous age, and in the end, became its victim. How could this be?

How and why Jesus became the victim of the Roman Empire was one of the first things his followers had to come to grips with in the wake of his tragic death. This fact would shape the community of his followers in a profound way: it meant that they could never see themselves at peace with the empire and its lord. The movement that Jesus created would declare its loyalty to another Lord and another empire, and it would place at its center the things that placed Jesus at odds with *the* empire. It would become a community that was profoundly countercultural.

To understand how Jesus' death as a victim of Rome became meaningful to his followers, we might try first to understand the Roman Empire and how Jesus' words and deeds brought him into conflict with it. His crucifixion was no accident. It was meant to serve notice to anyone who would follow him that the penalty for such ideas and activity would be humiliation and agonizing death. So what was the problem with Jesus? Or, rather, what was it about the Roman imperial age that put Jesus on a collision course with those who were its guardians?

The *Pax Romana*

Romans liked to speak of their spreading domain as a great *pax*, or "peace"—the *Pax Romana*.[1] But it was a peace established and maintained through violence and intimidation. Augustus Caesar, the chief architect of the great Roman *Pax*, boasted at the end of his life that he had "brought the whole world under the empire of the Roman people."[2] Indeed, he had. Spain, Gaul, the region of the Alps, Germany, Greece, Asia Minor, Persia, the Middle East, Egypt, Ethiopia, North Africa—all lay under Roman imperial control by the end of his reign in 14 C.E. This great expansion was accomplished by the relentless waging of war. So fearsome were Rome's legions that many kings and peoples simply requested annexation to the empire, rather than face the onslaught of Caesar's troops. They knew that resistance was futile. Those who dared try were simply exterminated or enslaved. The Roman *Pax* was anything but peaceful in coming.

Palestine itself provides an excellent illustration of how one of Rome's provinces would have experienced the *Pax Romana*. On the surface, Rome's relationship to Judea and its surrounds might have appeared quite amicable. For the first century of Roman domination, Judea still had its king, its temple, and its high priests. This was not unusual in the empire. It was customary for Rome to rule its provinces through local client kings, who could take advantage of local structures and institutions—like the Jerusalem Temple—to establish imperial authority and ultimately to collect the tribute. So it was with the Jewish king, Herod the Great, established in his rule initially by Marc Anthony, and later by Augustus himself. Herod did his job well, keeping the peace on behalf of Rome. The Jewish historian Josephus describes how:

> No meeting of citizens was permitted, nor were walking together or being together permitted, and all their movements were observed. Those who were caught were punished severely, and many were taken, either openly or secretly, to the fortress of Hyrcania and there put to death. Both in the city and on the open roads there were men who spied on those who met together. And they say that even Herod himself did not neglect to play a part in this, but would often put on the dress of a private citizen and mingle with the crowds by night, and so get an idea of how they felt about his rule. Those who obstinately refused to go along with his (new) practices he persecuted in all kinds of ways. As for the rest of the populace, he demanded that

they submit to taking an oath of loyalty, and he compelled them
to make a sworn declaration that they would remain friendly to
his rule. Now most of the people yielded to his demand out of
complaisance or fear, but those who showed some spirit and
objected to compulsion he got rid of by every possible means.
(*Ant.* 15.366–69; LCL)

Herod's methods were brutal, but probably typical for the more
remote corners of the empire. When he died in 4 B.C.E., there was naturally hope that his successor might prove less repressive. But Rome
was not interested in humanitarian ideals—at least not when it came
to administering its provincial districts. Herod had requested that
after his death his kingdom be divided up among his incompetent
and cruel sons. When Augustus confirmed this wish, the land erupted
into protest. Rome was swift in meeting this challenge to its benevo-
lent *Pax*. Varus, the Roman governor of Syria, moved in quickly with
his legions and sent his general, Gaius, into Galilee and Samaria to
destroy the major centers of resistance. Among them was Sepphoris,
just over the hill from Jesus' Nazareth. According to Josephus, Gaius
razed the city and enslaved its inhabitants. Afterward, Varus sent his
troops out to scour the hills and countryside for those who had participated in the rebellion. He rounded up two thousand of its alleged
leaders and had them crucified.[3] Such was the *Pax Romana* as a young
Jesus might have experienced it.

But the legions alone could not hold together so vast an empire as
the Romans had acquired by the beginning of the common era. The
Roman Empire was spread onto three continents, encompassing peoples as diverse as Ethiopians in the south, Britons in the north, Gauls
in the west, and Persians in the east. As large and powerful as their
legions were, no military force could bind together these disparate
lands. So how did they do it? Two enormous powers combined to
make the empire possible, one structural (or sociological), the other
ideological (or theological).

The Power of Patronage

The structure of the Roman Empire is a little difficult for moderns to understand. This is because modern, postindustrial society is structured more or less into horizontal layers, each layer comprising a "class" of persons: lower class, middle class, upper class, and so on. This was not true of preindustrial agrarian empires, like Rome. In the Roman Empire the lines of division were not horizontal, but vertical, or rather, the sloping pyramidal lines of patronage. Rome was not the industrial center of a large working-class culture. It was the home of influential persons—patrons—whose power and influence spread out through the empire like large slices of pie, economic pie. To get a piece of the pie, it was necessary to be taken up into one of those informal yet powerful spheres of influence that began in Rome, but extended on out into the furthest reaches of the empire, controlling every aspect of economic and political life.

What is patronage and how did it work? A patron is a person of considerable means, acquired through economic achievement, military prowess, or (most importantly) through birth. To hold on to the power that goes with his or her position, the patron must use it to the advantage of others, who come to be seen as the patron's "clients." He or she supports these clients, giving them access to the economic or political power he or she controls. For their part, the clients support their patron from below, working on behalf of his or her interests. These clients may, in turn, serve as patrons to others located below them in the social food chain, who become their clients. Thus the network widens to include more and more persons locked into patron-client relationships. This network of patronage becomes a kind of pyramid of dependency, strongly hierarchical in nature, with the means to life flowing up and down as persons meet their obligations and receive their rewards.[4]

Within the empire there were many such pyramids extending out from Rome, each related to an important person in the Roman hierarchy. As the drama of social and economic life unfolded, patrons and their clients competed for advantage in the drive to control more and more of the means to life. Thus loyalty became a crucial value in the success of a patron and his or her clients. Loyalty could be found most readily within a family, and so families and strong family ties became important in the empire. At the top of a patronal pyramid might be a prominent Roman family, a father and his sons, a tight inner circle of patrons and clients. But also at the bottom of the pyramid, where loyalty was no less important, families were held together by their relationship to a father, who might be the client of someone higher up in the pyramid. Indeed, Romans often came to think of an entire network of patron-client relations as a giant extended family.

One can now see how the empire could be held together once the legions had withdrawn. If one wished to get along successfully in the new social order, one needed to be connected. This was a feudal society, organized not horizontally but vertically, with all the lifelines of loyalty reaching ultimately to Rome itself. At the head of all these lines was the emperor. Augustus was the patron of the whole empire. In a sense, the empire was his to do with as he pleased. He held it through the power of his clients, whose own power came from their clients, who in turn had clients of their own, and so on down through the various pyramids of patronage into each and every family in every province of the empire. Augustus understood all of this very well. Thus he encouraged and celebrated precisely those values that were key to the success of patronage: *fides, pietas, familia*—loyalty, piety, and Roman family values.

Rome's Golden Age

The second great power binding the empire together was ideological, or better, theological. The spirit of these times for Romans was deeply religious. The *Pax Romana*, for them, was no ordinary time. It was the golden age foreseen in ages past as that great time of blessing and peace foreordained by the gods and destined to descend once again upon the gods' chosen people. The Roman peace was not a secular accomplishment: it was the gift of the gods. It was a reward for virtuous living. "Thy age, great Caesar, has restored to squalid fields the plenteous grain . . . , wild passion's erring walk controll'd, heal'd the foul plague-spot of the state, and brought again the life of old" (Horace, *Odes* 4.15, LCL).

At the center of this new and glorious age was Augustus himself. It was he who established the peace, he who secured the borders, he who added province after province to the greater glory and enrichment of Rome. Moreover, it was he who, personally, carried the favor of the gods. He became in the popular imagination nothing less than a messenger from the gods—God's own son. "Behold, at last, that man, for this is he, so oft unto thy listening ears foretold, Augustus Caesar, kindred unto Jove. He brings a golden age; he shall restore old Saturn's sceptre to our Latin land"—so prophesies Virgil's ghost of Anchises in the *Aenead* (6.756, LCL).

Augustus understood this ideology and the pious feelings that fueled it. Although Roman tradition discouraged him from promoting the idea that he was in truth divine, he bathed himself in nostalgic religious ideas and ceremony. He wanted to create the impression that the gods had indeed smiled upon Rome, and that he, the *Pontifex Maximus*—the high priest of the Roman people—was responsible for calling forth this blessing. So in 17 B.C.E. he revived the ancient custom of the Secular Games, a periodic celebration intended to mark the turning of the ages. It was a kind of national week of repentance and thanksgiving, with public sacrifices, prayers, processions, and pageantry, all done with great extravagance and marvelous entertainment value. It was a religio-political event celebrating the goodness and virtue of the Roman people and their leader, the high priest, Augustus Caesar. Horace composed a hymn for the occasion, to be sung by a choir of "chosen maidens and spotless youths." This excerpt captures the spirit of the celebration:

> If Rome be your handiwork . . . , then, O gods, make teachable your youth and grant them virtuous ways; to the aged give tranquil peace; and to the race of Romulus, riches and offspring and every glory.

> And whatever the glorious scion of Anchises and of Venus
> [Augustus], with sacrifice of milk-white steers, asks of you, that
> may he obtain, triumphant over the warring foe, but generous to
> the fallen. . . . Already Faith, Peace, Honor and ancient Modesty,
> and neglected Virtue have courage to return, and blessed Plenty
> with her full horn is seen. (Horace, *Carmen Saeculare* 37, 45-48.
> 49-52, 57-60; LCL)

Thus Augustus became the champion of ancient piety and traditional values: faith, peace, honor and shame, and good old-fashioned
virtue. These were the building blocks of a strong society, Augustus
believed. And Romans believed that he embodied these values in their
purest form. The empire was to them no accident. It was their destiny,
guaranteed by the piety and reverence of their political and spiritual
leader, Augustus.

This pious fervor was not confined to the hills and altars of Rome
itself. Indeed, one could find its strongest expression in the
provinces, where local leaders, connected to Rome through the web
of patronage, competed to demonstrate their loyalty to Augustus
and the empire through their own extravagant displays of piety.[5]
Provincial assemblies were created to promote and maintain the
imperial cult. Throughout the empire one can still find its remnants
today: temples in virtually every city dedicated to the gods, Roma and
Augustus. Time itself was made to pay him due homage. In the
province of Asia (Asia Minor) the assembled representatives of the
Greek cities voted that the celebration of the New Year be shifted so
that it would fall on September 23, Augustus's birthday.[6] Back home
in Rome, Augustus allowed the Senate to honor him by changing the
name of the eighth month from the traditional "Sextilis" to
"August," a remnant of the *Pax Romana* that remains with us still.[7]
From one end of the Mediterranean to the other, people were swept
up into the religious and political ideology that surrounded Rome
and its divine son, Augustus.

Another Empire, Another God

Jesus was born into an eastern province of Rome's vast empire during this golden age of Augustus. There, too, in Judea the cult of the emperor and the theology of empire were as strong as anywhere. Their chief promoter was Herod the Great. He was a client of Augustus himself, and he did his patron proud. Between 22 and 10 B.C.E. he built a lavish city on the Mediterranean Sea and created a harbor large enough to rival the great seaport of Alexandria in Egypt. The harbor he named "Sebaste," Greek for Augustus. The city he named Caesarea. In its center stood an enormous temple dedicated to the gods Roma and Augustus.[8] Though Jerusalem was the traditional seat of authority in Judea, the Roman governor resided in Caesarea. From here outward the patronal tentacles of the empire extended into the land—south to the cities of Sebaste, Neapolis, and Jerusalem, east to Scythopolis, and north to Sepphoris and Tiberias. All of these were cities with Gentile populations with strong Roman loyalties. The *Pax Romana* extended even to this remote land. Jesus would have grown up with it on his doorstep.

But what would it have meant for someone like him? Where did he and his family fit in Rome's imperial plan? Jesus was a carpenter, or more generally, an artisan (*tektōn*), or so tradition tells us (Mark 6:3).[9] In an agrarian empire, to be called a mere artisan is no compliment, for economic life is rooted in the land. To be part of things at all one must at least be connected to the land through agriculture. A carpenter—or any artisan or laborer, like a fisherman—was not. It is quite possible that the family of Jesus had fallen out of the mainstream.[10] Perhaps they had lost their land, as many had, during this time of Roman economic expansion and increased agricultural commercialization, or under the weight of the burdensome taxes, or tribute, paid to Rome, directly or through its vassals, the Herodians.[11] Philo, who wrote about Jewish peasant life in Roman Egypt at about this same time, gives a vivid picture of how such a thing could, and did, happen. His account is of how a certain man, appointed to collect the tribute, went about collecting from peasants in arrears on their payments:

> When some of his debtors whose default was clearly due to their poverty took flight in fear of the fatal consequences of his vengeance, he carried off by force their women and children and parents and their other relatives and beat and subjected them to every kind of outrage and contumely in order to make them either tell him of the whereabouts of the fugitive or discharge their debt themselves. . . . And where there were no relatives left, the maltreatment was passed on to their neighbors and sometimes even to villages and cities which quickly became desolate and stripped of their inhabitants who left their homes and dispersed to places where they expected to remain unobserved. (Philo, *Special Laws* 3.159, 162; LCL)

For those who were part of the empire, part of its systems of patronage, of collection and distribution, the *Pax Romana* might have offered at least some level of "peace." But for those who were not, life was anything but peaceful. Jesus and his family were not part of the empire. They lived on its margins, piecing together a subsistence living by working with their hands. In his company we find other such folk, similarly marginal to the empire: fishermen, prostitutes, lepers, beggars, persons disabled by life, the demon-possessed. None of these folk would have made good clients. They belonged to that category of persons the anthropologist Gerhard Lenski calls "expendables."[12]

Being expendable to the empire was in itself no crime. An expendable is an irrelevance. But Jesus turned out to be no ordinary expendable. He took cognizance of his situation and began to reflect on it. He began to speak of another empire, an empire for all the beggars, the hungry, the depressed, and the persecuted in his world (Luke 6:20b-23//Matt 5:3, 6, 4, 11-12 [Q]; *Gos. Thom.* 54; 69:2; 68). He began to speak of a new future, in which those who are first in the present order of things would be last, and the last would be first (Mark 10:31; Luke 13:30//Matt 20:16 [Q]; *Gos. Thom.* 4:2a). He also spoke of himself as one who would bring not peace but a sword (Luke 12:51//Matt 10:34 [Q]; *Gos. Thom.* 16). He spoke of this new empire in ideal, utopian terms as God's empire.[13] But it was not an empire whose reality was never to be known in the here and now. To the contrary, it is already spread out upon the earth; people just do not see it yet (Luke 17:20-21; *Gos. Thom.* 3; 113).

This sort of talk *was* a crime. Why, after all, speak of another empire, an empire that would truly be "of God," if there is nothing wrong with the empire bestowed by the gods through the auspices of the divine Caesar, Augustus? Here was an expendable who contemplated his situation and that of those around him, and dared to imagine a new world in which he and his were not expendable after all.

They were expendable to the empire, of course, because they had nothing to offer anyone who might see them as clients. What does a beggar have to offer a patron? Nothing. But this did not matter to Jesus. He was beginning to imagine life lived outside the realm of patron-client relations. He encouraged his mendicant followers to approach a house not as a beggar but as a bearer of the empire of God. They were to offer to those they meet care for their sick, and receive from them the gift of hospitality, he counseled (Luke 10:4-9//Matt 10:7-14 [Q]; *Gos. Thom.* 14:4). John Dominic Crossan has argued that this idea—that mutual care, nourishment, and support could deliver the means to life—was at the heart of Jesus' notion of an empire of God.[14] God has provided all that people need to live; if folk would only pursue the empire of God, all that is needed would fall into place (Luke 12:22-31//Matt 6:25-33 [Q]; *Gos. Thom.* 36). There is but one patron, whose gifts are meant for all, and that is God.

In a story he used to illustrate the nature and character of the empire of God, Jesus invoked a traditional Jewish symbol of God's future reign—the heavenly banquet. But unlike the banquets a patron might throw for his many clients, the table of God is open to all, regardless of one's loyalties:

> Someone gave a great dinner and invited many. At the time for the dinner he sent his slave to say to those who had been invited, "Come, for everything is ready now." But they all alike began to make excuses. The first said to him, "I have bought a piece of land, and I must go out and see it; please accept my regrets." Another said, "I have bought five yoke of oxen, and I am going to

try them out; please accept my regrets." Another said, "I have just been married, and therefore I cannot come." So the slave reported this to his master. . . . Then the master said to the slave, "Go out into the roads and lanes, and compel people to come in, so that my house may be filled. (Luke 14:16-24, alt.; cf. Matt 22:2-13 [Q]; *Gos. Thom.* 64)

Here a patron prepares a feast for his clients, but they insult his hospitality. Their relationship, it turns out, was a sham. But never mind. There is another way to celebrate, another way to create community. Open the table. Anyone can come. If God is the only real patron, then who can be denied?

Jesus began to reimagine the very basis for the patronage system, even the family itself. He once said something like this: "Whoever does not hate his father and his mother cannot become a disciple of mine. And whoever does not hate his brothers and sisters (and) will not take up his cross as I do, will not be worthy of me" (*Gos. Thom.* 55; cf. Luke 14:26//Matt 10:37 [Q]; *Gos. Thom.* 101:1-2). On another occasion, when his mother and brothers had come to see him, he said, "Who are my mother and my brothers . . . ? Here are my mother and my brothers! Whoever does the will of God is my brother, and sister, and mother" (Mark 3:35; cf. *Gos. Thom.* 99:2).

These difficult sayings are best understood when placed within the context of a feudal patronage system, in which the family plays a fundamental role in the distribution of what the empire has to offer. Recall that Augustus had espoused Roman family values more than anyone before or since. Why? Family loyalty was the linchpin of the entire system of patronage that held the empire together. Jesus pulled that pin, creating a new family with new loyalties. Their faith (*fides*) was directed to another empire, another God.

God and Caesar

What about the tribute? Here was the heart of the matter. After all, the entire system of patronage and brokerage was designed to insure the smooth flow of tribute to Rome and its selective redistribution to those whose loyalty could be trusted. Jesus was not foolhardy. He would have approached this question with great care, and perhaps cleverness. Mark includes a story about how Jesus was once approached by his opponents, who directly posed to him the question of the tribute, "'Should we pay it or not?'" Jesus replied, "'Bring me a denarius and let me see it.' And they brought one. Then he said to them, 'Whose head is this, and whose title?' They answered, 'The emperor's.' Jesus said to them, 'Give to the emperor the things that are the emperor's, and to God the things that are God's'" (Mark 12:15-17).

In modern American culture this reply has often been misunderstood as a blueprint for the separation of church and state, for dividing sacred from secular concerns. But this misses the point entirely. In Jesus' world there was no separation of church and state, sacred and secular. For Jesus, a Jew, there was *nothing* that did not belong to God.[15] "The earth is the Lord's, and the fullness thereof" (Ps 24:1). This was equally true of Romans, who thought of their expanding empire as divinely ordained, whose political leader was proclaimed the divine son of God. So what would Jesus have meant by this reply? In it he employs the skill of a clever street philosopher, constantly in danger of entrapment by his opponents. The classicists Marcel Detienne and Jean-Pierre Vernant coined a term to describe this common characteristic among the popular philosophers of the Hellenistic age: *metis*, or "cunning intelligence."[16] *Metis* is the art of the slippery reply, the clever rejoinder; it is the skill of the table-turner. The opponents of Jesus mean to trap him between the authorities on the one hand, and his tax-oppressed audience on the other. He eludes them with a reply that itself begs a question: "What *does* belong to God, and what to Caesar?" Now his opponents must reveal *their* loyalties. They are caught in their own trap. If they admit Caesar's claim, they will be stoned by the Jewish crowd; if they do not, they will be arrested. But no one in the crowd would have missed the clear subtext so elusively laid out by the unanswered question in Jesus' reply: God and Caesar are not the same, and one must choose between them.[17]

Casting out Legion

One of the things that put Jesus at odds with the empire was the apparent fact that he was an exorcist. He came from a traditional culture, in which belief in demons and spirits was common. Jesus shared this belief. In such cultures, there are people who have the ability to cast out (what are thought to be) demons. Jesus was such a person. Marcus Borg has called him a "spirit person" or "spirit-filled person."[18] In more technical terms we might call him a "shaman." The opponents of Christianity called him a *goēs*, or sorcerer—that is, an illicit holy man. This in itself made him "an enemy of the Roman people."[19] Why?

We might approach this question by looking at traditional cultures and their experience of spirit possession today. One very interesting study is I. M. Lewis's *Ecstatic Religion*.[20] Lewis noticed that in cultures where belief in spirits is common, people with little power, marginal people, or people suffering victimization in various social and political situations may become possessed by powerful spirits, which manifest themselves in outbursts of anger and frustration, harming themselves and others. Or sometimes the demon might even take on the characteristics of the victim's tormentor, now tormenting the victim in a very public way. Spirit possession may thus be a particularly powerful way of dramatizing to others one's personal sense of oppression when interpersonal or societal forces would make this otherwise impossible. Eventually an exorcist must be called in to attack the demon, and free its victim from its evil powers. Of course, in exorcising the demon he or she is at the same time symbolically taking on the power of the oblique oppressor as well. This makes the local holy man or witch a powerful mediator of cultural critique. This may be the reason why such figures are frequently marginal, or even illegal.

What sort of demonic forces might have bubbled forth as spirit possession in Roman-occupied Palestine, and what would it have meant for Jesus to confront those forces with the power to exorcise these unclean spirits? There is one story about Jesus' activity as an exorcist that certainly would have set Roman teeth on edge. The story is, in part, legend, but it looks so much like the scenarios for possession Lewis described, it might well be based in some distant historical memory. As told in the Gospel of Mark (5:1-20), Jesus encounters a demon-possessed man in the country of the Gerasenes. The man lives among the tombs, constantly howling and bruising himself with stones. Try as they might, the Gerasenes cannot subdue him. So he lives among the dead, a public spectacle of torment. When he sees Jesus, he runs to meet him, falls down in front of him, and begins to shout: "'What have you to do with me, Jesus, son of the most high God? I adjure you by God, do not torment me.' For he had said to him, 'Come out of the man, you unclean spirit.' Then Jesus asked him, 'What is your name?' He replied, 'My name is Legion; for we are many'" (Mark 5:7-9).

A demon named Legion. Imagine that, in a province that Rome more than once subdued by its legions, a province always standing under the threat of further violence should the Jews begin to chafe too severely under the burden of empire and rise up once again. Crossan is quite right in reading this story in light of Lewis's study of spirit possession.[21] Spirit possession—as with oppression, violence, and frustration—is not always strictly personal; it may also bear political markings. Crossan offers by way of analogy the remarkable example of the Lunda-Luvale tribes of the Barotse people of the former Rhodesia, studied by Barrie Reynolds in the 1960s, who, under European rule, began to experience spirit possession of a sharply political nature: "They always had . . . traditional ailments called *mahamba*, which resulted from possession by ancestral spirits. But they then developed a special modern version called *bindele*, the Luvale word for 'European,' which necessitated a special exorcistic church and a lengthy curative process for its healing."[22] Crossan summarizes the phenomenological connection clearly made across centuries and cultures: "*Legion*, I think, is to colonial Roman Palestine as *bindele* was to colonial European Rhodesia, and in both cases colonial exploitation is incarnated individually as demonic possession."[23]

Torment can come from many sources. The Gerasene demoniac bears in his body the torment and suffering of a subjugated people. Jesus responds with poetic daring, according to Mark: "Now there on the hillside a great herd of swine was feeding; and the unclean spirits begged him, 'Send us into the swine; let us enter them.' So he gave them permission. And the unclean spirits came out and entered the swine; and the herd, numbering about two thousand, rushed down the steep bank into the sea, and were drowned in the sea" (Mark 5:11-13).

In a Jewish context, this ending is none too subtle. Legion finds a fate that is doubly fitting of Rome's occupying forces: into the unclean swine, and then into the watery deep for their ultimate destruction. Jesus displays his holy powers in a conflict with the demonic Roman presence and wins. In Mark's story the Gerasenes, when they find out what has happened, beg Jesus to leave the area. An exorcist can get one into a lot of trouble.

On to the Temple

Imagine a person like Jesus in Jerusalem at Passover. Passover was the annual Jewish celebration of liberation, the commemoration of the end of Egyptian captivity. Rome understood how this festival in particular could be construed in the Roman province of Judea. The Roman prefect would have come from his normal seat in Caesarea Maritima to be present, as during all high holidays, and to make sure that the celebration remained focused on the past, not the present or future. Passover must have been a time of particularly great tension.

The Jewish historian Josephus relates an incident that illustrates how on-edge things could get during this most sensitive of times. The setting is a Passover celebration during the prefecture of Cumanus, who governed Palestine in 48–52 C.E. The scene is the Temple courtyard, an area surrounding the Temple, enclosed by a portico. A large Jewish crowd mingles in the courtyard, while Roman soldiers stand atop the portico watching for potential trouble.

"Thereupon one of the soldiers, raising his robe, stooped in an indecent attitude, so as to turn his backside to the Jews, and made a noise in keeping with his posture" (*War* 2.225; LCL). This, of course, enrages the crowd, which begins a chant for Cumanus to punish the soldier for his vulgarity. Some in the crowd begin to hurl stones up at the soldiers; fights break out. Fearing an all-out riot, Cumanus calls for more troops, who pour into the colonnades surrounding the courtyard and begin driving the people out the narrow gates. Josephus continues: "But such violence was used as they pressed round the exits that they were trodden under foot and crushed to death by one another; upwards of thirty thousand perished, and the feast was turned into mourning for the whole nation and for every household into lamentation" (*War* 2.227; LCL).

Imagine Jesus walking into that kind of tense situation. Imagine him speaking then, as he had so many times before, of a new empire, an empire of God in which the first will be last and the last first. And imagine the talk *about* him, how he cast out "Legion" in Gerasa, or how he had said that Caesar could not have what was rightly to be given only to God. Or simply imagine how a pious Jew would have felt walking into the locus of God's presence in Israel, the holy Temple of Jerusalem, and finding it policed by Roman troops looking on from the nearby fortress of Antonia, or perhaps watching from atop the Temple colonnades. Imagine how such a person as Jesus might have felt as he realized that the priests there were not troubled by this; they were part of it, woven firmly into the web of Roman imperial patronage. The high priesthood was at the time a matter of Roman appointment. Imagine how he might have felt as he was taken up into the mood of the crowd and felt the tension building around him and within him.

These are things about that final day in Jerusalem that we, of course, can never know. But we can imagine. We can imagine, as the Gospel writers did, how Jesus might have fallen into a rage and tried to disrupt activity in the Temple courtyard. We might even imagine him, as Mark does, spewing out prophetic contempt with words echoing Isaiah and

Jeremiah, "My house shall be called a house of prayer for all the nations, but you have made it a den of robbers" (Mark 12:17). If he had used these words, he would not likely have been referring to any petty thievery on the part of people selling doves and exchanging money in the porticoes. This word, *lēstēs* ("robber"), can mean much more than petty thief. A *lēstēs* is a marauder, a lawless pillager and bully who rides into town and takes what he wants. Jesus' words would have been aimed at the whole Temple apparatus in its incongruous role of arbiter of imperial power. Perhaps he even spoke of destroying the Temple (see Mark 14:58; John 2:19; *Gos. Thom.* 71). But this would not have been heard as a critique of the Jewish religion, or as an attempt to reform Judaism. It would have been heard as an indictment of the religion and politics of empire as it manifested itself in its peculiar Palestinian form: the Jerusalem Temple. If any of this took place, it would be difficult to imagine how Jesus ever could have walked out of that courtyard alive. His miraculous escape is perhaps the most fantastic part of the story, which many scholars believe is at least rooted in some historical episode.[24] In any event, Jesus did not live long after visiting the Temple. He was arrested. His trial would have been brief, if a trial was held at all. He was, after all, a mere carpenter, a nobody, an expendable. He was an expendable who cried out against the empire to which he meant nothing. Now he did mean something, however briefly, and so he was crucified. Jesus became the victim of the empire, an example to anyone else who might dare to imagine another empire under another God.

Another Age, Another Son of God

The death of Jesus, the victim of Rome's all-encompassing imperial claim, was not without meaning to those who followed him. They understood the challenge he was making to the empire and its worldview. They understood his invitation to see the world differently, to imagine another kind of imperial order, in which the first would be last and the last first, in which beggars, the hungry, the depressed, and the persecuted would have a place, in which those expendable to the empire would find their true value as children of God. That is, they understood why he was killed. His was a countercultural voice in a culture that did not tolerate dissent. When they decided to continue on with what Jesus had started, they knew that they were deciding once and for all to turn themselves against the imperial culture that surrounded them. Rome's golden age would not be their time; they imagined another future. Rome's chosen son would not be their savior; they proclaimed another Son of God.

This dissident mood pervades the literature of earliest Christianity, though it is often missed when read outside the cultural context of the Roman Empire. Take, for example, the Gospel of Mark. It begins with the line, "The beginning of the good news of Jesus Christ, the Son of God." This seems harmless enough. But if one were to have read this, say, in western Asia Minor, in the city of Priene, one would have walked each day past an inscription commemorating the introduction of the Julian calendar, which contained these words: "whereas the birthday of the god [Augustus] marked for the world the beginning of the good news, through his coming . . . ; therefore—may Good Fortune and Safety attend—it has been decreed by the Greeks in the province of Asia that the New Year shall begin in all the cities on September 23, which is the birthday of Augustus."[25] For earliest Christians, Augustus was not "the beginning of the good news." Mark understood this clearly, and so began his story with a counterclaim. His story is of another Son of God; his "good news" begins not with Rome's favorite son, but with Rome's victim—the one for whom there is a Roman cross waiting at the end of his story.

The Scum of the Earth

One sees this countercultural spirit especially in the writings of the apostle Paul. Though Paul had never known Jesus personally, he certainly picked up from his followers this dissident stance. Paul's career was marked by a constant struggle with Roman authorities: in and out of Roman jails, tortured, and—if legend preserves a kernel of truth—finally executed in Rome under the emperor Nero. Luke was not ill informed when he imagined the sort of accusations that would have been leveled against Paul and his companions as they attempted to bring their alternative "good news" to a place like Thessalonica, a major center of the imperial cult: "These people who have been turning the world upside down have come here also. . . . They are all acting contrary to the decrees of Caesar, saying that there is another emperor named Jesus" (Acts 17:6-7, alt.).

When Paul came to experience Jesus as his Lord, he also came to the realization that the *Pax Romana* was not a peace he could embrace. In Thessalonica, as elsewhere, his experience as a dissident in the empire was anything but peaceful (1 Thess 2:1-2). Later, when the Thessalonian church Paul left behind continued to experience harassment and trouble (1 Thess 3:1-5), Paul would encourage them by mocking the idea that Rome's program of *pax et securitas* was in truth peace and security after all: "When they say, 'There is peace and security,' then suddenly destruction will come upon them, as labor pains come upon a pregnant woman, and there will be no escape!" (1 Thess 5:3). As Dieter Georgi has persuasively argued, "peace and security" here is an "ironic allusion to the official theology and propaganda of the *Pax Romana*."[26] Later in this letter, Paul would share with the Thessalonian church his own apocalyptic vision of a future new age, when Jesus, himself a victim of Rome's peace, would return in a triumphal procession, "with a cry and command, with the archangel's call and with the sound of God's trumpet" (4:16), whereupon those who are left will go out "to meet the Lord" (4:17). The model for this scene, according to Georgi, is the ancient Near Eastern "legitimizing ceremony," whereby citizens go out to meet a visiting dignitary and escort him in through the gates of their city.[27] The ceremonious arrival of the emperor or his ambassadors must have been a familiar sight in a city like Thessalonica. But Paul does indeed have another "Lord" in mind. This procession is not for the keeper of the empire; it is for Jesus, the victim of the empire.

It was not just Rome and its emperor that Paul rejected. He rejected the values of the Augustan age itself. What his contemporaries regarded as wisdom, Paul regarded as foolishness. What the world regarded as foolish, he accepted as wise. This was the consequence of following a crucified Messiah. In his letter to the Corinthian churches known as First Corinthians, he writes: "Where is the one who is wise? Where is the scribe? Where is the debater of this age? Has not God made foolish the wisdom of the world? For since, in the wisdom of God, the world did not know God through wisdom, God decided, through the foolishness of our proclamation, to save those who believe. . . . We proclaim a crucified messiah, a stumbling block to Jews and foolishness to Gentiles" (1 Cor 1:20-21, 23). For Paul, following a crucified Messiah meant accepting a wisdom that was out of step with the Augustan age. Later in the same letter he continues: "Yet among the mature we do impart wisdom, although it is not a wisdom of this age or of the rulers of this age, who are doomed to pass away. . . . None of the rulers of this age understood this; for if they had, they would not have crucified the Lord of Glory" (2:6, 8).

What does it mean to follow a Messiah who was made the victim of Rome's empire? For Paul it meant seeing through what he had come to realize was a false claimant to God's hoped-for reign. The "rulers of this age" understood nothing. It meant turning one's values upside down: what seems wise is in fact foolish, and what is foolish is actually wise. It meant accepting one's fate as a fool, a person out of step with the spirit of the times. In his view, this was what some in Corinth had failed to see about following Jesus. He upbraids them, using himself as an example of one who is appropriately out of step:

> We are fools for Christ's sake, but you are wise in Christ. We are weak, but you are strong. You are held in honor, but we in disrepute. To the present hour we hunger and thirst, we are ill-clad and buffeted and homeless, and we labor, working with our own hands. When reviled, we bless; when persecuted, we endure; when slandered, we try to conciliate; we have become, and now are, as the refuse of the world, the off-scouring of all things. (4:10-13)

Here the Augustan values of strength and honor are mocked. The honorable life is not what an apostle of the crucified Messiah can rightly expect. Rather, such a person should expect the worst. The terms Paul employs in the final sentence could not be more derisive. One who follows the crucified Messiah will become the refuse of the world, regarded as filth to be thrown out with the trash. For Paul, being a loyal follower of Jesus means becoming the scum of the earth.

Life among the Scythians

This countercultural flavor was present in early Christianity for many generations—as long as Christians could still taste the humiliation of the cross, and the consequences of losing one's leader to the empire's executioner. Of course, there were also many compromises and attempts at accommodation. Paul himself, when writing to the church in Rome, would reverse his otherwise staunch stand against aligning oneself with the empire, even calling the emperor "God's servant for your good" (Rom 13:4)—if indeed Paul wrote these words.[28] One might suppose that such lapses in zeal are to be expected, especially when addressing people living in the very capital itself—in the belly of the beast. But the early church never lost the sense that Rome's empire was not really their place of peace. They looked for another day, another age to come.

Perhaps it is no accident that among the writings of the New Testament, the most stridently anti-Roman text is also the most thoroughly apocalyptic: the Apocalypse of John (Revelation).[29] John seems to have comprehended clearly that Rome and the church fostered different visions of the world's ideal future. While Rome nurtured the *Pax Romana*, John believed that true peace would come to the world only when the Roman beast was thrown into a sea of fire, never to be heard from again (Rev 19:20). Then and only then could the earth become a place fit for gods. His vision unfolds like a dream:

> Then I saw a new heaven and a new earth; for the first heaven and
> the first earth had passed away, and the sea was no more. And I
> saw the holy city, new Jerusalem, coming down out of heaven
> from God, prepared as a bride adorned for her husband; and I
> heard a loud voice from the throne saying, "Behold, the dwelling
> place of God is with humanity. He will dwell with them, and they
> shall be his people, and God himself will be with them; he will
> wipe away every tear from their eyes, and death shall be no more,
> neither shall there be mourning nor crying nor pain any more,
> for the former things have passed away." (Rev 21:1-4)

The power of these words is felt only when one successfully imagines
them on the lips of someone who had seen the inside of a Roman
prison. When John expresses his hope for deliverance from pain, tears,
and death one can be sure that this is not mere poetic fancy. He has
known pain and grief, and death surrounds him. This was the fate of
many who chose to embrace the crucified Messiah.

In fact, when we first hear of Christianity and Christians in the
wider literature of antiquity, it is to report on their illegal activity and
their arrest, torture, and execution. The report is in a letter of Pliny
the Younger, the newly appointed legate of Bithynia, to the emperor
Trajan, written in about 111 C.E.[30] Pliny had discovered in his province
a strange group of religious zealots such as he had never before
encountered. In order to find out the truth about this "depraved and
excessive superstition" he captured and tortured two slave girls said
to be "deaconesses" in the movement. Although he could find nothing particularly insidious about their activities, he nonetheless had
them executed. Their crime was not so much following Jesus—a figure
no doubt obscure and unknown to Pliny—but choosing not to worship the statue of the emperor and the images of the gods: disloy-
alty.[31] Pain, torture, and death: these were the fate of anyone who
refused to embrace the empire, and chose instead to hope for something else.

Christian resistance to Roman authority did not die out even as the
centuries wore on. In the third century we encounter it with astonish-

ing force in Origen's answer to the pagan critic of Christianity, Celsus. Celsus, writing a century before, had accused Christianity of being an illegal secret association. What is surprising about Origen's reply to this accusation is that he does not deny it. To the contrary, he justifies it in a most provocative way, comparing Roman authorities to the legendary savage barbarians, the Scythians:

> if a man were placed among Scythians, whose laws were unholy, and having no opportunity of escape, were compelled to live among them, such a one would with good reason, for the sake of the law of truth, which the Scythians would regard as wickedness, enter into associations contrary to their laws, with those likeminded with himself. . . . For as those persons would do well who should enter into a secret association in order to put to death a tyrant who had seized upon the liberties of the state, so Christians also, when tyrannized over by him who is called the devil, and by falsehood, form leagues contrary to the laws of the devil, against his power, and for the safety of those others whom they may succeed in persuading to revolt from a government which is, as it were, "Scythian," and despotic! (*Against Celsus* 1.1 [ANF 4.397])

Origen wrote these positively treasonous words in 248 C.E., just a year before the emperor Decius came to power and initiated the most widespread and systematic persecution of Christians that had yet been experienced in the empire. Small wonder that Origen was arrested, imprisoned, and tortured for his defiant effrontery.

Jesus the Victim

What does it mean for Christian faith that at the center of our tradition is a person whose life ended on a Roman cross, who was the victim of an imperial system that easily exploited its conquered serfs and cast off as expendable anyone who could not, or would not, contribute to the empire's greater glory? It means that Christian faith must be very suspicious of its imperial suitors, which have been many over the centuries. How easily has Christianity been co-opted by the various empires that have played host to it. How easily has the Christian agenda merged with the agenda of imperial domination, especially in the twentieth century. Can we honestly say that Jesus would have fit better amid the values and priorities of our own culture than he did in first-century Roman Palestine? Can we honestly believe that Jesus would not have ended up the victim of our culture, just as decisively as he became the victim of his own?

Recalling the earliest Christian attempt to understand the death of Jesus as the death of a victim can serve to remind those who would follow him today that this still involves embracing a vision of the future that is countercultural. Christians must still be willing to embrace ideas that will be considered foolhardy by most arbiters of culture today. Christians must still be willing to engage in cultural critique, even when such criticism might place in jeopardy one's pursuit of a successful life. North American Christians, especially, must realize that we live in the belly of the beast, in the very heart of empire. The *Pax Americana* is no less insidious and exploitative of the world's people than was the *Pax Romana*. And it is scarcely less violent with those who would challenge its authority and its vision. Recalling that Jesus was the victim of just this kind of *pax* should make us think twice if ever we are tempted to merge the *Pax Americana* and the Christian hope for the future into one glorious vision of world peace. Such a peace would not be God's peace—at least not as it appeared in the life of Jesus, the victim of the world's last great *pax*.

Jesus died the victim of an empire that is not so different from our own. If we are to take seriously the challenge that Jesus holds for human life today, we must take seriously the fact of his death. His death is not to be dismissed as meaningless, a mere prelude to greater glories to come. Jesus' death became meaningful to people, first, in its reality as the death of a victim. His death as a victim might hold meaning for us still, if we have the courage to face it—and to face the consequences of realizing how inhospitable the world remains to Jesus' vision of God's empire. We still proclaim a crucified Messiah. To proclaim the cross is to proclaim Jesus' death, his death as a victim. If we miss this harsh reality and rush immediately on to the resurrection, we risk eviscerating our faith before we ever really take to heart the challenge with which Christian faith began. It began with the death of a victim.

Martyr

*If any want to become my followers, let them deny
themselves and take up their cross and follow me.*
—Mark 8:34

To Die for a Cause

Though the followers of Jesus remained mindful that Jesus had died at the hands of the Roman Empire and its allies, they came very quickly also to understand that Jesus' death was not merely that of a victim. It had a purpose. But what was that purpose, and how was it related to the future his followers would now face without their teacher and friend? Why did Jesus die?

Those who had followed Jesus—nearly all of them Jews—were not without cultural resources for interpreting the unjust death of a righteous person. For centuries Jews had suffered under foreign rule. This was not the first time someone had suffered and died for dissenting from the version of life offered by those who ruled them. In Jesus' own day there were many who had died thus. Jesus' followers had themselves known oppression. They had seen dissidents before. They knew what a martyr was.

The Greek word *martys* means "witness." A martyr is someone whose death in the face of great opposition becomes a witness to others. The compelling thing about martyrs is their courage in remaining faithful to their principles in the face of dire threat, even to the point of death. The steadfastness of the martyr bears witness to two things. First, it testifies to the ultimate value of the cause for which the martyr was willing to give his or her life. Second, it provides an example of faithfulness for others to emulate.

A simple saying from the Gospel of Mark is supremely illustrative of martyrological thinking: "If any want to become my followers, let them deny themselves and take up their cross and follow me" (Mark 8:34). It is possible that Jesus said something like this, anticipating the trouble that he and his companions were likely to encounter. More important, though, is the interpretive value this saying came to have as Jesus' followers struggled to find meaning in his death. It expresses on the one hand his own willingness to face death, if need be, for God's new empire. On the other hand, it is an invitation to others to do likewise. His followers would now have to ask themselves: How important is this cause, really? This is the soul-searching question posed by the martyr's death.

The Death of God's Righteous One

In the period of Christian origins a number of popular stories—some of them very old—circulated among the Jews, which focused on Jewish heroes living in the court of a foreign ruler.[1] In these "court tales" the hero, caught in the web of foreign rule, must decide between bowing to the wishes of the heathen king or remaining faithful to the God of the Jews. The legends surrounding Daniel, Susanna, Esther, and the Maccabees all unfold in just this way. These great heroes of Jewish legend and lore all face great danger, torture, even death, but in the end remain faithful to God against the tyrant king.

Understandably, such stories were popular among Jews living under Roman rule. The example of their heroes was meant to inspire faithfulness and to strengthen Jews against the betrayal of their tradition. In his study of these court tales, George Nickelsburg is able to identify a set of themes, or plot, common to many of them.[2] Together they create the basis of a genre of story Nickelsburg called "The Story of the Persecution and Exaltation of the Righteous Man." In this generic storyline, the hero becomes the victim of provocation and conspiracy. Eventually he or she must decide between obedience to God and giving in to the demands of a foreign ruler. The hero trusts God, is obedient, but must as a consequence suffer persecution, slander, false accusation, trial, and ultimately condemnation. But this is not the end. The hero is rescued, redeemed, and ultimately vindicated against his or her enemies. At last the hero is exalted and made an example for all to see and—presumably—to imitate.

The pattern Nickelsburg saw was not limited to works of narrative fiction and martyrology. One finds it in the more poetic wisdom literature of the period as well. The martyrs had a lesson to teach, and it was taught in hymns, poetry, and classroom literature. One of the most compelling presentations of this idea of the suffering righteous one is found in a Jewish work from the first century B.C.E., the Wisdom of Solomon. In the following excerpt the author gives voice to the thoughts of the wicked who would oppress God's righteous one:

> Let us lie in wait for the righteous man,
>> because he is inconvenient to us and opposes our actions;
> He reproaches us for sins against the law,
>> and accuses us of sins against our training.
> He professes to have knowledge of God,
>> and calls himself a child of the Lord.
> He became to us a reproof of our thoughts;
>> the very sight of him is a burden to us,
> because his manner of life is not like that of others,
>> and his ways are strange.
> We are considered by him as something base,
>> and he avoids our ways as unclean;
> he calls the last end of the righteous happy,
>> and boasts that God is his father.
> Let us see if his words are true,
>> and let us test what will happen at the end of his life;

> for if the righteous man is God's child, he will help him,
>   and will deliver him from the hand of his adversaries.
> Let us test him with insult and torture,
>   so that we may find out how gentle he is,
>   and make trial of his forbearance.
> Let us condemn him to a shameful death,
>   for, according to what he says, he will be protected.
>   (Wisdom of Solomon 2:12-20)

So plots the wicked against God's righteous one. But it is to no avail. In the next chapter, there is redemption:

> But the souls of the righteous are in the hand of God,
>   and no torment will ever touch them.
> In the eyes of the foolish they seem to have died,
>   and their departure was thought to be a disaster,
>   and their going from us thought to be their destruction;
>   but they are at peace.
> For though in the sight of others they were punished,
>   their hope is full of immortality.
> Having been disciplined a little, they will receive great good,
>   because God tested them and found them worthy of himself;
>   like gold in the furnace he tried them,
>   like a sacrificial burnt offering he accepted them.
> In the time of their visitation they will shine forth,
>   and will run like sparks through the stubble.
> They will govern nations and rule over peoples,
>   and the Lord will reign over them forever.
> Those who trust in him will understand truth,
>   and the faithful will abide with him in love,
>   because grace and mercy are upon the holy ones,
>   and he watches over the elect.
>   (Wisdom of Solomon 3:1-9)

When Jesus' followers first began to formulate their convictions about him in light of his death, texts and traditions such as this one became important to them. They were grounded in the peculiar Jewish prophetic tradition that finds expression in the mysterious Suffering Servant Songs of Second Isaiah,[3] but given shape and form in the real experiences of Jews living under successive foreign rulers unsympathetic to their way of life. As such they offered a powerful framework for understanding the death of Jesus on a Roman cross. Like God's righteous servant, Jesus came to be seen as the target of enemies who conspired against him. He irritated his opponents, accusing them of transgressing against the law and of hypocrisy. He claimed to know God, to be a servant of God, even "God's child." His words and deeds were an offense, his manner of life strange. He boasted that God was his father. In the end, his enemies captured him and subjected him to the most shameful death. But he was not lost, ultimately. God redeemed him, accepted him "like a sacrificial burnt offering." One day, they hoped, he would return to rule the nations of the earth. In the meantime, those who trusted in God would know the truth, and they would abide in his love.

The followers of Jesus did not arrive at these ideas from out of the blue. Nor did these ideas derive naturally from the events of Jesus' life. They were the product of thinking about his life in light of a long Jewish tradition of considering the fate of God's suffering servants, God's "righteous ones." Certain aspects of his life—his countercultural lifestyle, for example—could take on special significance and become meaningful in new ways when viewed through the lens of this tradition. His shameful death was no longer a disaster, but could be seen as the expected fate of one who remained true to God in the face of wicked adversaries. His followers could see the cross as a powerful moment of witness, but not the end of Jesus' mission. Christians could hope for a new day, when Jesus would finally be vindicated before his enemies.

The Passion Narrative and the Wisdom Tale

Among the first written attempts to account for what had happened to Jesus was the story of his final days, trial, and death, known as the Passion Narrative. This is the source that many believe was used by the writers of Mark and John, and perhaps also another fragmentary Gospel, the *Gospel of Peter,* to give account of Jesus' death.[4] Not surprisingly, when Nickelsburg looked at the Passion Narrative against the backdrop of the Wisdom Tale, he found that the parallels were extensive.[5] Indeed, he could argue that it was this old Jewish tale of suffering and vindication that gave the Passion Narrative its basic plot and structure. The chart below, adapted from Nickelsburg's study and incorporating additions from Burton Mack's similar treatment, makes it possible to see how extensive the parallels are.[6]

Stories of Persecution and Vindication and the Passion Narrative as Used by Mark (items out of sequence are in parentheses)	
Elements of Nickelsburg's Wisdom Tale	In the Passion Narrative as used by Mark
Provocation	11:15-17
Conspiracy	11:18; 14:1
Decision	14:3-9, 35-36, 41-42
Trust	14:35-36
Obedience	14:3-9, 35-36
Accusation	14:57-61
Trial	14:53-64
Condemnation	14:64
Protest	
Prayer	14:35-36
Assistance	
Ordeal	15:29-30
Reaction	(14:63)
Rescue	(14:62)
Vindication	15:38 (14:62)
Exaltation	(14:62)
Investiture	
Acclamation	15:39
Reactions	15:39
Punishment	(15:38)

Nickelsburg's quite plausible theory of how his Wisdom Tale gave rise to the story contained in the Passion Narrative serves, of course, to underscore what most modern biblical scholarship affirms, that the Gospels and their sources are not historical archives. Committing to memory the things that took place, exactly as they took place, was not the task early Christians found laid at their feet in the years following Jesus' death. What was imperative for their own survival as a community was the task of discerning meaning in the life and death of the one who had brought them together in the first place. The writer responsible for the Passion Narrative did not begin with the question, What really happened? Whether he knew the details of Jesus' final days or not, he surely knew enough: that the one in whom they had come to believe was now dead, executed in shame on a Roman cross. Beyond this, any further historical detail would be superfluous. The important question was not what really happened. The questions—the truly important questions—were now, Were we right about him or not? Were we right to follow him? Was his cause just?

The writer of the Passion Narrative had somehow answered these soul-searching questions affirmatively. He had come to believe that Jesus was not a criminal; nor was he simply a victim. He was one of God's righteous ones, who died true to his convictions. So this author composed the story of Jesus' final days as the story of God's persecuted righteous one. He filled its episodes with allusions to the several psalms that speak of God's righteous sufferer and to the Suffering Servant Songs of Second Isaiah.[7] For Christians, Jesus would become the preeminent suffering righteous one. His faithfulness and obedience would become a witness to the value of his cause, and an example for anyone willing to take up the cross as their own fate.

A Noble Death

These ideas about death and persecution were not unique to Jewish culture in the period of Christian origins. They were part of a broader cultural view of what constitutes a meaningful death in the Hellenistic world. To die nobly for a cause, to remain true to one's principles to the very end—this was a time-honored ideal in Hellenistic culture generally speaking. In this period popular philosophers extensively discussed death and how to face it with equanimity and courage without compromising one's convictions.[8]

The most illustrious example of one who had died thus was Socrates. One of the most memorable scenes in all of literature is the death of Socrates, recounted in Plato's *Phaedo*. Already condemned for impiety and corrupting the young men of Athens, Socrates is met by his disciples one last time before he must die. As they arrive at the prison, he is just being released from his chains, for this is to be the day of his execution. As they enter the prison, his beloved Xanthippe bursts into tears at the sight of them. Socrates, nobly, asks his disciple Crito to see to her needs as she is led away, baby in her arms. Now, at length he discourses with his disciples: on how to endure pain and suffering, on how to face death, and on the nature of the world. When he has finished, Crito asks: "And have you any commands for us, Socrates?" He replies: "If you take care of yourselves you will serve me and mine and yourselves, whatever you do, even if you make no promises now; but if you neglect yourselves and are not willing to live following step by step, as it were, in the path marked out by our present and past discussions, you will accomplish nothing, no matter how much or how eagerly you promise at present" (*Phaedo* 115b-c [LCL]). Here is the real focus of the martyrological tradition: "to live following step by step . . . in the path" laid down by the martyr. The martyr asks of his followers only that they live as he lived, that they embrace the values he embraced, even if it should mean death in the end. At last Socrates drinks the hemlock and dies, in peace, true to his principles to the very end.

Socrates' death was the paradigmatic noble death; he was "of all those of his time . . . the best and wisest and most righteous man," says Phaedo (118a [LCL]). "Both in his bearing and his words, he was meeting death so fearlessly and nobly. And so I thought that even in going to the abode of the dead he was not going without the protection of the gods, and that when he arrived there it would be well with him, if it ever was well with anyone. And for this reason I was not at all filled with pity, as might seem natural when I was present at a scene of mourning" (*Phaedo* 58e-59a [LCL]). Plato's masterful depiction of Socrates' death was not meant to evoke pity or regret. His death was a witness—a martyr's death. In it we are to see how one might die nobly. Indeed, says Socrates, "is not [philosophy] the practice of death?" (*Phaedo* 80e-81a [LCL]). Perhaps not always. But when convictions place one in harm's way, the philosopher's highest calling is to die nobly, true to one's principles.

At least this is how the death of Socrates was appropriated in the Hellenistic philosophical tradition. In the first century C.E. the problem of death, and how to face it with dignity, was ubiquitous in philosophical discourse. This is perhaps understandable. Rome's empire was totalitarian. It could not tolerate dissent, and the philosophers often dissented. Then, indeed, philosophy was the practice of death. Many faced the choice that Socrates had faced: to live in compromise or to die with honor. For such folk, Socrates became a martyr, a model. The first-century Cynic philosopher Epictetus writes: "Socrates does not save his life with (the) dishonor (of escaping death by compromising his principles), the man who refused to put the vote when the Athenians demanded it of him, the man who despised the tyrants, the man who held such noble discourse about virtue and moral excellence; this man it is impossible to save by dishonor, but he is saved by death, and not by flight" (*Discourses* 4.1.164-65 [LCL]). Here death is not a disaster, an ending. It is salvation. Death in this tradition is transformed from defeat into victory. In fact, a noble death may become the capstone to a well-led life, one that transforms that life and makes it ultimately more useful to others.

Epictetus continues: "If we had been useful in our way of living, would we not have been much more useful to people by dying when it was necessary and in the manner called for? And now that Socrates is dead, the memory of him is no less useful to people. In fact, it is perhaps even more useful than what he did or said while he stilled lived"

(*Discourses* 4.1.168-69 [LCL, alt.]). For Epictetus, death was not the end of Socrates and his benefits for humankind. To the contrary, his manner of death transformed him into something more than what he had been in life.

The idea of dying nobly, with unflinching bravery and loyalty, was not limited to the philosophers. It was a standard theme in stories of military heroes, or anyone who was called upon to face death with dignity. It appears again and again, for example, in the tragedies of Euripides, as the ideal way for one to face whatever the gods might ordain, including and especially death.[9] In his study of the Noble Death tradition in Hellenistic literature, David Seeley identifies five key ideas that usually appear in various discussions and depictions of the noble death of individuals whose lives are seen as exemplary:[10] (1) The one who dies nobly dies in *obedience* to his or her principles, or often, to some higher (divine) calling or mandate. (2) In doing so, the hero demonstrates how to *overcome physical vulnerability*, to face torture and death without fear. (3) The standoff with the hero frequently involves a *military setting*—loyalty is often at stake. (4) Such a death is often seen as *vicarious* for others insofar as it may be imitated. Vicariousness comes through mimesis in this tradition. (5) Finally, there are often *sacrificial overtones* as the death of the hero is described and interpreted.

This idea of the Noble Death most certainly influenced Jewish writers of this period, as may be seen especially in the martyrological literature discussed by Nickelsburg and others. Perhaps the best example is to be found in the book known as Fourth Maccabees, a Hellenistic Jewish work written in the period of Christian origins, probably in Antioch.[11] Ostensibly, the book is a defense of the idea that reason—that is, "the mind making the deliberate choice of the life of wisdom" (1:15)—can rule over the bodily passions. To prove the point, the author takes the example of an aged priest, Eleazar, seven pious brothers, and their mother, all of whom were tortured to death during the Jewish struggle for freedom against Antiochus IV Epiphanes in the second century B.C.E. In spite of their gruesome ordeal, these martyrs all remained faithful to God. Their noble deaths two centuries earlier became an inspiration for Jews living under Roman rule, who faced many of the same challenges their ancestors had faced under Antiochus.

In Fourth Maccabees one may clearly see the marks of the Noble Death tradition, as described by Seeley.[12] The story unfolds in the context of a war—thus the military setting. The overarching theme of Fourth Maccabees is, of course, obedience. As the torturer stokes the fires that will soon sear his flesh, the elderly Eleazar takes his stand: "We, Antiochus, who firmly believe that we must lead our lives in accordance with the divine law, consider that no compulsion laid on us is mighty enough to overcome our own willing obedience to the law" (4 Macc 5:16).

Eleazar may speak with such confidence because in his resolve, he has overcome the sense of physical vulnerability that might cause him, out of fear, to capitulate to the tyrant's demands. He mocks Antiochus and his threats of torture:

> I will not violate the solemn oaths of my ancestors to keep the law, not even if you gouge out my eyes and burn my entrails. I am neither so old nor short of manliness that in the matter of religion my reason should lose its youthful vigor. So set the torturer's wheel turning and fan the fire to a great blaze. I am not so sorry for my old age as to become responsible for breaking the law of my fathers. I will not play you false, O law, my teacher; I will not forswear you, beloved self-control; I will not shame you, philosophic reason, nor will I deny you, venerable priesthood and knowledge of the law. (4 Macc 5:29-36)

Thus the ordeal begins, described in graphic detail by the author for his enrapt audience. Eleazar is stripped, scourged, and abused by his torturers. His friends try to offer him a way out. "Just pretend to taste the swine's flesh," they counsel. But he refuses. The death he dies is not a private, solitary act. It is public, a witness to others. He will not "become a model of impiety to the young by setting them an example of eating unclean food." In this sense his death is vicarious, "for others": it gives others an example to emulate. "Therefore, O children of Abraham, you must die nobly for piety's sake" (4 Macc 6:22).

So the torture continues: Eleazar is branded; an "evil-smelling concoction" is poured in his nose; he is thrown into the fire itself. At last, as he is about to expire, he lifts his eyes to God and prays: "You know, O God, that though I could have saved myself I am dying in these fiery torments for the sake of the law. Be merciful to your people and let our punishment be a satisfaction on their behalf. Make my blood their purification and take my life as a ransom for theirs" (4 Macc 6:27-29). Thus Eleazar's death becomes vicarious in another way: it is a sacrifice for the purification of the land.[13]

Obedient unto Death

The idea of the Noble Death was a common one in the culture of Hellenism and in the Hellenistic Judaism that emerged in the period of Christian origins. It may have been particularly strong in the city of Antioch, the home of a shrine to the Maccabean martyrs. Antioch was also a place where Paul spent a good deal of time early in his life as a follower of Jesus. It may also have been the home of the Gospel writers responsible for the Gospel of Mark and the Gospel of John. It is therefore not at all surprising to find many of the ideas associated with martyrdom and the Noble Death tradition in the literature of early Christianity.[14] Jesus was tortured to death by an empire that Christians regarded as tyrannical. This made the tradition of the Noble Death relevant. When one examines how the death of Jesus is treated in the texts and traditions that emerge, especially from Antiochene Christian circles, one sees immediately the profound influence of the Noble Death.

Let us begin with Paul. He, more than any other early follower of Jesus, is credited with the most active and imaginative interpretive effort in presenting Jesus, the crucified Messiah, to the wider Hellenistic world. But when Paul began to develop his characteristic preaching, he did not begin from scratch. He came into the Jesus movement relatively late, when many traditions had already been formulated. Some of these traditions he would have encountered first in Antioch.

One of the earliest pieces of Christian tradition we have is a hymn to Christ that Paul quotes in his letter to the Philippians. It is a complex hymn, blending ideas of the Hebrew prophets, language from the Roman imperial cult, and the mythic pattern of the descending/ascending redeemer known from many ancient Near Eastern religions.[15] But at the very center of this hymn is a single line—perhaps the only clearly Christian contribution to the hymn at all—in which we find that central theme of the martyrological tradition, obedience:

> Who, though he was in the form of God,
>   did not count equality with God a thing to be grasped,
> but emptied himself, taking the form of a slave,
>   being born in human likeness,
> And being found in human form he humbled himself
>   and became *obedient unto death,* even death on a cross.
> Therefore God has highly exalted him
>   and bestowed on him the name which is above every name,
> that at the name of Jesus every knee should bow,
>   in heaven and on earth and under earth,
> and every tongue confess that Jesus Christ is Lord,
>   to the glory of God the Father. (Phil 2:6-11)

Paul dictates this traditional hymn into a letter he is writing from a Roman prison cell, probably in Ephesus. He is in trouble, again. This time, he does not know whether he will live or die. Now he has received word from Philippi that the church he founded there is in trouble too. They have sent word to him, inquiring: What does this mean that you are in prison and we suffer here in Philippi? Perhaps some have raised questions about his credibility. How can a true apostle get into so much trouble (see 1:15-18)? But Paul does not see his current troubles as a mark against him. Rather, they are his opportunity to bear witness to the cause, their new way of life "in Christ." Thus Paul addresses the Philippians in terms that should by now be familiar: "I know that through your prayers and the help of the Spirit of Jesus Christ this will turn out for my deliverance, as it is my eager expectation and hope that I shall not be at all ashamed, but that with full courage now as always Christ will be honored in my body, whether by life or by death. For to me to live is Christ, and to die is gain" (1:19-21). Paul is prepared to die nobly. "I shall not be ashamed . . . , Christ will be honored in my body," he vows. And he urges the Philippians also to "stand firm," and not be frightened. It is their privilege to "suffer for his (Christ's) sake" (1:27-30). It is in the midst of this exhortation to bear up nobly for the cause of Christ that Paul includes the hymn, perhaps a hymn already familiar to the Philippians. Christ died nobly, obedient to the end. This is Paul's aim as well. As Jesus sacrificed his life for the cause of his new empire of God, so also now Paul will offer his own life for the sake of those who would be faithful to that new reality and hope. He is ready, he says, "to be poured out as a libation upon the sacrificial offering of your faith" (2:17).

This is how the martyrological tradition works. The martyr's death is vicarious insofar as it sets an example to be emulated by others.[16] Its benefits are experienced through imitation. Jesus' death became, in this tradition, the expression of obedience. He was no longer simply a victim. He died willingly, nobly, for a cause. His obedience unto death, "even death on a cross," became a model for his followers who might also find themselves imprisoned, tortured, even executed for the cause of God's new empire. Paul has taken this witness to heart. Now he offers himself as a sacrifice, obedient to the cause, even under the threat of death. He also expects that the Philippians will come to see their own suffering and threat of death in the same way. The death of Jesus has become part of the Christian way of living. This way of life always carries with it the threat of death. As Paul writes to another church—in Corinth—again, defending his record of constant trouble and conflict with the authorities: "We are afflicted in every way, but not crushed; perplexed, but not driven to despair; persecuted, but not forsaken; struck down, but not destroyed; always carrying in the body the death of Jesus, so that the life of Jesus may also be manifested in our bodies. For while we live we are always being given up to death for Jesus' sake, so that the life of Jesus may be manifested in our mortal flesh" (2 Cor 4:8-11).

Here are the themes found so prominently in the Jewish martyrological tradition, especially in 2 and 4 Maccabees, as well as in the Stoic tradition,[17] of bearing up nobly for the sake of one's principles: freedom from concern over what might happen to one's body and the consequent freedom to act in accord with one's conscience, in spite of dire threat. To be sure, Paul's perspective is unique: rather than his strength of "reason," Paul relies on the transcendent power of God working through his earthen vessel of a body to carry him through his trials. Nonetheless, the martyrological orientation of such talk is clear.

Consider Yourself Dead

While Paul used the traditions of the early Jesus movement in his preaching and writing, he was also an innovator, a creative practical theologian. The idea that Jesus' death was a vicarious death, at once his and ours, was intriguing to him. As he pondered this martyrological notion, he also had before him his own experience of Jesus as a spiritual force in his life. The spirit of Jesus, the risen Lord, had taken over Paul, such that he could say quite seriously, "It is no longer I who live, but Christ who lives in me" (Gal 2:20b). Finally, he had before him the liturgical life of the early Jesus movement, especially its practice of baptizing persons who wished to dedicate themselves to Jesus. In Paul's last known letter, to the Romans, all of these things come together in one of Paul's most elegant formulations expressing the significance of Jesus' death: Romans 6:1-11.

The issue that consumes Paul in this part of Romans is the question of sin. Recall that in Paul's version of Christianity, the Jewish law was not to be binding on the followers of Jesus. This raised a question for those who saw the law as the code by which righteousness could be distinguished from sin. In trying to live without it, was Paul not embracing a life of sin? "Are we to continue in sin that grace may abound?" he asks, rhetorically (6:1), supplying the words he imagines his critics to be thinking. To this he replies emphatically, "Not at all! How can we who died to sin still live in it? Do you not know that all of us who have been baptized into Christ Jesus were baptized into his death? We were buried therefore with him by baptism into death, so that as Christ was raised from the dead by the glory of the Father, we too might walk in newness of life" (6:2-4).

For Paul, baptism is baptism into Christ's death. What could he mean by this, and how did such an idea address the problem of sin? To understand Paul's meaning one must realize that for Paul sin is not just bad behavior. It is a cosmic power, a force loose in the universe to which we poor human beings are subject. Sin, for Paul, is the cumulative force of evil exercising power over humanity. Such an idea, foreign perhaps to moderns, was a common way of thinking in antiquity. The universe, for ancients, was full of such hostile forces against which mere mortals were powerless. Sin, as an evil power, exercised its control over a person through the flesh—the "sinful body," says Paul (6:6)—the seat of all the passions in Paul's ancient anthropology. If this was so, then ultimately a person's only escape from sin's power is death, when the body of flesh passes away. From out of this thought world Paul arrives at a new way of considering Jesus' death as a vicarious event. If Jesus' death is at once the death of anyone who would follow him, then in his death lies the key to ultimate freedom: freedom from the power of sin:

> We know that our old self was crucified with him so that the sinful body might be destroyed, and we might no longer be enslaved to sin. For he who has died is freed from sin. But if we have died with Christ, we believe that we shall also live with him. For we know that Christ, being raised from the dead, will never die again; death no longer has dominion over him. The death he died he died to sin, once for all, but the life he lives he lives to God. So you also must consider yourselves dead to sin and alive to God. (6:6-11)

But how could this be? How could a person really become united with Jesus in his death? Paul decides that this is the ritual meaning of baptism. He takes a concept that had been expressed primarily in a literary mode—the vicarious death of a martyr—and gives it ritual power. He can do this because Jesus has become for him more than a martyr. He is a divine being, an epiphany, a spiritual force in his own right. Worship and ritual "work" with him: one could be united with Jesus the Christ spiritually, ritually. That Paul chooses the ritual of baptism to bear this burden of meaning is quite understandable. On the one hand, death and water were connected in various ways symbolically and mythically in antiquity. Jews had long associated ritual washing with purification from sin and ritual uncleanness. All of this must have been wrapped up together in the poetics of Paul's new formulation of the meaning of baptism.

What is most impressive about Paul's interpretive work here is the extent to which he seems to understand how ritual really works in the life of a believer. However powerful and poetically effective a ritual might be, it is not magic. Ritual can create a real experience of altered reality, an intense moment—in this case—of freedom. But when the event is over, life stands waiting outside the door, ready to reassert itself when the priests have disrobed and the ritual fires have been extinguished. Paul understands all of this very well. Consequently, he does not say that those who have died with Jesus in the act of baptism have also been raised with him. That final and permanent freedom lies still in the future.[18] Rather, Paul carefully asserts that "as Christ was raised . . . , we too might walk in newness of life" (6:4). Life is still there, waiting to be walked. Baptism has not changed that reality. We are not dead yet! So, he insists, "you also must *consider yourselves dead to sin and alive to God*" (6:11). The future of freedom remains still to be constructed. "Let not sin therefore reign in your mortal bodies, to make you obey their passions . . . , but yield yourselves to God as people who have been brought from death to life" (6:12-13).[19] So long as we still have a body, we still have before us the martyr's challenge: obedience. The death of Jesus is vicarious, for others, only insofar as they choose to embrace his death and his life as their own.

The One Who Endures to the End

This idea, drawn from the tradition of the Noble Death, that the death of the martyr could have vicarious effects for others was a powerful one. As Paul worked out its implications in ritual, others continued the literary tradition of martyrology, telling the story of Jesus in a way that invited its imitation, in life and in death. The Gospel of Mark is one result of this literary effort.[20]

The idea of Jesus the martyr had obvious relevance to the writer of this first Gospel. Mark was written during or just following the years of the Jewish War for independence from Rome (66–70 C.E.). As a messianic Jew who believed in Jesus, Mark's author would have found no comfort with Rome. But his beliefs about Jesus would have put him at odds with most Jews as well—he was a heretic at a time when solidarity and loyalty to the Jewish tradition were in high demand. He was a person caught between the two sides of a war-torn world. He was also part of a community that found itself in this precarious situation as well. He and his community had come to a moment of truth. Are we right or are we wrong? Is following Jesus worth the risk we must now take? The issue of faithfulness and loyalty runs throughout Mark's Gospel.

We have already seen how the Passion Narrative took up the question of Jesus' death, as the death of God's persecuted righteous one. Mark knew this early text. But he wanted more from his narrative than just an account of Jesus' unjust death. He wanted to create a narrative that would involve his audience, that would tie their fate together with that of Jesus. So Mark took up the Passion Narrative, but he used it to write his own story of Jesus. In it he wove the Passion Narrative into a skillful plot that focuses the martyr's question on the lives of those for whom he wrote, always asking: Can you remain faithful in the midst of adversity?

One way he does this is by creating a narrative pattern to which Norman Perrin called attention some years ago.[21] Perrin noticed that the fate of John the Baptist and Jesus is essentially the same in the Gospel of Mark. Mark speaks of John as "preaching," (1:7), but then he is "delivered up" (*paradidonai*) to his enemies (1:14). Thereupon Jesus makes his own debut, like John, "preaching" (1:14). What is his fate? He too must be "delivered up" (*paradidonai*, 9:31; 10:33). As Mark approaches the Passion Narrative, he creates successive scenes in which Jesus predicts his own betrayal and death in Jerusalem. But the disciples cannot understand or accept what he is saying. Peter rebukes him (8:32); the disciples cannot understand his meaning (9:32); James and John can only speak of the glory that is to come (10:37). Finally Jesus asks them: "Are you able to drink the cup that I drink, or to be baptized with the baptism with which I am baptized?" (10:38), clear references to martyrdom. They reply, "We are able" (10:39). Are they?

Now, with the stage set, Mark heads into the Passion Narrative. Jesus provokes the authorities (11:15-17), who begin to conspire against him (11:18). What Jesus has predicted is beginning to take place. Mark enhances the developing tension. Jesus defends his authority against those who would question him (11:27-33). He prophesies against Jerusalem in parables (12:1-12). He gives a provocative answer to the question of whether to pay the tribute (12:13-17). He denounces the scribes (12:38-40). Something bad is going to happen to this man—one can sense it. But he wades deeper into the trouble, true to his cause, unflinching in the face of the growing danger.

Now Mark comes to what is arguably the high point of his entire narrative, at least for his audience: the apocalypse. Here Jesus foretells what is to happen in the future—about a generation away (13:30). When? "When you see the desolating sacrilege set up where it ought not to be (let the reader understand), then let those who are in Judea flee to the mountains" (13:14). Here Mark, with an inside nod to his audience, refers to the imminent destruction of the Jerusalem Temple. He is speaking of the very war that is just now raging around them. When will all of this take place? Now! says Mark. It is happening now! What will it mean for those who are reading these words? Jesus speaks to them out of the past, foretelling the future—their unfolding present:

> But take heed to yourselves; for they will deliver you up (*paradi-donai*) to councils; and you will be beaten in synagogues; and you will stand before governors and kings for my sake, to bear testimony before them. And the gospel must first be preached to all nations. And when they bring you to trial and deliver you up (*paradidonai*), do not be anxious beforehand what you are to say; but say whatever is given you in that hour, for it is not you who speak but the Holy Spirit. And brother will deliver up brother to death, and father his child, and children will rise against their parents and have them put to death; and you will be hated by all for my name's sake. But he who endures to the end will be saved. (13:9-13)

It is clear: John preached, and was delivered up; Jesus preached, and was delivered up. Now Mark's readers see their own fate. They will be called upon to preach, and they too will be delivered up.[22] How will they face this fearful prospect? Mark hopes that the martyr's story will now do what it is designed to do. Jesus, the persecuted righteous one, is to be their model. The disciples will flee (14:50). But Jesus will remain faithful to the end. Mark insists that his readers must emulate the steadfast faithfulness of Jesus, true to their cause to the very end. For those who can do this, there is reward: "But anyone who endures to the end will be saved" (13:13b).

This final admonition recalls to mind the words of Epictetus on the death of Socrates: "he is saved by death, not by flight." Mark hopes to convince his readers not to flee. Death may lie before them, but it is not to be feared. This idea, that death must not be feared, is central to the Noble Death tradition. Seneca argued that this was precisely why Socrates chose to face death, even when the opportunity of escape presented itself. In his letter to Lucilius (*On Despising Death*) he writes: "Socrates in prison discoursed, and declined to flee when certain persons gave him the opportunity; he remained there, in order to free humankind from the fear of two most grievous things, death and imprisonment" (*Ep.* 24.4 [LCL]).

This theme is indeed relevant to Mark and his audience. They live in fearful times. Throughout Mark's Gospel fear confronts those who would believe in Jesus. Fear is the enemy, the polar opposite of faith for Mark. "Do not fear, only have faith," says Jesus to those who fear that the ruler's daughter, whom he might have healed, is already dead (5:36). "Why are you afraid? Have you no faith?" asks Jesus when the disciples respond in fear to Jesus' powerful act of calming the sea (4:40).

As Mark's story unfolds, the disciples' fear intensifies. It comes to a head in Mark's depiction of Jesus' last meal with his followers (14:12-26), a scene surely reminiscent of the Socratic tradition. During the meal, Jesus invites his closest friends to eat with him from a common loaf and to drink from a common cup. Mark includes here the words of a Christian ritual that date back at least to the apostle Paul, which identify the broken bread with Jesus' body, and the wine of the cup with Jesus' blood.[23] Mark augments the tradition with words that might have been vaguely familiar from Isaiah's Servant Songs: the wine is Jesus' blood "poured out for many" (14:24).[24] The impending fate of God's Suffering Servant is underscored. They drink from the common cup and form a covenant, a pact sealed in the blood of Jesus. They are ready now to follow him, even into death. But even as they share in these symbols of ultimate commitment, the scene is charged with themes of betrayal and fear. Judas has already plotted to deliver him up (14:10-11; note *paradidonai*), and Jesus knows this and brings it into the midst of their ritual (14:17-21), filling the disciples with doubts and suspicions. As the meal ends, Jesus seems to suggest that this little covenant making has all been a sham. It has meant nothing. They will fail to follow through, he predicts: "You will all fall away" (14:27).[25]

And they do. In the Garden of Gethsemane, when Judas comes to turn Jesus over to the authorities, the other disciples are terrified and flee (14:50). Only Peter remains in the narrative, but just long enough to demonstrate what it really means to collapse in fear. He has promised Jesus, even "if I must die with you, I will not deny you" (14:31). But Jesus' prophecy that Peter will deny him, not once but three times before a rooster crows twice (14:30), now comes to pass as Peter loses

his nerve under cross-examination by a slave woman and an anonymous bystander as he lurks outside the high priest's residence where
Jesus is being interrogated inside (14:66-72). So much for brave promises made in private rooms. Meanwhile, Jesus alone endures the fate of
the suffering righteous one: falsely accused, convicted, and finally
beaten and spat upon (14:53-65; cf. Isa 50:4-9).

Fear even stalks the women, who, in contrast to the men who have
followed Jesus, have not all fled. They remain, and after the Sabbath
has passed they go to the tomb to tend to the body of Jesus (16:1-8).
But when they find the tomb empty, they are not emboldened by their
discovery. The angel standing guard instructs them to go and tell the
disciples what they have seen. But they do not, for they cannot. "They
said nothing to anyone, for they were afraid"—*ephobounto gar* (16:8).
With this awkward phrase, Mark brings his story to a close with a
colossal loose end. It demands the question: Who will have the courage
to tell the story? Who will bear witness? Who would be a martyr?

The Glory of Death

In many ways these concerns about survival, fear, and faithfulness
were John's concerns as well. The fourth evangelist wrote some years
after Mark, but he too faced times that posed a threat to him and his
church. It was a time when Jews and Christians were going their separate ways. Jews who were followers of Jesus found themselves having
to choose between the security of the larger community in which they
lived and the risky human experiment that was the emerging church.
John even avers that those who would dare to expose themselves in his
community by declaring their belief that Jesus is the Messiah might
face death (16:2). The pressure felt by those within John's church was
intense. Indeed, some might even have begun to renounce their faith
(16:1; 9:22).[26]

Like Mark, John turns to the martyrological tradition to try to
shore up the flagging zeal of his folk.[27] In presenting the death of

Jesus as that of a martyr, John had before him many of the same basic elements used by Mark. He probably had a passion narrative similar to that of Mark, likewise built on the idea of God's suffering righteous one. He was a Jew, quite likely from Antioch, and so must have known the Maccabean martyrological tradition well. He was also part of the larger Hellenistic world, with its philosophical discussions of how to die nobly, true to one's cause.

But John's creative act of building his own story of Jesus did not imitate that of Mark. There may be many reasons for this; John is a complex book. One reason, however, is clear. John had a different way of thinking about Jesus; he had a different Christology. In Mark, Jesus is a human being, the Son of man, who is designated as God's Son at the event of his baptism by John the Baptist (Mark 1:9-11). In John, Jesus is not a human being. He is "the Son of God, or God, striding across the earth."[28] He is the Logos of God, God's own Word, at one with God from the beginning of time. Apart from him, nothing in all creation came into being (John 1:1-5). This very "high" Christology may, in part, explain how Jesus faces the final days of his life in John. Through the final chapters of the Gospel, from Gethsemane to the arrest and trial scenes, and finally to the cross, Jesus is in control. In Gethsemane, for example, Judas brings an entire cohort (*speiran*) of Roman soldiers (about 600 men) to arrest Jesus (18:3). But with a word from God's Son—*egō eimi* ("it is I")—they all fall to the ground, powerless before him (18:6). These words, *egō eimi*, are not innocent in John. They are the epiphanic words of self-revelation spoken by the one who is God incarnate. In John, Jesus is no ordinary victim of Roman justice. He is a powerful, willing captive, orchestrating his own death according to a grand plan.

Initially this may seem to diminish the power of Jesus' death as a witness to others. What he, the Logos of God, could do was superhuman, not to be attempted by mere mortals. John does risk this conclusion. But the willingness of a martyr to embrace death, even to orchestrate its arrival, is not without precedent. Socrates rejected his friends' plot to spirit him away from Athens. He chose instead to die nobly, willingly, in control to the end. In the Christian tradition itself, to choose to die, to dream about it, to plan it out, became the highest expression of martyrological zeal. In one famous scene from a third-century Christian martyrological text,[29] the young and beautiful Perpetua, a girl barely past her teens, faces her executioners with a resolve that is almost superhuman. Her executioner is a young gladiator whose hand is trembling so much that he cannot make his sword perform the final deed. So Perpetua, to the astonishment of the crowd, reaches out, takes his hand, and guides the blade to her own throat.[30] Such is the martyr's zeal.

For a community that feels itself under siege, it was no doubt important to think of Jesus as in complete control of the situation. Nonetheless, in presenting Jesus as he does, John risks creating too great a chasm between Jesus, the cosmic Logos of God, and the normal people who must find in their own very human lives the wherewithal to follow Jesus. Thus, even though John's Jesus is in control in this narrative, almost orchestrating the unfolding drama of his death, John still tries to connect the fate of Jesus with that of his audience using martyrological motifs and ideas. Let us take, for example, the way John handles the final days of Jesus in Jerusalem, the ground covered by the Passion Narrative. Jesus and the disciples arrive in Jerusalem in triumphal procession. This much comes from the Passion Narrative. But as he arrives, he is already under a cloud. There is no need of an incident in the Temple to provoke the authorities; Jesus has been provoking them all along with his outrageous words. The threat of death already stalks him (see, e.g., 5:18; 7:19, 25, 32, 44; 8:59; 10:31; 11:45-53). Thus John has moved what would have been the next scene in the Passion Narrative, the Temple incident, up to the opening scenes of the Gospel, using it already in chapter 2 as a kind of first provocative act (2:13-22). Jesus has been arguing, provoking trouble, all along. In the end, even his miracles somehow provoke the authorities who begin to plot his death. Ironically, it is Caiaphas who provides the first hint that Jesus' impending death will not be an ordinary execution. With words invoking the Hellenistic Noble Death tradition of dying for others, the high priest describes Jesus' death as the vicarious death of a martyr:[31] "you do not understand that it is expedient for you that one man should die for the people, and that the whole nation should not perish" (11:50).

With the tension building, Jesus turns to face what awaits him in this last visit to Jerusalem, invoking familiar ideas from the martyrological tradition:

> The hour has come for the Son of man to be glorified. Truly, truly, I say to you, unless a grain of wheat falls to the earth and dies, it remains alone; but if it dies, it bears much fruit. He who loves his life loses it, and he who hates his life in this world will keep it for eternal life. If anyone serves me, he must follow me; and where I am, there shall my servant be also; if any one serves me, the Father will honor him. (12:23-27)

John has packed much into these verses: that in death a life is transformed; that to gain authentic life, one must be willing to part with life, "to hate life in this world"; that anyone who would serve Jesus must follow him, even into death. All of these ideas are developed from the martyrological tradition, as we have seen. Embracing this entire thought is the idea that Jesus' death is not a crisis or a catastrophe to dread. It is to be his moment of glory. Those who follow him into death, God will honor.

This is different from what we have seen in Paul or in Mark, where Jesus' death, though significant in martyrological terms, is still the nadir of the story. It is a crisis to be faced with dignity. In John, Jesus' death is the climax of the story, the moment in which he is to be glorified. And not he alone. In this act God is glorified as well: "Now my soul is troubled. And what should I say—'Father, save me from this hour'? No, it is for this reason that I have come to this hour. Father, glorify your name.' Then a voice came from heaven, 'I have glorified it, and I will glorify it again'" (12:27-28). Here John invokes the memory of Jews throughout time who have been martyred in faithfulness to God: "I have glorified it, and I will glorify it again." To die as a martyr is to glorify God. One sees this in the Maccabean literature (e.g., 4 Macc 1:12; 18:23). To die thus is to bring to oneself honor and glory—this too is a martyrological theme (e.g., 4 Macc 7:9). Glorious is the martyr's death in every respect. This is why John repeatedly refers to Jesus' death as his glorification (e.g., John 7:39; 13:31-32; 17:1).

With such sentiments John wends his way into the Passion Narrative, where we expect to follow, in close succession, the Last Supper, Gethsemane, and finally Jesus' arrest and trial. But before rushing on with the story, John pauses. In John's narrative, Jesus now retreats with his disciples for one final private discourse. The pause is long—chapters 13–17—and includes instruction on how to care for one another, how properly to understand him, and the nature of the world. He gives the disciples one last commandment: "I give you one final commandment, that you love one another. Just as I have loved you, you also should love one another. By this everyone shall know that you are my disciples, if you have love for one another" (13:34-35). And then, again: "This is my commandment, that you love one another as I have loved you. No one has greater love than this, to lay down one's life for one's friends. You are my friends if you do what I command you" (15:12-14).

Here are the basic ideas of the martyrological tradition. The fate of the martyr is united with those who would follow him in life and in death. As Jesus loved, so they are to love. As Jesus died, so must they also be willing to die for one another. His death is a witness to them, an act to be imitated. The relevance of this idea soon becomes clear as Jesus' discourse continues:

> If the world hates you, be aware that it hated me before it hated you. If you belonged to the world, the world would love you as its own. Because you do not belong to the world, but I have chosen you out of the world—therefore the world hates you. Remember the word that I said to you, "Servants are not greater than their master." If they persecuted me, they will persecute you; if they kept my word, they will keep yours also. . . . I have said these things to you to keep you from stumbling. They will put you out

of synagogues. Indeed, the hour is coming when those who kill you will think that by doing so they are offering worship to God. (15:18-20; 16:1-2)

The Farewell Discourse of Jesus in John is a long exposition of John's typical theology: the Logos of God is returning to the place whence he has come. But by lacing these chapters with ideas clearly drawn from the martyrological tradition, John manages to keep Jesus from drifting off into transcendental irrelevance. The Logos is also Jesus, the teacher and martyr. His life and death stand as a witness for how to live and die. As Jesus retires with his disciples and instructs them thus, one cannot help but think of that last meeting of Socrates with his companions. As Jesus goes forth from the upper room to face arrest with dignity, to defy his tormentors with words that witness to his resolve, to defy Pilate himself, one cannot help but think of the heroic witness of Eleazar, denouncing the tyrant whose instruments of torture have become powerless over him. In the end, Jesus dies with dignity. In the final death scene (19:25b-30) there is no cry of anguish, as in Mark. From the cross Jesus calmly sees to his mother's future; he drinks from a bowl of sour wine (again, vague allusions to Socrates' final acts); and then utters the final word: *tetelestai* ("it is finished"). This noble end is not a disgrace. It is a moment of accomplishment, of glory.

To Live and Die with Jesus

For the early followers of Jesus, his death was not simply the death of a victim. Jesus died as a martyr. A martyr (*martys*) is a "witness." For the early followers of Jesus, his death was a witness in a double sense. On the one hand, Jesus' faithfulness to his cause testified to the proposition that there are things worth dying for. Jesus died for God's new empire, that new way of being in the world he tried to exemplify in his words and deeds. His death was an invitation—a dare, really—to others to try to live as he had lived. On the other hand, it testified to the fact that it is possible to face such a death nobly, without fear. The martyr's death is ultimately an act of freedom: freedom from fear. Once one has learned to face death without fear, then there really is nothing to be feared. As Seneca tells his friend Lucilius, "death is so little to be feared, that through its good offices nothing is to be feared."[32] Jesus' death, as a martyr's death, is one that frees one from fear—not only the fear of death, but all such fears that would dissuade one from embracing Jesus' unusual way of thinking about human life and relationships. In this sense, the power of death, and of those who wield its instruments, is vanquished.

For Christians who embraced Jesus' dissident stance over against the empire and its ways, grasping this sense of freedom was very important. If Jesus could face false charges, arrest, torture, and death, even death on a cross, without fear, then what power should these things have over his followers as they pursued that same vision of God's empire for which Jesus had willingly died? As Paul wrote to those followers of Jesus living in the heart of Rome itself:

> If God is for us, then who is against us? He who did not spare his own Son, but gave him up for us all, will he not also give us all things with him? Who shall bring any charge against God's elect? It is God who justifies. Who is to condemn? It is Jesus Christ who died, yes, who was raised from the dead, who is at the right hand of God, who intercedes for us. Who shall separate us from the love of Christ? Shall tribulation, or distress, or persecution, or famine, or nakedness, or peril, or sword? As it is written, "For thy sake we are being killed all day long; we are regarded as sheep to be slaughtered." No, in all these things we are more than conquerors through him who loved us. For I am sure that neither death, nor life, nor angels, nor principalities, nor things present, nor things to come, nor powers, nor height, nor depth, nor anything else in creation, will be able to separate us from the love of God in Christ Jesus our Lord. (Rom 8:31-39)[33]

This is the power of the martyr's death: it enables one to live faithfully to God, free from fear of the consequences that might come from such an act of defiance. The martyr's death is an act that conquers the power of death itself, by showing that death is not to be feared. When one embraces the possibility of the martyr's death, then the martyr's life becomes possible too. This, finally, is the point of seeing Jesus as a martyr. The martyr frees one to live the martyr's life by showing one how to die the martyr's death, free from the all-consuming fear of death. The martyrological tradition gave early Christians a way of using the death of Jesus, terrifying though it was, as a source of power for those who would take up his dissident way of life, and his cause of a new empire of God.

What of those of us who would look to the ancient roots of Christianity for ways to understand Jesus and his fate as somehow significant for our own quest for meaningful existence: could the martyrological tradition prove meaningful even today? Are there things worth dying for? Are there causes worth living for? Certainly these are the questions raised by the ancient tradition of martyrdom. But early Christians did not pose these questions in the abstract like this. They had in mind a particular cause, a particular vision of human existence lived before God that they had come to see in Jesus' words and deeds. They—some—would willingly die for that vision, the empire of God. But the martyrological tradition has also been used to coax people to die for things far less noble, far less worthy than this unusual vision of life. From antiquity to modernity one sees this again and again in Christian history. There is a fine line between the martyr and canon fodder. Is the soldier drafted to fight a war in which he or she does not believe a martyr? Is a suicide bomber who blows up a bus full of anonymous bystanders a martyr?

So what shall we do with the martyrological tradition? Has history rendered us hopelessly cynical about the idea of dying for a cause? Perhaps. Nonetheless, the martyrological tradition remains important. For it offers an understanding of Jesus' death as "vicarious," as "for us," that is quite different from classical theories of atonement. In the martyrological tradition Jesus' death remains utterly connected to his life: he died obedient to his cause. To be moved by such a death is to be moved by the life that led to it. To be saved by such a death is to be set free from the fear that might prevent one from embracing that life as one's own. The life and death of a martyr are meaningless if those who witness them remain unmoved. They become vicarious "for us" only insofar as we embrace them as the life we would dare to lead and the death we would be willing to risk.

We may never be called upon to die for those things in which we believe most deeply. But the martyr's death is only the final act in his or her life. The courage to die for one's convictions is preceded by the courage to live out one's convictions. Martyrdom is not, finally, about death. It is about living life meaningfully, fully devoted to the things one believes in most deeply, free from the various fears, both profound and petty, that would usually dissuade one from such a course. To speak of Jesus as a martyr is to consider the values, ideas, and principles he lived and died for, and the God who comes to life in them, and to ask what it would take to bring that God to life once again in lives we might lead. What would it cost to do this? Would it be worth it? Would it be worth everything?

Sacrifice

Without constant sacrifice, the world would fall apart.
—Stanley K. Stowers,
"Greeks Who Sacrifice and Those Who Do Not"

*Those who will not or cannot conform to the rituals of a society
have no chance in it.*
—Walter Burkert, *Homo Necans*

It is common for Christians today to speak of Jesus' death as a sacrifice. But what do we mean when we speak in this way? Sacrifice is not a ready metaphor in our cultural parlance. How often, for example, does one actually witness the sacrifice of an animal in modern America? The very idea is repulsive to most. I suspect that the act of sacrificing an animal is even illegal in most states. This almost complete absence of sacrifice in our culture poses a difficulty for the theological use of this idea: we have no common cultural understanding of what sacrifice means. Small wonder that when one asks what it means to speak of Jesus' death as a sacrifice, all sorts of ad hoc answers come pouring out, many of which are woven around the modern post-Freudian experience of guilt and the personal quest for a guilt-free existence. Christ's sacrifice becomes the carte blanche by which one might stroll carefree through a world of injustice that demands a word of protest from our muted lips, peremptorily silenced by an insipid persuasion that "our debt has been paid." This is credit-card theology, where Daddy always pays the bill.

If our world is a world devoid of sacrifice, the ancient world of Christian origins was one in which sacrifice was ubiquitous. While strolling through the center of ancient Corinth, for example, as the apostle Paul would have done on any day of the week, one might observe the startling spectacle of animals falling under the sacrificer's ax in any of its temples, great and small. The air would have been pierced by the ritual scream of the women positioned around each high altar, cued to their climactic song by the raised hand of the priest poised to strike the decisive blow. The pleasant smell of roasting viscera and boiling meat would have filled the air, piquing the appetite for that rare taste of meat expertly cooked. Sacrifice was at the center of every ancient Greek city. It was the central theme of Hellenistic public life. It continued to be so throughout the Roman imperial period. The raw experience of sacrifice was constant in antiquity. What would it have meant to speak of Jesus' death as a sacrifice in *that* cultural setting?

Sacrifice in Antiquity

What do we know about the meaning of sacrifice in the ancient world? Surprisingly little, it turns out. Like so many things that form the common stock of a culture, the meaning of sacrifice seems to have been so self-evident that few ever had occasion to expound on it.[1] A good start can be made, perhaps, with mythology. How is it that Greeks came to sacrifice to the gods? The foundational myth occurs in Hesiod's *Theogony*.[2] Here we learn of how Prometheus kills an ox to be shared by gods and mortals, but by trickery and cunning secures for mortals the edible parts of the animal—the meat and the viscera— leaving for the gods only the bones. For this he would suffer a suffering of mythic proportions, chained to his Promethean rock. Those who told the tale, though, appreciated his deed. It is the story, after all, of how mortals, not quite gods, and yet more privileged than the animals, came to eat meat. The significance of sacrifice is, first of all, culinary.[3]

Lest this seem a little disappointing, consider the significance of eating meat in a peasant society. Meat in such a setting is a rare thing. Who gets to eat the meat? Who receives the best parts? How is it distributed? For the Greeks, and for all who were taken up into the sacrificial culture of the Hellenistic world, all of this is wrapped up in their sacrificial practices. Sacrifice was about the eating of meat. Virtually all red meat consumed in a Hellenistic city was sacrificial meat.[4] "To sacrifice" in Greek is also "to feast." "To butcher" in Greek is also "to sacrifice."[5] The *mageiros*, who strikes the blow at the altar, is at once "butcher," "cook," and "sacrificer."[6] This linguistic convergence underscores that for Greeks a sacrifice is a culinary event, and the eating of meat a sacred occasion. How important is sacrifice? How important is food? In a peasant economy, in which ninety percent of people live at subsistence level, food is the all-consuming issue. Who gets it? How much? When? These are the issues negotiated through Hellenistic sacrificial practice.

Consider a typical public festival in a Hellenistic city. Sacrifices would have been organized and financed by the elite of the city, the "first citizens"; the presiding priests come from among their ranks as well. The festival begins with a procession of priest, victim, and participants, with much music, pomp, and celebration. The animal victim is coaxed along, not led; it should come along willingly, implicitly giving its assent to the killing that is to take place. It agrees to the deed again upon arriving at the temple, as the participants shower the animal with handfuls of grain. As it shakes its coat free of the tiny granules that cling to it, this too is taken as a nod of assent. A prayer is offered, then a few hairs are clipped from the animal and cast into the waiting fire—an offering of firstfruits, the *aparchē*, or "beginning," of the sacrifice. Finally, the animal agrees once more before the altar itself, by lowering its head to drink from the water bowl placed before it: the willing victim appears to submit to the blow. This is not a violent act to be resisted. It belongs to the order of things; it is necessary. As the ax is raised, so are the voices of those who surround the proceedings, the women trilling in that distinctive high-pitched way that Westerners today still find both eerie and exciting. The ax falls, doing its work swiftly and cleanly (botching it now would be a very bad omen). The animal falls. Its blood—the animal's life—spills out, but is quickly collected to be sprinkled or poured upon the altar: a life taken is quickly returned to the gods. Now the viscera are efficiently removed. The liver is examined for omens. Then all these delicacies—liver, heart, lungs, spleen, and kidneys—are roasted and immediately consumed by the inner circle of celebrants. The rest of the animal is then butchered and cooked—usually boiled for tenderness. The bones are saved to reconstruct the skeleton, which, wrapped in fat, will be consumed by the altar fires, offering back to the gods their meager share.[7]

Finally, the cooked meat is distributed and the feasting begins. While modern anthropology has tended to focus on the act of killing as the central moment of the sacrifice,[8] for ancients living in a subsistence economy, where food is always an issue, and meat especially is a rarity, this distribution would have been the moment for which everyone was really waiting. In ancient Greece this distribution is said to have proceeded along egalitarian lines, each citizen participant receiving an equal share of the meat.[9] But in later Roman times, when the hierarchical systems of patronage and power, especially in the form of the imperial cult, had reshaped the contours of Hellenistic political life, the distribution would have reflected the top-down brokerage common to that era.[10] The first citizens of the city received the largest, choicest portions, second-rank officials the more common cuts. Further down the social food chain the shares would have become smaller and mean. Outside the circle altogether stood women, noncitizens, children, and foreigners. Their portions would come through those who might connect them to the civic, political, and religious life of the community: their husbands, fathers, and patrons. A sacrifice, finally, expresses and reinscribes the ordering of a community through the most elemental of human necessities: food. Here, as in all times and places, you are what you eat.

Thus the sacrifice, an offering aimed ostensibly at the gods, is also full of effects for the community that surrounds the altar. First of all, it defines the boundaries of the community. Sacrificing together, more than any other tangible act in antiquity, indicates one's membership in a group, whether that be a family, a club, a city, or, finally, an empire. Second, it provides a social index, or map, for the community gathered. Gender distinctions are reinscribed insofar as the inner circle of participants are all male; the very presence of women at the altar would pollute it.[11] And the more elaborate web of social standing, position, and hierarchy is traced out as the food is distributed in proper rank and order. By the end of the day, everyone knows how it is in the world, and all, by their participation, give their assent to this ritually created and ordered world. In the Hellenistic age, it was through sacrifice that culture found its coherence. "This essential act in Greek life is a moment when the world is set in place under the eyes of the gods."[12]

Though the details of sacrificial practice varied from culture to culture, even from city to city, this basic picture held true for most of the peoples of the Mediterranean basin throughout the period of Christian origins. This much was shared across many cultural lines: a sacred priesthood, the killing of a prized animal, the offering of cereal and wine as well, and the distribution of the food. These were the basic elements in Greek and Roman sacrificial practice. Jewish practice differed only in that the foundational sacrifice that created and sustained Israel as a people, by tradition offered originally on Sinai (Exod 24:1-11), and now daily in the Temple (Exod 29:38-46), was a whole burnt offering (*'olah*), consumed entirely by the altar fires as a fragrant gift to satisfy Yahweh. No Promethean trickery here to save the best parts for the human ones; everything "goes up in smoke," to God. But this was just one kind of sacrifice among the Jews. More common, and similar to Mediterranean practice generally, were the frequent "peace offerings" (*zebach shelamim*) to be made from the slaughter of any domesticated animal (Lev 17:1-9). Leviticus makes every slaughter a sacrifice, thus approaching the situation in the Hellenistic cities, where virtually all consumable meat was consecrated. Here too we find the same convergence of vocabulary around the practice of sacrifice and food preparation as one finds in Greek. *Zabach* means both "to sacrifice" and "to slaughter," and the *mizbeach* is both "altar" and "place of slaughter." By this regulation the consumption of meat was mediated through the priests and the Temple. To reiterate, in a peasant culture of subsistence, this is no small thing.

In another class of sacrifices the role of the priesthood in expressing and regulating the boundaries of community life was even more marked. These were the offerings designed to purge the community of the polluting effects of transgression or irregularity. In Israel these included the sin offering (*chatta't*) and the reparation offering (*'asham*). The sin offering was the remedy for conscious violations of the covenant (Lev 4:1–5:13), the reparation offering for unconscious or inadvertent violations (5:14–6:7). In each case the animal was given over to the priests, sometimes to be burned, sometimes to be consumed by the priests themselves (6:17-23). In any event, violation of the established order of things meant for the peasant the sacrifice of something very dear: food.

A similar practice existed among the Romans. Romans were particularly troubled by unusual events—so-called prodigies—that violated their sense of the expected, the normal.[13] A statue is seen to sweat. A goat grows wool. A wild animal runs unexpected through the city. Ravens whine, "as though being strangled."[14] When such things happened, they were to be reported to the Senate, which then decided whether the calamity constituted a true sign of discontent from the gods. If the Senate so decided, the matter was referred to diviners to determine the proper sacrificial remedy, which was then carried out by the priests (all of senatorial rank). Prodigies were usually associated with political, military, or economic crises, and taken to indicate the source of the crisis: divine displeasure. Defining the problem, specifying the remedy, and ultimately wielding the power to restore order and normalcy were prerogatives that lay firmly in the hands of Rome's ruling elite, the Senate.

What if the calamity was so great that no ordinary sacrifice would suffice to restore the divinely ordered world, placate the gods, and save the people from assured destruction? Sometimes nothing less than a *human* sacrifice would do. Many places in ancient Greece had the practice of selecting a person—usually from among the destitute and socially marginal—who might be ritually invested with the sins and transgressions of the people and ceremoniously driven from the city, thus bearing away all that had offended the gods. Such a one was called the *pharmakos*, a term closely related to the neuter noun *pharmakon*, which means drug or healing agent, even "charm." The *pharmakos* was the remedy, the means by which that which ails the city could be dispatched.[15] The Jews, of course, had a similar custom, only performed with a goat rather than an outcast (Lev 16:20-22). In Roman times the execution of a criminal might carry such sacrificial overtones.[16]

More ennobling was a person's *voluntary* sacrifice on behalf of his or her people. We have already learned in the last chapter of the ancient tradition of the Noble Death and martyrdom, and how this played a key role in the interpretation of Jesus' death among his followers. But now we should add that the ancient tradition of dying nobly for a cause, or more commonly for one's city or people, often took on the character of atoning sacrifice as well.[17] This popular theme in Hellenistic literature favors virgins and generals especially. Virgin daughters seem to be offered in pairs; for example, the legendary daughters of Erechtheus, sacrificed to satisfy the anger of Poseidon,[18] or the daughters of Antipoios of Thebes, Androcleia and Alcis, who were said to have sacrificed themselves to save their city.[19] Of generals there are plenty, including the Decii, father, son, and grandson, all of whom, by legend, gave themselves in battle as an expiatory offering (*devotio*) to the gods to save the Roman people.[20] P. Decius (son) summarizes the family legacy in words provided by the Roman historian Livy: "This is the privilege granted to our house that we should be an expiatory sacrifice to avert dangers from the State." This he says as he throws himself into battle against the Gauls. "Now will I offer the legions of the enemy together with myself as a sacrifice to Tellus and the Dii Manes."[21] With that, he says a prayer and spurs

his horse into the heart of the battle and is slain. This was how parti-
sans viewed Cato's death as well, as may be seen in the stirring oration
conjured up by Lucan in his epic poem on the Roman Civil War: "Let
my blood redeem the nations, and my death pay the whole penalty
incurred by the corruption of Rome," says Cato. "My blood, mine
only, will bring peace to the people of Italy and end their sufferings."[22]
His model for such self-sacrifice is Decius: "As hordes of foemen bore
down Decius when he had offered his life, so may both armies pierce
this body, may the savages of the Rhine aim their weapons at me."[23]

As we have seen in the last chapter, Jews had their own martyrs,
whose deaths they came to see as sacrificial in just this way. In the traditions of early Judaism, the great heroes of the Maccabean literature—
the old priest Eleazar, the seven brothers and their mother, all of whom
were tortured to death by Antiochus IV Epiphanes during the early
days of the Maccabean revolt—provide the best-known instance of this
development. It occurs already in one of the earlier Maccabean books,
Second Maccabees (second century B.C.E.). Here the last to die of the
seven brothers confesses, "we [Hebrews] are suffering for our own sins"
(7:32). By their deaths, the seven brothers and their mother hope to
obtain for Israel the mercy of God, and "to bring to an end the wrath
of the Almighty that has justly fallen on our whole nation" (7:37-38).
The idea that these heroes died an expiatory death persisted and
became relevant again during the Roman imperial period. Then
among the Jews of Antioch, the Maccabean martyrs were remembered
once more. In Fourth Maccabees, written during the first century C.E.,
their deaths are regarded as a sacrifice, an expiation for the sins of the
people. Thus the old priest Eleazar prays shortly before he expires, "Be
merciful to your people and let our punishment be a satisfaction on
their behalf. Make my blood their purification and take my life as a
ransom for theirs" (4 Macc 6:28-29).[24] Of his death, and that of the
brothers and their mother, the narrator of this text concludes:
"Through the blood of these righteous ones and through the propitia-
tion (*hilastērion*) of their death the divine providence rescued Israel,
which had been shamefully treated" (4 Macc 17:22).

These deaths, of course, are examples of the ultimate sacrifice one might make. But in purpose, and sometimes even in form, they are of a piece with those offered around the public altars, however large or small. The very existence of these ancient communities, whether we are speaking of Athens, Rome, or Jerusalem, depends on sacrifice. In Mediterranean antiquity, a community is a group gathered around an altar. The gods have ordered the world and created every people, each in its place. At the center of each place is an altar, the table at which both gods and mortals gather, where food is both offered and consumed. To sacrifice reconfirms this order—a people in their place, together with their gods. But the place must be fit for the gods; it must be holy. This too is part of the ordering work accomplished by sacrifice. In Judaism, the blood of the sacrificial victim had a sanctifying power. Sprinkled on the altar, it had the power to cleanse the place of sin's soiling effect.[25] It removed the dirt—"matter out of place," to quote Mary Douglas.[26] Sacrifice sets things aright; it puts everything and everyone in their proper place. Sacrifice settles things. When the community begins to dissolve and fall apart, there can be only one solution: sacrifice. This is why Cato throws his life down on behalf of the ideals of Republican Rome. It is why Augustus would years later prohibit all manner of strange and upstart private religious associations and permit only the ancient and time-honored collegia of Rome to offer *proper* sacrifices.[27] It is why Eleazar bears up under torture, even death, as a witness to the gravity of following Israel's law. These sacrifices all aim to set things aright. When all is right once again, sacrifice keeps it so. The hearth burns; the animals are brought; everyone eats; the gods are satisfied and so are the mortals.

Jesus the Sacrifice

Now given all this, what would it mean for the followers of Jesus to begin speaking of his death as a sacrifice? First and foremost, we should expect that this kind of talk would have been closely connected to the processes of social formation that were unfolding in the first years of the Jesus movement. It is not an image located in the personal dimensions of ancient life, but in the sphere of public and private *group* life. This is where we should try to explore the image in early Christian usage: in the context of forming communities. How might early gatherings of the Jesus movement have begun to speak of Jesus' death as a sacrifice?

Imagine yourself in a city such as Corinth, walking into a gathering of these early Christians—followers of Jesus, really, for we cannot assume that they have a firm group identity just yet. They gather at week's end, like other groups of common purpose, to eat and to talk.[28] First comes the eating, then the talking. The talk is of one not present, the founder, who is dead. They speak of what he said, and did, and what he stood for and valued. And then the talk turns to his death. The story is told of how it happened. Perhaps it is familiar to you—the death of God's righteous one—tricked, betrayed by friends, suffering a tortured death, but faithful to the end, and finally exalted by God for his faithful witness. We know this as the martyr's story in Jewish tradition, even a noble death among the Greeks. Now it is told of Jesus, too. But what does it mean, really? The talk continues on into the evening. Perhaps someone says something like this:

> For while we were still weak, at the right time Christ died for the ungodly. Indeed, rarely will anyone die for a righteous person—though perhaps for a good person someone might actually dare to die. But God proves his love for us in that while we still were sinners Christ died for us. Much more surely then, now that we have been justified by his blood, will we be saved through him from the wrath of God. For, if while we were enemies, we were reconciled to God through the death of his Son, much more surely, having been reconciled, we will be saved by his life. (Rom 5:6-10)

These are words, of course, from the apostle Paul. They speak on the one hand of the Messiah's willing death—a martyr's death—but at the same time of the reconciling effect that Jesus' death has for those who follow him, unworthy though they may be. This sort of talk, as we have seen, was right at home in the Hellenistic milieu of Christian origins. The martyr's death is not just a death that bears witness to a cause. It can also be a sacrifice reconciling sinners with their God. This is how Lucan understood Cato's death. It is how Jews in Antioch understood Eleazar's death. It is how the followers of Jesus came to understand his death as well.[29]

When such passages in Paul are read today one might easily overlook the martyrological aspects of the text. "Jesus died for our sins" is understood in purely sacrificial terms. But this cheats the context within which this idea was at home, and from which the idea drew much of its power. The saving aspect of the martyr's death cannot be separated from the exemplary aspects of his life. The career of the martyr is in part vicarious precisely through the example it sets for others.[30] Notice that in this instance Paul speaks of the reconciling power of Jesus' death (v. 10a), but it is by his *life* that his followers are saved (v. 10b).

Though Paul's voice is the first one we hear explicating the meaning of Jesus' death in just this way, he was not alone in this, nor was he the first to do it. Earlier in Romans Paul makes rough-and-ready use of an early Christian (pre-Pauline) tradition that brings together the martyrological tradition and these sacrificial notions in the same way (even though the modern translation tradition makes this a little difficult to see on first glance). I will cite it first in the NRSV:

> But now, apart from the law, the righteousness of God has been disclosed, and is attested by the law and the prophets, the righteousness of God through faith in Jesus Christ for all who believe. For there is no distinction, since all have sinned and fallen short of the glory of God; they are now justified by his grace as a gift, through the redemption that is in Jesus Christ, whom God put forward as a sacrifice of atonement by his blood, effective through faith. He did this to show his righteousness, because in his divine forbearance he had passed over the sins previously committed; it was to prove at the present time that he himself is righteous and that he justifies the one who has faith in Jesus. (Rom 3:21-26)

It would be difficult to think of a passage of greater importance to the Reformed understanding of Christian faith. This is unfortunate, for this is also one of the most difficult passages to understand in English, and, unbelievably, even more mystifying in Greek. It is a place—not untypical for Paul—where the apostle blurts out parts of thoughts and traditional formulas with little attention to syntax or sentence formation. What is more, the words he uses are ambiguous in the most crucial places. The NRSV smooths all this out for the reader of English, but in so doing it must resolve all of Paul's broken thoughts and ambiguities into cogent sentences. Here, as much as anywhere in the New Testament, translation is the first act of interpretation, and the only one that really counts.

By far the most important of these ambiguities occurs in the phrase rendered here "faith in Jesus" (vv. 22 and 26). To a believer used to thinking about "justification by faith," this is quite natural. But believing *in* Jesus is probably not what is meant here. A more apt translation of the phrase would be "faith *of* Jesus."[31] Now, how might one be justified, redeemed, or saved by the faith—or faithfulness—*of* Jesus (v. 26)? And how might one speak of God's righteousness being disclosed through the faith *of* Jesus (v. 22)? Again the martyrological context for speaking of Jesus' sacrificial death proves crucial to understanding just what Paul is trying to say. It is always through the martyr's *faithfulness* that God's righteousness is called forth and God's mercy rekindled. It is the martyr's faithfulness, even unto death, that redeems the people in God's eyes. This is the meaning of the first half of the passage. We might translate it as follows:

> But now the just nature of God has been made clear—apart from the law—even though the law and prophets bear witness to it—through the faithfulness of Jesus the just nature of God (has been made clear) to all who have such faith. For there is no distinction, all have sinned and fallen short of the glory of God—but—they have been judged righteous as a gift, by his grace, through the redemption that is in Jesus Christ. . . . (vv. 21-24)

The thought is not yet crystal clear because Paul is fumbling with the language, trying to use a tradition, but qualifying and explaining it all the way through. But Paul seems to be working with the idea, common in the Hellenistic era, that one person's faithfulness could call forth mercy from the gods. This becomes clearer as Paul continues:

> whom God proposed as a sacrifice, because of his [Jesus'] faithfulness—at the cost of his blood. In passing over former sins—in his divine forbearance—God thus demonstrated his just nature . . . (Rom 3:25)

Here it is not as though God sends his son Jesus to earth with the purpose of being a sacrifice, as might be suggested by the NRSV ("God put forth . . .").[32] Rather, God observes the faithfulness of Jesus and proposes that his blood be treated as an expiatory sacrifice. The martyr becomes a sacrifice. Thus Paul finishes the thought:

> as proof of his [God's] just nature in the present time, showing that he himself is just and declares righteous the person who is so from the faith of Jesus. (Rom 3:26)

This last phrase, "from the faith of Jesus," I have left just as vague as Paul himself leaves it. It could mean that the follower of Jesus is declared righteous because Jesus was faithful unto death, and so atoned for the sins of those who follow him.[33] On the other hand, it could mean that the follower is declared righteous if she or he too demonstrates the same kind of faith as that shown by Jesus.[34] The latter seems to fit Paul's argument better, though it chafes against traditional Reformed theology. Indeed, in the next chapter of Romans Paul will offer Abraham as an example of one who was justified by his (own!) faithfulness. The latter interpretation also seems to fit better into the martyrological framework within which these ideas are offered. The martyr's death is expiatory, and so satisfies God; but it is vicarious also by its exemplary nature: it shows the kind of faithfulness that is pleasing to God, and is thus to be emulated.

Given what we have seen in the Hellenistic world—including early
Judaism—it is not at all difficult to imagine how Jesus the martyr
became Jesus the sacrifice. And given the ubiquity of sacrifice in
ancient life, it is easy also to see how this idea could have flourished
in Christian circles and taken on a life of its own. As the people of
the Jesus movement began to reflect on this idea of Jesus as a
sacrifice, they did not always do so in an explicitly martyrological
framework. For example, in Romans 8:3 Paul can speak of God sending his son to be a "sin offering" (*hamartia*), thus detaching sacrifice
from its martyrological context and grafting it into the idea of the
descending/ascending redeemer sent from God. He speaks similarly
in 2 Corinthians 5:21: "For our sake he made the one who knew no sin
into a *sin offering*, in order that in him we might become the righteousness of God." Here the cultic context of sacrifice shows its influence. Now Jesus is the perfect sacrifice, unblemished, without sin, as
must be all victims offered to satisfy God's anger. All of this would
have been easily understood by the Jews, Greeks, Romans, and others
who came into contact with Christianity. The metaphor was as common as life itself.

Why Sacrifice?

But this answers the question of *how* early Christians came to speak of
Jesus as a sacrifice: it was probably in connection with the understanding of Jesus' death as a martyr. But this leaves many more questions yet unanswered. Why did this sacrificial metaphor prove to be so
powerful for Jesus' followers in coming to grips with their own existence in the wake of his violent death?

To explore this question further we will need once again to visit
that imaginary early Christian gathering in Corinth, paying close
attention to what is said, and by whom. Since sacrifice is about eating,
it is not surprising that we find some interesting things said about
sacrifice in connection with the meal part of this gathering. As the

meal begins we learn that it is a commemorative meal. As the first loaf is broken, someone says: "The Lord Jesus on the night when he was betrayed took a loaf of bread, and when he had given thanks, he broke it and said, 'This is my body that is for you. Do this in remembrance of me'" (1 Cor 11:23-24). A broken body, offered "for you." The martyrological theme, with its sacrificial overtones, is clear.[35]

But then, after the meal someone speaks a word about the last cup of wine as well: "This cup is the new covenant in my blood. Do this, as often as you drink it, in remembrance of me" (1 Cor 11:25). Now the sacrificial overtones take on a more distinctive cast. The sacrifice of Jesus' blood is to be understood in terms of the Jewish covenant sacrifice, the sacrifice offered at Sinai that created the bond between the people of Israel and Yahweh, and in so doing, created Israel as a people (Exodus 24), or perhaps the talk of a "new covenant" is to echo the prophetic renewal tradition (Jeremiah 31). The words explicitly invoke the Jewish tradition, but the idea that sacrifice creates, defines, and delineates a people is not unique to Judaism, as we have seen. This is the basic function of sacrifice in the Hellenistic world. It creates community. To speak of Jesus as a sacrifice is to recognize, first, that it is in him that this new community finds it existence. His death draws them together. But how?

The words we have just read from Paul are repeated almost verbatim in the Gospel of Mark. There they are found in a poignant depiction of the last time Jesus eats with his closest followers gathered for the traditional Passover meal just outside Jerusalem (Mark 14:12-31, especially vv. 22-25). Their narrative setting gives them more power yet: Passover commemorates the birth of Israel, the creation of a new people. Another detail underscores the orchestration: those gathered with Jesus are twelve in number, like the original tribes of Israel. Mark sees this as the moment when a new people is born. But this new people consists not just of "the twelve." This symbolic meal is presaged by two meals in Mark involving great throngs of people of every sort, stuck in the wilderness, hungry, and yet miraculously fed by Jesus

(6:30-44; 8:1-10). He is, for Mark, a new Moses, re-creating the passage from bondage to freedom.[36] All of this is fairly straightforward.

But to catch the full effect of what Mark is doing through these passages one should cast an eye to the sort of people who inhabit Mark's narrative, who are brought with Jesus on the journey and joined with him in the new community. There are many ordinary people—the ever-present "crowd," in Mark's story. But there are others, too, whom Mark names and calls attention to especially: lepers, the demon-possessed, foreigners, women—even menstruating women. This table, this meal, this sacrifice is for the unclean and any who would deign to eat with "unclean hands" (Mark 7:2). As he approaches Jerusalem and his final meal there, Jesus warns that he will have to die for what he has been doing. At one point he takes a child—perhaps a street urchin—embraces it, and says: "Whoever welcomes one such child in my name welcomes me, and whoever welcomes me, welcomes not me, but the one who sent me" (Mark 9:37). The table he would die for is one to which even children are invited. All of this is very important. For when this table is transformed into an altar, it will play host to a sacrifice that is for the unclean, the marginal, and the unimportant.

In my view, this is crucial to understanding just why the followers of Jesus found it meaningful to think of his death as a sacrifice. Like a sacrifice, his death created of his followers a community who would be devoted to the same things to which Jesus devoted himself. In this way Jesus' martyrdom could be thought of as a sacrifice, and their meals to commemorate his death, as sacrificial meals. But there is more: they thought of his death not just as a covenant sacrifice. It was also expiatory—an atoning sacrifice. Such a sacrifice removes the stain of the unclean, the offense of the sinner. Just think of the makeup of one of these early communities gathered in Jesus' name. In addition to lepers, the demon-possessed, foreigners, and women, there were also prostitutes, tax collectors, and sinners. Various unclean types turn up in the narratives of these early communities—tanners, for example. Slaves, too, were part of the mix. Paul says of the Corinthian community, "Consider your call, brothers and sisters: not many of you were wise by human standards, not many were powerful, not many were of noble birth" (1 Cor 1:26). This statement of course indicates that some in the Corinthian community were indeed persons of wealth and power, but Paul stresses that most of those who had come to make up this community were *not*. They were "weak," "despised," "nothings" in the world (1 Cor 1:27-28). Those who were "of noble birth" were choosing quite consciously to take leave of their privileged social location by associating with "the low and despised in the world." Paul himself is perhaps the most obvious example of this. He was probably a person of means, educated, perhaps even a Roman citizen, but by his own choice to join a disreputable religious movement he became, in his own words, "the scum of the earth" (1 Cor 4:13). For these "nothings" and those who chose to associate with them, Jesus' death became the sacrifice that made them something: clean, redeemed, drawn together in a community of adopted children of God (Rom 8:14-17).

Imagine a prostitute in the following of Jesus. She comes into this movement, is welcomed to the table, and becomes part of a new community. She—an unclean prostitute—is, for the first time, considered clean. In the company of Jesus she is human. She is no longer an expendable piece of meat, no longer a prostitute. Then Jesus is killed, crucified as a common criminal. Now she must decide: is what she experienced over now, or was it real—real enough to continue as a reality for her? Is she clean or not? Is she a prostitute or not? The city that knows her is of no help to her. A patron who wants what he thinks he deserves from a prostitute says, "You *are* a prostitute. You think you are not? You think you are clean just because Jesus said you were? That's a joke! He's dead, and you're a prostitute. You always were, and you always will be, scum." Here is her challenge. So she says, "I am not a prostitute. I am not unclean. You want something for my sins? You want a sacrifice to atone for me? *Jesus* is my sacrifice. His death was 'for me.' His blood atones for everything I ever did, and everything you ever did to me. You think he was killed—a common, unclean criminal execution—but I say his death was a sacrifice . . . for me." So she gathers at week's end with others who knew Jesus: lepers, tanners, fishmongers, tax collectors, slaves, unaccompanied women, maybe a few street urchins. They eat a meal like they ate with Jesus, they remember what he died for, and they convince themselves once again that it was all true. His death becomes the sacrifice that makes them clean and whole, worthy to come to the table—now "altar"—and eat in the presence of God.

We Abstain!

Early Christian meals might naturally have been saturated with talk of sacrifice. This was, after all, the central theme of sacred meals in antiquity. But now we must attend to something quite peculiar about these early meals. Indeed, all this talk about sacrifice could easily deflect attention away from what is by far the most striking, and from the ancient point of view, most disturbing aspect of these gatherings: in early Christian worship there is, in reality, no sacrifice. No animals are killed. No libations are poured on an altar. There is no altar. A religion without sacrifice: it is not just unusual in the Hellenistic world, it is subversive.

To understand the significance of this great absence in early Christian worship one must recall all that was said earlier about sacrifice and the central role it played in Hellenistic culture. This was not simply a matter of religious sensibility, of style, or of taste. One must think beyond the stark separation of sacred from secular that so marks the social geography of modern Western life. Such a divide did not exist for ancients. Sacrifice was the central expression of ancient religious life, but through sacrifice the social and political world was also given its definitive shape and organization. The world, in this conception, is divinely ordered and maintained, and the human role in this divinely ordained stasis is to sacrifice. "Without constant sacrifice, the world would fall apart."[37]

Practically speaking, sacrifice functioned thus by creating and managing the reality of *place*. An altar is first of all a place, a center for communal life. To be associated particularly with a place, a center, is to be located in the culture and to have an identity. Of course, one might be located multiply in a culture, with several overlapping identities. One might be a citizen of a polis—thus located in a city. One might also be a Roman citizen, part of the empire. Most people had families, yet another location. In addition there were various other temples and religious associations to which one might belong. Each of these "places" revolved around an altar at which sacrifices were offered on a regular basis, from the family shrine, to the city hearth, to the great imperial temples dedicated to the gods Roma and Augustus. To gather at an altar was to mark one as belonging to a particular place.

This was true in a geographic sense, but also in terms of social location. Not everyone could approach the great altar of Athena in Athens. Within the groups gathered at various levels of social and political importance, a social ordering was reflected in the ceremony and, most importantly, in the distribution of the meat and the partaking of the meal. Through sacrificial practice, the whole world was set in place, and each person located somewhere within it. In the Roman imperial period this was especially crucial. For in a totalitarian, strongly hierarchical regime it is above all imperative to know that everyone has a place, and is in fact *in place*. The maintenance of imperial power and control depends utterly on this. The Roman historians Beard, North, and Price summarize what was at issue in the sacrificial practices of the empire:

> What was at stake for emperors, governors, and members of civic elites was the whole web of social, political, and hierarchical assumptions that bound imperial society together. Sacrifices and other religious rituals were concerned with defining and establishing relationships of power. Not to place oneself within the set of relationships between emperor, gods, elite and people

was effectively to place oneself outside the mainstream of the whole world and the shared Roman understanding of humanity's place within that world. Maintenance of the social order was seen by the Romans to be dependent on maintenance of this agreed set of symbolic structures, which assigned a role to people at all levels.[38]

Earliest Christians, by choosing not to sacrifice, refused to place themselves within the "web of social, political, and hierarchical assumptions that bound imperial society together." They did this by omitting sacrifice from their own religious life. They refused thus to "place" themselves. But more significantly, they did this by refusing to participate in the whole public and private structure of sacrificial life. They would not attend sacrifices in the local temples. They would not sacrifice to the emperor or his gods. Most importantly, they would not eat the meat that came from the sacrifice of animals to the gods.[39]

This matter of eating sacrificial meat deserves closer scrutiny, for within early Christian groups it became a matter of great dispute. By understanding what was at stake in eating such meat, we might better understand the significance of Christian abstinence from it.

To begin, we should recall three things. First, in an agrarian peasant culture meat is a rare thing. People who live at a subsistence level do not eat much meat; any opportunity for such a rich source of sustenance was therefore highly prized and cause for much celebration. Second, the consumption of meat—what portion, how much, how often—was directly related to one's social location. Meat was expensive; it is as simple as that. Gerd Theissen makes this point by quoting from the rabbinic tractate *b. Hullin* 84a: "A man having one *maneh* may buy a *litra* of vegetables for his bowl; if ten a *litra* of fish; if fifty *maneh* a *litra* of meat."[40] Grain is basic. Vegetables are a step up from that. Fish is a luxury. But meat is in a class all by itself. Finally, given these realities, it is quite understandable that in the Hellenistic world, the consumption of meat was indeed always a special occasion, marked in its significance by sacrifice. In fact, as we have already seen, virtually all the meat consumed in the Hellenistic world would have derived from sacrifice. There were great celebrations involving public sacrifices to commemorate great events; there were regular events on the sacred calendar of the empire or of individual cities; there were games and contests; there were smaller gatherings of religious associations and collegia; there were private, "invitation only" gatherings at the great temples and their accompanying banquet facilities.[41] These were the occasions at which meat was made available; each began with a sacrifice, from which the meat was distributed. If an altar marks one's place, it is the meat of sacrifice that draws one close and holds one in place.

Small wonder that the issue of whether one should eat meat that came from a sacrifice emerged as significant for early Christians. Eating meat—publicly—was to involve oneself in the whole web of social and political life, and the religious substance that held it all together. It was more than the issue of practicing idolatry, seen, as it usually is, as an abstract or purely theoretical religious issue. To eat meat was to participate in the world, the empire, and all that it stood for. This was the empire that had executed Jesus as a common criminal. This was the empire that would not tolerate the vision of a new empire so treasured by his followers. To eat meat was to cross the line, to "re-place" oneself in the world from which one had just taken leave. To eat meat, to participate in sacrifice, was to participate in the great cultural project of sustaining the world *as it is*. How could the followers of Jesus do this if they looked forward to another, very different world to come?

Apparently, some did find a way, for the record shows that this was a matter of dispute in various Christian communities. Theissen's analysis clarifies why.[42] For peasants, and even more so for the marginal and expendable types who became part of these communities, to pass up any opportunity for food would have been a grave choice. If you were hungry already, to turn away from the pleasant smell of roasting meat was almost too much to ask. And if you were among the few people of means who joined these communities, abstaining from meat would have meant severing all ties and relationships binding you securely into the social and political web that had nurtured you and treated you so well. It would have meant extricating yourself from all patronal relations, all peer associations, all institutional sources of support. For such a person, the loss of place would have involved taking leave from a place that had in so many ways been rewarding. Eating sacrificial meat was more than consumption, more than mere worship. It meant conviviality, commensality, and community.

We first encounter eating sacrificial meat as an issue in Paul's early Corinthian correspondence. It is a little surprising that Paul should have such a strong reaction to the practice of eating meat that had been offered to an idol. True, Jews typically did not eat meat that had been offered to a pagan god,[43] but Paul had notoriously dispensed with Jewish dietary practices that would hinder commensality between Jew and Greek (Gal 2:11-14). Nonetheless, in this case he is adamant that members of the Corinthian churches should not eat sacrificial meat. The situation calls for explanation.

Some in the Corinthian community have apparently justified eating sacrificial meat on the grounds that the gods to whom the sacrifice had been made were not really gods after all, and so their participation in such activities could not compromise their devotion to the one true God (1 Cor 8:4-6). Paul is not convinced by this explanation, even though he grants that in theory it might be true. He knows that this is not finally a theoretical matter. Rather, he is concerned about the consequences such activity will have for the whole community. He asks, "What if someone who doesn't share your sophisticated theoretical understanding[44] of these things sees you eating at a temple feast and thinks, if it is all right for him to do that, why shouldn't I?" (8:10). Paul is realistic here: he knows that meat is a powerful draw, powerful enough to draw people away from his abstaining, countercultural community. So, he concludes, "If food is a cause of their falling, I will never eat meat" (8:13). Paul clearly knows what meat eating means in his culture: it is about finding one's place in the community; it is about participation. To be at table is to be united with those who share the table. Thus later in his argument he says of their own meals: "The cup of blessing that we bless, is it not a sharing in the blood of Christ? The bread that we break is it not a sharing in the body of Christ? Because there is one bread, we who are many are one body, for we all partake of the one bread" (10:16-17).

Eating in this sacral way is about expressing one's place, one's belonging to a community. Those who commune together are partners, he argues, and, even though the pagan gods are not really gods, but demons, "I do not want you to be partners (*koinōnous*) with demons," he says (10:20b). Paul is not concerned here with mystical or physical union with lesser deities (by consuming the flesh of the deity, for example). Rather, he speaks in a manner reflecting Hellenistic sacrificial practice. To participate in a sacrificial meal is to be at table with one's chosen companions (*koinōnoi*), including the god, who is also present at the meal. In such meals it was common to set aside certain portions of the meat, placing them on the god's table, or *trapeza*—hence the common name *trapezōmata* for these portions.[45] "You cannot partake of the table (*trapezēs*) of the Lord and the table (*trapezēs*) of demons," he argues (10:21b). Paul clearly knows, as everyone of his culture did, that eating meat is a public statement of belonging. Notice, as his argument continues to resolution, that Paul is not concerned about eating meat in private, where the question would become a purely theoretical question of principle (10:23-27). His concern, rather, is those *public* occasions when eating meat could be seen as a statement (10:28-29). When it comes to that, one's statement should be clear and unequivocal: we abstain![46]

Paul's measured approach to this question would have sounded wishy-washy and weak-kneed to the early Christian prophet responsible for Revelation. From the letters attached to the beginning of the Apocalypse proper we can see that eating sacrificial meat had also emerged as an issue in the churches of western Asia Minor, to which the letters are addressed. It appears specifically in two of these letters, the letter to Pergamum (2:14) and the letter to Thyatira (2:20). In each case the prophet is adamant. Against such persons who eat sacrificial meat the heavenly Christ will make war "with the sword of my mouth" (2:16). At Thyatira the practice is apparently allowed by a woman prophet, whom John insults with the name "Jezebel" and promises to "strike her children dead" (2:23)—a reference presumably to her followers. These searing words are to be understood within the context of Revelation as a whole, which portrays the prophet as the most ardent defender against a great cultural onslaught that was challenging the integrity of these churches at the end of the first century. This was probably during the reign of Domitian, who insisted on order and cultural uniformity as a way of holding off the chaos that always threatened so large an empire as Rome's. Christians who refused to participate in local cults suffered persecution and martyrdom along with all dissidents of that period.[47] But the prophet John would not brook any cultural accommodation whatsoever, even in these extreme circumstances. By the end of the Apocalypse, one can only conclude that martyrdom is preferable by far to the horrors that await those who cave in and "worship the beast" that is Rome.

We are fortunate to have from about that same time a record of just such a confrontation between Christian dissidents and the empire, but told from the point of view of the empire itself. It rings remarkably true to the picture one gets from Revelation. Pliny the Younger governed the Roman province of Pontus-Bithynia early in the second century C.E. Among his letters to the emperor Trajan we find the first mention of Christians in pagan literature. Christians had come to Pliny's attention because they had formed illegal "political associations." Pliny investigated. He rounded up several members of the group, but discovered only

> that they were in the habit of meeting on a certain fixed day before it was light, when they sang in alternate verses a hymn to Christ, as to a god, and bound themselves by a solemn oath, not to do any wicked deeds, but never to commit any fraud, theft, or adultery, never to falsify their word, nor deny a trust when they should be called upon to deliver it up; after which it was their custom to separate, and then reassemble to partake of food—but food of an ordinary and innocent kind. (*Ep.* 10.96 [LCL])

This picture was confirmed for Pliny when he tried "to extract the real truth" by torturing two of the movement's leaders, both female slaves. Were they harmless, or dangerously seditious? Pliny devised a test: the accused should repeat an invocation to the gods, offer adoration to the image of the emperor and the gods, and finally curse Christ. Many did this; but others did not. The latter Pliny ordered executed. This is the true test of sedition: will they sacrifice to the emperor and the gods or not? Why this? As Pliny notes a little later in the letter, before his intervention the temples of the region had all but been abandoned, their festivals neglected, and sacrificial animals had "met with but few purchasers." This was the problem. The Christian refusal to sacrifice struck right at the very heart of Hellenistic civilization and the Roman imperial system that had been built upon its trusses. The altar, sacrifice, meat: without these the Hellenistic world would have fallen into chaos. If there was one thing that Rome feared, it was chaos.

Thus it was that the Christian refusal to sacrifice would remain a point of conflict with the empire for as long as sacrifice remained at the center of public religious and political life. We encounter it again, not surprisingly, at the center of the first great systematic persecution of Christians during the reign of Decius (249–251 C.E.), under whom many Christian dissidents were martyred. We have from that period a papyrus document attesting to the vindication of a certain (presumably) Christian suspect, which illuminates the issues involved. The document, a certificate of sorts, is dated to 250 C.E., and comes from the Fayum district of Egypt, where Christians were required to appear before a local commissioner and perform the requisite sacrifices to satisfy the imperial edict. The "certificate of sacrifice" reads as follows:

> To those chosen to superintend the sacrifices in the village of Alexander's Island; from Aurelius Diogenes, son of Sabatus, of the village of Alexander's Island, aged seventy-two, with a scar on his right elbow. I have always sacrificed to the gods; and now in your presence in accordance with the terms of the edict I have

sacrificed and [poured a libation] and have [tasted] the sacrificial
victims. I request you certify this. Farewell. I, Aurelius Diogenes,
have presented this petition.[48]

From this we may thus infer the requirements of the edict: one must
sacrifice to the gods, pour a libation of wine, and eat of the sacrificial
meat. These were the spiritual essentials necessary to holding the
whole imperial system together. It is noteworthy that nothing is said
here of worshiping the emperor. Loyalty, per se, was not the nub of
the issue. The issue was whether you were part of the ongoing, recognized religious and social life of the empire. Beard, North, and Price
comment:

> Decius did not specify which gods were to be the recipients of the
> sacrifices—and it would seem that local gods were as acceptable
> as specifically Roman ones. In this case the demand was not that
> Christians should worship Roman deities, but they should par-
> ticipate in the sacrificial system as a whole with its offering of
> incense, pouring of libations and tasting of sacrificial meat. Sac-
> rifice (not particular gods or festivals) here delimited and
> paraded the true subjects of Rome.[49]

Taking Leave

Many Christians in the early years of the church did not consider
themselves to be true subjects of Rome. They recalled Jesus' proclamation of another empire, an empire of God, and looked forward to the
day when the empire they had come to despise would cease to be. This
is the spirit in which one should understand the Christian refusal to
sacrifice. Why was this spirit so strong among early Christians?

Jonathan Z. Smith has noticed something about religion in the
Hellenistic world that may help us to understand this dissident ethos
more clearly. Smith observes that in the world of antiquity there are
two kinds of religion: he calls them the "locative" type and the
"utopian" type.[50] Central to the locative type is the concept of place—

locale. These ancient, tradition-steeped religions center on a place—a city, an altar, a hearth. But they also give place; they locate people by orienting them to a place, and assigning each a place in the divinely ordered world. Sacrifice was *the* expression of "locative" religion, as we have seen. This is why sacrifice was important to Rome, why Rome recognized local cults and encouraged them, and why Rome cultivated its own sacrificial traditions, disseminated them throughout the empire, and integrated the figure of the emperor into this sacrificial legacy. It was, finally, the emperor who ordered the world, and to him that each owed his or her place in the world that was.

But many in this finely tuned world of empire did not like their place. It was a world that thrived on the backs of slaves. It was a world that had little use for the disabled, for abandoned children too young for labor, for women cast outside the world of men, for the sick, the weak, and the mentally ill. In a world so fixed on "place," it was a time particularly prone to "*dis*-place." War, social upheaval, and economic coercion all disrupted the personal lives of millions of people, leaving them without place, or in a new and strange place that did not feel like home. For such people the locative religions simply—sometimes suddenly—lost their relevance. Why rejoice in place, when the place you occupy is no cause for celebration? For such persons, this new experience of place called for a "radical revaluation of the cosmos."[51] Smith speaks of a "cosmic paranoia" that begins to set in—though one should wonder whether an ancient slave's experience of the world as turned utterly against him could justly be called "paranoia." Among such people there emerged a new way of being religious. Smith calls this the "utopian" way, understood in terms of the original Greek meaning of this word: "no place." This way of being religious centers not on place, but on *leave-taking*. It is diasporic, mobile, transitional. In a more speculative mode it contemplates departure from the world that is; it hopes for a better place. The religions of this type are "savior" religions, for the most part, in which a savior descends to earth from the heavenly realms to lead the lost to a new and better place, their true and final "home."

In the Hellenistic world there were many such religions, or branches of older, locative religions, that responded to the experience of being "no place." Christianity was one. Its memory of its own origins was of a radical leave-taking—from village, home, family—in those who followed Jesus. Many of its early leaders were itinerants, like Paul. Its rank and file included slaves, prostitutes, "sinners," the unclean, the disabled, unattached women, and many others who, by their association with such unseemly, un-placed types, found themselves taking leave of the places they had been taught to honor as their own. Not all or even many of these early Christians literally left their homes and families. But their dissidence took a form that was perhaps far more threatening than the itinerant life of the wandering beggar. They took leave of the altar. For the Roman governor, Pliny, this was the crisis. And who did he find leading this exodus-in-place? Two female slaves. Is there a worse place to be in the ancient world than the place of a female slave? This is one of the most remarkable things about Christianity as it unfolded in the days of the Roman Empire: it inspired people to consider their place in the world and to question it. Even slaves found in this movement the wherewithal to see their place as really "no place," and to hope, imagine, and perhaps even begin to live into a new place. But the first steps in this journey were always the most daring: to step away from the altar and into the chaos of really having "no place."

For the followers of Jesus, his death became a powerful moment of clarity. When Jesus was executed as a dissident in the Roman Empire, what became clear to them was that the world they had known could not tolerate the radical reordering implied in the way Jesus had spoken to them about human life and relationships. The Roman Empire could not tolerate the empire of God. So they took leave. They left the empire and their assigned places in it, and they stopped doing the thing that created, affirmed, and maintained the whole imperial placement system: they stopped sacrificing.

This act became the occasion for much interpretive work. Thus early Christians soon discovered in the Jewish prophetic tradition an antisacrificial message that spoke truth to them. One can see this, for example, in the Gospel of Matthew, where the narrative occasion says much about the social context in which this critique of sacrifice became most relevant. Matthew sets the scene: Jesus is dining with "tax collectors and sinners," giving place to those who have no place at a clean and respectable table. His opponents complain to his disciples: "Why does your teacher eat with tax collectors and sinners" (Matt 9:11)? But Jesus overhears them, and replies for them, "Go and learn what this means, 'I desire mercy, and not sacrifice'" (Matt 9:13, citing Hos 6:6). What does this mean? Of what relevance could sacrifice have to this situation? A meal begins with sacrifice. A sacrifice insures that the meal is respectable, clean, with participants that are all respectable and clean. With the sacrifice, everyone is "placed" at the table. But a "sinner" is without place, unclean—"matter out of place." This may have been true for many in the Jesus movement. For those without proper place, and those who chose to associate with them, sacrifice became an encumbrance, and finally irrelevant.

But the death of Jesus also gave his followers a less obvious and more ironic opening for critiquing the culture of sacrifice. We have seen how early Christians could come to speak quite naturally of Jesus' death as a martyr's death, with atoning significance for his followers. We have also seen how they could contemplate their existence as a new community, and extend the sacrificial metaphor using, from the Jewish world, the concept of covenant sacrifice. Jesus became for them the sacrifice that drew them close to God and to one another. But even while working this out, early Christians were also aware that the death of their Jesus was not really a sacrifice. He died on a cross, not an altar. He died battered, pierced, and torn, not a perfect, unblemished lamb, a virgin, or even a hero. The place of his sacrifice was not the innermost *sactum sanctorum* of the Temple, but a stinking pile of bones and bodies outside the city walls. Consider the irony of claiming that this death was a sacrifice. Indeed, it was an antisacrifice.

In the Epistle to the Hebrews the irony of this claim is played out most fully. Here, in one of the few texts in the New Testament where one finds any sustained reflection on the idea of Jesus as sacrifice, we can see how early Christians could critique the culture of sacrifice and at the same time speak of Jesus' death as a sacrifice of a higher, spiritual order. In this remarkable text the whole breadth of the sacrificial tradition comes into play. Jesus' death is an atoning sacrifice (e.g., 9:11-14); it is a covenant sacrifice (e.g., 9:15-22); and finally, it becomes the sacrifice to end all sacrifices:

> Thus, when he came into the world, he said, "Sacrifices and offerings you have not desired, but a body you have prepared for me [cf. Ps 40:7-9]; in burnt offerings and sin offerings you have taken no pleasure [cf. Lev 4:14] . . . ," then he added, "See, I have come to do your will." He abolishes the first in order to establish the second. And it is by God's will that we have been sanctified through the offering of the body of Jesus Christ once for all. (Heb 10:5-6, 9-10)

For the author of Hebrews, the sacrifice of Christ is the end of sacrifice: "For by a single offering he has perfected for all time those who are sanctified" (10:14). What is left but to draw near to God "in full assurance of faith" (10:22). Ironically, sacrifice is brought to an end by sacrifice itself.

This spiritualization of sacrificial concepts, and its implied withdrawal from sacrificial practice, is often seen today by Christians as central to the idea that Christianity has superseded Judaism and gone beyond it. Yet the authoritative Scriptures to which the author of this epistle appeals, and the techniques he uses to explicate them, are all Jewish.[52] Hebrews, in my view, is not an anti-Jewish tract aimed at "Judaizers."[53] Rather, from *within* the Jewish tradition itself the author of Hebrews encourages an antisacrificial ethos in the midst of a broader Hellenistic culture that depended on sacrifice to create and order its social world. This was appropriate, for whoever the original addressees of this epistle might have been, it is clear that they had at some point run afoul of the current social map and those charged with its maintenance. They have suffered public shaming and ridi-

cule, imprisonment, and dispossession (10:32-34), a common fate
for those who dared to assume a dissident stance over against the
empire, who refused to accept their assigned place. They have also
begun to weaken in their resolve (10:23-25). Under these circumstances, the author of the Epistle to the Hebrews offers parenesis
structured around themes that are fitting to the dissident life: bold-
ness (*parrēsia*),[54] endurance (*hypomonē*),[55] hope (*elpis*),[56] and faithfulness (*pistis*).[57]

In Hebrews 11 an elegant encomium on the virtue of faithfulness
underscores the importance for these early Christian dissidents of
accepting the utopian (no-place) implications of what they had chosen to do. In it, the author delves into the great Jewish epic tradition
of leave-taking and associates it with the challenge of being resolute
and faithful. Of Abel, Enoch, Noah, and Abraham he says:

> These all died in faith, not having received what was promised,
> but having seen it and greeted it from afar, and having acknowl-
> edged that they were strangers and exiles on the earth. For people
> who speak thus make it clear that they are seeking a homeland. If
> they had been thinking of that land from which they had gone
> out, they would have had opportunity to return. But as it is, they
> desire a better country, that is, a heavenly one. Therefore God is
> not ashamed to be called their God, for he has prepared for them
> a city. (11:13-16)

The author continues with Moses, the Israelites, Rahab, and others,
finally turning to matters that may have more direct relevance to the
fate of dissidents living in his own community of faith:

> Some were tortured . . . , mocked, scourged, in chains and impris-
> oned . . . , stoned, sawn in two, killed with the sword, they went
> around in skins of sheep and goats, destitute, afflicted, poorly
> treated—of them the world was not worthy—wandering over
> deserts and mountains, and in dens and caves of the earth. (Heb
> 11:35-38)

In the epic tradition of Israel, faithfulness often means accepting rejection, being displaced, wandering in search of new and promised lands, new places with new altars. Out of this tradition, the author of Hebrews builds an ethos fitting for people who had taken leave of those altars around which they had once found their place. They are now "strangers and exiles," whom Ernst Käsemann so aptly named in his classic study, *The Wandering People of God*. Now, however, we can see that the author of this epistle has not presented Christian existence in this manner out of a general desire to translate the gospel into terms that would be intelligible to Gentiles steeped in gnostic mythology, as Käsemann had thought.[58] Rather, this notion of being cut loose, without place, free, is the authentic religious response to the experience of alienation and dissatisfaction felt by so many early Christians, as well as by many others in Hellenistic antiquity who expressed their utopian ethos using various mythic schemes to imagine their eventual escape from this hostile world.

Of central importance in this utopian discourse was the question of sacrifice, the temple, the altar—the cultic tether that held everyone in place. That is why, in the face of adversity, suffering, even possible martyrdom, the author of Hebrews does not speak of faith only as endurance, but also as leave-taking.[59] The one who follows Christ follows him "outside the camp," away from the old sanctuary and its altar to a new city that is to come, with new sacrifices of a different sort:

> We have an altar from which those who officiate in the tent have no right to eat. For the bodies of those animals whose blood is brought into the sanctuary by the high priest as a sacrifice for sin are burned outside the camp. Therefore Jesus also suffered outside the city gate in order to sanctify the people by his own blood. Let us then go to him outside the camp and bear the abuse he endured. For here we have no lasting city, but we are looking for the city that is to come. (13:10-14)

Jesus died as a sacrifice that really was no sacrifice. His sacrificial death was in reality a brutal state execution. As such it became for

Jesus' followers the sacrifice to end all sacrifices. It became an event that would stand once and for all as the great threshold over which the followers of Jesus would pass out of the ordered world of their past, a world that had cast Jesus out, and into some unknown future. Jesus' fate took him out of the ordered world, the city, "outside the camp," into that great beyond of chaos and no-place. His followers now took this fate to be their own. Behind them lay the polis and its hearth, the empire and its gods, the Temple and its altar. Before them lay the mysterious journey into faith: a life of trusting God to bring them to some new and better place, a "city that is to come." Christ's death had freed them from both the tyranny and the security of place, to embrace in fear, trembling, and joy the prospects of no-place. So the unclean and unsettling death of Jesus became the sacrifice to end all sacrifice, and an invitation to take leave of one's home fires to seek life in the liberating and terrifying experience of no-place.

Epilogue

The Resurrection of a Nobody

*And when we say also that the Word, who is the first-birth of God, was
produced without sexual union, and that he, Jesus Christ, our Teacher,
was crucified and died, and rose again, and ascended into heaven, we
propound nothing different from what you believe regarding those who
you esteem sons of Jupiter. For you know how many sons your esteemed
writers ascribed to Jupiter: Mercury, the interpreting word and teacher of
all; Aesclepius, who, though he was a great physician, was struck by a
thunder bolt, and so ascended into heaven; and Bacchus too, after being
torn limb from limb; and Hercules, when he had committed himself to
the flames to escape his toils; and the sons of Leda, and Dioscuri; and
Perseus, son of Danae; and Bellerophon, who, though sprung from
mortals, rose to heaven on the horse Pegasus. And what shall I say of
Ariadne, and those who, like her, have been declared to be set among
the stars? And what of your emperors who die among yourselves,
whom you deem worthy of deification, and in whose behalf you
produce someone who swears he has seen the burning Caesar
rise to heaven from the funeral pyre?*
—Justin Martyr, *1 Apology* 21

When someone today begins to speak of "the resurrection,"
most of us will likely assume that it is Jesus' resurrection
to which the speaker refers, not the resurrection of someone else. True, in the world of the tabloids one might find an occasional rival to *the* resurrection: an Elvis sighting, the face of the Virgin
Mary on the side of a weathered building in Kansas. But it is usually
no contest. "Jesus is risen!" is serious religion; "Elvis lives!" is not.
This is not just because most of us find it slightly preposterous to

elevate a rock-and-roll idol to divine status. Martin Luther King Jr., Ghandi, even Lou Gehrig could not give Jesus much serious competition today. *The* resurrection is unequivocally *Jesus'* resurrection for us. This is because most of us do not really believe in resurrection from the dead, except, of course, in the case of Jesus. He is in a class by himself. His resurrection is what makes him who he is: the unique, divine Son of God.

This way of thinking about the resurrection places us in a completely different frame of mind from those ancients who might have heard for the first time the claim that Jesus had been raised from the dead. Ancients, for the most part, had no trouble believing in resurrection per se. It was a common element of most ancient religions, and a fate thought to have been shared by many prophets, martyrs, and heroes. King, Ghandi, and Gehrig would have been good candidates by ancient standards. Jesus, on the other hand, was not. To most who had heard of him, he was not a prophet but a small-time pretender. His death was an execution, not a martyrdom. His life of poverty and his death in disgrace were far from heroic. Not much chance there for a godlike happy ending. Resurrection was not for nobodies.

A famous grafitto (see page 105) discovered in the mid-nineteenth century on the Palatine Hill in Rome illustrates the difference most strikingly.[1] The crude etching, meant as a joke, is of a man with the head of an ass hanging on a cross. Next to the cross a small boy kneels in adoration. An inscription reads: Alexamenos worships his God. A similar grafitto in an adjoining room identifies the boy, Alexamenos (perhaps a slave), as a Christian. Today the image is almost universally repelling. Then, difficult as it is to imagine, it was probably thought a pretty good joke. Elvis on a crucifix—that just about captures what "Jesus is risen!" might have sounded like to most respectable people of the ancient world.

For ancients, the Christian resurrection proclamation was not unique. When Justin Martyr wished to explain this aspect of Christian faith to the emperor, Antoninus Pius, in the second century, he had plenty of analogies to which he might refer. To be sure, the Christian

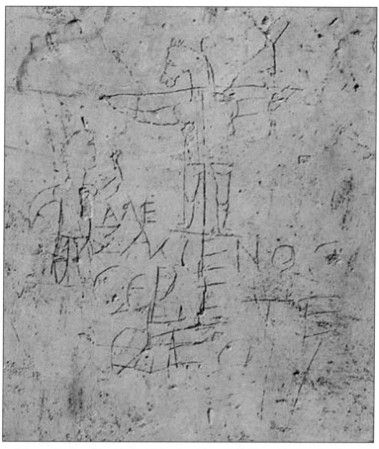

"Alexamenos worships his God." Reprinted from Rodolfo Lanciani, *Ancient Rome in the Light of Recent Discoveries* (Boston: Houghton Mifflin, 1888), 122.

accounts of Jesus' resurrection do have unique features, as do all particular religious narratives. But the basic idea that someone who had died might come back to life was not unique. Even in the New Testament itself Jesus' resurrection is not unique. Lazarus is raised from the dead in John 11, as is the unnamed daughter of Jairus in Mark 6:35-43. Paul sees Jesus' own resurrection not as a unique event, but as the first of many—"the first fruits of those who have fallen asleep" (1 Cor 15:20), as he puts it. In his account of Jesus' crucifixion, Matthew incorporates this end-time hope as the dead begin to come back to life already at the moment of Jesus' death, emerging from their tombs and to wander the city with him three days later (Matt 27:52-53). In the second century, Irenaeus does not blanch to claim that he and other Christian leaders could themselves raise the dead.[2] Ancients also believed in the resurrection of great heroes, all the "sons of Jupiter," and most importantly in the world of Christian origins, the resurrection and exaltation, or "apotheosis," of the emperor, welcomed to heaven at the end of his life as the divine son of God. In such a world, the hard part about the Christian resurrection proclamation would not have been believing in resurrection. The hard part would have been believing that Jesus, a nobody, had been raised from the dead.

Herein lies the great difference in the way ancients and moderns proclaim their faith in the risen Lord. For moderns, resurrection is impossible, except, of course, in the case of Jesus. It thus has become a unique event in our imagination, an event that proves we are right about Jesus, the Son of God. For ancients, resurrection is quite possible. It is what happens to sons of gods and heroes. But Jesus did not fit well into this fraternity. Ancients readily believed in resurrection; they just would not have thought Jesus to be a likely candidate. His death was not heroic. He was born a peasant and died a criminal. Yet his followers said of him what others said of Hercules, Aesclepius, or Caesar. Why?

The Meaning of Resurrection

To answer this question, we might turn first to the New Testament itself. Here we find the earliest surviving witness to the resurrection proclamation in one of Paul's letters, First Corinthians: "For I delivered to you as of first importance what I also received, that Christ died for our sins in accordance with the scriptures, that he was buried, that he was raised on the third day, in accordance with the scriptures" (1 Cor 15:3-4). This ancient tradition actually predates

Paul, as the phrase he uses to introduce it clearly indicates: Paul was taught this, and so now passes it on. Reference to "the scriptures" probably indicates the learned origins of the tradition. Someone has taken the time to reflect on Jesus' death and has decided that his death was the sort that carries meaning, the sort of death one finds discussed in Scripture.

Now, as in most cases where Paul makes use of Christian tradition, he is doing so here for the purpose of winning an argument. The nature of the argument in 1 Corinthians 15 is often misunderstood. The dispute was not over whether Jesus had been raised from the dead, as one might assume from the way such passages as 1 Corinthians 15:14 are used today, typically on an Easter Sunday morning: "if Christ has not been raised, then our preaching is in vain and your faith is in vain." This is misleading. No, the question Paul addresses has to do not with the fate of Jesus, but with the fate of others who have died: is there a *general* resurrection of the dead, or not? This is clear from Paul's opening salvo in the debate: "Now if Christ is preached as raised from the dead, how can some of you say that there is no resurrection of the dead?" (15:12). The logic of his argument in the verses to come will unfold as follows: "If you all agree that Jesus has been raised from the dead—and you do, don't you?—then you have to agree that there will also be a general resurrection of the dead." As Paul says in verse 20: "But in fact Christ has been raised from the dead, the first fruits of those who have fallen asleep." His resurrection is not unique, but the first of many that are to come.

The reason why some in Paul's Corinthian churches were denying the general resurrection is disputed. It may be that they thought in baptism they had already been transformed into the immortals they were destined to be. The resurrection, in their understanding, had already taken place in baptism.[3] Paul's own ideas on the meaning of baptism are suggestive of this view (see especially Romans 6).[4] Or it may be that this dispute was simply the result of ethnic diversity within the Pauline communities. Greeks and Romans believed in the resurrection of certain extraordinary individuals, but not in a general resurrection. In any event, not believing in the future resurrection of the dead left the community with a problem: what happens when someone dies? Inadvertently, Paul may have already answered this question, if in Corinth he had said something akin to what he would later say in his letter to the Romans: "the wages of sin is death" (Rom 6:23; cf. 5:12, 21). On such a view, death could be seen quite easily as punishment for sin. The person who dies before Christ's return is only confirmed as a sinner, not worthy of the empire of God after all. That this is what some in Corinth did indeed believe is suggested by Paul's words in 1 Corinthians 15:29a: "Otherwise what do people mean by being baptized on behalf of the dead?" Apparently some of the Corinthians thought that even after the wages of sin had been earned, surrogate baptism could save the dead person from his or her fate.[5] Of course, Paul knew that he now had these surrogate baptizers in checkmate: if the dead are truly dead and gone, for what, or how, could baptism really save them? "If the dead are not raised at all, why are people being baptized on their behalf" (15:29b)? For the dead to enjoy the fruits of surrogate baptism they would have to come back to life at some point in the future. God would have to raise them from the dead.

But this little trick of an answer is not the main thrust of Paul's argument in 1 Corinthians 15. His real argument is that Christ has been raised from the dead—something to which all the Corinthians would certainly agree. This was the content of the preaching and witness Paul had brought to them to begin with. But if, as they now seemed to believe, "there is no resurrection of the dead," then one must also say that "Christ has not been raised," and Paul's preaching was in vain, and their faith too (15:13-14). But why should these things be so linked? Why, if there is no resurrection to come, must one also say that Christ has not been raised? Remember, for Paul the resurrection of Jesus was not a unique event. Jesus was the "first fruits of those who have fallen asleep." The resurrection of Jesus, for Paul, was part of a great, unfolding cosmic drama in which the powers of the world were being overthrown. Paul writes:

For as by a mortal came death, by a mortal also has come the resurrection of the dead. For as in Adam all die, so also in Christ
shall all be made to live. But each in his own order: Christ the first
fruits, then at his coming those who belong to Christ. Then
comes the end, when he delivers the kingdom to God the Father
after destroying every rule and every authority and every power.
For he must reign until he has put all his enemies under his feet.
The last enemy to be destroyed is death. (15:21-26)

Paul's framing of the resurrection proclamation within an apocalyptic scenario reminds us where the idea of resurrection comes from
in the Jewish tradition. Both resurrection and apocalypticism address
the same fundamental issue: What happens when life and death do
not bear witness to good and evil?[6] When the evil live, and the good
die, where is God? Does God care? As Jews suffered endlessly under a
succession of foreign rulers with no apparent sign that faithfulness to
the God of their ancestors could bear any fruit at all, prophets and
visionaries raised a cry, a protest to the injustice they knew in this
world. "Mortal, can these bones live?" God asks the prophet Ezekiel
(Ezek 37:3). Out of the genocidal experience of exile comes the
prophet's stunning vision of the dry bones of the house of Israel coming together again, "bone to its bone . . . sinews . . . flesh . . . and skin"
(Ezek 37:7-8). By the will of God the bodies of all those slain, now laying silent in the valley of the dry bones, are reconstituted, reassem-
bled, and finally resuscitated to live again: "Thus says the Lord GOD:
'Come from the four winds, O breath, and breathe upon these slain,
that they may live.' And I prophesied as God commanded me, and the
breath came into them, and they lived, and stood on their feet, a vast
multitude" (Ezek 37:9). With a word from the prophet, the hope and
promise of a just and merciful God is given new life.

Ezekiel was not alone. Isaiah, too, found hope in the idea of resurrection (Isaiah 24–27). Later, as Jews suffered under a series of foreign
rulers, the idea of resurrection became a varied but constant element
in the Jewish response to the experience of evil and injustice in the
world. One finds it in Daniel (12:1-3) and the early Enoch literature

(*1 Enoch* 22–27) from the third century B.C.E., and in the later Enoch material (*1 Enoch* 92–105), *Jubilees* (23:11-31), and Second Maccabees (chap. 7, passim), all from the second century B.C.E. Closer to the period of Christian origins, it appears in the Wisdom of Solomon (chaps. 1–6, passim), Baruch (chaps. 49–51), and 4 Ezra (chap. 7). The idea that God would someday intervene in one last great cosmic battle, raise the righteous dead, and destroy their enemies was at home among a people who suffered long under brutal foreign rule. In chapter 2, I dwelt at some length on the effect of this legacy, as found especially in Fourth Maccabees, on the development of the early Christian idea that Jesus died as a martyr, true to his cause. The martyr's story, with its final chapter of vindication, became the narrative home of resurrection in the Christian story, as it had been among Jews for centuries. It is this rich tradition to which the creed Paul cites in 1 Corinthians 15:3-4 refers when it declares that Christ died, was buried, and was raised on the third day "in accordance with the scriptures."

Paul knew this tradition and the experience that made it relevant, as did many early followers of Jesus. Paul had spent time in a Roman prison and apparently had his own brushes with martyrdom. For him, the resurrection (first of Jesus, then of all who belong to Christ) was the assurance that his own attempts to live a life faithful to the cause of Jesus were not in vain. And if it were not so? "Why am I in peril every hour? . . . I die every day! What do I gain if, humanly speaking, I fought with beasts at Ephesus? If the dead are not raised, 'Let us eat and drink, for tomorrow we die'" (1 Cor 15:30-32).

Throughout 1 Corinthians 15 Paul talks the talk of the martyr. Those who have died, and who risk death, will not be lost. This is the importance of resurrection. His concept of the resurrection is bodily. This was very important in view of the martyr's experience of suffering. The martyrological literature dwells on the physical pain of torture, on the vulnerability of the body, and on the need to rise above the dread of what one's enemies can do to one's body.[7] For the martyr, release from the vulnerable, physical body and the restoration of that body, but now in an invulnerable, imperishable form, would be the very definition of salvation. So Paul says of the resurrection of the bodies of those who have died, following the analogy of the sown seed: "What is sown is perishable, what is raised is imperishable. It is sown in dishonor, it is raised in glory. It is sown in weakness, it is raised in power. It is sown a physical body, it is raised a spiritual body" (1 Cor 15:42-44).

Paul's concept of the resurrection is *bodily*, but *not physical*. Jesus and those who are to follow him in resurrection have "spiritual bodies," not physical bodies. For the martyr this is crucial. This is how the torturer's power, the power of death, is broken. When the martyr sheds the physical body to put on the spiritual body, he or she is freed from the vulnerability that comes with physical existence. The torturer's iron cannot touch a spiritual body. So Paul says, quoting that great restoration text, Isaiah 25, "Death is swallowed up in victory," and then, twisting Hosea's words of vengeance into a martyr's victory chant: "O death, where is your victory? O death, where is your sting?" (1 Cor 15:54b-55).

Jesus' resurrection, as the first of all who would follow after him, was the assurance that his life and the lives of those who, like Paul, found themselves in the perilous position of being a dissident in the Roman Empire were not without purpose. Indeed, they believed that their lives carried God's own purpose for a new world lived out in rebellion against the old. Should the old world still prevail against them, they believed that redemption awaited them beyond the suffering they might temporarily endure in this life. Jesus was a martyr. He died for the righteous cause of God's new empire. To say that God raised him from the dead was to say that his cause was indeed just, that his empire was truly God's empire. "Jesus is risen" finally means "Jesus was right."[8]

The only remarkable thing about these thoughts—and it is truly remarkable—is that someone thought them about *Jesus*. One might well think them about the heroic brothers and their brave mother of Maccabean fame, whose public witness was nothing less than astonishing. One might well think them about a better-known figure, like John the Baptist, who stood up to kings and humiliated the powerful. Most loyal subjects of the empire would have thought such thoughts about the emperors, especially Julius Caesar and his adopted son, Augustus. Julius was martyred; Augustus was the hero who avenged his death and established peace once again. Here were God's true sons, sent to bring peace and prosperity to the whole world. The *Pax Romana* itself bore witness to their authenticity.

But what of Jesus? He was no hero. He led no armies. He inspired no rebellion. The following he attracted was small and comprised people of the lowest station, marginal in their shame and dirt—expendables. He was executed as a criminal of the lowest sort, without heroic struggle or a moving speech to ignite his followers. Crucifixion offered no honor. He died quickly, a sign of weakness. What is remarkable about the early Christian resurrection proclamation was that it claimed *Jesus* had been raised from the dead—Jesus, not Caesar.

Resurrection Proves Nothing

So how did earliest Christians come to believe in the resurrection of Jesus? How did the followers of Jesus come to believe that he was a martyr, that his cause was just, and that they too should give themselves over to that cause, in spite of the dangers it posed? For many theologians and historians of early Christianity, the answer to this lies in the resurrection itself. For them, the resurrection of Jesus was that singularly astonishing event that convinced his followers they had been right about him all along. Had it not been for the resurrection, it is argued, they all would have given up and gone home, discouraged and disappointed. In short, without the resurrection, there would have been no Christianity.[9] But I am not convinced by this.

The evidence for the resurrection of Jesus is by itself not very compelling. It may seem compelling to Christians today, but this is only because our tradition has taught us to regard everything in the Bible as beyond question. It is also because most of us do not have much at stake in believing in the resurrection of Jesus. Martyrdom is not an issue for us. Precisely the opposite is more the case. We are encouraged and rewarded by our church and our culture for believing in the resurrection of Jesus. But what if believing in Jesus meant leaving house and home and risking a dissident lifestyle that could very well place one in mortal danger with the empire? What if it meant challenging the values of a culture that did not bear dissent with calm accepting? Would the early Christian resurrection proclamation have been enough to convince one that all these sacrifices were indeed worthwhile? I doubt it.

Paul's way of thinking about the resurrection was particularly problematic. He insisted that the dead will be raised as "spirits," that they will have "spiritual bodies," not physical bodies (1 Cor 15:35-58). Further, he thought of the risen Jesus himself as a spirit, experienced internally in moments of ecstasy, as in that moment when God chose "to reveal his son *in* me" (Gal 1:16), as Paul says.[10] From then on, Paul thought of himself as coming under Christ's control, of being "in Christ," even of having "the mind of Christ." To the sophisticated ancient observer of Christianity what Paul was experiencing was a simple and common case of spirit possession. To speak of Christ as a spirit, a *pneuma*, was to speak of him not as a god but as a mere ghost, doomed to wander the earth like so many other tortured souls of criminals who met with a similar violent end.[11] To outsiders, Paul's Christianity might have seemed to be nothing more than vulgar grave religion.[12] Paul's experience of the Spirit of Christ convinced him only because it was his own experience, quite real and very powerful.

The author of the Gospel of Mark was probably aware that outsiders could arrive at such a negative view of the Christian resurrection proclamation. This is perhaps why he takes at least two resurrection appearance stories and treats them as though they were not. The transfiguration of Jesus (Mark 9:2-8) is the better known of these, probably a mountaintop postresurrection appearance story originally.[13] The other is embedded in the story of Jesus walking on water in Mark 6:48-50.[14] This one in particular reads like a ghost story. As Jesus appears mysteriously walking across the waves in the dim wee hours of the morning, the disciples scream, for "they thought it was a ghost" (v. 49). Mark was probably leery of this, or any spooky postmortem appearance stories, and steered clear of them altogether. Instead, he presents the witness of the empty tomb (Mark 16:1-8). To Christians accustomed to finding epiphanies of Jesus at the end of their Gospels, this abrupt ending to Mark may seem rather incomplete. But Mark's empty tomb story would have appealed more widely to readers in the Jewish and Hellenistic world, who would have heard similar stories told of heroes who had been rescued from dire straits and translated directly to heaven to live in safety with the gods.[15] In Mark's Gospel Jesus becomes a respectable hero, saved from his foes in a surprise ending—a miraculous escape.

But, of course, an empty tomb is hardly definitive proof, even for the mildest of skeptics. In the Gospel of Matthew the chief priests are made to offer the obvious retort: "Tell people, 'His disciples came by night and stole him away while we were asleep'" (Matt 28:13). In the Gospel of John even Mary succumbs to this conclusion when, after discovering the tomb empty, she encounters Jesus in the garden but does not recognize him. Instead she complains to him, thinking that he is the gardener in charge: "they have taken away my Lord, and I do not know where they have laid him" (John 20:13). An empty tomb is really nothing but a missing body in need of an explanation: stolen or raised from the dead?

The solution to this problem, of course, is to produce the body—alive. This is what Luke does by adding a particularly graphic appearance story to Mark's earlier narrative. In Luke the risen Jesus appears not as a mysterious spiritual presence, as with Paul, but as a living, breathing, *eating* body:

> As they were saying this, Jesus himself stood among them. But they were startled and frightened, and supposed that they saw a ghost (*pneuma*). And he said to them, "Why are you troubled, and why do questions arise in your hearts? See my hands and my

feet, that it is I myself; touch me and see; for a ghost (*pneuma*) does not have flesh and bones as you see that I have." And when he had said this he showed them his hands and his feet. And while they still disbelieved, out of joy, and marveled, he said to them, "Do you have anything here to eat?" They gave him a piece of broiled fish, and he took it and ate it in front of them. (Luke 24:36-43)

One might suppose that Luke, with this "eat the fish" test, has finally settled the matter of whether Jesus was a mere ghost or a true hero. "Touch me and see, for a ghost does not have flesh and bones as I have." Without those flesh and bones Luke must think that the broiled fish would have fallen directly onto the floor! But with this story Luke has probably crossed the thin line, even for ancients, dividing the sublime from the ridiculous. Luke has also wandered about as far as one can get from Paul, who insisted most adamantly, "flesh and blood cannot inherit the empire of God!" (1 Cor 15:50).

If John the evangelist had known Luke's story, he would not have liked it. He knew that in the heat of conflict and under the pressure of threat to life and livelihood, such proofs are not satisfactory. His arch-skeptic, Thomas, voices the outer limit to which such ridiculous demands might stretch: "Unless I . . . place my finger in the mark of the nails, and place my hand in his side, I will not believe" (John 20:25). Presently Jesus appears and gives Thomas the opportunity to do just that. "Put your finger here, and see my hands; and stick out your hand and put it in my side. Don't be an unbeliever, be a believer!" taunts the Johannine Christ (20:27). The ridiculous has now become the macabre, as John parodies the attempt to prove what he knows must be accepted and believed on entirely different grounds. "Have you believed because you have seen me? Blessed are those who have not seen, and yet still believe" (20:29). Jesus' scolding of Thomas is really aimed at the many in John's community who longed for a sign, a miracle, anything to see them through the dire times in which they were living. But it is in such times that the flimsiness of faith based on miraculous proofs is easily exposed.

The followers of Jesus needed more than a miracle. Miracles were a dime a dozen in the ancient world, and resurrection was part of every ancient religious tradition. For the followers of Jesus, believing in the miracle of God raising someone from the dead was not a problem. The problem was believing that God would raise *Jesus* from the dead.

Why Did They Believe?

Why, then, did the friends and followers of Jesus believe that God had raised him from the dead? If sightings of the risen Lord would not have convinced the unconvinced, nor empty tombs, nor fantastic stories of a fish-eating, perforated, bodily Christ, what then would have convinced the followers of Jesus that he was not dead, but raised by the God of their ancestors and taken up into heaven to live on, seated at the right hand of God?

As we have seen, in the Jewish tradition the presupposition for any claims that God had raised someone from the dead was not the appearance of the departed in ghostly form, the discovery of an empty tomb, or any other such postmortem proof that God had chosen to intervene against the forces that killed him. Resurrection, as vindication, presupposed only that one of God's righteous ones had been slain in faithfulness to God. This is how the followers of Jesus felt about him. These were the few who heard his words as God's Word, who experienced his deeds as epiphanic. We might find it hard to imagine that something like the first beatitude could inspire that kind of loyalty and devotion. Perhaps one would have to be a beggar to know how splendid those words sound: "Blessed are beggars, for yours is the empire of God." Perhaps one would have to experience the interminable loneliness of the permanently unclean to know how powerful and transforming a simple invitation to table could be. Perhaps only an enslaved prostitute could experience gracious acceptance and the offer of freedom so powerfully that death could seem utterly irrelevant to its continuing effect. For these few friends and followers, Jesus was a hero of no less stature than Eleazar, the slain priest of Fourth Maccabees. He was their Elijah, their Moses, their Adam. They believed in him thus, not because of his resurrection. They believed in him thus because of the way he touched their lives. And because he had touched their lives in this profound way, they believed in his resurrection.

One of the earliest forms of the resurrection proclamation is a simple formula (actually three different forms), repeated several times in Paul's letters, that speaks of God as the one who "raises Jesus from the dead."[16] This turns out to be a very Jewish way of speaking about God in the period of early Judaism. In the traditional Jewish liturgy, which likely derives from the period of Christian origins, the second of the Eighteen Benedictions says, "Blessed are you, Yahweh, who makes the dead to live." This is not very far from that simple early Christian formula; indeed, Paul seems to quote the second benediction itself in Rom 4:17, praising the God of Abraham, "who gives life to the dead."[17] The parallel is suggestive. Let us imagine a gathering of Jesus' early followers sometime not long after his death. Jesus sponsored such gatherings in his lifetime, probably around a meal, and so his followers would have continued on in his memory, gathering for meals and to share stories of Jesus then, and life now. There would have been blessings and traditional prayers offered around the loose structure of a meal, eventually a prayer for the bread and a prayer for the wine. Among them someone like Paul could well have heard something like: "Blessed are you, Yahweh, who raised Jesus from the dead." To the prayers would have been added a hymn, perhaps the hymn Paul records in correspondence to the Philippian church (Phil 2:6-11), whose middle verses went something like,

> And being found in human form,
>   he humbled himself
> and became obedient until death, even death on a cross.
> Therefore God has highly exalted him,
>   and given him the name that is above every name . . .
>   Lord Jesus Christ.

The extraordinary christological claims that appear in this traditional, pre-Pauline hymn to Christ are not predicated on stories of an
empty tomb or miraculous appearances. The song proceeds directly
from death to exaltation, and the only prerequisite for this giant leap
is "obedience until death." This is martyrological language thrust
into song.[18] The followers of Jesus first proclaimed his resurrection in
celebration of his life.

Jesus was a visionary who attracted a loyal following. He had a
cause, the empire of God. All those who followed him believed in this
cause and in him, one of God's righteous ones. If the enemy were to
find and kill him, his followers would have believed with all their
hearts that the God of their ancestors, the God of justice and righteousness, would redeem him from suffering and restore him to life.
They believed God would raise him from the dead because they
believed in him. It did not matter to them that he was a nobody. They
were themselves nobodies and outsiders. Jesus was a nobody who
convinced them that they were somebody to God. This nobody was
their hero, their prophet, *their* "son of Jupiter." This is why, when at
last he was killed, they proclaimed his resurrection. They could have
done this on the day he died, and probably did.

Did Anything Really Happen?

But in addition to the martyrological talk, Paul also speaks to the
Corinthians of other, more mysterious things—of "appearances": "he
appeared to Cephas, then to the twelve. Then he appeared to more than
five hundred brothers and sisters at one time, most of whom are still
alive, though some have fallen asleep. Then he appeared to James, then
to all the apostles. Last of all, as to one untimely born, he appeared also
to me" (1 Cor 15:5-8). What shall we make of this tradition? Did Jesus
really appear to Peter, James, other of his followers, and even to five hundred people at one time? Did such things happen, or was this simply
the tradition taking shape around certain figures of authority?[19]

I think that this tradition represents something that did happen, but probably not something so clear and unambiguous as one might conclude from Paul's manner of expression in 1 Corinthians 15. To understand this tradition we should probably begin with Jesus himself, and the sort of experiences he and his followers had during his lifetime. Jesus was a "spirit person," to quote Marcus Borg.[20] The movement he began was probably one in which ecstatic religious experiences—experiences of the Spirit—were important and defining. Jesus himself was an exorcist, an activity in antiquity normally involving the manipulation of spirits, or being manipulated by them.[21] The tradition of Jesus' baptism links his status as a Son of God to the descent of the Spirit upon him, an idea that persisted into the Pauline churches, where followers of Jesus possessed by the Holy Spirit cried out "Abba," thus testifying to the fact that they too were children of God (Rom 8:14-16; Gal 4:6-7). These passages and a host of others from Paul's letters, the Gospels, and Acts give a clear picture of the early Jesus movement also as a spiritually charged religious following. The followers of Jesus continued to have ecstatic religious experiences after his death, just as they had had them before.

What did they make of these spiritual experiences? Paul's references to them are instructive. Sometimes Paul speaks of the work of "the Spirit." Sometimes he speaks of the work of "God's Spirit," the "Holy Spirit," the "Spirit of Life," or the "Spirit of the Lord." And sometimes he speaks of the work of the "Spirit of Christ."[22] The following passage from Romans, in which Paul discusses this life in the Spirit, illustrates just how interchangeable all of these terms are for Paul:

> But you are not of the flesh; you are in the Spirit, since the Spirit of God dwells in you. Anyone who does not have the Spirit of Christ does not belong to him. But if Christ is in you, though the body is dead because of sin, the Spirit is life because of righteousness. If the Spirit of the one who raised Jesus from the dead dwells in you, the one who raised Christ from the dead will give life to your mortal bodies also through his Spirit that dwells in you. (Rom 8:9-11)

For Paul the Spirit is the Spirit of Christ is the Spirit of God is the Spirit "that dwells in you." It is this Spirit that gives them life, that "is life."

The spiritual life that Jesus cultivated with his followers before his death did not cease to exist when he died. It continued. Only now, his followers could speak of this spiritual activity not simply as God's Spirit moving among them, but as Christ's Spirit, or the "Spirit of his Son" (Gal 4:6). Why? Because it was through Jesus, their Christ, that they had first come to experience God in this new way. Now, as they continued to experience the Spirit of God after Jesus' death, they would name it also as they had first discovered it, as the Spirit of Christ. This is how I would understand Paul's statement in 1 Corinthians 15 that on one occasion more than five hundred people had experienced the risen Christ at the same time. This probably does not refer to a gigantic Jesus appearing before a crowd of hundreds. It refers to spiritual ecstasy, experienced by many in the act of gathering for worship. These moments of spiritual ecstasy, experienced individually and in communal worship, now became experiences of the risen Christ. For many, they became the defining experience in following Jesus, so much so that Luke, in Acts, offers a stylized depiction of this sort of ecstatic, spiritual experience as the thing that gave birth to Christianity itself (Acts 2:1-13). Perhaps in the inner dimensions of the spiritual lives of figures like James and Peter, who had been particularly close to Jesus, these experiences took on the more personal character of an encounter with their former teacher and friend, his tortured body now transformed and freed from his former suffering. These "appearances" of Jesus became for them the reauthorization for continuing what he had begun, their apostolic mandate.

A Matter of Decision

When all is said and done, of course, the spiritual experiences of ancient Christians do not prove that Jesus was raised from the dead or that he was the Son of God. For ancients these things might just as easily have been dismissed as ghost stories. Moderns might speak of them as mass hysteria, or as the grief experience of seeing again a loved one who has recently died, as happens quite commonly today. The ambiguity of these experiences underscores once again the fact that Christian faith does not really have its origins in such experiences. Rather, the followers of Jesus spoke of their ecstatic religious experiences in this way—as experiences of the risen Jesus—because of a conviction whose origins must be traced back to another beginning. Their conviction about him began on a day long before his death, on an afternoon, or a morning, when, out of the blue, they heard Jesus say something, or saw him do something that moved them, deeply. In his company they came to know God. In his words they heard the Word of God. In his activity they experienced the empire of God. They became committed to him and his vision of a new empire, a new world coming into being. They believed in him. When he died, they knew that the Spirit of God they had experienced in his words and deeds was not thereby snuffed out. Their Jewish tradition of martyrdom and redemption gave them the words by which to proclaim this: God raised Jesus from the dead. Now, as the spiritual life of the community of his followers continued, they could speak of it not just as the life of the Spirit, or of God's Spirit. It now became also life in the Spirit of Christ.

The followers of Jesus did not believe in him because of the resurrection. They believed in the resurrection because they first believed in him and in the spiritual life he unleashed among them.[23] This is, finally, what the resurrection proclamation is about. It is about the decision to believe in Jesus and to give oneself over to the Spirit to be discovered in his life.

Killing Jesus (A Conclusion)

*Christ crucified rules, and it may be that the true business of
modern Christianity is to crucify him again and again so that
he can never get a word out of his mouth.*
—Barbara Ehrenreich, *Nickel and Dimed*

W hen Jesus was killed by authorities charged with keeping
the Roman *Pax*, his friends and followers were not without
cultural resources for dealing with the violent end of his
life. As they began to reflect on Jesus' death, they soon came to see it
not as a tragedy or calamity, but as an inevitable part of his life, an end
fitting of the kind of life Jesus led. They began to develop ways of
speaking of the death of Jesus that would connect it with his life and
draw attention to his life as decisive for their own lives.

One way that these early followers of Jesus could speak of his death
was simply as the death of a victim—a victim of Roman imperial
power, a dissident to the great Roman vision of a single empire
encompassing the whole known world, standing alone, without rival
or alternative. They knew that to be a follower of Jesus was to embrace
the foolishness of raising a dissident voice and an alternative vision to
the Roman *Pax*. "We proclaim a crucified Messiah," says Paul, who is
both the "power of God" and the "wisdom of God" (1 Cor 1:23-24).
Power that is weakness; wisdom that is foolishness—these were the
realities that determined Paul's new life in being a follower of Jesus.
To be a follower of Jesus was to become a "fool for Christ's sake." It

meant embracing weakness, not strength; shame rather than honor. It meant welcoming vilification, persecution, and slander. It meant becoming "the refuse of the world, the offscouring of all things" (1 Cor 4:8-13). As Jesus' dissident life led to his death as a victim of imperial power, so also many of his followers led dissident lives that in turn earned them the fate of victim as well.

But the followers of Jesus soon began to speak of his death not simply as the death of a victim, but as the glorious death of a martyr. The rich and varied Jewish martyrological tradition was perhaps the most fertile and productive interpretive field for early Christians. From it come the idea that Jesus' death was a sacrifice, and the belief that God could, and would, raise Jesus from the dead. But the direction in which the martyrdom tradition points is not forward, into the heavenly future life the martyr is said to enjoy, but backward, to the way of life, the values, and the cause for which the martyr was willing to die. The martyr's death is a witness—a witness to the ultimate value of the cause for which he or she died, and a witness to the way of faithfulness to that cause, a way that may well lead to death. The martyr must be willing to pay the ultimate price for the convictions she or he holds. But before one might be willing to die for a cause, one must first be willing to live for it. Thus the New Testament Gospels, all of which make use of the martyrological tradition, present Jesus' life not simply as a prelude to his death, but as the *way of life* one must embrace as one follows Jesus to the cross.

This was true of Paul as well—though this is often obscured by the fact that Paul very seldom discusses Jesus' life and only occasionally makes use of his words. But of all the characters that appear in the New Testament, it is Paul who emulates the life of Jesus most thoroughly. If Mark's fictive rich young ruler turns away from Jesus when he learns of the rigors of renunciation Jesus requires, Paul did not. Paul took up the life of Jesus and made it his own. This he says of his own struggles with life as a dissident voice in the empire: "we are always carrying in the body the death of Jesus, so that the life of Jesus might be made manifest in our body; for in living we are always given up to death for Jesus' sake, so that the life of Jesus might be made manifest in our mortal flesh" (2 Cor 4:10-11). For Paul and others who came to understand Jesus' death as a martyrdom, embracing his death was really about embracing his *life*. The martyr's death means nothing apart from the life to which it bears witness. This is why for generations the Jesus movement would be known simply as "the way." Following Jesus meant embracing his way of life.

Finally, the followers of Jesus also spoke of his death as a sacrifice. To speak thus may seem at first glance finally to take leave of Jesus' life and to draw his death into theological abstraction. A sacrificial lamb is born to die, nothing more. But this was not how the early followers of Jesus made use of the metaphor of sacrifice to interpret his death. The idea that a *person* might become a sacrifice for sin originally came out of the martyrdom tradition. In the Maccabean literature, for example, it is because of the martyr's extraordinary faithfulness to God that his or her death might be regarded by God as atonement for the sins of the people. It is the martyr's extraordinary life and faithfulness unto death that finally turns God's anger, and stirs God to come at last to rescue the suffering people of God. Ironically, in the New Testament it is Caiaphas in John's Gospel who gives clearest expression to this idea: "do you not understand that it is expedient for you that one man should die for the people, and that the whole nation should not perish" (John 11:50).

But even when the idea of Jesus' death as a sacrifice was not explicitly tied to the martyrological tradition from whence it came, it remained connected to Jesus' life in a very creative way. As Jesus' followers pondered his death as a sacrifice, and considered this within the context of a culture in which sacrifice was the glue that held every stick of the social infrastructure firmly in place, they began to see how Jesus' death could function cultically to free them from that infrastructure, and their cultically sanctioned places in it. Like the sacrifices that held together family, clan, city, and empire, they found that their common meals—sacrificial meals, as all meals were—could become a place of new identity and new social formation. And as they began to walk away from the sacrificial fires that held the old world together, they discovered once again the freedom to become something new in this new microsociety, "the body of Christ," held together by the sacrifice of Jesus' own body. At these new tables—altars—where slaves and prostitutes sat as equals with merchants, scholars, and even the occasional state official, they received a new identity and purpose. But this was exactly what people had experienced in the table fellowship of Jesus himself. Jesus gathered at table the clean and the unclean, those with honor and those with none, prostitutes, sinners, beggars, and thieves. Around those tables all became equals, members of a common family, heirs to a new empire, the empire of God. After his death, as the tables of the Jesus movement became the altars around which a new society was formed, this process of personal and communal transformation continued. Thus what Jesus had meant to people in life was translated into a cultic parlance, and enacted once again through the appropriation of his death as a sacrifice.

And what of Jesus' resurrection? Here, at last, do we not finally take leave of his life? Is not the resurrection a thing of a different class altogether, an event so powerful and transforming that nothing in Jesus' life could carry much significance after that? Not at all. On the contrary, apart from Jesus' life the resurrection proclamation would never have been ventured in the first place. If we were to take the Gospel accounts of the resurrection as historical, they would not be convincing to anyone outside the inner circle of Jesus' devoted companions—and even some of them express doubts in these stories. I do not regard them as historical, but I do imagine that people in the Jesus movement did indeed have the kind of spiritual experiences Paul and others came to understand as postresurrection manifestations of the risen Christ. But why did they understand them thus? Why did they not see these powerful spiritual experiences as instances of spirit possession—as the ghost of Jesus coming back to haunt them, like so many other criminals and victims of violence and betrayal? Why did they say "God has raised Jesus from the dead?"

They said this because they had faith in Jesus. Those who said it first had known him. They believed in him and in his cause. To them, he was a martyr, not just a victim. In the ancient Jewish context of Christian origins, resurrection is part of the martyr's story. Resurrection is vindication. Could God raise Jesus from the dead? Any ancient would have answered yes to that question. But *would* God raise Jesus from the dead? To this question, only his followers could answer yes. And they said yes to it because they believed that Jesus' life had revealed him to be one of God's righteous ones. They believed that in his words were God's Word. They believed that in his deeds, Jesus had done the will of God. Resurrection, too, was a way of proclaiming the significance of Jesus' life.

I have become convinced that in each of these ways of interpreting Jesus' death, the followers of Jesus were in fact drawing attention to his *life*. His death mattered to them because his life had mattered to them. They spoke of his death in ways that affirmed his life, and reaffirmed their own commitment to the values and vision stamped into his life by his words and deeds. In his life, they had come to know God. To the followers and friends of Jesus, his death was important in its particularity—as the fate of him who said and did certain things, who stood for something so important to him that he was willing to give his life for it. That something was the vision of life he called the empire of God. They too believed in this vision of a new empire. If this vision was indeed *God's* empire, then the bearer of this vision was not dead. No executioner could kill what he was. To kill Jesus, you would have to kill the vision. This is what the cross could not do.

When Christian believers and theologians approach the question of Jesus' death today, these are generally not the concerns that lie close to hand. The things Jesus said that lead to his death are not at issue. What he lived or died for is of no concern. The event of Jesus' death has lost its particularity, its connection to the course of real human events that brought it about. In this abstracted status, Jesus' death has become for us a mythic event connected to the universal problem of death and the mysterious and frightening end of human

life. As we fret over the moral and ethical failures of our lives and
dread the perils and punishments that might lie beyond the grave, we
are comforted by the knowledge that Jesus died "to save us from our
sins." His resurrection assures us of our own immortality. If Jesus
came to fulfill his cosmic destiny and die on the cross so that we
might be saved, then anything else he might have done in his life—his
own aspirations, his own values and vision, his carefully chosen words
and daring prophetic deeds—pales by comparison. Ethics are never as
important as salvation. With salvation it is life itself that hangs in the
balance, our lives, which we desperately seek to preserve, even in the
face of death, whose threat confronts us all. Thus Jesus' death and resurrection have become the universal saving events in which we find
God's graciousness extended even to us, hopeless sinners, who have
no intention of giving up the lives we live, oblivious to the vision of
human life Jesus espoused and the God he embodied.

The eclipse of Jesus' death and resurrection in their particularity,
and their elevation to the status of mythic events in a cosmic struggle,
is invited perhaps by the way Paul and other early Christians placed
Jesus' death and resurrection at the center of their own traditional
apocalyptic hopes. Apocalypticism casts the struggle between good
and evil in terms of a great cosmic battle, with the forces of God
arrayed against the armies of the evil one. In Jewish apocalypticism
the power and victory of God is marked by the resurrection of all
those who have been slain by the forces of evil. In the final struggle
their faithfulness and sufferings are vindicated. This is the framework
in which Paul interpreted the resurrection of Jesus: he was the firstfruits, the first of those countless ones slain in the struggle against
evil to come back to life (1 Cor 15:20). The resurrection was for Paul a
signal, a cosmic alarm clock sounding the arrival of the final battle,
which would begin any day. But Paul and others who interpreted
Jesus' death and resurrection in this way did not detach the death and
resurrection of Jesus from his life. The cosmic battle they believed
they were witnessing was being waged over a specific idea, a real cause.
The struggle in which they were engaged was the struggle for the

vision of human life their crucified Messiah had espoused. For Paul, to experience the resurrection of Jesus was to become possessed by his Spirit, to share "the mind of Christ," and to embrace the life of Christ as his own. Paul and others formed communities that would be the "body of Christ," embodying the life of love and mutual care that Jesus had died for. What he died for, they would now live for, until God would finally establish the empire of God as the universal rule of love and justice in the world.

As time passed, however, and that first generation of friends and followers who had known Jesus and actually remembered his life passed from the scene, the connection between the particulars of Jesus' life and the mythic structures of cosmic battle became ever more tenuous and eventually were lost. The struggle became less and less a struggle for a particular set of values connected to Jesus, and more a clash of powers. The power of Christ was pitted against the religion of the Jews, against the pagan gods, and ultimately against the universal foe, death itself. One can see this already in the Apostles' Creed, where the life of Jesus has been diminished to a mere comma, a blank space residing quietly between "born of the Virgin Mary" and "suffered under Pontius Pilate." The elements of the Christian creed are the elements of the cosmic drama common to many ancient religious traditions: miraculous birth, death, resurrection, ascension. Jesus became simply another of the many dying-rising savior gods of antiquity, association with whom would assure safety in this world and the next. His table fellowship would for some become a mere dispensary for the "drug of immortality," the *pharmakon athanasias*, as Ignatius would come to speak of the communion bread (*Ephesians* 20).

Jesus Christ would eventually become the greatest Savior-God of all. His cross would become a logo, a talisman emblazoned on the shield of Constantine and his soldiers to protect them in battle. Jesus became a partisan, whose name would strike fear in the heart of anyone who by chance had not been born under his sign. In the Middle Ages his cross would become a sign of terror, before which Jews and Muslims would cringe in supplication, begging mercy from marauding hordes of crusaders, or stand in defiance only to be slain. The symbol of weakness Paul embraced became the symbol of merciless power, where it remains today for many Christian believers. One can see this still in its infinitely trivialized American form on any given Sunday afternoon—where the warriors of sport pause to cross themselves as a solemn prelude to the touchdown victory dance that is sure to follow, taunting those poor unfortunates inexplicably abandoned by Jesus in their moment of greatest need. Today the cross is for winners, not losers.

Is Jesus dead? Not yet. But what the cross could not do, Christians could. We are killing Jesus. Jesus was a sage, or if one prefers, a prophet. Sages and prophets live by their words and deeds. In this sense, for most of us who assemble in the name of Jesus, he is dead. His words and deeds mean little to us, if anything at all. We do not look to Jesus for a way of life, but for salvation. "He died that we might live." Indeed. It seems we have to kill him in order that we might live whatever lives our power and privilege will allow us to lead. When real life is at stake, most of us will take personal salvation over the empire of God any day. So we prefer our Christ crucified, a once living Jesus silenced by a higher calling.

But this was not so for the friends and followers of Jesus. For them, the empire of God *was* salvation. They saw God's care for them in the communities of mutual care and love founded in Jesus' name. They experienced the acceptance and welcome they received around the tables of the Jesus movement as redemption. Beggars, lepers, prostitutes, and expendables of every sort—the "nothings" of the world, as Paul puts it—embraced Jesus' empire of God as their one great hope and longing. Others did too—people like Paul, who gave up lives of considerable status and importance to enter into these communities of the new empire. Why did they do it? They were responding to the compelling vision of Jesus, who lived on for them, alive in their midst. For them, this was no existential metaphor for commitment. Jesus was really alive, spiritually present with them. Whatever it might mean to speak thus today about Jesus—to say that he is "alive" in our midst—it must above all else mean that he somehow still offers us the vision of a new empire, into which we are still invited in a very real way. Apart from his words and deeds, the living Jesus would have meant nothing to those who encountered him in the private and public places of antiquity. Neither can Jesus be alive to us apart from his words and deeds. He is alive to *us* only as he was alive to them, as a real invitation into a way of life we can see reflected in his own life, and the God to be encountered there.

Notes

Prologue: The Crucifixion of a Nobody

1. On the connection between Christian anti-Semitism and the way Christians have chosen to remember Jesus' death, see James Carroll's compelling account in *Constantine's Sword: The Church and the Jews—A History* (Boston: Houghton Mifflin, 2001).

2. For crucifixion as a Roman form of punishment see Paul Winter, *The Trial of Jesus*, 2d ed., rev. and ed. T. A. Burkill and Geza Vermes, SJ (Berlin: de Gruyter, 1974), 90–96; also Richard Horsley, "The Death of Jesus," in *Studying the Historical Jesus: Evaluations of the State of Current Research*, ed. Bruce Chilton and Craig Evans, NTTS 19 (Leiden: Brill, 1994), 409–13.

3. Josephus, *War* 2.66-75; *Ant.* 17.286-98.

4. Josephus, *War* 2.308-9.

5. This is Crossan's term in *Jesus: A Revolutionary Biography* (San Francisco: HarperSanFrancisco, 1994), 127.

6. For discussion see Ekkehard W. Stegemann and Wolfgang Stegemann, *The Jesus Movement: A Social History of Its First Century*, trans. O. C. Dean Jr. (Minneapolis: Fortress Press, 1999), 118.

7. Most scholars seem to agree that the Temple incident depicted in Mark 11:15-19 (also Matt 21:12-13 and Luke 19:45-46) and John 2:14-16 recalls an actual event that ultimately brought about Jesus' death; see, e.g., E. P. Sanders, *Jesus and Judaism* (Philadelphia: Fortress Press, 1985), 61–76; John Dominic Crossan, *The Historical Jesus: The Life of a Mediterranean Jewish Peasant* (San Francisco: HarperSanFrancisco, 1991), 355–60; Richard Horsley, *Jesus and the Spiral of Violence* (San Francisco: Harper & Row, 1987), 292–300; Marcus Borg, *Jesus, a New Vision: Spirit, Culture, and the Life of Discipleship* (San Francisco: Harper & Row, 1987), 174–76; but cf. Robert J. Miller, "Historical Method and the Deeds of Jesus: The Test Case of the Temple Destruction," *Forum* 8, nos. 1-2 (1992) 5–30, for a contrary view.

8. Crossan, *Jesus: A Revolutionary Biography*, 154.

Victim

1. Klaus Wengst's sobering treatment is most helpful: *Pax Romana and the Peace of Jesus Christ*, trans. John Bowden (Philadelphia: Fortress Press, 1987), 7–55.

2. The reference is to Augustus's *Res Gestae Divi Augustus*, an autobiographical account of his accomplishments written near the end of his life. A copy of the document was found inscribed in the temple of Rome and Augustus at Ancyra: *CIL* 3.769-99; for a translation, see Naphtali Lewis and Meyer Reinhold, *Roman Civilization*, 2 vols. (New York: Harper & Row, 1966), 2.9–19.

3. As recounted by Josephus in *Ant.* 17.288-95.

4. For ancient practices generally see Thomas F. Carney, *The Shape of the Past* (Lawrence, Kans.: Coronado, 1975); for Roman practices see Paul Veyne, "The Roman Empire (Where Public Life Was Private)," in *A History of Private Life*, vol. 1: *From Pagan Rome to Byzantium*, ed. Paul Veyne, trans. Arthur Goldhammer (Cambridge: Harvard Univ. Press, 1987), 95–115; also Peter Garnsey and Richard Saller, "Patronal Power Relations," in *Paul and Empire: Religion and Power in Roman Imperial Society*, ed. Richard Horsley (Harrisburg: Trinity, 1997), 96–103.

5. The older view that the imperial cult was simply political, and therefore superficial, is currently under revision following the work of, among others, S. R. F. Price, *Rituals and Power* (Cambridge: Cambridge Univ. Press, 1984).

6. *OGIS* no. 458; for discussion, see Lewis and Reinhold, *Roman Civilization*, 2.64.

7. This decree was passed in 27 B.C.E., but not accepted by Augustus until 8 B.C.E., just a year after the Asian province began celebrating his birthday as the New Year (see previous note). The decree is discussed in Macrobius, *Saturnalia* 1.12.35 (for text and discussion see Lewis and Reinhold, *Roman Civilization*, 2.65).

8. For a description and study of the ancient city see Kenneth G. Holum, et al., *King Herod's Dream—Caesarea on the Sea* (New York: Norton, 1988).

9. Note that the manuscript tradition is at odds over whether Jesus was remembered as a *tektōn*, or merely the son of a *tektōn*, a dispute that perhaps reflects the unseemly background all of this implies.

10. For this correction to earlier notions of Jesus coming from a "middle-class" background we are indebted to John Dominic Crossan, *Jesus: A Revolutionary Biography* (San Francisco: HarperSanFrancisco, 1994), 23–26, making use of the work of Gerhard Lenski on the structure of ancient agrarian societies in *Power and Privilege* (New York: McGraw-Hill, 1966). Crossan also

notes, following Ramsay MacMullen, that *tektōn* was a common term of deri-
sion in Roman times. See MacMullen, *Roman Social Relations: 50 B.C.–A.D. 384*
(New Haven: Yale Univ. Press, 1974), 17–18, 107–8, 139–40, and 198 n. 82.

11. For the commercialization of agriculture and concentration of land in
the hands of fewer and fewer large owners see Ekkehard W. Stegemann and
Wolfgang Stegemann, *The Jesus Movement: A Social History of Its First Century*,
trans. O. C. Dean Jr. (Minneapolis: Fortress Press, 1999), 104–13; for the
tax/tribute situation in first century Palestine see 113–25. On commercialization under Herodian and later Roman rule see also John Dominic
Crossan and Jonathan Reed, *Excavating Jesus: Beneath the Stones, Behind the Texts*
(San Francisco: HarperSanFrancisco, 2001), 54–70.

12. Lenski, *Power and Privilege*, 281–84.

13. The use of the term "empire," rather than "kingdom" or "reign," may
at first seem jarring, but this is what Greek *basileia* means in the Hellenistic
world. The challenge to Rome's imperial vision implied by the provocative
use of this term was intentional, in my view.

14. John Dominic Crossan, *The Historical Jesus: The Life of a Mediterranean
Jewish Peasant* (San Francisco: HarperCollins, 1991), 332–48.

15. Cf. Richard Horsley, *Jesus and the Spiral of Violence* (San Francisco:
Harper & Row, 1987), 309–10.

16. Marcel Detienne and Jean-Pierre Vernant, *Cunning Intelligence in Greek
Culture and Society,* trans. Janet Lloyd (Atlantic Highlands, N.J.: Humanities,
1978).

17. Is the story historical? Quite possibly, though the arguments do not
fall clearly one way or the other. It coheres with the charge brought against
Jesus in Luke's version of the trial before Pilate: "We found this man pervert-
ing our nation, and forbidding us to give tribute to Caesar, and saying that
he himself is Christ a king" (Luke 23:3). This was clearly an issue with the
early followers of Jesus, and so probably with Jesus himself.

18. Marcus Borg, *Jesus, a New Vision: Spirit, Culture, and the Life of Discipleship*
(San Francisco: Harper & Row, 1987), especially 23–75.

19. On the dim view of magic taken by Romans see Mary Beard, John
North, and S. R. F. Price, *Religions of Rome* (Cambridge: Cambridge Univ.
Press, 1998), 1.211–44; 2.260–87. By the beginning of the first century C.E.,
magic of all sorts was considered illegal under the "Cornelian law on mur-
derers and poisoners," passed under Lucius Cornelius Sulla in 81–80 B.C.E.,
which remained in force at least until the late third, or early fourth century
C.E., as shown by commentary on the law from Justinian (*Digest* 48.8.3),
Paulus (*Opinions* 5.23.14-19), and its reiteration in the *Theodosian Code* 9.16.3;
see Beard, North, and Price, *Religions of Rome*, 2.261–63. For further discus-

sion of magic and its perceived threat to the Roman Empire, see Ramsay MacMullen, *Enemies of the Roman Order: Treason, Unrest, and Alienation in the Empire* (Cambridge: Harvard Univ. Press, 1966), 97–127. That pagan opponents of Christianity regarded it as *supertitio*, and its adherents (including Jesus himself) as magicians, is well known from Justin Martyr (*First Apology* 30; *Dialogue with Trypho* 69.7) and Origen (*Against Celsus* 1.6, 28, 68; 4.33; 6.38-41; 8.37).

20. I. M. Lewis, *Ecstatic Religion: An Anthropological Study of Spirit Possession and Shamanism* (Baltimore: Penguin, 1971).

21. Crossan, *Jesus: A Revolutionary Biography*, 88–91.

22. Crossan, *Jesus: A Revolutionary Biography*, 91, citing Barrie Reynolds, *Magic, Divination and Witchcraft among the Barotse of Northern Rhodesia*, Robins Series 3 (Berkeley: Univ. of California Press, 1963), 133–38.

23. Ibid.

24. See, e.g., E. P. Sanders, *Jesus and Judaism* (Philadelphia: Fortress Press, 1985), 61–76; Crossan, *Historical Jesus*, 355–60; Horsley, *Jesus and the Spiral of Violence*, 292–300; Borg, *Jesus: The New Vision*, 174–76; but cf. Robert J. Miller, "Historical Method and the Deeds of Jesus: The Test Case of the Temple Destruction," *Forum* 8, nos. 1-2 (1992) 5–30, for a contrary view.

25. The inscription is to be found in *OGIS* 2.48–60 (no. 458, lines 30-62); the translation (alt.) is from Lewis and Reinhold, eds., *Roman Civilization*, 2.64–65.

26. Dieter Georgi, *Theocracy in Paul's Praxis and Theology* (Minneapolis: Fortress Press, 1991), 28. The connection is also well documented by Wengst, *Pax Romana*, 76–79; and Helmut Koester, "Imperial Ideology and Paul's Eschatology in 1 Thessalonians," in *Paul and Empire*, ed. Horsley, 161–62.

27. Georgi, *Theocracy*, 26; see also Koester's remarks in "Imperial Ideology," 158, 160.

28. See especially James Kallas, "Romans XIII.1-7: An Interpolation," *NTS* 11 (1964) 365–74; W. Munroe, *Authority in Paul and Peter: The Identification of a Pastoral Stratum in the Pauline Corpus and 1 Peter* (Cambridge: Cambridge Univ. Press, 1983), 16–19; and J. C. O'Neill, *Paul's Letter to the Romans*, PNTC (Harmondsworth: Penguin, 1975), 207–9.

29. On the thoroughly anti-imperial stance of the Apocalypse of John see most recently Steven J. Friesen, *Imperial Cults and the Apocalypse of John* (New York: Oxford Univ. Press, 2001).

30. Pliny, *Ep.* 10.96.

31. On the mix of piety, power, and politics that characterized the imperial cult see especially Price, *Rituals and Power*.

Martyr

1. For discussion, see Lawrence M. Wills, *The Jew in the Court of the Foreign King: Ancient Jewish Court Legends,* HDR 26 (Minneapolis: Fortress Press, 1990).

2. George W. E. Nickelsburg, *Resurrection, Immortality, and Eternal Life in Intertestamental Judaism,* HTS 26 (Cambridge: Harvard Univ. Press, 1972), especially 48–62.

3. For the relationship between the songs of Second Isaiah and the hymns of the Wisdom of Solomon 2 and 4–5, see ibid., 62–65.

4. The existence of a pre-Markan passion narrative is to be sure a fractious debate not to be settled here. For an informative if tendentious discussion, see Burton L. Mack, *A Myth of Innocence: Mark and Christian Origins* (Philadelphia: Fortress Press, 1988), 249–68. Mack notes well the troubling apologetic interests involved in the quest for a pre-Markan passion narrative as an historically reliable account of Jesus' final days. Yet Mack's conclusion, drawn from the work of Werner Kelber, et al., in *The Passion in Mark: Studies on Mark 14–16* (Philadelphia: Fortress Press, 1976), that Mark created the passion sequence on his own is unsatisfactory since it necessitates the dependence of the Gospel of John and the *Gospel of Peter* on Mark for the episodes they all share in common, something I find unlikely. Preferable, in my view, is the analysis of Helmut Koester, who argues instead that Mark, John, and the *Gospel of Peter* all rely on a common source (*Ancient Christian Gospels* [Philadelphia: Trinity Press International, 1990], 220–30). Consequently, I would continue to foster the theory of a pre-Markan passion narrative, but without the usual accompanying assumption of its basic historicity. The *fictional* work Mack and others ascribe to Mark must simply be moved back to a pre-Markan stage.

5. "The Genre and Function of the Markan Passion Narrative," *HTR* 73 (1980) 153–84. Nickelsburg's treatment is the most elegant, but his insights about the use of the tradition of the suffering righteous one were anticipated by several, including C. H. Dodd, *According to the Scriptures: The Sub-Structure of New Testament Theology* (New York: Scribner's, 1953); Barnabas Lindars, *New Testament Apologetic: The Doctrinal Significance of the Old Testament Quotations* (Philadelphia: Westminster, 1961); Eta Linnemann, *Studien zur Passionsgeschichte,* FRLANT 102 (Göttingen: Vandenhoeck & Ruprecht, 1970). Detlev Dormeyer's study, *Die Passion Jesu als Verhaltensmodell: Literarische und theologische Analyse der Traditions- und Redaktionsgeschichte der Markuspassion,* NTA 11 (Münster: Aschendorff, 1974), adds independent weight to the discussion.

6. Mack, *Myth of Innocence,* 267.

7. For a list of allusions in the passion narrative to the psalms of the righteous sufferer and the Servant Songs of Second Isaiah, see Joel Marcus, "The Role of Scripture in the Gospel Passion Narratives," in *The Death of Jesus in Early Christianity,* ed. John Carroll and Joel Green (Peabody, Mass.: Hendrickson, 1995), especially 207–9 and 214–15.

8. Among recent treatments of the Noble Death tradition and its significance for understanding the New Testament are David Seeley, *The Noble Death: Greco-Roman Martyrology and Paul's Concept of Salvation,* JSNTSup 28 (Sheffield: JSOT Press, 1990); and Arthur J. Droge and James D. Tabor, *A Noble Death: Suicide and Martyrdom among Christians and Jews in Antiquity* (San Francisco: HarperSanFrancisco, 1992). Earlier, see Martin Hengel, *The Atonement: The Origins of the Doctrine in the New Testament,* trans. John Bowden (Philadelphia: Fortress Press, 1981), 1–32.

9. Sam K. Williams, *Jesus' Death as Saving Event: The Background and Origin of a Concept,* HDR 2 (Missoula, Mont.: Scholars Press, 1975), 153–61.

10. Seeley, *Noble Death,* 13, 83, 87–99, *et passim.*

11. For the Antiochene provenance of Fourth Maccabees see especially André Dupont-Sommer, *Le Quatrième Livre des Machabées,* Bibliothèque de l'École des Hautes Études 274 (Paris: Librairie Ancienne Honré Champion, 1939), 69–73; Moses Hadas, *The Third and Fourth Books of Maccabees* (New York: Harper & Brothers, 1953), 109–13; and Williams, *Jesus' Death as Saving Event,* 248–53. This judgment seems persuasive to me, *pace* the judicious treatment of this still disputed matter by H. Anderson, "4 Maccabees: A New Translation and Introduction," in *OTP* 2.534–37.

12. Seeley's analysis of Fourth Maccabees is most helpful: *Noble Death,* 92–99. Seeley is not the first, however, to see the significance of the Maccabean literature for understanding the martyrological background of early Christian interpretation of Jesus' death. Eduard Lohse developed it in his study, *Märtyrer und Gottesknecht: Untersuchungen zur urchristlichen Verkündigung vom Sühntod Jesu Christi,* FRLANT 64 (Göttingen: Vandenhoeck & Ruprecht, 1963), especially 66–72. Williams's study, *Jesus' Death as Saving Event,* upon which Seeley builds, advanced the discussion by locating the martyrological ideas evidenced especially in 4 Maccabees within the Hellenistic intellectual tradition of sacrificing oneself for a cause; similarly, Marinus de Jonge, "Jesus' Death for Others and the Maccabean Martyrs," in *Text and Testimony: Festschrift for A. F. J. Klijn,* ed. T. Baarda, et al. (Kampen: Kok, 1988), 142–51.

13. The idea that the noble death could be "sacrificial" and atoning is significant for early Christian notions of Jesus' death as a sacrifice, and the subject of Williams's study, *Jesus' Death as Saving Event.* I will take up this important subject in the next chapter.

14. For Antioch as the home of both the Maccabean tradition and certain early Christian traditions, and the importance of this geographic coincidence in accounting for the emergence of these ideas in early Christianity, see Williams, *Jesus Death as Saving Event*, 233–54.

15. See David Seeley's helpful analysis in "The Background of the Philippians Hymn (2:6-11)," *Journal of Higher Criticism* 1 (1994) 49–72.

16. This is Seeley's insight; see *Noble Death*, 92–94, *et passim*.

17. For the Stoic parallels here see Victor Paul Furnish, *II Corinthians*, AB 32A (Garden City, N.Y.: Doubleday, 1984), 281.

18. Note the "caution required by the apostle's eschatology" (Ernst Käsemann, *Commentary on Romans*, trans. and ed. Geoffrey W. Bromiley [Grand Rapids: Eerdmans, 1980], 166).

19. That Paul must balance his indicatives here with imperatives underscores his realism about the continuing human situation—so Günther Bornkamm, "Baptism and New Life in Paul (Romans 6)," in *Early Christian Experience*, trans. Paul L. Hammer (New York: Harper & Row, 1969), 71–86.

20. The martyrological aspects of Mark are emphasized especially by Mack, *Myth of Innocence*, especially 320–21, 340–49.

21. Norman Perrin, *The New Testament: An Introduction* (New York: Harcourt, Brace, Jovanovich, 1974), 144–45; idem, "The Evangelist as Author," in *Parable and Gospel*, ed. K. C. Hanson, FCBS (Minneapolis: Fortress Press, 2003), 58.

22. The use of the term *paradidonai* may reflect the terminology of the Servant Songs of Second Isaiah (Isa 53:6, 12)—so Joel Marcus, *The Way of the Lord: Christological Exegesis of the Old Testament in the Gospel of Mark* (Louisville: Westminster John Knox, 1992), 188–89. That the Servant Songs could take on collective significance in Jewish exegesis of Isaiah (Marcus, *Way of the Lord*, 190–93) perhaps offers Mark the poetic license to identify John, Jesus, and anyone who would follow them with Isaiah's suffering righteous servant.

23. See 1 Cor 11:23-25.

24. Isa 53:12 (MT).

25. The martyrological aspects of the Last Supper in Mark are brought out especially by Dennis Smith in *From Symposium to Eucharist: The Banquet in the Early Christian World* (Minneapolis: Fortress Press, 2003), 247–53.

26. On the Johannine situation and the question of martyrdom see the benchmark study by J. Louis Martyn, *History and Theology in the Fourth Gospel*, rev. ed. (Nashville: Abingdon, 1979); also, idem, *The Gospel of John in Christian History: Essays for Interpreters*, Theological Inquiries (New York: Paulist, 1978), 90–121. One should bear in mind, however, that there is no evidence of widespread persecution of Christians by Jews in this or later periods. John's

experience is a local experience, and we know it only through his perception and presentation of it.

27. The complexity of themes and issues in John serves often to obscure what otherwise might be quite obvious. The martyrological aspects of John are seldom commented upon, though a notable exception is Paul Minear's subtle treatment in *John: The Martyr's Gospel* (New York: Pilgrim, 1984).

28. Wilhelm Bousset, *Kyrios Christos: A History of the Belief in Christ from the Beginnings of Christianity to Irenaeus,* trans. John E. Steely (Nashville: Abingdon, 1970) 217.

29. *The Martyrdom of Saints Perpetua and Felicitas*; for the text in translation see Herbert Musurillo, *The Acts of the Christian Martyrs* (Oxford: Oxford Univ. Press, 1972), 106–31.

30. *Perpetua and Felicitas* 21.

31. Hengel, *Atonement,* 14–15.

32. *Ep.* 24.11.

33. For the martyrological sense of the passage, particularly of the quotation from Ps 43:23, see Käsemann, *Romans,* 245–52, especially 249–50.

Sacrifice

1. Anthropology has not passed on the opportunity to fill in this lacuna of meaning; the theories are as impressive as they are imaginative. See William Robertson Smith, *The Religion of the Semites* (1889; reprint, New York: Schocken, 1972); Emile Durkheim, *The Elementary Forms of Religious Life,* trans. Joseph W. Swain (New York: Macmillan, 1915); Henri Hubert and Marcel Mauss, *Sacrifice: Its Nature and Function,* trans. W. D. Halls (Chicago: Univ. of Chicago Press, 1964); Walter Burkert, *Homo Necans,* trans. Peter Bing (Berkeley: Univ. of California Press, 1983); René Girard, *Violence and the Sacred,* trans. Patrick Gregory (Baltimore: Johns Hopkins Univ. Press, 1977).

2. *Theogony* 535ff.

3. For this insight, and the approach that follows from it, see the collection of essays from colleagues at the Center for Comparative Research on Ancient Societies edited by Marcel Detienne and Jean-Pierre Vernant, *The Cuisine of Sacrifice among the Greeks,* trans. Paula Wissing (Chicago: Univ. of Chicago Press, 1989).

4. Marcel Detienne, "Culinary Practices and the Spirit of Sacrifice," in ibid., 11. Only the meat of smaller animals, like chickens or fish (usually), was not sacrificed.

5. Jean-Pierre Vernant, "At Man's Table: Hesiod's Foundation Myth of Sacrifice," in *Cuisine of Sacrifice*, 25–26, citing Jean Casabona, *Reserches sur le vocabulaire des sacrifices en grec, des origins à la fin de l'époque classique* (Aix-en-Provence: Ophrys, 1966). *Hierō* can mean either "to slaughter" or "to sacrifice" in Homeric and Classical usage. Later the term *thyō* can mean "to sacrifice," "to feast," or "to slaughter" (LSJ, s.v. *thyō*). For the unity of sacrifice and feasting, see Dennis E. Smith, *From Symposium to Eucharist: The Banquet in the Early Christian World* (Minneapolis: Fortress Press, 2003), 67–69.

6. Detienne, "Culinary Practices," 11.

7. This basic description of a Greek sacrifice comes from Burkert, *Homo Necans*, 3–7, with assembled details from Homer and the Greek tragedians. Helpful details and insights are also to be found in Jean-Louis Durand's essay, "Greek Animals: Toward a Typology of Edible Bodies," in *The Cuisine of Sacrifice among the Greeks*, edited by Marcel Detienne and Jean-Pierre Vernant, 87–118 (Chicago: Univ. of Chicago Press, 1989).

8. Note this critique from Stanley K. Stowers, "Greeks Who Sacrifice and Those Who Do Not," in *The Social World of the First Christians: Essays in Honor of Wayne A. Meeks,* ed. L. Michael White and O. Larry Yarbrough (Minneapolis: Fortress Press, 1995), 297–98.

9. Detienne, "Culinary Practices," 13. Plato speaks of the *geras*, or "meat privilege" (*Phaedrus* 265e; *Politicus* 287c), whereby the choice pieces of the animal are given first to the dignitaries present, but the more ancient practice seems to have been strictly egalitarian, with equal portions of meat distributed to all by lottery.

10. See especially the discussion by Stowers, "Greeks Who Sacrifice," 323–29. Stowers's perspective is a corrective to those who have tended to view Hellenistic sacrificial practice in terms of the Homeric ideal of citizens sharing equally in the distribution of the sacrificial meat. Yet, even before the changes brought on by the early imperial period, the distribution of meat portions was not strictly egalitarian, with multiple and choice portions going to city and cult officials before the common portions were distributed to the gathered crowd. A late-fourth-century Attic inscription lists the following recipients and their allotted shares: "Five pieces each to the presidents / Five pieces each to the nine archons / One piece each to the treasurers of the goddess / One piece each to the managers of the feast / The customary portions to others" (*SIG* 271; as cited by Royden Keith Yerkes, *Sacrifice in Greek and Roman Religions and Early Judaism* [New York: Scribner's, 1952], 107–8).

11. For the principle, and its notable exceptions, see Detienne, "The Violence of Wellborn Ladies: Women in the Thesmophoria," in *Cuisine of Sacrifice,* ed. Detienne and Vernant, 129–47.

12. Durand, "Greek Animals," 104.

13. See Mary Beard, John North, and Simon Price, *Religions of Rome*, vol. 1: *A History* (Cambridge: Cambridge Univ. Press, 1998), 37–38, for a discussion of the phenomenon; and vol. 2: *A Sourcebook*, 172–74, for examples.

14. Pliny, *Natural History* 10.33 (LCL).

15. For discussion see Martin Hengel, *The Atonement: The Origins of the Doctrine in the New Testament*, trans. John Bowden (Philadelphia: Fortress Press, 1981), 24–28; and Adela Yarbro Collins, "Finding Meaning in the Death of Jesus," *HR* 78 (1998) 185–87.

16. See Hengel, *Atonement*, 19, n. 65.

17. See Hengel, *Atonement*, 19–24, for discussion and the examples that follow.

18. Lycurgus, *Oratio in Leocratium* 24.

19. Pausanius, *Description of Greece* 9.17.1.

20. For the father, see Livy, *Roman History* 8.9; for the son, see Livy, *Roman History* 10.28; for grandson, see Plutarch, *Pyrrhus* 21; and Dionysus of Halicarnassus, *Roman Antiquities* 20.1.

21. *Roman History* 10.28 (LCL).

22. *Civil War* 2.314-15 (LCL).

23. *Civil War* 2.305 (LCL).

24. H. Anderson, trans., in *OTP* 2, 552.

25. This basic understanding of how the sprinkling of sacrificial blood works as a cleansing agent, not of the sinner, but of the cultic sanctuary, is the insight of Jacob Milgrom, "Israel's Sanctuary: The Priestly 'Picture of Dorian Gray,'" *RB* 83 (1976) 390–99; reprinted in idem, *Studies in Cultic Theology and Terminology*, SJLA 36 (Leiden: Brill, 1983), 75–84.

26. *Purity and Danger: An Analysis of the Concepts of Pollution and Taboo* (London: Routledge and Kegan Paul, 1966), 35.

27. For a discussion, see Wendy Cotter, "The Collegia and Roman Law: State Restrictions on Voluntary Associations, 64 B.C.E.–200 C.E.," in *Voluntary Associations in the Graeco-Roman World*, ed. John S. Kloppenborg and Stephen G. Wilson (London: Routledge, 1996), 74–89.

28. On the significance of meals in the early Jesus movement see Burton L. Mack, *A Myth of Innocence: Mark and Christian Origins* (Minneapolis: Fortress Press, 1988), 80–83; Hal Taussig and Dennis E. Smith, *Many Tables: The Eucharist in the New Testament* (Philadelphia: Trinity, 1990), 48–50; and Dennis Smith, *From Symposium to Eucharist*, 173–80, especially on meals in the Pauline tradition.

29. That early followers of Jesus came to understand his death as sacrificial primarily through the Jewish and broader Hellenistic martyrological tra-

dition is argued most impressively by Sam K. Williams, *Jesus' Death as Saving Event: The Background and Origin of a Concept*, HDR 2 (Missoula, Mont.: Scholars Press, 1975). See also the remarks of Rowan Williams, *Eucharistic Sacrifice: The Roots of a Metaphor* (Bramcote: Grove, 1982), 13–15.

30. The point is pressed by David Seeley, *The Noble Death: Greco-Roman Martyrology and Paul's Concept of Salvation*, JSNTSup 28 (Sheffield: JSOT Press, 1990), especially 87–94.

31. See Richard B. Hays, *The Faith of Jesus Christ: An Investigation of the Narrative Substructure of Galatians 3:1—4:11*, SBLDS 56 (Chico, Calif.: Scholars Press, 1983), 170–74, for discussion and literature.

32. Note that for Paul, in Romans, Jesus is designated Son of God by his resurrection (Rom 1:4).

33. So Hays, *Faith of Jesus Christ*, 173; see also his n. 135, commenting on the thesis of Goodenough (see n. 34 below).

34. This is closer to the approach taken by E. R. Goodenough in Goodenough and A. T. Kraabel, "Paul and the Hellenization of Christianity," in *Religions in Antiquity: Essays in Honor of Erwin Ramsdell Goodenough*, ed. Jacob Neusner, SHR 14 (Leiden: Brill, 1968), 45.

35. Smith, *From Sympoium to Eucharist*, 188–91.

36. Mack, *Myth of Innocence*, 216–19, 222–24; also Reginald H. Fuller, *The Foundations of New Testament Christology* (New York: Scribner's, 1965), 171; and Ferdinand Hahn, *The Titles of Jesus in Christology: Their History in Early Christianity*, trans. Harold Knight and George Ogg, Lutterworth Library (London: Lutterworth, 1969), 379.

37. Stowers, "Greeks Who Sacrifice," 328.

38. Beard, North, and Price, *Religions of Rome*, 1.361.

39. Similarly Williams, *Eucharistic Sacrifice*, 6. Williams, however, stresses the efforts of later Christian apologists, like Justin Martyr, to overcome the charge of subversion by depicting the Eucharist as a sacrifice that ought to be seen as a "normal and acceptable traditional form of piety" (8). But one should probably understand Justin to be putting the best possible spin on a practice that was conceived and perceived as subversive to the state.

40. Gerd Theissen, "The Strong and the Weak in Corinth," in *The Social Setting of Pauline Christianity: Essays on Corinth*, trans. John H. Schütz (Philadelphia: Fortress Press, 1982), 126.

41. See the succinct summary by Theissen in ibid., 127–28; or the more recent and all-inclusive survey by Dennis Smith in *From Symposium to Eucharist*, 13–172.

42. "The Strong and the Weak," 125–32.

43. Alan F. Segal, *Paul the Convert: The Apostolate and Apostasy of Saul the Pharisee* (New Haven: Yale Univ. Press, 1990), 231–32.

44. For *synedeisis* as "consciousness," not "conscience," see Richard A. Horsley, "Consciousness and Freedom among the Corinthians: 1 Cor 8–10," *CBQ* 40 (1978) 581–85.

45. David Gill, "*Trapezomata*: A Neglected Aspect of Greek Sacrifice," *HTR* 67 (1974) 123–27.

46. Cf. Richard A. Horsley's excellent treatment of this issue in 1 Corinthians in "1 Corinthians: A Case Study of Paul's Assembly as an Alternative Society," in *Paul and Empire: Religion and Power in Roman Imperial Society,* ed. Richard A. Horsley (Harrisburg: Trinity, 1997), 242–52, esp. 247–49.

47. There is little evidence that Christians suffered general persecution during this time frame. Nonetheless, we should probably assume that they suffered to the same extent that all dissidents to the empire suffered, and more severely in some places than in others; see Frederick J. Murphy, *Fallen Is Babylon: The Revelation to John,* New Testament in Context (Harrisburg: Trinity, 1998), 5–17.

48. Ludwig Mitteis and Ulrich Wilcken, *Grundzüge und Chrestomathie der Papyruskunde,* I, 2 (Leipzig: Teubner, 1912), no. 124, as cited and translated in Beard, North, and Price, *Religions of Rome,* 2.165.

49. Beard, North, and Price, *Religions of Rome,* 1.239. Note, however, that in places where the Roman cultus was particularly established and prominent, the Christian affront was understood to be directed more specifically to Roman religious customs (so Beard, North, and Price, *Religions of Rome,* 1.239–41).

50. Jonathan Z. Smith, *Map Is Not Territory: Studies in the History of Religions,* SJLA 23 (Chicago: Univ. of Chicago Press, 1993), xi–xv and 67–207, passim; and idem, *Drudgery Divine: On the Comparison of Early Christianities and the Religions of Late Antiquity* (Chicago: Univ. of Chicago Press, 1990), 121–25.

51. Smith, *Map Is Not Territory,* 138.

52. On the various techniques for interpreting Scripture in Hebrews see Harold W. Attridge's succinct summary in *The Epistle to the Hebrews,* Hermeneia (Philadelphia: Fortress Press, 1989), 23–25.

53. Passages such as 7:11-19, often used to make this case, are not anti-Jewish. Rather, the author typically critiques aspects of Jewish (cultic) tradition by making use of other Jewish traditions.

54. 3:6; 10:19; 10:35.

55. 10:36; 12:2; 12:7.

56. 3:6; 6:11.

57. Especially 11:1-40; see below.

58. Ernst Käsemann, *The Wandering People of God: An Investigation of the Letter to the Hebrews,* trans. Roy A. Harrisville and Irving L. Sandberg (Minneapolis: Augsburg, 1984), 174–82.

59. Attridge (*Epistle to the Hebrews,* 22): "fidelity [in chap. 11] encompasses both the more static virtue of endurance, exemplified particularly in Israel's martyrs (11:35-38) and in some aspects the story of Moses (11:25, 27), but also the 'dynamic' virtue of movement. In the exemplars of faith, this movement is not entry but exit."

The Resurrection of a Nobody

1. Rodolfo Lanciani, *Ancient Rome in the Light of Recent Discoveries* (Boston: Houghton Mifflin, 1888), 122.

2. *Against Heresies* 2.32.4.

3. The matter of what the Corinthians actually believed is disputed. The view expressed here is held by a number of scholars, including Ulrich Wilckens, *Weisheit und Torheit* (Tübingen: Mohr/Siebeck, 1959), 11; Ernst Käsemann, *New Testament Questions of Today,* trans. W. I. Montague (Philadelphia: Fortress Press, 1969), 125–26; J. H. Wilson, "The Corinthians Who Say There Is No Resurrection," *ZNW* 59 (1968) 90–107; James M. Robinson, "Kerygma and History in the New Testament," in idem and Helmut Koester, *Trajectories Through Early Christianity* (Philadelphia: Fortress Press, 1971), 33–34; and Jürgen Becker, *Auferstehung der Toten im Urchristentum,* SBS 82 (Stuttgart: Katholisches Bibelwerk, 1976), 74–76; although see E. Earle Ellis for a skeptical assessment: "Christ Crucified," in *Reconciliation and Hope,* ed. Robert Banks (Grand Rapids: Eerdmans, 1974), 73–74.

4. That such a view developed among the followers of Paul is shown by 2 Tim 2:17-18, which attributes it to a certain Hymenaeus (also mentioned as an opponent of the Pastor in 1 Tim 1:20) and Phyletus.

5. The question of how to understand surrogate baptism in this text is also a thorny problem. Most scholars take the plain sense of the text to be that people in Corinth were being baptized vicariously on behalf of dead relatives or friends. See, e.g., Hans Lietzmann, *An die Korinther I-II,* HNT 9 (Tübingen: Mohr/Siebeck, 1949), 82; Hans Conzelmann, *1 Corinthians: A Commnetary,* trans. James W. Leitch, Hermeneia (Philadelphia: Fortress Press, 1975), 275; and Andreas Lindemann, *Der Erste Korintherbrief,* HNT 9/1 (Tübingen: Mohr/Siebeck, 2000), 350–51.

6. Robert Martin-Achard, "Resurrection: Old Testament," *ABD* 5.683: "We draw attention to the fact that the theme of the resurrection asserted itself in

the Jewish milieu at the very moment when apocalyptic views were developing in answer to the distress being undergone by faithful Jews. By the victory over death . . . justice was rendered to the Yahwistic faithful."

7. One of the great themes of Jewish and Hellenistic martyrological literature is the overcoming of physical vulnerability; see David Seeley, *The Noble Death: Greco-Roman Martyrology and Paul's Concept of Salvation,* JSNTSup 28 (Sheffield: JSOT Press 1990), 96–97, 118–24, 126–27, 128–29, 131–32.

8. The importance of this simple point, seldom emphasized, is seen especially by Ulrich Wilckens, *Resurrection: Biblical Testimony to the Resurrection—An Historical Examination and Explanation,* trans. A. M. Stewart (Atlanta: John Knox, 1978), 124–32.

9. Most recently, e.g., N. T. Wright, *The Resurrection of the Son of God* (Minneapolis: Fortress Press, 2003), 696: "the combination of empty tomb and appearances of the living Jesus forms a set of circumstances which is itself *both necessary and sufficient* for the rise of early Christian belief. Without these phenomena, we cannot explain why this belief came into existence, and took the shape it did." Others have doubted it, however. See especially Rudolf Pesch, "Zur Entstehung des Glaubens an die Auferstehung Jesu," *ThQ* 153 (1973) 201–28, who argues that postresurrection visionary experiences and the like "did not occasion the origin of Easter faith, but confirmed this faith" (152). So also most notably Edward Schillebeeckx, *Jesus: An Experiment in Christology,* trans. Hubert Hoskins (New York: Seabury, 1979), especially 379–97. Though Schillebeeckx does allow that the disciples scattered after Jesus' crucifixion, he does not postulate the resurrection as that seminal "event" that brought them back together. Their "conversion" from fear involved foremost the "remembered aspects of their life shared in fellowship with Jesus and of Jesus' whole line of conduct." Though they had failed, they "had not in the end lost their faith in Jesus" (382).

10. Scholars have been slow in persuading translators to abandon the traditional rendering of this verse using the word "to" rather than "in," even though most translations now note that Paul does not really say "to me" in the Greek of this verse, but "in me" (*en emoi*).

11. The Greek word *pneuma* has many meanings: spirit, wind, breath, and ghost.

12. Hans Dieter Betz, "Zum Problem der Auferstehung Jesus im Lichte der griechischen magischen Papyri," in *Hellenismus und Urchristentum: Gesammelte Aufsätze,* vol. 1 (Tübingen: Mohr/Siebeck, 1990), 230–61, especially 254–58.

13. As first proposed by Julius Wellhausen, *Das Evangelium Marci* (Berlin: Reimer, 1909), 71. The mountaintop setting, the luminous appearance of Jesus and his companions, Moses and Elijah, and the idea in popular Jewish

lore that these latter two figures had been translated to heaven, are generally regarded as evidence that the story was originally a postresurrection appearance story. Jesus has now joined the company of those whose fate was finally to dwell with God in heaven. Mark easily transforms it into a story designed to predict Jesus' fate.

14. Rudolf Bultmann, *Die Geschichte der synoptischen Tradition, Ergänzungsheft,* 81; more recently, John Dominic Crossan, *The Historical Jesus: The Life of a Mediterranean Jewish Peasant* (San Francisco: HarperSanFrancisco, 1991), 405.

15. Adela Yarbro Collins, *The Beginning of the Gospel: Probings of Mark in Context* (Minneapolis: Fortress Press, 1992), 138–43.

16. The formula exists in three basic forms: (1) a participial construction describing God as "the one who raised him [Jesus] from the dead" (Rom 4:24; 8:11a, b; 2 Cor 4:14; Gal 1:1); (2) a simple finite construction: "God raised him [Jesus] from the dead" (Rom 10:9; 1 Cor 6:14; 15:15); and (3) a relative construction modifying Jesus as the one "whom he [God] raised from the dead" (1 Thess 1:10). See Paul Hoffmann, "Auferstehung Jesu Christi: II/1. Neues Testament," in *TRE* 1.479–80.

17. So Hoffmann, "Auferstehung," 486.

18. For the martyrological overtones of Phil 2:8 see Seeley, *Noble Death,* 103.

19. That the contest over apostolic authority shaped the early Christian resurrection proclamation is clear. See Hans von Campenhausen, *Ecclesiastical Authority and Spiritual Power in the Church of the First Three Centuries* (Stanford: Stanford Univ. Press, 1969), 13–23; Pheme Perkins, *Resurrection: New Testament Witness and Contemporary Reflection* (Garden City, N.Y.: Doubleday, 1984), 193–214; Crossan, *Historical Jesus,* 395–416.

20. Marcus J. Borg, *Jesus, a New Vision: Spirit, Culture, and the Life of Discipleship* (San Francisco: Harper & Row, 1987), 23–75.

21. For a fascinating treatment, see Stevan L. Davies, *Jesus the Healer: Possession, Trance, and the Origins of Christianity* (New York: Continuum, 1995).

22. The Spirit: Rom 7:4; 8:4-6, 13, 16, 23, 26-27; 1 Cor 2:10; 12:4, 7-11, 13; 14:2; 2 Cor 1:22; 3:6, 8; 5:5; Gal 3:2-5, 14; 5:5, 18, 22, 25; 6:8; Phil 2:1; 1 Thess 5:19; God's Spirit: Rom 8:9, 14; 1 Cor 2:11, 14; 3:16; 6:11; 7:40; 12:3; 2 Cor 3:3; Phil 3:3; the Holy Spirit: Rom 5:5; 9:1; 14:7; 15:13, 16, 19; 1 Cor 6:19; 12:3; 2 Cor 6:6; 13:14; 1 Thess 1:5-6; 4:8; the Spirit of Life: Rom 8:2; the Spirit of the Lord: 2 Cor 3:17; the Spirit of Christ: Rom 9:2; or Jesus Christ: Phil 1:19; cf. the Spirit of his Son: Gal 4:6.

23. On this point see especially Willi Marxsen, "When Did Christian Faith Begin?" in *Jesus and the Church: The Beginnings of Christianity,* trans. and ed. Philip Devenish (Philadelphia: Trinity, 1992), 76–95.

Bibliography

Anderson, H. "4 Maccabees: A New Translation and Introduction." In *OTP* 2.531–64.

Attridge, Harold W. *The Epistle to the Hebrews*. Hermeneia. Philadelphia: Fortress Press, 1989.

Beard, Mary, John North, and Simon Price. *Religions of Rome*. Vol. 1: *A History*. Vol. 2: *A Sourcebook*. Cambridge: Cambridge Univ. Press, 1998.

Becker, Jürgen. *Auferstehung der Toten im Urchristentum*. SBS 82. Stuttgart: Katholisches Bibelwerk, 1976.

Betz, Hans Dieter. "Zum Problem der Auferstehung Jesus im Lichte der griechischen magischen Papyri." In *Hellenismus und Urchristentum: Gesammelte Aufsätze*, 1.230–61. 3 vols. Tübingen: Mohr/ Siebeck, 1990.

Borg, Marcus J. *Jesus, a New Vision: Spirit, Culture, and the Life of Discipleship*. San Francisco: Harper & Row, 1987.

Bornkamm, Günther. "Baptism and New Life in Paul (Romans 6)." In *Early Christian Experience*, 71–86. New York: Harper & Row, 1969.

Bousset, Wilhelm. *Kyrios Christos: A History of the Belief in Christ from the Beginnings of Christianity to Irenaeus,* trans. John E. Steely (Nashville: Abingdon, 1970).

Breytenbach, Cilliers. "'Christus starb für uns': Zur Tradition und paulinischen Rezeption der 'Sterbformel.'" *NTS* 49 (2003) 447–75.

Bultmann, Rudolf. *Die Geschichte der synoptischen Tradition, Ergänzungsheft*. Edited by Philipp Vielhauer and Gerd Theissen. 5th ed. FRLANT 29. Göttingen: Vandenhoeck & Ruprecht, 1979.

Burkert, Walter. *Homo Necans: The Anthropology of Ancient Greek Sacrificial Ritual and Myth*. Translated by Peter Bing. Berkeley: Univ. of California Press, 1983.

Campenhausen, Hans von. *Ecclesiastical Authority and Spiritual Power in the Church of the First Three Centuries*. Translated by J. A. Baker. Stanford: Stanford Univ. Press, 1969.

Carney, Thomas F. *The Shape of the Past: Models and Antiquity*. Lawrence, Kan.: Coronado, 1975.

Carroll, James. *Constantine's Sword: The Church and the Jews—A History*. Boston: Houghton Mifflin, 2001.

Casabona, Jean. *Reserches sur le vocabulaire des sacrifices en grec, des origins à la fin de l'époque classique*. Aix-en-Provence: Ophrys, 1966.

Charlesworth, James H., ed. *The Old Testament Pseudepigrapha*. 2 vols. Garden City, N.Y.: Doubleday, 1983–1985.

Collins, Adela Yarbro. *The Beginning of the Gospel: Probings of Mark in Context*. Minneapolis: Fortress Press, 1992.

———. "Finding Meaning in the Death of Jesus." *HR* 78 (1998) 175–96.

Conzelmann, Hans. *1 Corinthians: A Commentary*. Translated by James W. Leitch. Hermeneia. Philadelphia: Fortress Press, 1975.

Cotter, Wendy. "The Collegia and Roman Law: State Restrictions on Voluntary Associations, 64 B.C.E.–200 C.E." In *Voluntary Associations in the Graeco-Roman World*, edited by John S. Kloppenborg and Stephen G. Wilson, 74–89. London: Routledge, 1996.

Crossan, John Dominic. *The Historical Jesus: The Life of a Mediterranean Jewish Peasant*. San Francisco: HarperSanFrancisco, 1991.

———. *Jesus: A Revolutionary Biography*. San Francisco: HaperSanFrancisco, 1994.

———, and Jonathan L. Reed. *Excavating Jesus: Beneath the Stones, Behind the Texts*. San Francisco: HarperSanFrancisco, 2001.

Davies, Stevan L. *Jesus the Healer: Possession, Trance, and the Origins of Christianity*. New York: Continuum, 1995.

de Jonge, Marinus. "Jesus' Death for Others and the Maccabean Martyrs." In *Text and Testimony: Festschrift for A. F. J. Klijn*, edited by T. Baarda, et al., 142–51. Kampen: Kok, 1988.

Detienne, Marcel. "Culinary Practices and the Spirit of Sacrifice." In *The Cuisine of Sacrifice among the Greeks*, edited by M. Detienne and J.-P. Vernant, 1–20. Translated by Paula Wissing. Chicago: Univ. of Chicago Press, 1989.

———. "The Violence of Wellborn Ladies: Women in the Thesmophoria." In *The Cuisine of Sacrifice among the Greeks*, edited by M. Detienne and J.-P. Vernant, 129–47. Translated by Paula Wissing. Chicago: Univ. of Chicago Press, 1989.

———, and Jean-Pierre Vernant. *Cunning Intelligence in Greek Culture and Society*. Translated by Janet Lloyd. Atlantic Highlands, N.J.: Humanities, 1978.

———, eds. *The Cuisine of Sacrifice among the Greeks*. Translated by Paula Wissing. Chicago: Univ. of Chicago Press, 1989.

Dodd, C. H. *According to the Scriptures: The Sub-Structure of New Testament Theology*. New York: Scribner's, 1953.

Dormeyer, Detlev. *Die Passion Jesu als Verhaltensmodell: Literarische und theologische Analyse der Traditions- und Redaktionsgeschichte der Markuspassion.* NTA 11. Münster: Aschendorff, 1974.

Douglas, Mary. *Purity and Danger: An Analysis of the Concepts of Pollution and Taboo.* London: Routledge and Kegan Paul, 1966.

Droge, Arthur J., and James D. Tabor. *A Noble Death: Suicide and Martyrdom among Christians and Jews in Antiquity.* San Francisco: HarperSanFrancisco, 1992.

Dupont-Sommer, André. *Le Quatrième Livre des Machabées.* Bibliothèque de l'École des Hautes Études 274. Paris: Librairie Ancienne Honré Champion, 1939.

Durand, Jean-Louis. "Greek Animals: Toward a Typology of Edible Bodies." In *The Cuisine of Sacrifice among the Greeks,* edited by Marcel Detienne and Jean-Pierre Vernant, 87–118. Translated by Paula Wissing. Chicago: Univ. of Chicago Press, 1989.

Durkheim, Emil. *The Elementary Forms of Religious Life.* Translated by Joseph W. Swain. New York: Macmillan, 1915.

Ellis, E. Earle. "Christ Crucified." In *Reconciliation and Hope: New Testament Essays on Atonement and Eschatology Presented to L. L. Morris on His 60th Birthday,* edited by Robert Banks, 70–75. Grand Rapids: Eerdmans, 1974.

Friesen, Steven J. *Imperial Cults and the Apocalypse of John: Reading Revelation in the Ruins.* Oxford: Oxford Univ. Press, 2001.

Fuller, Reginald H. *The Foundations of New Testament Christology.* New York: Scribner's, 1965.

Furnish, Victor Paul. *II Corinthians.* AB 32A. Garden City, N.Y.: Doubleday, 1984.

Garnsey, Peter, and Richard P. Saller. "Patronal Power Relations." In *Paul and Empire: Religion and Power in Roman Imperial Society,* edited by Richard A. Horsley, 96–103. Harrisburg: Trinity, 1997.

Georgi, Dieter. *Theocracy in Paul's Praxis and Theology.* Translated by David E. Green. Minneapolis: Fortress Press, 1991.

Gill, David. "*Trapezomata*: A Neglected Aspect of Greek Sacrifice." *HTR* 67 (1974) 123–27.

Girard, René. *Violence and the Sacred.* Translated by Patrick Gregory. Baltimore: Johns Hopkins Univ. Press, 1977.

Goodenough, E. R., and Thomas A. Kraabel. "Paul and the Hellenization of Christianity." In *Religions in Antiquity: Eassays in Memory of Erwin Ramsdell Goodenough,* edited by Jacob Neusner, 35–80. SHR 14. Leiden: Brill, 1968.

Hadas, Moses. *The Third and Fourth Books of Maccabees.* New York: Harper, 1953.

Hahn, Ferdinand. *The Titles of Jesus in Christology: Their History in Early Christianity.* Translated by Harold Knight and George Ogg. Lutterworth Library. London: Lutterworth, 1969.

Hays, Richard B. *The Faith of Jesus Christ: An Investigation of the Narrative Substructure of Galatians 3:1—4:11.* SBLDS 56. Chico, Calif.: Scholars Press, 1983.

Hengel, Martin. *The Atonement: The Origins of the Doctrine in the New Testament.* Translated by John Bowden. Philadelphia: Fortress Press, 1981.

Hoffmann, Paul. "Auferstehung Jesu Christi: II/1. Neues Testament." *TRE* 1.479–80.

———. *Die Toten in Christus: Eine religionsgeschichtliche und exegetische Untersuchung zur paulinischen Eschatologie.* NTA 2. Münster: Aschendorf, 1966.

Holum, Kenneth G., et al. *King Herod's Dream—Caesarea on the Sea.* New York: Norton, 1988.

Horsley, Richard A. "1 Corinthians: A Case Study of Paul's Assembly as an Alternative Society." In *Paul and Empire: Religion and Power in Roman Imperial Society,* edited by Richard A. Horsley, 242-52. Harrisburg: Trinity, 1997.

———. "Consciousness and Freedom among the Corinthians: 1 Cor 8–10." *CBQ* 40 (1978) 581–85.

———. "The Death of Jesus." In *Studying the Historical Jesus: Evaluations of the State of Current Research,* edited by Bruce Chilton and Craig Evans, 395–422. NTTS 19. Leiden: Brill, 1994.

———. *Jesus and the Spiral of Violence: Popular Jewish Resistance in Roman Palestine.* San Francisco: Harper & Row, 1987.

Hubert, Henri, and Marcel Mauss. *Sacrifice: Its Nature and Function.* Translated by W. D. Halls. Chicago: Univ. of Chicago Press, 1964.

Käsemann, Ernst. *Commentary on Romans.* Translated and edited by Geoffrey W. Bromiley. Grand Rapids: Eerdmans, 1980.

———. *New Testament Questions of Today.* Translated by W. I. Montague. Philadelphia: Fortress Press, 1969.

———. *The Wandering People of God: An Investigation of the Letter to the Hebrews.* Translated by Roy Harrisville and Irvine L. Sandberg. Minneapolis: Augsburg, 1984.

Kallas, James. "Romans XIII.1-7: An Interpolation." *NTS* 11 (1964) 365–74.

Kelber, Werner, ed. *The Passion in Mark: Studies on Mark 14–16.* Philadelphia: Fortress Press, 1976.

Koester, Helmut. *Ancient Christian Gospels: Their History and Development.* Philadelphia: Trinity, 1990.

———. "Imperial Ideology and Paul's Eschatology in 1 Thessalonians." In *Paul and Empire: Religion and Power in Roman Imperial Society*, edited by Richard A. Horsley, 158–66. Harrisburg: Trinity, 1997.

———. "Jesus the Victim." *JBL* 111 (1992) 3–15.

Lenski, Gerhard E. *Power and Privilege: A Theory of Social Stratification*. New York: McGraw-Hill, 1966.

Lewis, I. M. *Ecstatic Religion: An Anthropological Study of Spirit Possession and Shamanism*. Baltimore: Penguin, 1971.

Lewis, Naphtali, and Meyer Reinhold. *Roman Civilization: Selected Readings*. 2 vols. New York: Harper & Row, 1966.

Lietzmann, Hans. *An die Korinther I-II*. HNT 9. Tübingen: Mohr/Siebeck, 1949.

Lindars, Barnabas. *New Testament Apologetic: The Doctrinal Significance of the Old Testament Quotations*. Philadelphia: Westminster, 1961.

Lindemann, Andreas. *Der Erste Korintherbrief*. HNT 9/1. Tübingen: Mohr/Siebeck, 2000.

Linnemann, Eta. *Studien zur Passionsgeschichte*. FRLANT 102. Göttingen: Vandenhoeck & Ruprecht, 1970.

Lohse, Eduard. *Märtyrer und Gottesknecht: Untersuchungen zur urchristlichen Verkündigung vom Sühntod Jesu Christi*. FRLANT 64. Göttingen: Vandenhoeck & Ruprecht, 1963.

Mack, Burton L. *A Myth of Innocence: Mark and Christian Origins*. Philadelphia: Fortress Press, 1988.

MacMullen, Ramsay. *Enemies of the Roman Order: Treason, Unrest, and Alienation in the Empire*. Cambridge: Harvard Univ. Press, 1966.

———. *Roman Social Relations: 50 B.C.–A.D. 384*. New Haven: Yale Univ. Press, 1974.

Marcus, Joel. "The Role of Scripture in the Gospel Passion Narratives." In *The Death of Jesus in Early Christianity*, edited by John Carroll and Joel Green, 205–33. Peabody, Mass.: Hendrickson, 1995.

———. *The Way of the Lord: Christological Exegesis of the Old Testament in the Gospel of Mark*. Louisville: Westminster John Knox, 1992.

Martin, Dale B. *The Corinthian Body*. New Haven: Yale Univ. Press, 1995.

Martin-Achard, Robert. "Resurrection: Old Testament." *ABD* 5.680–84.

Martyn, J. Louis. *The Gospel of John in Christian History: Essays for Interpreters*. New York: Paulist, 1978.

———. *History and Theology in the Fourth Gospel*. Rev. ed. Nashville: Abingdon, 1979.

Marxsen, Willi. "When Did Christian Faith Begin?" In *Jesus and the Church: The Beginnings of Christianity*, 76–95. Translated and edited by Philip E. Devenish. Philadelphia: Trinity, 1992.

Milgrom, Jacob. "Israel's Sanctuary: The Priestly 'Picture of Dorian Gray.'" *RB* 83 (1976) 390–99. Reprinted in idem, *Studies in Cultic Theology and Terminology*, 75–84. SJLA 36. Leiden: Brill, 1983.

Miller, Robert J. "Historical Method and the Deeds of Jesus: The Test Case of the Temple Destruction." *Forum* 8, nos. 1-2 (1992) 5–30.

Minear, Paul S. *John: The Martyr's Gospel*. New York: Pilgrim, 1984.

Munroe, Winsom. *Authority in Paul and Peter: The Identification of a Pastoral Stratum in the Pauline Corpus and 1 Peter*. SNTSMS 45. Cambridge: Cambridge Univ. Press, 1983.

Murphy, Frederick J. *Fallen Is Babylon: The Revelation to John*. New Testament in Context. Harrisburg: Trinity, 1998.

Musurillo, Herbert. *The Acts of the Christian Martyrs*. Oxford Early Christian Texts. Oxford: Oxford Univ. Press, 1972.

Nickelsburg, George W. E. "The Genre and Function of the Markan Passion Narrative." *HTR* 73 (1980) 153–84.

———. *Resurrection, Immortality, and Eternal Life in Intertestamental Judaism*. HTS 26. Cambridge: Harvard Univ. Press, 1972.

O'Neill, J. C. *Paul's Letter to the Romans*. PNTC. Harmondsworth: Penguin, 1975.

Perkins, Pheme. *Resurrection: New Testament Witness and Contemporary Reflection*. Garden City, N.Y.: Doubleday, 1984.

Perrin, Norman. *The New Testament: An Introduction*. New York: Harcourt, Brace, Jovanovich, 1974.

Pesch, Rudolf. "Zur Entstehung des Glaubens an die Auferstehung Jesu." *ThQ* 153 (1973) 201–28.

Price, S. R. F. *Rituals and Power*. Cambridge: Cambridge Univ. Press, 1984.

Reynolds, Barrie. *Magic, Divination and Witchcraft Among the Barotse of Northern Rhodesia*. Robins Series 3. Berkeley: Univ. of California Press, 1963.

Robinson, James M. "Kerygma and History in the New Testament." In idem and Helmut Koester, *Trajectories Through Early Christianity*, 20–70. Philadelphia: Fortress Press, 1971.

Sanders, E. P. *Jesus and Judaism*. Philadelphia: Fortress Press, 1985.

Schillebeeckx, Edward. *Jesus: An Experiment in Christology*. Translated by Hubert Hoskins. New York: Seabury, 1979.

Seeley, David. "The Background of the Philippians Hymn (2:6-11)." *Journal of Higher Criticism* 1 (1994) 49–72.

————. *The Noble Death: Greco-Roman Martyrology and Paul's Concept of Salvation.* JSNTSup 28. Sheffield: JSOT Press, 1990.

Segal, Alan F. *Paul the Convert: The Apostolate and Apostasy of Saul the Pharisee.* New Haven: Yale Univ. Press, 1990.

Seland, Torrey. *Establishment Violence in Philo and Luke: A Study of Non-Conformity to the Torah and Jewish Vigilante Reactions.* Biblical Interpretation Series 15. Leiden: Brill, 1995.

Smith, Dennis E. *From Symposium to Eucharist: The Banquet in the Early Christian World.* Minneapolis: Fortress Press, 2003.

Smith, Jonathan Z. *Drudgery Divine: On the Comparison of Early Christianities and the Religions of Late Antiquity.* Chicago Studies in the History of Judaism. Chicago: Univ. of Chicago Press, 1990.

————. *Map Is Not Territory: Studies in the History of Religions.* Chicago: Univ. of Chicago Press, 1993.

Smith, William Robertson. *The Religion of the Semites.* Reprint. New York: Schocken, 1972.

Stegemann, Ekkehard W., and Wolfgang Stegemann. *The Jesus Movement: A Social History of Its First Century.* Translated by O. C. Dean Jr. Minneapolis: Fortress Press, 1999.

Stowers, Stanley K. "Greeks Who Sacrifice and Those Who Do Not." In *The Social World of the First Christians: Essays in Honor of Wayne A. Meeks,* edited by L. Michael White and O. Larry Yarbrough, 293–333. Minneapolis: Fortress Press, 1995.

Taussig, Hal, and Dennis E. Smith. *Many Tables: The Eucharist in the New Testament.* Philadelphia: Trinity, 1990.

Theissen, Gerd. "The Strong and the Weak in Corinth." In *The Social Setting of Pauline Christianity: Essays on Corinth,* 121–43. Translated by John H. Schütz. Philadelphia: Fortress Press, 1982.

Vernant, Jean-Pierre. "At Man's Table: Hesiod's Foundation Myth of Sacrifice." In *The Cuisine of Sacrifice among the Greeks,* edited by M. Detienne and J.-P. Vernant, 21–86. Translated by Paula Wissing. Chicago: Univ. of Chicago Press, 1989.

Veyne, Paul. "The Roman Empire (Where Public Life Was Private)." In *A History of Private Life.* Vol. 1: *From Pagan Rome to Byzantium,* edited by Paul Veyne, 95–115. Translated by Arthur Goldhammer. Cambridge: Harvard Univ. Press, 1987.

Wellhausen, Julius. *Das Evangelium Marci.* Berlin: Reimer, 1909.

Wengst, Klaus. *Pax Romana and the Peace of Jesus Christ.* Translated by John Bowden. Philadelphia: Fortress Press, 1987.

Wilckens, Ulrich. *Resurrection: Biblical Testimony to the Resurrection: An Historical Examination and Explanation.* Translated by A. M. Stewart. Atlanta: John Knox, 1978.

———. *Weisheit und Torheit: Eine exegetisch- religionsgeschichtliche Untersuchung zu 1. Kor. 1 und 2.* BHT 26. Tübingen: Mohr/Siebeck, 1959.

Williams, Rowan. *Eucharistic Sacrifice: The Roots of a Metaphor.* Grove Liturgical Study 31. Bramcote: Grove, 1982.

Williams, Sam K. *Jesus' Death as Saving Event: The Background and Origin of a Concept.* HDR 2. Missoula, Mont.: Scholars Press, 1975.

Wills, Lawrence M. *The Jew in the Court of the Foreign King: Ancient Jewish Court Legends.* HDR 26. Minneapolis: Fortress Press, 1990.

Wilson, Jack H. "The Corinthians Who Say There Is No Resurrection." *ZNW* 59 (1968) 90–107.

Winter, Paul. *The Trial of Jesus.* 2d ed. Revised and edited by T. A. Burkill and Geza Vermes. SJ 1. Berlin: de Gruyter, 1974.

Wright, N. T. *The Resurrection of the Son of God.* Minneapolis: Fortress Press, 2003.

Yerkes, Royden Keith. *Sacrifice in Greek and Roman Religions and Early Judaism.* New York: Scribner's, 1952.

Index
of Ancient Sources

Double Lives

Also by Jane Barnes:

I, KRUPSKAYA

Jane Barnes

DOUBLE
LIVES

Doubleday & Company, Inc.
Garden City, New York
1981

All characters in this book are
fictitious, and any resemblance
to persons living or dead is
entirely coincidental.

DOUBLE LIVES was completed
with the assistance of a grant
from the National Foundation for the Arts
during 1976–77.

ISBN: 0-385-15647-2
Library of Congress Catalog Card Number 79-7795

For J. D. C.

1

"Red lips kiss my blues away," Christopher Nicholas whispered in a dream.

He was a grown man in army uniform—just after the war—and he was in his cubicle at Groton. He was adult, but his boy's fear was fresh, as gripping as if he were a boy again, subject to the masters and bullies and school heroes all over again, subject to the fear of being unmasked, discovered, *exposed!* But the future depended on people so deep inside the government they'd come out the other side, people like him, who were the secret wild cards in the deck of laws.

"Red lips kiss my blues away," he whispered to Ellie Snow, who was sitting at the foot of his bed, looking as she had in the old days, back when she was still mighty good kissing. Transparent skin, hair so blond it was almost silver, and irregular mouth—shockingly large when she grinned. And she had just the right blend of wit and witlessness. Important that a woman be beautiful, but not too smart. Smart enough to be a worthy receiver of his feeling, but not so smart she would see how tenderhearted he really was, not so smart she'd ridicule him.

He reached for her, but she fended him off. "What's the matter?" he asked, knifed by her rejection. "Remember Dance Weekend? Remember how we crept off to the bushes? Ellie, you let me do more than kiss you then."

"That was fifteen years ago," she pointed out. "I'm a married woman. Why, I'm a twice-married woman. I'm twice as respectable as I used to be."

"That's what I hate about women! If they aren't killers, they're only superficial."

"I say, that's a little strong, isn't it? Though there's nothing like a good stiff insult to arouse me, dear. Where there's danger, hope is still alive!"

But as she turned to him, arms outstretched to embrace him, she began to look more like her recent, older, drunken self. Her cheeks became their unhealthy purple color and veins were visible close to the surface of her skin. Her silvery blond hair grew gray and wiry and was cut so short it stood on end all over her head as if electrified. As if she'd just come from having shock treatments.

"Ellie, I just remembered," he said primly, recoiling from the monster life had made of her. "I've met a wonderful girl to whom I must be true. Joanne Gillian Goddard. Miss Porter's '39, runner-up Agawam Hunt Tennis

Championship '38 and winter '39, model and girl-about-
New York '39 to '42, war work in the office of the International Red Cross, Washington, D.C., '42 to '46."

"Nothing, I suppose, like your first wife, Brearley '29,
Vassar '33, Junior League '33 to '66. I still see her, ya
know, and pleash don ever imagine you can criticize me
after what you did to her."

"I didn't ask for the editorial. And I haven't said a
thing about your boozing, which I might as well tell you
has gone too far. You'll admit you're looped, won't you?"

She put a thin, aged finger to her temple and pondered
this question. "Am I looped? Plastered, squiffed, smashed
or bombed? Ish a Pope a Cafolic? Don't ashk such shtu-
pid qeshions. But don't think I haven't done something
with my life either. Don't forget: I schlept with Kennedy!
And what he told me about you and Castro would make a
beet blush."

His eyes flew open. He was in a panic. His heart raced.
He ached in every limb.

Though the curtains were drawn, he knew from the
quality of bright grayness in the room that it was around
seven. Why had coming home made a coward of him?

After eighteen years with the CIA, he had retired two
weeks before, in June 1966. He was fifty-five years old. He
had faced death before and not been afraid. Somehow it
was different here in his own bed, more truly an extinction
than it had been on the battlefield. Here in his family he
died every time he held his tongue; but at work self-
sacrifice and service had returned him to himself a thou-
sandfold. Here his self-restraint, discipline and sense of
responsibility all made him feel miserably unappreciated.

The longer he lay there, the calmer his heart became,
but lying there made him feel lonely. He got out of bed
and woke Joanne. Or tried to. She was the kind of person

who could sleep through an air raid, but today he wanted her to get the children up for breakfast; then he would take them to The Bleakers for their first morning of work on the old farmhouse.

Joanne brilliantly impersonated a person who was awake. Very clearly, enunciating every word in her sentence, she told him she would be right up, and would go and wake the kids. He was completely fooled, went to start coffee and cook bacon. This was a job he felt uniquely qualified to do because he understood that the strips had to be taken from the pan before they got too brown. He alone in this family seemed to know that bacon continued to cook after it had been laid on the paper towels, and though he possessed this crucial knowledge, he was not always allowed to put it to good use. People usually got up whenever they felt like it, and breakfast was cooked at all hours of the morning. He had seen much ruined bacon, but this was the first day he'd had a chance to exert some control over this area of incompetence.

He carefully covered the bottom of the frying pan with bacon, watching the white fat slowly become translucent with the heat. It began to snap and hiss, and he turned every piece over, but as he did he grew increasingly suspicious of the silence from the bedroom. He wiped his hands on his handkerchief and went back to find his wife still sound asleep. When he shook her, she immediately turned on her recording of an awake person.

"I'll be right there," she said brightly, loudly, as if he was in the other room and she was just getting her clothes on. Her eyes were shut; her face and body were utterly relaxed. She was like someone operating under posthypnotic suggestion. Christopher had a technique for dealing with her when she was like this. He had developed it when they were first married and she had talked in her sleep. He had asked her questions which were progressively harder to answer until she'd had to think so hard she'd woken up. After several weeks of waking to the sound of her own voice talking about old boyfriends, Joanne's reserve sank to a deeper level and she stopped talking at night. Now, floating these false balloons of dialogue, it was as if she'd forgotten his training.

"What day is it?" he asked.

"One of these days," she murmured, frowning slightly.

"What will happen one of these days?" he went on, having to use one hand to hold Foster off. The old black labrador could not stand to see a circumstance which might be affectionate without trying to get in on it himself. He bumped Christopher's ear with his cold, wet nose while Christopher asked again, "What's going to happen one of these days?"

"One a theesh daysh," she repeated drunkenly.

"Where are you, Joanne?"

"Somewhere, somehow," she muttered, growing crosser as she was brought up to consciousness.

"Do you know that I was involved in several attempts to assassinate Castro?"

Her eyes opened and she blinked when she saw him with his face so close to hers, fending off Foster. When the dog saw she was awake, he laid his nose on the bed, wriggling his whole body, snuffling and brimming with enthusiasm for this early-morning lovefest. "Hello, Foster," she murmured.

"Time to get the kids up," said Christopher, straightening and looking at his wristwatch. "We've got to be at The Bleakers in an hour."

And then he smelled his bacon burning. The kitchen

was filled with smoke and the crisp smell of scorched meat. What if it were his hand in the grease? How brave was he really? Germans poured scalding water down a man's throat to get him to talk. Could he have borne that pain? Always hated the thought of being burned. Tested himself in fantasies. Read books about men who never broke down—captured spies who died instead of talking. Hated himself for not bearing the little pain he'd been given in life when there were so many others who'd suffered so much more and said so much less.

He started a new pan of bacon, seared by the stupidity of having let the first batch scorch. Broke eggs to make the omelette. Heard two of his children, Katherine (twenty) and Bucky (sixteen), grumbling, fighting, joking. They shut up when they saw Hitler was cooking breakfast. They couldn't have fun when he was around, the family killjoy. Sorry he put such a strain on their good times. Sorry to get in their way. Sorry to be such an old bore. Sorry to always be so serious, even though his friends thought he had a pretty good sense of humor. As a matter of fact, he knew people who sought him out just because he was considered sort of an amusing fellah.

His wife floated in, surrounded by veils of cigarette smoke, smelling like toothpaste, Chanel Nº 5 and Jergen's Lotion. She took over the cooking of breakfast as if he weren't there, but Christopher would not stoop to letting her see that he was bothered. He poured a cup of coffee for himself and sat down in a large leather chair by the fireplace, away from the table where the children were sitting. Joanne served the plates, poured orange juice, milk, coffee, and yet, in the process of serving breakfast her humor and vitality began to govern, if anarchy can be said to have a government. She told a story about three brothers who were all called Sam, all sons of a man named Sam. Christopher would not have believed it from anyone else, but things had a way of growing funnier and funnier as they came into Joanne's vicinity. Christopher could imagine a painfully sensitive person (like himself, say), poetic yet isolated, well, even tragically isolated in some ways, encountering one Sam after another and going mad with the strangeness of the surrealistic repetition. For him, of course, there would be the dark, unshareable suspicion that Uncle Sam was trying to push him over into insanity so that everything he said could be discounted as the raving of a maniac.

But there were no barbs in Joanne's brush with the absurd, only foolishness, offered with real goodwill, as proof of which Joanne went first, playing the fool to give others the courage to try. She was like the person who plunges into the cold water and then bursts joyfully through the surface, waving everyone in after her. She drank the soup to show it was safe. She was fearless, without a shred of vanity or pride. She had no respect for institutions and this made her feel she was outside the whole question of obedience. If she did what he asked, it was because she wanted to and not because she accepted his system as a whole. Now, when she did everything at once—the work at the stove as well as the job of entertaining—she imagined she was providing the common human denominator through which they all could mix: parents and children, fat and thin, young and old, funny and dull. Maybe she didn't do this purposely. Maybe she had no idea what she was like or what her effect on others was. But whether she did or didn't, this time she was wrong. She could not stir him into her batter like a tablespoon of salt. She could not be equally friendly with both sides without betraying one of her loyalties. She could not divest herself of all her authority, like someone getting down on the floor to play with a dog, and expect him to do the same. Precisely because she made herself childlike and so appealed to the children, he had to stand apart, maintaining the standards.

"Goddamn it," he said. "Where the hell is Diana?"

"Still asleep," said Bucky, savoring the trouble he knew his information would get his seventeen-year-old sister into.

"Not for long," said Christopher, and started up from his chair.

Just then Diana straggled in, unkempt, cross, looking for a fight, saying, "I see everyone's off to the usual cheerful start."

"Since you think so, you can start the working day without breakfast. We're due to meet Nathan in five minutes," Christopher retorted, cocking his wrist importantly to see the time.

"Don't tell me you're finally going public?" Diana asked rudely.

"What do you mean?" Christopher was shocked by Diana's assault on unwritten family rules. When he was present, he was boss. And his work was virgin territory. People didn't speak of the Agency unless they were invited to.

"Just that it's hard to take a piss without seeing graffiti about the CIA written on the walls."

"Diana," her mother protested. Joanne's whole body seemed to shrink away, withdrawing toward a modesty which forbade disrespect, open rebellion, the cruel truth. Her head gave a little, graceful shake of reprimand and resignation. "How dare you speak that way to your father?"

"She doesn't know what she's saying," Christopher said with disgust. (If only they'd done it *right*. If only Kennedy hadn't called off the air cover, and the Cuban invasion had really had a military chance.) He could tell from the fear on Diana's face that she'd scared herself by going as far as she had, and he let her fear of having trespassed be her punishment. He got up and left. His children trooped out after him, following three steps behind in a funeral procession of respect.

As soon as they were out their own front door, they could see The Bleakers, a small eighteenth-century farmhouse several hundred yards away. Once the property's central building, it had been maintained for rental purposes ever since the Nicholases converted the large dairy barn. This past year the farmhouse has been vandalized by winter tenants, and Christopher, who only discovered this fact in May, had never expected to have it in shape for summer lease. Then, just as the family was leaving Washington for Saunderstown, the Bakers had called, desperate for a place to live in Rhode Island. Arnold Baker taught a special history course for students in technical universities; that summer he was going to be lecturing on the U.S. labor movement to engineering students at U.R.I. The Bakers had learned about the house because Christopher had forgotten to take it off the university's list. They had already investigated the place, and when Christopher started to explain about its condition, Arnold said they thought the house would be livable. As a matter of fact, as there was really no place else for them to go, and as they had an eighteen-year-old son and had participated in Quaker work camps involving just such projects, they offered to fix the place up as payment. Christopher had donated his children to the labor force and it was a deal.

The Bakers turned out to be the kind of people who made him feel like T. E. Lawrence. Though they'd spent their lives regarding Christopher's type as infamous, they treated him like a celebrity when they met him in person. Christopher felt it was his job to right the balance of admiration. Though they differed on every issue—from the dropping of the atom bomb (Christopher for, the Bakers against) to the current buildup in Vietnam (Christopher for, the Bakers against)—they were all governed by a desire to work for what they felt was right. Christopher maintained that a belief in belief gave him and the Bakers the largest thing people could have in common. As long as people agreed it was worse to be faithless than it was to be 60 percent right, they were in the same ball park. The *only* ball park as far as Christopher was concerned.

His greeting to Nathan was excessive. The big, broad-shouldered boy was standing outside, waiting for them as they approached. Christopher waved "hello," said "hello" heartily, and followed this up by shaking hands "hello." It was his way of going overboard in the interest of proving his democratic sense of equality with the boy, his parents and their opposing political views. Nathan caught the ball and threw it back; he waved, heartily countergreeted and vigorously shook hands. His blue eyes shone beneath tufted, mustard-colored eyebrows. He had pimples, but of a rare sort in that they weren't that unattractive. They were dry and flat and their redness contributed to his healthy appearance. His face was diamond-shaped, the face of a jester and an owl.

Christopher's children seemed like unlikely candidates for any transformation, but Nathan Baker's mechanism of cheer and efficiency soon had ground them up and redistributed them according to their sizes and his plans. He escorted them into the house, explaining that his father had gone to the university for the day, but that they had discussed things, and that if it was all right with Mr. Nicholas, they might as well do everything that needed to be done and not just the two tasks they'd spoken of the night before at dinner. Unable to resist this raw onslaught of energy and purpose, Christopher said that sounded fine to him, and then found himself and his children all whirled upstairs. Nathan pointed out the window onto the landing to the slightly inclined roof over the front porch. In several places the shingles had rotted and Nathan urged Christopher to put the girls to work tearing the shingles up. A new set would be cheaper than having to replace the whole roof and would be necessary in the next year or so if the asphalt tiles were left to deteriorate further.

"Go to it, girls," said Nathan, opening the window and waving them through with his hand. (Later, Katherine said she had no idea if she was stepping to her death or not, only that Nathan had so unquestionably taken command that she had to do what he bid.)

Downstairs in the farmhouse there were three rooms, and two of these were built on either side of a chimney. There was a fireplace in the kitchen and the living room, and along the wall to the side of the hearth in the living room there was a great hole knocked in the plasterboard. Nathan wanted to take down all the walls and lay insulation before putting up new plasterboard. This seemed completely sensible, though Christopher was beginning to feel quite dizzy from the adrenalin injection of Nathan's new ideas. It seemed thoroughly possible that he was imagining things when he turned and then involuntarily ducked to avoid what he thought was a tiny missile dive-bombing his head. In the moment of confusion, Christopher was fleetingly suspicious that Nathan had distracted him so he would make a better target.

The missile turned out to be a common swallow that somehow had gotten into the room and, in an incredible display of pride, had treated the dwellers of this nest as the invaders of her own.

"This has happened before and it's another reason to tear down the walls and put up new plasterboard," said Nathan, shutting the door to the kitchen so the bird would not fly into the rest of the house. Then he opened a window, raised the screen and waited with the others on the far side of the room. Finally, after several foolish attempts to fly through the closed window, the bird flew through the open one. "The nest is under the eaves, but there's room at the top of the plaster for her to slip through if she makes a mistake. I don't know if it was badly built in the first place, or whether some board or other filling has fallen down between the two walls, but in that corner there is nothing separating the inside from the outside. I think I should get to work in here, and Bucky can tackle the job in the kitchen. It's a question of prying off the scorched boards around the window. Later on, when you've got the new stove to replace the old one, we can paint that wall and the new window frame."

Again, Nathan's organization, if only because there was nothing to resist or counter it, had swept them up like so much shot, wrapped them up and fired them from the cannon of his powerful plans. In another moment they were all at work, except Christopher, who felt both annoyed and relieved not to have a specific job. As a way of asserting himself, but also of fulfilling a sense of duty he alone could explain, he went from Nathan in the living room to Bucky in the kitchen to the girls upstairs. Christopher actually shared some of Nathan's work and helped Bucky wedge the screwdriver between the wall and the window frame. But he felt useless as he did this. He felt they were even humoring him by letting him think he was helping, and so, when he reached the girls he did not even pretend that he had anything to offer. He merely joked with Katherine a little from the window and then turned to go, but found his way blocked by a box of old toys. He reached down and took three colored balls off the top, and after several false starts he juggled them successfully, whistling as he did for the girls' attention. It was a trick he had learned at college, but it now gave him a strange sensation of decadence, as though he had descended through uselessness into some hell of evasion where he played "knick knack paddy whack" at 10 A.M. like an old man in his senility. As he started out through the kitchen he saw Nathan's mother, Amy, and the sight of her, at that moment, made him want to crush her. Suddenly, the thought of the critical left wing and the whole idea of her feminism made him want to state his position. And more: he wanted to demonstrate to her that his position incorporated hers but was one step beyond in refinement of logic and understanding of the way things really worked.

What struck Christopher at the time was that he almost started the conversation in the middle, though this came as no surprise to either of them. Their differences were so clearly defined that their awareness of them were what they had in common, *all* they had in common at any given moment.

"I enjoyed talking to your husband about his father the other night," Christopher began. "Of course, with my background, hearing about these guys who worshiped the Russian Revolution is like news from outer space. I mean, my parents were wealthy Republicans and they thought I was a Bolshevik when I went to work for FDR. Hell, I felt like a Bolshevik myself, and it felt great! But the point is really that since the war the main issue has been communism versus the free world. Women's rights are interesting, but they're about number ten in importance."

"Some people say just the opposite—that if women were running the world instead of men you wouldn't have wars. It's obvious that weapons have a meaning to men that they don't to women."

"What does that mean?"

"That bombs are phallic symbols."

He snorted. "Are you kidding? This is for the birds."

"No, as a matter of fact, it seems so obvious that you must be neurotic to deny it."

He took a step closer, baffled by her rudeness. He was used to silky treatment in the hands of women; he knew he was sought after for dinner parties and as a dinner partner. He would have liked to give this woman a punch in the snoot. (Was Diana going to grow up to be like this?) Maybe Mrs. Baker couldn't help it. She was a feminist, after all, meaning she wasn't good-looking. At the same time, he had to admit her feistiness had a sort of ammoniac challenge. It made his brain reel, but it also made him feel awake. "I'm not denying that bombs are phallic symbols. I'm just saying you haven't said anything by saying that they are."

"I think you have," she replied calmly. "Hearing you deny it confirms my feeling that the world would be a better place if everyone in government were psychoanalyzed."

"That is brilliant, that is truly brilliant. Do you think you're going to keep the communists out of Asia by asking Lyndon Johnson how he feels about his mother? And how about you, Mr. Dulles? Does this gun remind you of some part of the human anatomy? Think hard, Mr. Dulles, take your time."

Madam Baker was taking in every word, but with a wry attitude that embarrassed him. He was blowing off steam; he wasn't making any point. He wanted her to understand that he'd had experience with strong women, knew they were sometimes frustrated, and yet felt they should recognize, as he did, that they really had more power than was fair in family life and personal relationships. Most smart, rational people would agree to that, but not this woman. But then some faces had aged and creased as naturally as bark, and hers wasn't one of those either. Her skin was of a certain doughy sort that lay in three long loaves on her forehead, separated by deep, permanent wrinkles of concentration. Her hair was short and not exactly wavy, though it had some curl—perhaps bend was a better word, expressing the sense he had that each wiry hair had been taken over someone's knee to give the general impression of a mass of dents. To his prejudices she seemed like a failed Greenwich Village poetess, the type who wrote bad verses and chanted them tunelessly in coffeehouses. Why be so cruel? What do you care if some suburban beatnik thinks she knows how to run America? Much worse having the New York *Times* think it knows.

He paused, and then went on more simply, as though admitting something which was hard for him to admit. "My mother was a remarkable person, very intelligent, very potent, of the old school. You know, born in the 1880s, didn't go to college, and she ruled her family and its little world like a feudal lord. She treated Wall Street and the White House like a Tartar king sizing up Moscow. You must know the type," he plunged on, feeling confused.

When he blinked, he found a movie being shown on his inner lid. It pictured the Groton dining hall with all its surfaces shining. Beyond the two square columns, the darker wing with the kitchen looked like a second-rate turn-of-the-century hotel. Christopher opened his eyes and saw a film about an unattractive woman called Mrs. Baker, saying, "I think I know the type you mean. It's the barbarian chieftain who signs a peace treaty with the princes of civilization. According to the treaty, the chieftain turns over all his country's raw materials and the princes promise not to go to war against him. As if the princes were doing the barbarian a big favor."

Suddenly, it was as though Christopher were six or younger, dealing with a monstrous female giant. He seemed to have fatal knowledge of her. She wanted something from him, but would never give him what he wanted in return. It was terrifying, but his training came through. He let himself be ruled by what he'd learned in OSS. Dropped by parachute behind enemy lines in Brittany. Had to figure out if this unfamiliar territory was the terrain described in briefing. Was this unfamiliar, unattractive woman the same woman who was in his fantasy? Which film was real? He heard his own voice saying, "My mother would have made a good judge. She had an eye for who had what kind of power, and she had a terrific social conscience. Campaigned for Hoover in the back seat of a roadster."

"But she wasn't a suffragette, was she?"

"No," he admitted, controlling a deep, childish urge to hang his head.

"Those are the ones who most support the injustice in the system. It's the ones who've been maintained as mascots in the most privileged way. They're the ones who do the most dirty work for the smallest share of the spoils."

"Well," he murmured manfully, "it's very complicated, that much is clear." He smiled sweetly and bowed out into the blooming summer day, where he was still starring in a dream about a memory. He was a boy again, his hair cut in bangs, and wearing a dress, standing by himself at an operating table in the middle of the Groton dining room. At the table nearest him a woman kept waving. A familiar, froggy beauty: look once you saw the frog, look again you saw the beauty. Between waves she leaned in confidence to share a joke with the rector, a formidable man with a ruddy John Bull face. The woman had a marvelous, terrifying laugh, regal to the last degree. Heads had rolled under the edge of that mirth, decapitated by its keen relish and chuckling, mocking arrogance. In public she cavorted with lions—Goren, Hoover, the rector—but at home she was happily married to a pussycat. (Which did she really prefer?)

Boys even younger and smaller than Christopher, dressed in white waiters' coats, wheeled in a dessert. It was an immense marzipan head of Stalin, represented in all his feline, gloating ugliness. The confection had been dyed so that the features matched their proper colors. The head had brown eyebrows and moustache, green eyes and a sickly green complexion. The slick, fat lower lip was shiny crimson. The creation ballooned before Christopher, completely obscuring his view of his mother and the rector, though the headmaster's voice was audible as he prayed and called Christopher to the task of carving the Prize Day Dessert.

The man's booming voice was there in Christopher's ears as he streamed by the lilac hedge, and then he was surrounded by cheers and whistles and applause, resounding in the sky while he made his way across the lawn, pleased beyond all description to be given this honor. He'd been picked to prove that Groton boys were men! When he closed his eyes, he took up the long knife lying beneath Stalin's slightly double chin. He blinked again and began to cut slices off the tips of the features, carving one side of the face so that he would have a sheer surface to work from. The bits of nose and lips and moustache were the proper size for servings, and he scooped them onto plates held for him by the boys waiting on tables. As he flattened one side of the marzipan sculpture, he had to get up on the table to slice the top through to the bottom. He hoisted his skirts and scrambled aboard, but as he did he saw his clothes were covered with blood. Had he cut himself? He couldn't find the wound if he had. This was no time to be ill or faint, and he forced himself to continue.

He cut into Stalin's forehead and now blood streamed down Christopher's frilly front. A long, precise slice fell from the tyrant's head and Christopher leaned over to cut it up into squares, dripping fresh blood into the colorless sweet. He felt tears rising in his eyes. Any more of this and he'd be sick. Could he carve his way through the whole head? Was he man enough to be a butcher?

2

On her way out to the roof with Katherine, Diana muttered crossly, "Hey, Dad, I thought competition was the best teacher. I thought that was one of your big mottoes, big boy." Well, if competition was so great, how come there were several chains of command, all of them beginning with der Fuehrer, in plain English, her father? She sensed that the greatest concentration of seriousness took place when her father worked with Nathan in the living room. Nathan had taken on the heaviest, but also the hardest, physical labor; when her father lent himself to such a task, the future of society seemed to depend on his efforts. Yet when he moved over to help Bucky, then Bucky's work seemed more important. At the same time, a whole new system of values seemed to be in effect. Her younger brother's job was not as hard as Nathan's, but when her father gave Bucky the boost of his personal prestige, it seemed to Diana that sincere exertion had acquired precedence over brute achievement.

When her father had come up to the roof with the girls, it was their turn to be raised to the first power, not because of their work, which pretty much ceased while he was with them, but through his special relationship with Katherine. This consisted of elaborate jokes about how he'd sold them all down the river, and how horrible it was to slave in the broiling sun—jokes that affirmed his and Katherine's appreciation for one another in a world apart from the one preempting most of their time. In this hierarchy—the hierarchy of leisure—Diana felt she'd gone up in the world, but only through her sister's place in their father's heart.

After Christopher had left them and gone on to juggle by himself, both she and Katherine had plummeted. Then solitary fantasy and pure play were raised up as the highest values. While der Fuehrer played, anyone who labored seemed a beast of burden. While he labored, anyone who played seemed frivolous. Oh the unfairness, the unbearable unfairness! That he should rule anything he touched!

Diana raged and tore off shingles, hurling them away with blind abandon.

"Hey!!" cried Katherine. "Man is the animal that better watch what he's doing."

"It makes me so furious," Diana muttered, ripping and flinging. "We have to do what he wants, but he does whatever he pleases."

"Slowly, slowly, little pet, who is 'he'? Our Father who art in Heaven, or our father who art talking to Mrs. Baker in the kitchen?"

Katherine's tone stilled Diana's craving, craving. It gave her herself in some endearing essence, and though she knew the tone as peculiarly her mother and sister's, she always sought it in the strange world outside. When she heard it she felt recognized and lovable, appeased, willing to be as obedient as any minister could wish. Now, as Katherine pointed with her nose toward the window, Diana followed the pointer to see parts of her father and Mrs. Baker, triangles and rectangles visible between the stairway and the ceiling, and in between the bannisters.

"That's the one," Diana said grimly.

"Mad at Dad, eh?"

Well, yes and no. Between Dad and Mrs. Baker, it was a toss-up. Not so much in terms of being more mad at one than the other, but more in the complexity of her feeling about both. Mrs. Baker was a new woman to add to Diana's repertoire, offering the reverse of whatever Diana's radar detected in her mother's attitude. Mrs. Baker's tone was dark, honey-colored, consuming and heated, charcoal-broiling the fuel of the forbidden. From her came invitations and perceptions that went fishing in Diana's deepest uneasiness, and in Mrs. Baker's presence she was conscious of having pushed through the swinging doors of what she typically expected from her own sex— the combination of affectionate petting with the hint that she must try harder to obey. But she could not puppy up to Mrs. Baker. The woman seemed to call Diana's energy to some serious understanding of itself. This was a far cry from the stifled scream she usually felt in her father's presence.

"Yeah, I'm mad at Dad. Aren't you?"

Katherine scanned the sky, and then seemed to find the cues to her higher calling in a cloud, a small puff in the distance. Diana found the cloud all right, but she did not see in it half of what Katherine saw. "I believe Daddy is at a juncture of loneliness and anguish," Katherine said prophetically. "I feel for him in his isolation. Many cross the desert without knowing it is a desert. Many crawl across the burning sand and see oases where they stop and drink, so willing to believe in water that they will not admit they're gulping sand. Some few journey the broiling dunes without hope, without illusion, quenching their souls with abstraction. Daddy's like that—horribly honest, horribly afflicted, very idealistic."

"You really think so?"

"I'd say there was a fifty-fifty chance."

"Oh great, first you're Ardmelia, the stargazer, and one minute later you're Katherine, the hacker. Which one is the real you so I can copy her?"

"If you're so smart, let's see you do Ardmelia."

With both hands clasped on her heart, Diana swayed back and forth on her knees, intoning to the sky, "What is a Nicholas? A Nicholas is a being who refuses to acknowledge death. Yes, death: the wall. Life is art, family life a discipline. And those of us trained to be Nicholases are trained to live up against the wall, yes, the wall! Or death."

"Death, death, death, whadya always have to make such a goddamn big deal outa something that happens everyday?"

"Hey, wait a minute. This is still another Katherine. Woah, I've never met this one before."

"I'm being Chace. That's the tough-guy way he talks."

"So, you finally admit it—Chace Harsh is your boyfriend. I knew it. What's he like? Pretend to be him. Do him some more."

"Look," said Katherine, hanging her head and sticking out her jaw. "One time my brother and I found the hired man swinging from the rafters and we were only kids. It scared the shit out of us, but do you hear me talking about being up against a goddamned wall? No! And if you ask me, your father's just a guy who's going nuts because he has to sit around the house all day. Jeezus, I'd go nuts. Five years ago the whole country was behind him. Those CIA guys were heroes. Today—pffft—they aren't worth the water in your spit."

"Is that what Chace said?"

"He did. He's really up on that kind of thing, reads the newspapers."

"Planning a career in politics?"

"No, painting. He's a painter or wants to be. He goes to Yale, as I believe you know from reading my mail, but he goes and studies painting every summer with a teacher in Italy, Herr Muehler, a German. The man he studies with is actually in America now. They're traveling around together."

"Sounds scary. And now for two important questions. Will they like me? And is Chace a grown-up or not?"

To the first query Katherine quickly, sweetly answered, "They're going to love you." But then she stopped to think before answering the second. Finally, she said, "Chace does grown-up things like read the newspaper and pursue his career, but he isn't a grown-up through and through."

Though they did not define 'grown-up' and had never categorized people this way before, they both knew instantly what it meant. Their closeness was constantly cresting on these discoveries of ideas they'd shared all along without knowing it. Katherine was vague, peppery, grandiloquent. Diana was humorous, mutable, and extreme. Yet it was as if their skins were clothes taken from the same closet. Though Katherine was a more romantic, more desirable girl than Diana, still their faceless spirits were indistinguishable. Though Katherine had a boyfriend, still she saw a grown-up man as a fate, a Responsibility come to claim her. Maybe Responsibility for Katherine wore a crown of flowers at a rakish angle; still, Responsibility was male. Clomp, clomp, clomp he came with his boring demands and boring ego and boring hobbies. If there was anything Diana hated it was a male stamp collector and, after that, any male who liked to build model airplanes. If there was anything Diana really despised it was a male who knew all the different kinds of cars. And wanted her to listen to them. No, that was going too far. She wasn't so mad at men because their hobbies were dull (though many men seemed to have dull hobbies); she just didn't like the idea that there was someone out there to whom she owed something without her ever having been consulted about whether she wanted to give it or not. Thanks nature, thanks a lot.

The mere thought of Mr. X coming nearer all the time, and possibly having already begun to pester her in the pale shadow of his future self, Nathan—this thought was enough to make Diana merge completely with Katherine. Hee, hee, he'll never find me in here, she thought gleefully as she disappeared into absolute conformity with Katherine's spiritual shape. This was not an easy trick. Where Diana was unfinished and open, Katherine had a low ceiling, particularly in the area of sociability. For a person who hated everyone, Diana could talk to anybody. She recognized the necessity of passing time. Katherine would only talk to people living on mountain peaks as high as her own. The air was very thin up there, Diana discovered, adjusting the earthy level of her own thoughts to the pure ether of Katherine's abstractions.

And then there was the problem of what to do with her own rough-draft emotions, which kept occurring in all their rejectable irrelevance. During lunch, when her mother came over with sandwiches for everyone, Diana maintained the cool front of a Greek temple. From the inside, her face felt the way Katherine's looked from the outside, but the very sort of feelings she would most have liked to be rid of continued to plague her. As Katherine and Diana came into the kitchen, their mother greeted them with a friendly smile. But she was saving her real conversation for Amy Baker, who brought the boys in from the living room, giving Diana a tap on her rump (giving Diana a tap on her *rump?*) and passing on to resume the discussion with Joanne.

For a while, the voice which spoke the loudest to Diana was the one resounding on her fanny. Mrs. Baker's touch said, don't forget, we're in league, you and I. I know you're not your family's daughter. And then, once she'd heard this, Diana heard other messages broadcast by Mrs. Baker's posture. Her shoulders invited Diana to look at her mother in a new light, at least to look at her from the point of view of the outsider Mrs. Baker knew Diana really was.

"Summer vacation is terribly tough on a man like Christopher. I mean, it's always hard for him to be at home, doing what he feels is nothing. But this summer is ten times worse because of Vietnam, and the black rioting and the whole student protest. He has strong feelings about all those things, but he's out of it now. And, of course, he also feels he's failed, and he's lost his place because he dropped the ball. I'm sure you can imagine how

bitter the feeling of failure is to someone as proud as
Christopher, someone who's given his life to his country."

Diana, the outsider, saw a tall, lean, handsome brunette
making excuses; Mrs. Baker's shoulders vibrated their
agreement. Diana, the insider, saw her mother's will to
coziness leading her to lay herself bare to another person
who wasn't seduced by openness. She felt like a thief,
robbing Peter to pay Paul, stealing her love from her
mother to satisfy Mrs. Baker and then pinching it back to
assuage her own sense of loss. Either way it was looting
because her mother didn't know what was happening,
and had no idea that her friendliness, taking the form
of describing her husband's career, was being fingered by
her daughter. Joanne told Mrs. Baker about Christopher's
start as a brilliant young lawyer under FDR—how he,
aged twenty-eight, in the company of several other
whippersnappers, conceived and wrote the legislation for
the Housing Act.

"His parents were wealthy New York Republicans, and
they were horrified," Joanne said proudly; and Diana, listening like a safecracker, delicately twisting the dial of
her parents' marriage, heard the subtlest, faintest click:
she'd found the proper combination. The door swung
open, and there, sitting deep inside the safe, was the radi-
ant gold of her mother's goodness. Diana's heart sank, she
was dragged down off of Katherine's cloud, seeing what
she'd always known, that her mother's generosity was the
family jewel, kept under lock and key by a miserly man.
She had always known that—this was nothing new—except that Mrs. Baker's back and arms, and now her eyes
as she turned and looked at Diana, all these made her
wish she could rescue her mother or that her mother
would rescue herself.

As Mrs. Baker's gaze sought out her feelings, Diana's

glance fell as though pulled down by the heavy sunken treasure of her love. She felt Mrs. Baker would possess her if she looked her in the eye, and yet Diana was incredibly tempted to give herself and her riches away. And this longing, added to her other conflicts, made her feel her head was going to burst. Unfortunately, at that very moment Nathan got a plate for himself, and like the big fat nitwit that he was, drew up two chairs, one for Diana, one for himself. This made her furious, though there were many shades within this fury, sub-rages having to do with wanting and not wanting to rise to Mrs. Baker's invitation (in case she was inviting), and feeling frustrated with her mother for not championing her own cause.

She overheard her mother say something about "the wreck rate in our generation," strained to hear the rest, meanwhile having to pretend to be listening to Nathan, who was telling her about hummingbirds. (He was? *He* was unreal.) To hear better, Diana looked at her mother, not because she could lip-read but because seeing a person's expression often helped her understand what was being said. Her mother, she discovered, was watching her and Nathan. She could tell her mother was taking note and wondering hopefully, has Diana met her match at last?

Her mother had it all wrong! And this gave Diana another rage she couldn't express, though Nathan didn't seem to notice she was shaking with clashing, inarticulate angers, and he continued to stoke her furies by trying unsuccessfully to get her to talk. Bucky pulled up beside them and gave Diana his you're-such-a-fairy look. He said, "Guess you guys got the one really easy job."

She doused him with a bucket of spleen. "Shut up, you stinkerfatsoidiot."

"Do you feel unsafe in the presence of this forward

hussy? Come, sirrah, let us seek shelter thither," said Nathan, drawing back in comic alarm and adding another degree of purple to Diana's rage-reddened face. The degree consisted in her deep annoyance with what she considered Nathan's chalky sense of humor. If he couldn't really be funny, he shouldn't try. She hated it when people substituted pomposity for real comedy. It was just like a drip to think that talking fake Shakespeare was the same as being witty. And it was just her bad luck to have a humorless drip get a crush on her. . . .

"Are those two Nicholases at each other's throats?" Joanne asked. "Do you need help separating them, Nathan?"

"NO!" bellowed Diana and leapt to her feet. Now that her temper had surfaced, it was like a case of runaway hives. It covered everything; everything aggravated it. She was enraged to see her mother's eyebrows rise, infuriated when her mother's blue eyes swelled fearfully and grew moist with childlike sensitivity. When her mother began to puff on a cigarette to compose herself, Diana tacitly accused her of seeming more like a teenager pretending to be an adult than a woman in her forties with the authority of her experience. Diana's face broke out in blotches, which was normal enough for one of her tantrums, but which was embarrassing in this situation because she didn't want Mrs. Baker to know about the maniac side of her character. Diana might have gotten away with a mysterious huffy exit, she just might have if she hadn't detected a defensive ghost of amusement on her mother's lips. Thatidiotassholejerk!

She turned to appeal to Mrs. Baker, to claim the sympathy she had played at stealing, but she was nearly drowned by a wave of impressions relating to the agony of meeting the woman's eye. Diana could not bring herself to take outright what she had so far only gathered in secret. Quickly, without having squarely faced Mrs. Baker, Diana whirled on her mother. New amusement, new *confident* amusement had risen in her mother's expression, but Diana was still wrestling with her mother's original insecure derisiveness, and though Diana speedily took in the shift, she couldn't muster words fast enough to express how mad she'd been in the first place and how much madder she was now. Joanne opened her mouth, but Diana couldn't bear to have her mother say anything until Diana had said everything on her own mind and said it ALL AT ONCE, though this, she realized simultaneously, was impossible because half of what she felt was inadmissible, relating as it did to her top secret love affair with Mrs. Baker.

Diana began to sputter. Mrs. Baker and her mother exchanged a look of astonishment. Diana knew she must look hilarious grimacing and beeping, but it drove her wild to appear comic just when she was struggling with the most serious matters, trying to separate her legal emotions from her illegal ones, particularly as it was so crucial for her to get it out about her legitimate feelings, namely, those that dealt with her mother's imbecility. But her mother couldn't tell an important revelation when she saw one, and started to speak. Unable to utter the slightest fraction of what she was feeling, completely overwhelmed by frustration and impatience, Diana yelled, "Don't ever speak to me again! EVER!"

This was clearly the most ridiculous thing she could have possibly said, but to show them she somehow meant business Diana dramatically spun on her heel and rushed out the kitchen door. She was beset by energy and tore over the lawn, dizzy with adrenalin. Her hard, bare feet flew instinctively toward the beach, dancing over large

pebbles and rocks, crisscrossing from one side of the un-
paved road to the other to follow the smooth ground. It
was only by running at top speed that she got any impression of stretching or straining, and then the limitations
she felt had nothing to do with her power, only bodily
shape. As her bent knee rose before, she felt the curve of
her lean rear, but the exertion was effortless—like the free
ride she got when she rode her bike into the vacuum
behind a truck.

The road began to slope through woods and passed between stone walls built two centuries before by slaves. On
her right as she ran there was now a pine grove, while the
left side of the road opened into a meadow planted with
alfalfa. A hundred yards in front of her was the back of a
square white building, showing a handsome stone chimney that tapered to a kind of waist halfway up the wall.
The June sun bleached the white house with its frank
light and exposed the subtle variations of gray and tan in
the chimney stones. At this time of year, during the day,
the excitement in the landscape was in the greens, but the
rocks which muscled their way through the surface of the
tough New England terrain, and the sand along the
curving coastline, as well as the boulders which formed
the northern point—all this stone contained amazing
depths and shades of color. Blacks and browns dominated, but when the tides withdrew from the point, the
slick rocks showed yellows and roses and dark purples.
The water had washed the beach with bands of mottled
pebbles, stripping the sand with powdered blues and
whites and oyster grays. At the bottom of the alfalfa field,
on the other side of the grassy footpath, the beginning of
the beach was marked by a jagged line of broken boulders. In the daytime sun they looked like works produced
by nature grunting; yet these same crude rocks attained a

rich mauve in the evening, and at dawn they had the placid dignity and calm of gray elephants at rest.

Diana slowed to a trot and stopped beside the beach house. While she caught her breath, she put her foot on the log laid down as an indication of where cars should park. For a moment, she felt clarified and complete, as though she had finally found her true average between her entrancement and the recent violence of her tantrum. She looked out over the bay, absorbing her impressions calmly for once. She took in the Jamestown Bridge to the south, Conanicut's deep green shore across the water and the Quonset naval base in the distance to the north. The horizon might have been drawn with a ruler. The sky was immense and beneath this wide, clear dome the coast (even where it was built up) had perfect miniature proportions.

She relived her previous scene, taking it back to the moment when Nathan sat down beside her. The embarrassment Diana felt about exploding tapped at her shell; but like a dreamer incorporating external noises to preserve her sleep, Diana quickly rewrote the scene, transforming the embarrassment as fast as it grew. She allowed it into her rewritten recollection as mutual recognition of unhappiness between Mrs. Baker and herself, a signal passed vibrationally while Diana shook with thwarted love and fury.

It wasn't all that farfetched. Anything could happen in a weird world. And after Diana ran off, perhaps Mrs. Baker, knowing the girl suffered as she, too, had suffered, perhaps Mrs. Baker found an excuse and followed Diana to the beach. Perhaps Mrs. Baker was at this very moment catching sight of a lone figure by the beach house, a sensitive person, no, a *painfully* sensitive person, highly poetic and yet tragically isolated. Diana turned, wearing the mournful look of this sensitive, poetic, isolated person, but her dream had not come true. Mrs. Baker was not in sight. Yet she could still come, and feeling sure she would, Diana trotted down the grassy slopes to the beach, and began to walk toward the ponds, which, in the diminished perspectives of the noon sun, seemed to have receded to a point below the bridge.

As she went, Diana addressed wordless, poetic thoughts to the ocean, but her hands, by constantly getting in her way, kept interrupting the flow of her unspoken dialogue with nature. She folded them in front of her and then felt them pressing her ribs in a way that hampered her breathing as she walked. She tried letting them hang at her sides, but the blood ran into them until they swelled up like two udders. She grew cross and held her hands in front of her as though to scold them, then gave up and sat down, afraid that if she got any more involved in the problem of where to park her hands while she walked she would lose her grip on her high level of wonder.

Maybe Mrs. Baker had just reached the beach house and had only this minute caught sight of Diana; maybe Mrs. Baker was at that very moment moved by the skinny farmer's boy or a girl staring out to sea. The thought that her appreciation of nature was being seen by the very one for whom it was intended whipped Diana to a last tense pitch of rapture. The smells of the beach and its colors, the rank odor of decay and seaweed drying at low tide, the deep blue bay reaching to the azure sky: all these marinated keenly in her vinaigrette senses. More from ambition than falseness, to carry the moment to its grandest conclusion, Diana drove herself to prayer, "O God," she breathed. "O life, o sky, o me, o my life. . . ."

It didn't work. Her aspiration all fell back on top of

her. She was stunned with depression and peered to see if she really might have been caught in the act of being an idiot. Not a moment too soon. A big, broad-shouldered person, definitely a boy, all too probably Nathan, was bounding down the beach in her direction. Her depression waxed, and she was so depleted she could neither hide nor overcome the bleak feeling the fact of his approaching gave her.

"Diana, Diana," Nathan called as he bore down on her. "What's wrong? What happened? I hope I haven't made you mad." He was wearing track shorts; and when he stopped in front of her, his big thighs bulged above his knees like the long beaver hats worn by guards at Buckingham Palace. His legs were attractively, even prettily, covered in blond hair that cascaded down over his broad, faceted knees and down his calves.

She longed for sympathy, but his sympathy wasn't the right one. She was horrified to find herself crying in front of him and wailed, "Now look what you've done. Go away."

"But what, *what* have I done?" he cried, pleading in a voice that both worried her and made her mad at him for needing help. By stealing the show, however, or shifting its focus, he helped push her back under her own control.

"Take it easy," she advised, sniffling. She wiped an eye with a downward stroke of her hand, which she then pulled across her runny nose.

"I can't take it easy. I won't," he declared and threw himself to his knees in the sand. "I know I irritate you. You irritate me. But that's part of it. We were meant to fight it out. Don't tell me it's impossible. That's what makes it interesting. I'm sick of the possible. The possible is what's wrong with everybody else."

Talk about unrealistic. Talk about simpleminded. The

guy was off his rocker. Plus he looked like a king-size Donald Duck, quacking his heart out on the beach in broad daylight.

"Shit," he said and got up, brushing the sand from his knees. A look of grave self-disgust crossed his face. "That didn't come out right."

"It sure didn't," she agreed.

"Well, but you can go fuck yourself because it's your fault it didn't come out right, buddy. You make it impossible to be natural around you. It's your fault I went down on my knees. It's because you're such a snot. You drove me to it. You just make it impossible to be any self I like when I'm with you."

"Why is it my fault? I don't care what self you put on. They're all the same to me."

"That's what you think. What you don't realize is that I'm your type. I'm going to make you see that."

What kept running through her mind was the difference between his voice at this moment and the way he'd sounded in another conversation they'd had a few days before. The tone of his emotions then had been so nervous, even frail, but all they'd been talking about was stupid stuff like communism. Now, though he was revealing what would be for her the most intimate feelings, and running the risk of seeming utterly ludicrous, now he seemed blithe and free, completely at home. Could he really be like her? Of two or three or four minds, and trying to find out which one was the key to open the world of experience? Maybe he was just trying to make her *think* he was like her—an Old Mother Hubbard with so many selves she didn't know what to do. Her mind began to worry this observation, to try and realize what it meant, and whether it was accurate; and, at the same time, she was so overcome with fatigue that she thought she would faint if she did not lie down right away.

Lash, lash, leave me be mind! Why didn't anyone mention that the atmosphere was full of everyone's Morse code? Or was she the only one picking it up? Maybe she was Superman's humanoid sister, designed with a receiver meant to pick up signals from Krypton. But Krypton was gone! Superman was gone! And she was equipped to pick up all this stuff she couldn't understand. Sleep was coming over her like a trance of honey, thick and sweet and heavy in the hot sun. She murmured, "I think I have to have a nap." As she spoke, she wilted onto the warm sand. She thought she heard him say, "I'll guard you," but she was asleep before she could express the sarcasm such a remark would have prompted if it was real.

In ten minutes she was awake again, somewhat dazed, a little refreshed, though uneasily conscious of how, by succumbing to her exhaustion, she had let things out of her hands. She felt as if she'd literally slept on his proposal; that in itself her slumber had been a kind of acquiescence. As they walked back up the hill, they said nothing more of what had gone on, but she felt she'd accepted some queer responsibility she didn't want.

3

On Saturday, when there was no work to be done, Christopher noted with disapproval the aimless way his children milled around the house. Their purposelessness proved to him that he had been absolutely inspired to arrange the work project at The Bleakers. If he hadn't done it, he saw that they would be spending the summer doing what they were doing that day: wasting a beautiful morning by lounging around the living room, talking, smoking, snacking, joking. He himself was sitting there, but he was not idle.

It was one of the best times for the living room, the

morning hour when its mixture of hard elegance and relaxed charm, its size and the variety of fabrics all harmonized as a beautiful background for the architectural space. The room occupied half the hayloft, once the entire top floor of the house. It was twenty-five feet from floor to ceiling, all paneled in blond wood. The window facing Narragansett Bay was eighteen feet high, supported by two vertical beams and two horizontal ones. Rose curtains fronted by fishnet hung on either side of the ten-foot width. The vast amount of material from floor to ceiling brought a royal magnificence to the big room, but at night, when the curtains were drawn, the rose curtains made the converted loft cozy despite its scale.

On the south side of the room, opposite the window, a wall had been constructed to divide the second story of the house. It now presented a plaster monolith, interrupted only by the black hood over the fireplace and balanced by the balcony to the right, over the end of the corridor as it gave way to the dining table at the front of the room. The wall was painted a pale, pale purple, and in its size and singleness of color it celebrated certain principles of modern art. The smooth plaster enhanced the color's airiness. The room's changing light heightened its complexity. Because of the scale, the wall allowed the life within its space an incredible degree of play, yet there was no distracting busyness. The wall's effect could subside, providing a serene canvas for the variety and richness of the rest of the room.

No paintings had ever been hung on the wall. By itself it was a study of pure form and color, and one of Christopher's favorite uses of the room was to sit in a chair, facing the wall, dwelling on the great expanse, his thoughts progressing toward the generality inspired by the sheer abstract size of the area. Today the sound of his children's talk gave him the subject of his meditation. Diana and Bucky were teasing Katherine about some boy, Chace Harsh. Though he recognized that jealousy of this Chace ran neck and neck with his irritation, Christopher let his annoyance gallop away with him. To begin with, Katherine, the family beauty, was too young to have a serious boyfriend. Why didn't she go learn Latin? There were years and years for her to have boyfriends!

And why wasn't Bucky outside using the tennis court Christopher had built just so his children could always get out and practice? Why didn't he go make himself a great player instead of merely a good one? He'd made the Groton team, but that was only the first step. Instead of driving himself up to the next stage of achievement, the guy sat around inside talking to his index finger. His son's dependence on this comic routine summed up for his father exactly why his only heir was still called by his babyish nickname and not Christopher, Jr., as he'd been baptized. The boy had recently emerged from plumpness, and like someone who'd recovered from a long childhood disease and who was not yet sure of his health, Bucky treated his new muscular body as a stranger. He tended to pamper it, as if afraid he might at any moment lapse back into his old baby fat. Under pressure, he did lapse into a chubbier self, the sweetly inept caboose to his sisters' slimmer lives. But he had to learn, as everybody had to, that beyond every hurdle is another hurdle, that life builds character but also takes character. And, Christopher thought with a sigh, until you get used to it, character is just another form of unhappiness.

As for Diana, well, she had so much to repair in her life that the last place she should be was sprawled in an overstuffed chair, teasing her older sister. Just for starters, what was she going to do about college? She had graduated from prep school, but she had not gotten into college. She had no idea about jobs, and this was a girl who was saying with all the confidence of a person with a real future, "Katherine, just relax, be easy, and let me see if I can jog your memory. Does the following ring a bell? 'Dear Doll Face, You're so beautiful, it's disgusting. I suppose you've been eating orchids all your life . . . !'"

"God, you are *incredible!*" cried Katherine, laughing with outrage. "You've been steaming open my mail again . . ."

"No, it was open already when I found it," Diana protested and laughed at the same time.

Bucky, meanwhile, began to address his index finger, holding it before him as though it were a ventriloquist's dummy. He spoke first in his own voice and then in an effeminate squeak meant to represent the persona of the index finger. "What kind of world is it when sisters read each other's mail?"

"I dunno," he squeaked. "Doggy dog? Spy versus spy? Hush-hush?"

Christopher began to move from his specific teenage children, working his way up and around the wall by developing a brief against the whole younger generation. He got halfway into his indictment when Joanne appeared before him, looking like a warrior—tall and strong and streamlined. Her brow was knit. She was smiling and frowning at the same time, as if to ask, are you approachable? The expression emphasized the forward, wolfish angles of her face. Her prominent, pretty nose, very straight in its descent, was saved from arrogance by the benevolence of its tip. Good nature softened the aristocratic sharpness of the bones, protruding in her cheeks and wrists and her collarbone, visible through the open collar of her shirt.

"The party?" she asked exploratorily. "Remember you wanted to talk about it with the kids?"

"The party?" he echoed, wrinkling his lip, unable to remember what she meant.

"Whoops, I'll be right back," she said in response to the sound of the phone ringing in the kitchen. (The place was a madhouse. Between calls for Katherine and calls for Joanne, the phone never stopped ringing.)

"Ellie!" his wife's voice cried. "How are you? No, of course, we haven't forgotten you! We were just talking about you, about asking you to come to a great big party we're giving at the end of the summer . . ."

"Oh, *that* party." Christopher groaned softly to himself. Ellie's call had interrupted his meditation, partially by ruining his concentration and partially by reminding him of the wrecks in his own generation. Ellie had been the glamor girl of his set after the war. She had been his drinking companion after his only divorce, during her second (or third?) marriage. According to legend, Joanne had looked up to Ellie like a freshman with a crush on a senior. For Joanne, ten years younger, Ellie's sharp tongue and her looks and her inimitable clothes had symbolized the unattainable heights of Christopher and his friends. Even more than Christopher's first display of feelings, Ellie's kindness to Joanne had made Joanne dare to believe she belonged. Joanne remained loyal to what Ellie had been, though she paid for this loyalty by frequently having to be on the listening end of the long-distance phone while Ellie, now the alumna of several fancy mental hospitals, told and retold the story of her divorces, her heroic list of one-night stands (including one, she claimed, with then Senator Kennedy), her problems with the bottle, with pills, with her only daughter who'd committed suicide.

"Well, now we have to give the party," Joanne said, returning from the phone. "It was the only way I could put Ellie off until August."

"Hey, what party?" asked Bucky.

"This is going to be the pot of gold at the end of your slave labor," said Joanne. "We're going to give an immense party. We'll shoot the works, get a band, dancing girls, you name it."

"*All right!!*" said Bucky, straining for the tone of an experienced gay blade. "This sounds more like me."

The phone rang and Joanne went to get it. In a moment she was back to tell Katherine it was long distance for her. Then Joanne asked Bucky to come help her get the garage door open, and Christopher was left with Diana.

"I like your friend Nathan," he said, though he meant something less casual and more righteous, something like, I think Nathan is about the only person in your generation with any real stuff.

Still, though he couldn't blame her for reacting to his tone, he was offended when Diana snapped back, "He's your friend, not mine."

"Well, he's your age after all. I thought you'd be interested in him. He's an outsider the way you want to be, but he's an articulate critic of the system. I mean he's an outsider with a program . . ." He continued, but she ceased to hear his words.

While her father talked, Diana's hot reaction to what he was saying made her recoil into detachment. From there she could admire what she often admired about his unorthodox but noble face. He was a dark blond with a high roan complexion. His features were large and irregular except for his eyes, which were extraordinary: almond-shaped and royal blue. They were set deep in his

skull so that his eyelids arched beneath poetic hollows—
an attribute masked by the pink, semitransparent frames
of his eyeglasses. His nose had been broken in a college
hockey game and did a swan dive, leaping from his forehead, flying free of his cheeks and ending in the perfectly
articulate, theatrically flared nostrils. But as he came
closer, so that he was leaning over her as he finished
speaking, when he was near enough to kiss, his hand-
someness and distant manner paralyzed her. The Colgate
invisible guard seemed to have dropped down between
them, preventing the tooth decay she might have otherwise caused to the big teeth showing through his parted
lips.

When he was through, she nodded her head word-
lessly, thinking, yes, I know what you really mean. I understand that you regard me as a failure, and that's why
you have to drag in this goody-goody nit Nathan to com-
pare me with. She left the room and went downstairs and
got his tennis racket out of the closet. If she had ever
wanted reassurance, he had shown her she could not have
it from him, a man who only dealt with beauty.

She took his racket outside and began to hammer it
against one of the long, low, flat rocks surfacing like the
backs of whales in the lawn. What you're getting at is
that you think it's fine for boys to break the rules, but not
for girls. Right? That it's unattractive for girls to stick out
like sore thumbs, and only an unattractive girl like me,
who's already out of it, could go on living for a minute
once she didn't get into any dumb college. And you think
your only hope is to palm me off on creephead Nathan because I can't do anything right on my own, so I might as
well go piggyback on a jerk because I couldn't get anyone
else in any case and at least his interests are vaguely like
mine. Her inner voice reached a screaming pitch as she

brought her father's racket down a last few violent times. The wooden head was completely smashed. The nylon strings were in the frazzled disarray her nerves had been in before she worked her anger off.

Now, however, in contrast to the racket, she was all of a piece again, though that piece happened to be a vengeful one. Without a second thought (not that thinking would have stopped her) she crept back upstairs, found her parents' bedroom door open and no one there; tiptoeing stealthily to the fiend's side of the bed, she dropped the remains of the racket on her father's pillow. Then Diana stole downstairs to the bathroom, where she began to address her image in the mirror as if it belonged to some poor fool to whom she was a wise adviser.

"Let's be absolutely frank. The truth may be terrible, but at least it gives you a sure place to start from," said Diana, beginning silently to cry. "You might as well accept the fact that you're absurd. Your father has just confirmed this, though, of course, he didn't come right out with what he really feels. He didn't say you were ugly but sexy in some dirty way. But it's what he meant."

He could, in fact, have told her she was beautiful and she would have still felt he meant she was a parody of what was feminine, capable perhaps of rousing desire but no feeling in the heart of any man. As though she herself was the way the lowest men were supposed to be: a beast. And like a beast, she was ugly, wearing the outward mask of her inward loathsomeness. If men desired her sexiness, she believed it was because it offered some twisted variation on what they really wanted—what was really beautiful. And she had proof of this in the type of men who seemed to notice her. Boys her own age did not come near her, but wayward types—garage mechanics, men driving on the highway, unshaven bums, tough-looking older strangers—often eyed her knowingly. If she was ever going to be popular at a dance, it would have to be one composed of the scary outsiders who seemed to recognize her as one of them.

There was a knock at the door.

"Who is it?" Diana asked brokenly.

"Katherine. Let me in. Hurry!"

Diana opened the door, her tears beginning to subside in Pavlovian response to Katherine's agitated tone. No drama of hers would ever be equal to any of Katherine's. This was a fact, and Diana was learning to be resigned to it, knowing her only hope for promotion was through participation in the marvels of her older sister's experience and thoughts and high maxims. She readied herself to listen, though Katherine first paid her the compliment of asking if anything was wrong.

"Nothing, the usual. I look like a judge. Daddy hates me," Diana said, dismissing it.

Katherine laughed, saying, "Come on, you know he doesn't. He's just bad at expressing his feelings."

"Not to Mummy."

"Well, they've been married for a million years. And they love each other."

"Pfff—marriage is just legalized sex."

"How can you say that?" Katherine cried, truly shocked. "Look at Mummy and Daddy. They adore each other."

"Maybe it's a big fat act. How do we know it's real?"

Katherine stared hard at Diana, and then did something both strange and characteristic. She slid away from the situation like smoke evaporating up a chimney. For Diana, her sister's withdrawal was incredibly tantalizing. Katherine was so completely an exception to every rule that everything her sister did struck Diana as beautiful,

rare, unique. Oh, even more than unique: Katherine, as
she stood staring out the window, was blue but still
peachy, tinkling, intricate. Gazing on her sister's face,
Diana doted on its combination of the adorable and the
exquisite, of a milky complexion and vivacious green eyes,
of flat planes and tiny, fragile features. Suggestions piled
on images; theater piled on suggestions. As she immersed
herself in Katherine, a balloon of poignancy swelled up
inside Diana, followed by the word "discretion," and then
Diana saw a girl getting off a train (huge clouds of steam
nearly obscured her) holding a small carpetbag and being
met by a man in a Chesterfield coat and wearing chamois
gloves.

And yet, for all its soft mysteriousness, Katherine's
beauty rested firmly on a simple structure: that of her
small Roman nose, descending from her forehead in an
unbroken line. Her particular relation of nose to brow was
characterized in Katherine's Potomac school yearbook in
a drawing which fascinated Diana. The caricature introduced Diana to the idea that people's qualities, physical
or spiritual, were separable from the people who had
them. For years, whenever she was bored at school, Diana
had drawn the caricature of Katherine's nose in the mar-
gin of her textbooks. It made Diana feel strangely powerful to represent her older sister, to have the essential
Katherine there on the page of the book while the walking, breathing Katherine wandered somewhere else far
away. And now, as Katherine stared off into space, as
though answering a higher call, Diana kept a grasp on her
sister by clinging to the sight of her nose. Katherine could
disappear into abstraction, but she left her profile both as
a sign she would return and as a form she could return to.
For an instant, it was like being with a perfect wax model
of a person. Diana looked out into space, too, as if by as-

suming the same outward pose she could evoke the same inner spirit. Nothing happened, though Katherine began of her own accord to thaw, to come down off the high mountain of thought, bringing with her this commandment: "Man is the animal which falls in love."

"He is?" Diana asked, awestruck before the realms of detachment and law opening before her. She felt as if all previous reflections on life were less than inadequate— they were cheap and fragmented, and she was cheap and pathetic ever to have thought of herself as a thinker when she had not begun to imagine principles anywhere near the level of insight and fusion of Katherine's. Not that Diana was exactly, precisely sure what Katherine's statement meant, but it had the ring of immense truth. For once, for a moment, Diana felt her hurtling sensations embraced by order.

"There is a way that traveling out from yourself brings up things of a peculiar nature, that is, you come on yourself unexpectedly, and whole areas of desolation gape; in fact, you meet face to face the conflict in our society between the breakdown of traditional values and will."

"God," breathed Diana, receiving a rush of elevated hints and glimmers, and feeling the lack of simple coherence was her own fault. And then, inspired, she asked, "Are you the animal in love called man?"

"Are you snoopy or what?"

"Well?"

"Who knows." Katherine sighed. "How would you like to be in love?"

"Not me, but I don't want to do anything I'm supposed to do."

"What if someone fell in love with you? What then?"

"I guess if Mick Jagger fell in love with me, I could put up with it."

"Just remember, if you ever need a confidante, someone to talk to, to tell your most intimate secrets to, you know who you can call on."

"You?"

"Me," said Katherine, tapping her chest with her thumb. "And don't hold back if you have any sexual problems. They're my specialty."

Katherine and Diana got giggling so hard and in such perfect harmony that their laughter died down and flared like parts of a duet. Their unison was disturbed by a new knock which silenced them momentarily, and then their twin guiltiness sent them into fresh, identical gales of giggling.

"OK, OK, break it up," said Bucky. "Daddy wants to see you, Diana."

"What for?" she asked. She was now in such a good humor, she'd temporarily forgotten that her father had tried to kill her.

"I'm not sure, but I think it's got something to do with his tennis racket."

"Oh-oh," murmured Diana, though she was still so involved in Katherine's spell she felt invulnerable.

"She'll be right there," Katherine called breezily.

"I bet," said Bucky. "Just hurry the fuck up."

"I'm coming, I'm coming, keep your pants on," said Diana, opening the door.

Bucky ruefully made way for his sisters, obeying what he first thought was life's cruelest, fastest law: that the fat exist to serve the thin. Standing at the bottom of the stairs, Katherine said, "I'd better wait for you here."

"Good, and now sic semper tyrannis, hic, haec, hoc, agricula, agriculae . . ." muttered Diana, as she trotted up the stairs. "Daddy?" she called pleasantly. "Daddy, did you want to see me?"

He called her into the study where he was sitting with Joanne. Diana was sorry to see her mother there, indicating by her presence that she had discussed the whole matter with her husband and approved whatever line he was going to take. Her own mother! A woman who could spin a moment into human gold, this wonderful person had sided with her husband's hairshirted approach to life.

Maybe while you're here she lets you think you're boss, but when the cat's away, mister . . .

This was not the time to right the wrong of her mother's subjugation. This was the time to somehow seem repentant for a crime committed so long ago it might have been done in a former life. When her father held his smashed racket up to her, Diana had to admit that its destruction looked like the work of an insane person. It could never be repaired, and once more the fretful spray of strings reminded her of nerves, though now of someone else's nerves, a poor, antisocial murderer's or a violent idiot's. Not hers, at least not anymore. But what could she say? Moods would be moods. She had been in a bad one when she bashed his tennis racket to smithereens, but she'd probably never be in that extreme state again in her life. Did this mean she was going to have to spend sixty years in the pen for a passing fancy?

She looked at her feet, saying softly, "I guess I was mad at you for comparing me to Nathan." That sounded dumb, so she added, "I don't know why." That really sounded dumb, so she added again, "Sometimes I frighten myself." Maybe she could come in under the James Dean clause, covering Darkly Mysterious Adolescent Behavior.

"It goes without saying that you'll pay the cost of the racket. But, more seriously, Diana . . ." She steeled herself for the lash. "More seriously, I forbid you to play tennis for the rest of the summer. You want to bail out of the system? You don't want to be compared to anyone, won't compete with anyone? Well, see how you like sitting on the sidelines. See how you feel when you're forced to let your ability go to waste. Maybe that will teach you self-control if nothing else will."

She dropped her gaze to the floor, counted twenty, lifted her eyes to her father, counted two and dropped them sorrowfully again. In the laboratory behind her play face she developed this last polaroid glimpse. It had been taken, of course, without his realizing, while he delivered his last blast of silent sternness, and while he still held Exhibit A: the fright wig of strings. Thanks to the brain's modern technology, Diana had the unrecognizable tennis racket enlarged in seconds. It looked like a piece of a corpse. Y-e-e-ch! No wonder her dad had overreacted. He who lives by the letter bomb might die by the morning mail! Shivers ran through her as she pictured her father coming into his bedroom and seeing the crazily tortured limb on his pillow, sent anonymously as a warning. *Beware! Your own leg could be next.* In his position she might have been a little freaked out herself. But from here on in she was also going to have to be more careful. Now that there was no one else for him to shoot, he was going to be gunning for her.

4

Chace Harsh arrived on Friday afternoon, bringing something for everyone. He brought word games, his tennis racket, a bear costume and his painting teacher, Herr Muehler. He also brought a noticeable change in the weather, so that the undistinguished month of June, having turned in a typically cloudy performance, brightened Friday, cleared with a sort of vengeance as if to challenge doubters with a real display of its talent. The temperature rose; a fresh wind swept the sky of its clouds and the sun poured itself like gravy over the deep lawn and red tennis court and the bay.

Having two new people in the house created new space
in the cramped corridors of communication. Joanne felt
herself drawing a deep breath of relief and then expanding to enjoy the new possibilities. She had not seen
Chace's family in years, but their acquaintance (which
for Christopher went back to childhood) made the boy
deliciously familiar to her. Having him turn up as Katherine's boyfriend brought old selves to Joanne's surface,
come alive again with no diminishment of their eagerness
or hunger or curiosity.

Events and scenes had a poignant, appetizing reso-
nance. She was reminded of nothing in particular and her
youth in general. She was in a state of spongy awareness,
conscious of the slightest details of emotion and pleasure,
struck by their novelty and by their melancholy. It was as
if she were remembering the present for the first time.
When the men gathered on the tennis court for doubles
on Friday afternoon, Joanne went out to watch with Herr
Muehler and the girls. She felt her own mother hovering
near in the straw hats she used to wear when she watched
the Nonquit tennis tournaments. And then Herr Muehler
evoked the man who'd immortalized her unusually high
arches many summers ago. She had been a young girl
when she sat for Herr Fischer in Munich, and when she
posed Herr Fischer had been about the same age as Herr
Muehler now was in the present.

"This is a foolish thing to ask," she murmured, her head
turning left and right in unison with his as they watched
a long, dramatic rally, "but did you by any chance ever
know a sculptor from Munich named Herr Fischer?"

"He was my teacher, if you will believe it, for two
years. Before the world war where I deserted from," he
said, applauding a remarkable smash by Christopher,
whose turn it now was to serve. (He was playing with

Diana's racket; his hand and muscular arm dwarfed the grip.) He stood at the base line, contemplating his feet; even at rest, his grace as an athlete was apparent. Just as it seemed he had forgotten where he was, what he was doing, Christopher looked up and took a step into position. Bucky steeled himself for his father's unanswerable serve. Christopher tossed the ball, his arm stretching like a swan's neck. His right foot came off the ground as he reached, throwing his weight onto his left leg, heaving his body into the arc of the racket. This went up and down like a flung tomahawk, sending the speeding ball to the back corner of the service line. Bucky swung and missed, aced. Christopher stepped to address the other court and delivered a serve which no one saw, though everyone was poised. To his own great surprise, Chace got his racket on it and hit a high pop fly over the fence behind his host. Diana had been laboring over "somersault," trying to find the two words it supposedly contained; but she left the puzzle to get the ball, trotting to retrieve it, and throwing it back over the fence in a display of the athletic ability she was normally dedicated to suppress.

This was how it seemed to Joanne, whose perceptions were riding high on the coincidence of Herr Muehler having known Herr Fischer. She wasn't at all sure it was true, and she couldn't have cared less. His claim added to the charm of his admiration for her. She'd felt it the minute he'd walked in the door, took her hand, kissed it, then raised his admiring eyes to hers, saying, *"Gnädige Frau."* Such a sweet old fraud: no pretense on that score. But she had always had a soft spot in her heart for frauds. Who else was willing to talk the high baloney of romance? Not Christopher, not any of the men she had respected. And yet she loved compliments and filigree, though she knew the men most apt to talk the language of love were usually the least devoted.

There was only one moment in life when poetry was truly justified, truly felt. That was a glorious summer day in the youth of an innocent boy and girl. You only fell in love once, though you might want to fall in love many other times. You were only innocent once, only felt the grand pangs once, though you might be reminded of them again and again in your feelings for others. There were many different feelings, stronger ones, even deeper ones, but never so poetic, so poignant as the feelings of the first love.

But then why did her receptivity keep tilting anxiously toward Katherine? Her oldest daughter's blurred loveliness aroused sensations of bruised blue, the color Joanne always felt when she felt someone unhappy was near her. Yet why should Katherine be miserable? She had everything: youth, beauty, an adorable boy who was in love with her. But there were shadows darkening all around, even at Joanne's back, where she knew the actual shade of the old apple tree had lengthened, and covered her rock garden and had perhaps touched her chair. She lifted her head and started to turn and saw Nathan standing there.

"Aha! I thought you had all gone this weekend to the march in New Jersey," she said.

"It's not much of a march," Nathan replied, looking a little cross. "Concerned Clergy Against the War in Vietnam? In South Orange, New Jersey? It's not going to stop the war. It's peanuts. My parents went to see their friends. I'm saving myself for Clear Lake."

"Clear Lake?"

"It's going to be where the big SDS roundup is held at the end of the summer. I'm helping to organize it. So I had a lot to do here. You know, writing letters, working on the program." All of this spoken in a slightly defensive tone, as though Joanne might suspect him of staying for some reason beside his stated one. She did suspect him. More: she knew with all the confidence of her intuition that he'd stayed on to see Diana. It was his bad luck to have chosen this weekend when Chace was there. Chace had already so inflamed Diana's enthusiasm that, in addition to showing off her boyish athletic skills for him, she'd begun to imitate his rolling, sailor's walk. At this minute Diana was again poring over "somersault," trying to crack its code in a desperate effort to beat everyone in that sweepstakes for Chace's attention. She was sitting cross-legged beside her sister, holding the slip of paper so they both could see it. But Katherine was clasping her knees and rocking back, gazing away over the stone walls through the line of rustling trees directly behind the court. She was still broadcasting bruised blue, but her distress was now vying with Nathan's in Joanne's awareness. She felt his was like an itchy dark suit; his unhappiness took the form of constraint, while Katherine's was a kind of leaking away of her energies. Nathan was uncomfortably awake, like someone whose bed is full of sand, but Katherine was slipping from them all into a sea of vagueness.

"Herr Muehler," said Herr Muehler, getting to his feet and holding out his hand, "I rise to congratulate an idealist."

Nathan relaxed a fraction to take the shorter man's hand. Herr Muehler was bald, with tufts of white hair around his tanned crown. Holding the top of his head with one hand, while shaking with the other, he explained, "I was drafted in the First World War into the

German Army. But I . . ." He illustrated by walking his two fingers through the air.

"You deserted?" Nathan asked. The old man grinned and nodded. He tapped his temple with pride. Pretty brainy, eh?

"Nathan Baker, Herr Muehler," Joanne said, rising to go.

"War is hell," said Herr Muehler, and rubbed it out of existence with his hands, which he operated like windshield wipers before him. Then he shook a long index finger didactically, saying, "When I walked away from the Cherman Army, I walked into a Zen monastery. They teach by hitting you on the head with a board. And laughing at you. They love to laugh, but they are as hard as wooden tables inside. What was I supposed to do? I sat all day, meditating. No smokes. No drinks. The master says, 'War is exercise.' But then I made friends with the cook, who every night goes out to drink. He's not crazy. He's not a monk. But then they found out, they won't let me stay. I go back to Munich. I live a little. Draw, paint, have my girls. And then what? This clown, this duck, Hitler, is lifting legs in the street." Here Herr Muehler began to goose step comically in a narrow circle on the lawn, and to mock the *heil* sign by doing it with such an idiotic expression on his face that Joanne's breath was taken away. She had never seen Hitler so rudely spoofed. Or had she seen *The Great Dictator?* She thought she had. Maybe she had just never seen a German make such brutal fun of Hitler. Volumes of tragic emotion disintegrated into a dust heap. She didn't think that was at all funny, and yet she was laughing (or was she gasping?) at Herr Muehler's droll, stiff-legged walk, his ridiculous robot's arm, his mocking face. He came full circle for the last time and offered his hand again to Nathan. "That's when I took off to Italy. So long ducks and clowns."

"Pleased to meet you," Nathan said, insisting on the plainness of his tone. Inspired to self-parody? Joanne wondered. Afraid to laugh at Germans for fear of insulting this German?

Meanwhile, the commotion had also brought Nathan to Diana's attention, and Joanne saw her daughter look from her would-be boyfriend to her new hero, Chace. Man-to-man, Diana's glance seemed to say, I hope you'll understand he means nothing to me. You know how foolish tenderhearted people can be. As the men were oblivious to everything except the ferocious contest on the court, Diana's confidential message was only perceived by her mother, who turned, inviting Nathan for dinner as she went to prepare it.

She had veal chops browning in two pans of butter and oil when Herr Muehler joined her in the kitchen. He asked her to give him a useful task, and she felt he was like a troubador seeking to bind himself in service to her. Pleased, flattered, she laid a melon, purple grapes, pears and apples before him; she gave him a sharp short paring knife and a deep wooden bowl to cut the fruit into. He bent himself to his work, speaking beautiful high baloney, she was sure. "You remind me of a woman I loved more than my own life. I was almost crazy with feeling. It was awful. I would have liked to take a gun to love. But my wife did it for me. Then I didn't know which was worse, life with love or life without it. It was dying either way. It was all a question of courage and dying. It was just the breaks being born."

Joanne understood him, loosely translated, to have said that she reminded him of a woman he had once loved more than his life, for whom he almost committed suicide until he'd been spared by seeing how love, even desperate and adulterous love, was the essence of life. If it hurt as much to love as not to love, then why not love? Once you were born, you had no choice, really, except to love. He chose a very serious form of flirtation, but she believed she knew why. He was a youthful character, and yet he must be sixty-five; he was of an age to know how vulnerable all the pretty feelings were. Of course, this made him appreciate love's sweetness much, much more.

"Tell me of yourself. Of your childhood," he urged.

"I grew up in Providence. Right down the road."

"Start at the beginning."

She did. While she turned the chops, washed the rice and put it on to boil, she painted a broad picture for him, filled with detail. Her family had been part of a social group, including the Browns and Lippetts and Goddards, which had once made up Rhode Island's ruling class. In the colonial era they built ships and distilled rum. Later they ran the trade to Europe and India, owned textile mills, set up banks, became senators. Their grip began to loosen in the last half of the nineteenth century, though their finances continued, to an amazing extent, to be bound up in the resources of the whole nation. When the railroad tracks were laid through the Midwest, a relative of the Browns and Hazards was involved in the surveying. Through his foresight, there were people in Providence who bought up huge tracts of land in Iowa, Illinois and Ohio. (These would be sold off slowly, so that young men and women in 1956 were still financing their graduate educations and European tours with property picked up in 1870.) Many of the Providence Republicans had money in the railroad itself, and their investment in oil and crops and beef spanned the country on a bridge of dollar bills. When their power diminished, after the textile mills went South, after horse sense and good luck lost in earning power to mechanical inventiveness, after the rise of electronics and jewelry and Italians in Rhode Island, these White Protestant families continued to be prominent as lawyers, philanthropists, scholars and socialites. They were prominent, but no longer at the center. Like almost everybody else in the twentieth century without an advanced degree in physics, these New Englanders were not entirely sure any longer what made the economy, let alone the world, go round.

"My family was typical. My grandfather made a small fortune, and my father managed it. He could afford to go into politics. He was a Republican congressman and then the senator for Rhode Island. Mother would take us all to Washington for the winter and Watch Hill for the summer. We kept our house in Providence and moved back there after Daddy left the Senate."

Herr Muehler wanted to know how she met Christopher and where, jostling many layers of feeling she'd forgotten, and was sad to recall, not because they were painful (some actually were) but because they had once been so strong, and still they'd been swept away like everything else in life's flood. Yet she also knew Herr Muehler was drawing out her special narrative gift, her purring, streaming, witty way of telling tales. She heard her own voice glowing with its most attractive tone; insights lighted her descriptions; details leapt up in her memory (how Christopher's great uncle died in his mistress' bed the day he had all his teeth pulled and false ones put in). Still, there was another quality which made her fascinating, one of which she was conscious because when it took over she felt welded together as long as it was there. She could not name this quality, though she saw its light reflected in Herr Muehler's listening eyes. It

was like the most delicious sauce, both in its having wonderful flavor but also in its having a moment when all the
ingredients, intensified by heat, could fly apart, and this
time hadn't, though then it was all too good to last.

In this case, it lasted while she told how she met Christopher in Washington at the end of the war. And while
she quickly described their youthful characters, she was
at work preparing the more complicated analysis of their
different sorts of backgrounds. Though Christopher was
her social equivalent, few coins minted in Providence, no
matter how equal as currency, could match New York
lucre for flourish. His family boasted more bygone piracy
in its acquisition of wealth and greater contemporary ur-
banity. If she did not go up in the world, in any hard
sense, by marrying Christopher, still their combined physical magnetism and doubled charm made her rise in everybody's estimation.

Though her inspiration stretched far ahead of what she
was saying, to the outer reaches of this thought, she was
denied the chance to deliver it. The tennis players barged
in, sweaty and thirsty and smelly, bursting with their
game's postmortem, which they wanted everyone to share.

"We had you, we really had you," wailed Bucky. "We
had you in the second set and I blew it by double-faulting
three times in a row." The fat boy he had been flared momentarily. Bucky stamped his black, ankle-high sneaker,
but the older, more streamlined adolescent followed this
by letting his hand flop resignedly against his hairy thigh.

"We were better, you shouldn't feel badly," said Bill
Outerbridge, a neighbor who had played as Christopher's
partner.

"It's true," Christopher agreed. "We played awfully
well. Way above our heads and yours too, I guess."

"Whaddya mean? You can't hurt my team with his

crummy psychological warfare. We expecta see you guys on the court tomorrow. Then we'll see who plays over whose head."

"Yeah, it's a shoo-in. These bums don't stand a chance in real competition. Matter of fact, I'd play with you except I'm so good they don't let me play here anymore."

Would the real Chace please stand up? Despite Diana's perfect imitation of Chace's way of speaking, Joanne could still tell their teeth apart. Chace accompanied everything he said with a half-grin, as if he were laughing at his own inexplicable gruffness. His self-mocking smile showed his sharp, sizable canines, which clearly identified him as the real Chace Harsh. His reverent copycat, Diana, took his act seriously, and played him with a kind of stricken admiration. Her version of Chace involved occasional Bogart-like grimaces, during which her own even teeth revealed to her mother that she was, after all, Diana, her second daughter, as opposed to Frank Harsh's first son.

The whirlwind had destroyed her idyll with Herr Muehler, but for once she had risen to her own inner heights and stayed there. Her happiness continued, stable and calm, while she drew the curtains before the big window, and went around turning on the lights before dinner. Her mood did not alter while she bathed or dressed in a long, soft, mauve gown or stepped into her gold evening slippers. She hummed while she finished dinner and set the table with her daughters, covering it first with the flowered cloth and then the gleaming silver forks and knives and candlesticks. Squat silver salt-and-pepper urns went at either end, the cobalt blue glass visible as a thin rim above the white salt. An antique silver toothpick holder went in front of Christopher's place, containing the wooden toothpicks he loved to use at the

end of the meal and for which he would substitute his
fingernails if the toothpicks weren't provided.

Her happiness was in her and yet it was also in the
flowers she arranged around the room. She saw the ecstatic core burning in the Pekingese faces of the pansies,
with their velvet petals and complex expressions. Joanne
closed her eyes to bear the unexpected smell of cold
cream coming from the first harvest of summer roses. The
house itself was a center of ecstacy to her then, and the
light on her blue linen sofas, the light on her piano and in
the corner, illuminating a Meissen china seal—the dewy
beauty of its head topping the absurd comma of its body
—the light shone with the power generated by her strong
emotions.

Her husband was there, handing her a highball glass
with fresh ice cubes making oily swirls as they melted in
the caramel-colored scotch. And dinner began to smell
unbearably good, but now the others were coming into
the richly lit living room, having bathed and put on clean
clothes so that they were all newly presented to each
other. Conversation which had arrived at joking familiarity by the end of the afternoon was formal again; people had reacquired their reserve and shyness. Still, beneath the flutter there was the ease of people who
confidently expected the evening to return to a previously achieved intimacy. Though Joanne herself hardly
spoke, conversation kept coming around to her, as though
the happiness she felt in herself and at the center of
things was a source of inspiration to everybody else.

Later, when the plates had been passed out; after people had eaten the veal chops and rice under the creamy
sauce; after salad and dessert; after they had talked generally about the Vietnam War, about the cold war, about
the last war and the differences between the weapons

used and the attitudes of the public and the soldier and the press and our allies; after Katherine, her brushed blond hair falling over her peachy cheek, had served coffee, Joanne said they had to think about the music they wanted to have at the party when The Bleakers was finished. She said she was worried that there would be generational differences about the kind of music people would want. She was sure the younger generation would want rock 'n' roll, but that the older generation would want something, well, dancier. She had an idea for a compromise, though she wasn't sure she could find a band to play what she had in mind. She went and put on the record of the sort of music she meant. Unexpectedly, her husband asked her to dance, as if, she felt, to reassert his supremacy over her too numerous admirers. This, though he had dominated the discussion all during dinner. They danced the shag, their steps so polished after years of dancing that they seemed to be skating back and forth in front of the victrola, and then all around the sofas, smiling openly and gazing like new lovers into one another's eyes.

In another moment everyone was dancing with them, but, in the manner of the new generation, without partners. Someone changed the record to "Tell Me What I Say." Everybody danced with everybody; in a circle and in chains and in a cluster. Herr Muehler never moved. He swayed rhythmically in one place, dressed in his best baggy plaid pants, a velvet vest and shirt with a flowing bow like those worn by nineteenth-century artist-bohemians. His head was tipped back and he rolled it from side to side, waggling his hands like a minstrel singing "Mammy." His lids were closed blissfully, and his mouth was slightly open so that his tongue was sometimes gleamingly visible. Gradually, he became the hub of the dancing universe. The circle formed around him; people danced into the center, incorporating Herr Muehler into their own routines. Joanne sashayed to the middle and he reached out, taking her hands in his small meaty ones. Still without moving his feet, he swung her right, then left, imparting through their handclasp a profound, intimate sense of recognition. She experienced it as an exchange of similarities, their ability to step aside and let the great forces of nature sweep through them. She squeezed his beefy hand, found her strong selflessness answered by his, and spinning between, spinning out and, finally, as she danced back into her place in the circle, she felt their moment spinning up, up into the fumes.

5

Being in love meant you didn't have to be the person you were born. No, at long, wonderful last, Diana felt she'd escaped that bore, that idiot, that ugly nonentity. She had fallen completely in love with Chace, literally had tripped on the sound of his voice and plunged several stories to her new life at the beginning of his. It was like merging with Katherine, only multiplied by ten. She was like a transistor radio with one station: WCHACE. Imitating him involved no will. Suddenly, she *was* him, galvanized into being him the instant she heard his gruff-tender voice at the door. She heard him from her room and like a snake, hypnotized by the fakir's tootling flute, she felt herself called to a complete knowledge of what he meant —not just in content (a mere "hello") but also in all its implication. "That's it," Diana thought. "That's really how everything's knit together."

In a flash, she had deserted Katherine's premises, and had begun to organize behind Chace's first principles. Katherine sent emotion up the hill to the aerie of idealism; Chace kept it down to earth where he chopped it up for firewood. To be Katherine, you had to pull your feelings up, up, out of the fray, up into the clouds where you could set them to music and sing the high, high purposes of man. To be Chace, you could let your feelings be as low and rank as they spontaneously were, but you also constantly denied their hold on you. You could feel with all your heart that your father was a tyrant, but you made fun of yourself for feeling that way. You could go ahead and love your mother with all your might, but you never forgot how ridiculous it was to care for anyone. As all Diana's different, contradictory sentiments rushed to obey the laws of Chace, she marveled at how, when she used to be Katherine, she had failed to account for so much of the evidence of her senses. As she hurtled into place, she remembered her awful temper, recalled how she'd blow up in front of everybody and realized that her problem had been the too radical suppression of her emotionally volatile self. Now that she was Chace, she was sure things would go more smoothly. She'd let her nature out a little bit at a time, but always snipping off each piece cleanly lest she get attached to anything she'd said or done and grew to have expectations. If you didn't try to follow up what you felt, if you just expressed yourself truthfully without imagining that reality would give anything back, then you, too, could find happiness.

Oh, it was great to be a boy, though she was sorry she couldn't play tennis with the rest. Oddly enough, now that she was one of the guys, Diana was more inclined to feel that you had to have rules and that you couldn't let girls like her get away with murder. Were women inherently immoral after all? What if everybody went around smashing up tennis rackets for obscure personal reasons? Well, maybe not so obscure. Her dad had behaved like a despot, but since her conversion (some would call it a sex change) she saw how things needed running. Though her punishment kept her from showing her tennis talent in front of Chace, she didn't mind appearing to him as a black sheep, and she acknowledged that the glamor of being a sinner depended heavily on the existence of law.

If only Nathan hadn't come along. He cramped her style. She could not be as completely Chace-like as she wanted, though she never for a moment thought of being anybody else. There were moments when she flagged, or stopped to catch her breath, but there was never an instant when she wasn't being her hero. It was only a question of degree, of whether she was being Chace more or less. Even when they were dancing, when the whole dinner party jumped to its feet and began, each one, to rock 'n' roll and twist and swirl—even then she was Chace, though appearances led Nathan (among others) to believe she was Diana. She knew he thought he was dancing with her, despite the fact there were no couples, only general bobbing. (The laws of connection in partnerless dancing were real, but as meandering and difficult to follow as the strings in the game of spider at birthday parties. For each participant, as for every dancer, there was a prize, a partner, but between the player and his treasure there was a web of crisscrossing strings woven through each other and strung over branches and under bushes and around posts. Every player's string was involved in the tangle, but his eye could not separate his own string from the web. He had to wind up his twine and claim the favor to clearly realize the relationship so confusingly wrapped up in the others.)

After dancing, everyone went to bed except Chace, Katherine, Diana (Chase II), Herr Muehler and Nathan. Herr Muehler's mood became restless, and he roamed around the record player muttering (almost growling) to himself. He paced across the room to the piano and back again, drumming his fingers on the cabinet, snarling softly, then loudly enough so that the other four looked in his direction. Herr Muehler did not explain himself.

"He's drunk," said Chace. "It always makes him weird. Sometimes he gets going about his wife, who's dead or in jail. Either she shot one of his mistresses or vice versa. Hard to tell."

Herr Muehler slammed his fist on the cabinet and swore incoherently, "Idiots! . . . Money bags! . . . Nazi Pig Imperialists! . . ."

"Christ, we're in for it. If he gets going about goddamn politics we'll never hear the end of it. Last week he got drunk at home and wouldn't go to bed until someone took him to a voting booth."

"Whadja do?" Diana asked.

"Finally, he was so drunk I put him in a closet and told him it was a voting booth. He pulled a hanger for the Socialist ticket and felt much better."

Herr Muehler rambled into their midst, still muttering, and Chace said, "Come on, we don't wanna hear a big fat lecture. Why doncha just go out and give the moon a piece of your mind?"

Herr Muehler shook his fist at Chace, then shook his

head, spitting all the while, or hissing, stuttering with rage, but not without a distant hint of comedy, suggesting (somehow) that Chace was the incarnation of all wrong. Herr Muehler stamped his foot, hitched his pants up, grimaced, laughed violently and emptily, and so managed to convey the bitter irony of his—Muehler's—having to be teacher to one who'd failed to learn what was most important.

"*Fertig!*" Herr Muehler said, his only clear word so far, and thrust his hands out in a breast stroke of exasperation. "Finished!" he howled and left the room. In a moment they heard the downstairs screen door slam behind him.

"Don't worry," said Chace. "It happens all the time. Whenever he gets soused, he wants the world to join the revolution, but by then he's so drunk he can't get a word out straight."

"I wish he'd started talking about it earlier," said Nathan. "I would really like to hear about his experiences in Germany during the war."

And I wish you'd left a little earlier, Diana thought, wondering what made Nathan stay. She had the strange, even unpleasant, feeling that Nathan thought he was saving her from being a third wheel. As if by making it a double date, he preserved the other couple's privacy. He didn't seem to understand that if he left the three of them in peace, there would just be her, herself and her former self. They would have been quite comfortable together, thank you. And not only was Nathan wrecking a perfectly happy threesome, he'd confused Chace to the point where he was treating Nathan both as the only other boy in the room and as Diana's boyfriend.

This drove her to new heights of Chacedom—like a person waving with great frenzy from a crowd on the dock to a friend in the crowd on the incoming ship's deck. She swaggered, plunging her thumbs into the waist of her skirt. (She regretted this feminine touch terribly, and swore she would never again be false to her real self, as she had been earlier when she put a skirt on in imitation of Katherine.) Diana stood with her legs set wide apart in front of the fireplace, frustrated beyond telling by the fact that Chace settled his arm around Katherine, that they seemed to sink back into the pillows of the sofa as if they were starting to withdraw, as if they were waiting for the others to go and leave them alone. But how could they treat her as other? Why didn't Chace recognize her? (What would he do if he did?) Why didn't he see that she was he?

"Yeah, well, there's only one way to get really good at anything," said Diana, as Chace-like as she could make it. "You have to go get rolled over by the people who are better'n you are. I mean that. You know what Matisse said?" she asked, discovering that one of the odd features of being another person meant that everything she knew about his interests suddenly came alive in the very terms most recognizable to him. "I'll tell ya what Matisse said. He said you gotta always go against the greats. And if you never get as good as they are, tough."

"Yeah, well, he's right," said Chace, friendly but tired, as if Diana were sapping his strength by being him.

"Yeah, well, like let's get out of here. I'm going crazy. You know some people just can't be contained in little lives, little houses."

"Little houses?" Nathan said, using his hand to ask whether she was referring to the immense converted hay-loft as small.

"Sure, I suppose you think just because I came from a wealthy family that I can't suffer, too. I'm not saying I ever went hungry, but I can tell you, I've felt the big squeeze."

Though she addressed these words to Nathan's person, they were meant for Chace. But his station had gone dead! Come in WCHACE, come in! Finding herself cut off, she grew more urgent, more obvious in her broadcast. She turned to him and Katherine, saying, "Don't you want to get outta here? Howsa bout a walk to the beach?"

Chace yawned, or perhaps he faked a yawn, laying his actor's foundation so she would believe him when he excused himself on the grounds of being too tired.

"Yeah, well," Diana rushed on, growing more repelled by herself as she became more flagrant. She was breaking all her own strictest rules. If you were going to work behind enemy lines, you couldn't blow your cover like this. Enemy lines? Well, when you go and sit in a man's identity, you've put part of your own in alien territory, but you don't want to let everyone in on the secret. "Yeah, well," she repeated just to keep the floor. She didn't know what to say, really, but if she let Chace speak she saw he was going to make excuses she didn't want to hear. "Yeah, well, let's get going," she finally announced, conscious of how feeble her command sounded.

"Yeah, well, you know, Diana," Chace said, his voice as light and kind as a young girl's, full of the surprise a young girl feels when she realized (to her amazement) that someone is in need of her kindness. "You guys go on without us . . . I'm bushed."

"OK, OK, I know you two wanta go play hide the baloney. Well, just don't let me come between you," Diana said. Immediately, a hundred knives descended, but not one of the sharp horrors she felt did the job she wanted done: not one of the hundred knives cut her

tongue out. She could not believe she said what she'd
said. And looking at the stunned faces of Katherine and
Chace, she saw she'd not only stumbled onto the truth,
but that by spitting it out so coarsely she'd also stripped
away the veils protecting their lovers' sensitivities.

Until she'd flung the cat out of the bag, the act had
been mistily shrouded, as was proper for the true romance
of two perfect people. Diana saw now—now that she'd
made Chace hang his head, now that she'd caused Katherine to sink into introspective misery—that they were not
just perfect, but that they each also had a perfect relation
to gender. She, meanwhile, was an absurdity, becoming
Chace and then becoming attracted to him—as if it were
possible to be queer for the opposite sex. But that's how
she felt when she'd most become him. She'd felt they
were buddies, sailors on leave, and that the whole point
of picking up dates was just to have new corners off
which to angle the shots of friendship. But then her pal
had betrayed her and really found a girl he liked, leaving
Diana in a state of yearning and weirdo signaling; after
all, she was a girl pretending to be a boy involved in male
bonding.

If she was not an absurdity—a lady fairy—if such a
thing was possible, then she was a fiend for having made
her sister, her one true self, so unhappy. For a perfect person Katherine's face seemed suspiciously disturbed, so
disturbed that Diana was touched, fleetingly, by the fear
that what was wrong in this picture had eluded her completely. It occurred to her that Katherine's problems were
both different and possibly worse than her own, and
though this thought splashed across her mind like a
bucket of water, it also evaporated in an instant, leaving
Diana's floorboards bare of any other person but herself.

Once again her mind had only her own feelings to go

on. As crazy as they'd seemed seconds before, they now seemed crazier, careening along a spiral of insights about having become her sister's boyfriend in an attempt to steal him. She saw that possibility now, not just in its cruelty to Katherine, whom she loved, but also in its sexual pathos. She'd tried to sneak up on Chace from behind, like a ghost taking possession of a living body. She'd competed in the only way she'd known how. Not in an all-out contest, ladies and gentlemen of the jury; no, nothing so simple as that. She was guilty of trying to get inside his self, as opposed to his pants, which any normal, self-respecting jealous sister would do. . . .

Oh, ladies and gentlemen of the jury, I am guilty. I admit it. Don't go on with this trial. Sentence me to death and get it over with. "I'm so sorry," she cried. "I'm so sorry," and ran from the room.

I'm not alone, she noticed, hearing the clump of Nathan's foot on the stair. But then I couldn't be alone even if he hadn't come. I don't *have* anyone to be alone with! And she was out the door into the warm, moonlit night. He was beside her, his arm brushing hers as they walked along the road to the beach. He didn't say anything. She knew he was being sympathetic and yet she felt his sympathy came with a condition. It could only be received if she herself took on the proper shape. His kindness was like a stencil laid on wet paint; it imposed sense from the outside. The word he was asking her to conform to was masculine, implying that she was foolish and feminine and in need of him.

This infuriated her, as he always infuriated her. He seemed to think he was doing her a favor, but one which she should darn well obey. (Some favor.) Still, her own repetitive anger toward him was boring. She was tired of the person she became in his presence, but because there was no real way to get rid of him, there being nothing to get rid of (they weren't going steady, thank God, or engaged, to say the least), she felt her irritation wearing so thin that it had almost been rubbed entirely through to a new attitude. What this would be was obscured by the threadbare veil of resistance still cloaking all the other feelings she might have for him.

Not that she imagined she was going to wake up and find herself in love with him. For that to happen, they would have to be spontaneously overwhelmed by a wild, powerful, irresistible and mutual obliteration. As far as she could tell, this could not occur even if her resistance disappeared entirely, cured overnight by some miracle drug. Even if she got to like him a whole lot better than she did right now, she would still be very careful about what she told him. She wouldn't want him to know much more than he already did about her feelings on any subject, and she did not think she would have an improved idea of what he was really like either. As it was, his feelings were extremely mysterious to her, not that she cared except that it made her twice as secretive as she was anyway, which, according to her own informal survey, was about three times more than the average. Of course, she had something real to be secretive about. Her strange feelings for his mother, just for starters. God, if she told him he'd probably think she was a lesbian! He was just queer enough to think she was queer!

He wasn't so queer, however, that he didn't put his arm around her waist as they passed through the second gate in the stone walls. When he did this, her own inner clamor suddenly went still. She listened for the feelings of her waist and looked around her—as if the sensations she awaited might as easily come at her from the outside as from within. The moonlight swept everything with silver,

turning trees and stones and bushes into a field of chiaro-
scuro. As they made their way down the road of mercury,
they were watched by the cows pastured in the meadow
below the first gate. These creatures perked up when they
heard the disturbance of pebbles, and came to the
wooden fence, watching with a kind of silly, fearful gravity and yet adding to the mysteriousness of the occasion.
Their hides showed only black and white. The mas-
siveness of their heads contributed to the brute delicacy
of their nostrils and jaws. As Diana and Nathan passed,
the beasts followed them with nodding concentration, as
though they were forest elders musing on the fates of
those who wandered late at night.

Then, as they passed through the next and last gate, entering the shadiest portion of the way to the beach, she
began to feel a band of heat at her waist, a belt of pleasure where his arm encircled her. She leaned back into his
embrace, but as she yielded to this desire, or in the instant that she first felt it, she also experienced a terrible
fear. What was she afraid of, she wondered? That he
might misunderstand and think she had some romantic
interest in him? What did she care about his feelings? If
she didn't have the simple heartlessness to experimentally
enjoy his embrace, then she was even more pathetic than
she already knew she was. She snuggled up to him, determined to prove to herself that she was the real thing and
not just an armchair hellion.

He reached farther around and pulled her closer, and
suddenly she could feel a swivet coming on. It got its
start in a murky but powerful sense of how limiting it
would be if she was generally thought to be his girl
friend. It could ruin her life! Everything depended on
Diana's floating independence, on her ability to receive a
message anytime, anyplace, on any frequency. She had to

broadcast back under false identities, if necessary, but if people got the idea that she was Nathan's girl friend they might mistake the false fake identity for the real imposter.

Not that Nathan had the vaguest idea of the risk he was exposing her to: the risk of losing the possibility of true love by making her give in to being his apparent one. As her anger developed, it gathered in her objection to his political ideas along with her fury against him personally, and soon these had blown up into a great, shaking rage. There it was, a twister darkening her inner horizon, swirling darkly where no mood had been before. It was coming this way. Fast. As it approached, it sent out advance bulletins that tended to justify its arrival: everyone wanted to have things his own way, but most people knew this was a childish desire and didn't try to impose their programs on unsuspecting bystanders. "What kind of world do you think this would be? You probably think my mother should go to work in a factory. Oh, that would be wonderful, great, no more beauty or sympathy just because *you* think you've got all the answers."

By the time these words burst out of her, she was well into the middle of her tornado, but it was the first that Nathan knew of her state. He stepped away from her and stared. She might have expected the look of surprise and concern on his face when he heard himself attacked, but when she saw it she grew incensed. What had apparently begun as the storming of his arrogance—"Youbigdumbfuckerassholeidiotbaby, what makes you think you're so much better than anybody else?"—this storm slightly shifted its direction when she saw by his expression that he was going to pretend not to know what she was talking about. She marched on his self-delusion, yelling, "Don't look at me as if I were some kind of raging maniac just because I happen to be doing the talking for once. And if

I happen to be screaming it's just to get it through your thick skull that just because I don't mention my problems doesn't mean I don't have them. It's just that I don't complain, but you, ninnyfucker, I have about seven thousand thoughts per minute of which you realize one or two, if I'm lucky," though by reminding herself of how little she thought he knew about her, she raised the question of how she'd let things slide between them this far without impressing their inequality on him—that is, the inequality of her having more insight into him than he had into her. The joy of anger gave way to the rage of frustration. It made her mad that he was unknowing and even madder that she had to be the one to tell him, especially as *she* was what he didn't know about. If they'd been in love, he would have known everything. But they weren't, so she was forced to educate him, forced, really, to boast about her complexity, to go to these embarrassing extremes just to get him to be slightly aware of what she was like, "all because you don't have any idea of what goes on in my head, but that's only a tiny example of what you don't know or understand. You couldn't anyway, if you tried, because I mean no one knows. Life is just that way, and if you want to know the truth, you've had it because you're a mama's boy and that makes you completely out of it, so shut up," she said, expelling the tail end of the squall, feeling in its wake a great peace and clarity, feeling very much as she did after a good meal; that she'd like to have the whole thing all over again.

While she was blowing her stack, Nathan followed her tirade with his feet. He stepped forward. He stepped back. He stepped to one side and then the other, as though he was chasing her thoughts, which were swerving violently within a tiny area. He jogged on tiptoe; he stood his ground, but when she ended abruptly, he stumbled drunkenly like a man who'd been shot. For an awful instant she thought he was going to fall to his knees again. His pupils were dilated as they had been the fateful day at the beach. But, fortunately, he did not go so far, though he was horribly abject—she could not understand why he did not feel as braced and satisfied as she did—or why he said, miserably, "Jesus Christ, why didn't you give me any warning? God, you make me feel like shit, but I can't even tell what I've done wrong."

Hummmm, he was taking it pretty hard. Her brother always fought back. In retrospect, she could not really remember now why such a subtle point had made her quite so mad. (And how pretty it was out tonight. How calm, how still!) Even if everyone thought she was Nathan's girl friend—which they wouldn't because she never would be—but even if they did, it would just be one more mask among many. If, in her disguise as a girl, she could disguise herself as a sailor for Chace, why should she worry about the restrictions of one more pretense? She shouldn't have gotten so mad, though she felt wonderfully well, so wide and clean, she could not completely regret having lost her cool. Re: temper, she realized she was a geyser, a sort of Old Faithful of fury, bound to go off about once every forty-eight hours. As a matter of fact, her worst problems arose if she couldn't go off, or if she misfired, as when she'd blown up at her mother *in front of* Mrs. Baker. (Blush City!) Right this minute, however, as they walked the rest of the way to the beach, she felt entirely egoless and solved: she could give the rest of her life away to charity.

And Nathan just then seemed to need some funding. He was in a bad, sad mood, and for a guy who was usually your cheerful, chalky, helpful, wholesome 4-H'er he sure was being melodramatic. His brow was deeply knit. He stared deeply out to sea. He sighed deeply, dug his foot deep into the sand. (This was not the first time she'd noticed this Byronic excess in the dark moods of the straight-laced. Whereas her emotions were always sloshing right through her unbuttoned restraints, and thereby having at least a natural intensity to recommend them, prim people always overdid the ketchup.)

Well, she was going to have to go heavy on the corn relish if she wanted to get out of this one without an enemy. "Nathan," she said, pleading softly, though she almost had to laugh at the private joke of her insincerity. She thought of how Katherine might appreciate it, but that was dangerously laugh-provoking, so she thought of it no more. "Nathan, sometimes I'm frightened by my own violence." (Had she gone too far in the direction of amusing herself? Was she going to laugh right out loud?) "I wish I hadn't let my violence out on you. I've really gotten to admire you. I respect your conviction," she added in an attempt to restore some truthfulness to her eulogy. As a matter of fact, the side to him that pledged allegiance to the left was just what bored her, but she admired conviction in the abstract. God, if one thing would ever be true of her for longer than five minutes, she would be a much happier person.

But back to her private endowment to Nathan's hurt feelings. How was her charity going? So-so. A tremor of response passed through him on the word "admire." On top of the corn, she could see he wanted a whole feast of compliments. This could have been funny if it was happening to someone else. Hadn't she often been struck by the comedy of he-men melting under the pressure of flattering remarks from a bombshell? Isn't poochum moochum the biggest, strongest man I've ever met? (Bombs away!) But she hated to think she was going to have to cater to this he-man's appetite for mush. In many ways it made her mad that these big, supposedly scary beasts were just assholes under their beards. The least they could do was live up to their reputations as he-men. But, OK, OK, she didn't want Nathan to hate her. She might hate him; hell, she might hate everybody, still, she didn't want them to do the same to her. "Nathan, I feel really badly. You've been kind to me, and I guess what really impresses me is that you're very smart, but you can be kind to someone like me even though I don't agree with you and also am not very nice at times."

Wham! His intelligent lips were kissing her smartly. This was not the way she had dreamed it would be, baby outlaw that she was, without even one notch on her gun. Yes, this was her first kiss. Where were the lights, camera, action? Why wasn't the wind sweeping back her long black hair and her floor-length skirt? Why wasn't he the dark stranger who'd arrived that morning on the stagecoach, who, in a matter of hours, had turned her life on its head? Where was the custardy dissolution and union of souls? Would she ever draw another breath? Or would she suffocate, the victim of a head-on collision with a socialist?

Ah, that was better. His mouth loosened a little. Their faces adjusted to one another so she could inhale, they took little steps to bring their bodies into better alignment. It was still not all that she'd expected, but it was fascinating. She was a darkness in which his lips moved like minnows. She ceased to be physically specific. His feeding mouth gave her shape by defining the lines of her sensation. His tongue crept out and then surged into the cave formed by her sea's receding around his tongue. There was a revolution of feeling in her chest. Pain rolled over, becoming pleasure. Holding his tongue gave her the impression of feeling both sides of the profile that their meeting made in her imagination. His hands began lightly to rove, without being searching, as if he was vaguely outlining what he was going to come back to later to sculpt in detail. These swift, soft caresses were incredibly sweet. She adored being brushed by his hands. She had always loved candy, and now, turning slightly to move fresh surfaces under his touch, she discovered her sweet tooth for foreplay.

6

The morning after the night with Nathan on the beach, Diana stayed in bed, recalling the encounter. Actually, she did not recall it so much as close her eyes and his lips were trailing from her mouth, or turn her head, experiencing the rush of his breath beside her ear. She was wrapped in arousal, muffled by it. Her strongest urge was to hold herself in her arms or to lie with one arm clenched between her legs and the other covering her small breasts. Then she was wonderfully contained in the blur of memory and fantasy. Over and over she recalled how one minute they'd been standing apart like two empty coats in the night, and then the next thing she knew she was water, brimming and grave and tingling. She swam in her physical recollections, full in herself and feeling the fullness as if it were tangible, though it was only there when she closed her eyes.

Her desire was like a lake's seiche, moving back and forth within her own shores. It wasn't even that sexual. She had no desire to go on, only to curl up in the sensual puddle of her memories. She probably would have gone right back to the womb if Katherine hadn't come in to say her presence was required at the breakfast table.

"Hey, I'm really sorry about last night."

"What about it? What did you do?"

"Don't you remember how stupidly I acted? I didn't do it to be mean. I was so sorry that I said that thing about hiding the baloney. God, just saying those words makes me want to tear my hair. I mean, I really can't believe I was such an asshole."

"Diana, that's what we did," said Katherine in a sudden flash of frankness.

"That's . . . what . . . you . . . did?"

"Yes."

"You . . . hid . . . the . . . baloney?"

"Yes," said Katherine, staring at Diana with a totally serious look. Her great emerald eyes said, this is it.

"Goddamn it," said Diana, "there is just no getting away from fucking. It's everywhere. Now I'm going to have to do it."

"Why?"

"Just to get it over with. To see if I can do it. I wouldn't be surprised if I couldn't. What does it feel like?"

"It hurts, but it feels good at the same time. It's like when you have a loose tooth and you push it back and forth. You know how that hurts and feels good at the same time?"

"Hmmmmm. I hope you know you're probably pregnant."

"We used a thing."

"I certainly hope so."

"Well, Diana, what do you think of me?"

"I think you're a different person. I don't know what I think. Except now I've got to do it to find out what you're like now you've done it. I can't have my sister becoming a completely different person."

"Who are you going to do it with?"

"I guess I'd have to do it with Nathan, right?"

"Have you been necking around?"

"Pretty much," said Diana, studying her nails maturely.

"I think you're too young."

"Are you kidding? I'm about ninety-two. We're both overage for virgins. But now you're in a new category. And I'm getting out of here."

"What if you get pregnant?"

"It would be a lot of fun if we both got to go to the unwed mothers' home together. But time's awasting," said Diana, standing at military attention beside her bed. "'Tis a far better thing that I go to do than I have ever done. . . ."

"Ka – the – rine, Di – ana," someone called from upstairs.

"Co – ming," Diana yelled.

"Well, maybe not the first time," Katherine said speculatively.

"So now you've done it you're going to talk dirty all the time. It's shocking," said Diana, pulling on jeans and a shirt chosen for their geometry—for their angular, self-containing shapes. At all times, nudity was a form of vagueness to her, making her feel she was nothing but eyes, as though her body was a ghost trailed from her vision. Once she was dressed, cut off at the frayed cuffs of an old pink Brooks Brothers shirt and at the ankles by the cubism of her dungarees, she felt that she had acquired some character, some shape.

Upstairs they found their brother and parents sitting at the kitchen table with Herr Muehler. Outside, on the porch, Chace was painting. From behind he seemed all triangles: the large triangle of his back—his broad, thin shoulders and tapered waist; though the shape of his head was not severely triangular, still it was reminiscent of the form, as well as his hand holding the brush. Though she had definitely lost Chace to Katherine, and vice versa, Diana couldn't help but be moved by the sight of these geometric forms. She had so much in common with him! He was naturally well formed and, well, she sought forms to contain her. And then—she had to just bring it right out in the open—he was so sickeningly attractive. It was terrible to know she'd never have him for her own.

Diana felt a slight pang of guilt about still coveting her sister's boyfriend. She peeked to see if Katherine might be watching, but Katherine was looking down at her own thumb, which she held with her other hand as though it were something of surprising interest. Diana went back to watching Chace, dwelling on his hands as a kind of parallel activity to Katherine's. His hands were stunning. The knuckles were poised gracefully above the brush; each segment of each finger was clearly, cleanly defined. He held the brush as though he were about to let it go, but there was nothing limp about the way he dabbed the paper with pale watercolors, only fluency in the relation of hand to brush and brush to color and color to swirling shapes and dancing forms. The day was overcast, and he was painting the pearl coalescence of the sky and water.

Then, as always, fatally drawn to her own embarrassment, Diana saw her feet walking out through the
door. Her body went along for the ride. She stood behind
Chace, looking at his work. She fuzzily heard the voices
from the breakfast table, jokes about Herr Muehler's
hangover, and pieces of his story about where he'd gone
last night. As far as he could recall, he'd wandered down
the highway and fallen into an argument with a "For
Sale" sign, but had failed to wrestle it to the ground.
Though Diana only paid vague attention to Herr
Muehler's account, the sound wired the air between her
and Katherine. She was on one side of the murmur and
Katherine was on the other, and though her own snoopy
feet propelled her to Chace's side, Diana also felt she was
in the vanguard of Katherine's exploratory curiosity. As
if Katherine was waiting to see how Chace treated her—as
if by doing *it* Katherine had lost the power to know what
to expect from him. Any fears Diana had of interfering
were assuaged by her sense of serving as Katherine's foot
soldier, of helping at long last instead of hindering.

"It's good," she said, stepping closer to look at the
painting.

"Thanks, but if I were a real painter I'd tear it up," he
said, restraining a smile. He frowned, looking back and
forth between her and the leather case into which he was
tucking his glasses. Without these he became his true age
of twenty-two again, though his hands kept their matu-
rity, imparting their grace and reverence for the integrity
of whatever object they held. "A real painter, see, would
destroy everything until he was sure he was doing his
masterpiece. I should be ready to train myself for years
just to paint one true color. Instead of this junk," he
grumbled, half-smiling and jerking his thumb in the direction of his work.

"You mean you wouldn't want to show your work?" she asked. There was some oppression in the sunless day, a cottony heat that dulled her reactions and reminded her of suspended Sunday afternoons at boarding school.

"I mean, it's like you said Matisse said. You gotta go against the greats. And if you never get as good as they do, tough," he said, lapsing into inarticulateness. Though he still had a slight grin, his mockery was meant for himself, as if he could sympathize with anyone who thought his seriousness was absurd. He looked past Diana, making her glance back too; she saw Katherine behind the screen door. Diana's sense of gravity began to tilt in her sister's direction. Katherine's vulnerability reawakened Diana's worry and yanked it all toward her sister. Katherine seemed as undefended as a five-year-old, as magically wide-eyed, as impressionable, as crushable. Diana's strongest impulse was to stand in front of Katherine and to protect her from the sharp particles in the air, not to mention Chace's bristling masculinity. He was waiting with suppressed explosiveness, straining with his shoulders toward the door, but rooted to the porch through his feet in their scuffed, roan-colored shoes.

"Have you had breakfast?" Katherine finally murmured.

"Yeah," he blurted aggressively, almost cruelly. What's it to you? If he sounded angry, he also cut himself off from all practical excuses for going inside. He fell backward, as though pushed by his own ferocity, and sat down wearily in one of the aluminum porch chairs.

"Well, you girls, eat up," Christopher urged, draining his coffee cup. "I want to take Chace and Herr Muehler to The Bleakers."

"What for?" Diana asked, coming into the kitchen, moving protectively to Katherine's side at the stove.

"Just to show them what you all have done," said Christopher.

"Can I go in bear drag?" asked Bucky, whose interest in the costume was rivaled only by Diana's.

"It's too hot for the bear suit," Herr Muehler said, and went on to describe a terrible experience he'd had in New York City on a boiling day inside the bear suit. "I thought if I got into it naked, I would be all right. Everything was fine on the way to where we were going. We took a taxi there. Then we had to walk back. I thought I would die, but, of course, I could not take the suit off, only the head, and if you think it's funny to walk around the city like a bear, it's even stranger to walk with your bear head in your hands, absolutely wet inside your outfit."

"We call that a *misfit*," said Christopher, and tapped the kitchen table with his fingertip.

"Christopher, you now remind me of what I have been meaning to tell you," said Herr Muehler.

"What is that?"

"I am a man after your own heart," said Herr Muehler, raising his poetically aged face to Christopher, addressing him with generous, brotherly sympathy. It was a face that had grown young in its expression, though it was ancient in its wrinkles. A smooth, silky beauty shimmered in the air before the old face. His gleaming brown eyes were hard and wet and shot Christopher with a piercing look of love. "The man who married your wife is me, but that's beside the point." As he said this, Herr Muehler patted Joanne's hand. "More important. Weren't you hush-hush in Paris?"

"I was hush-hush in OSS during the war, then later I was hush-hush, as you call it, in Germany. Paris was never my base of operations."

"Well, I wanted you to know I was hush-hush in Italy during the fifties."

"You were, eh? Those were the great years at the Agency. There were more smart people working at the CIA than in all the rest of government combined."

"Well, what happened? What's your opinion of what happened?" Chace asked, drawn from the porch by the conversation.

"I'll tell you what happened to me," Herr Muehler said. "I was painting in my studio one day, and someone called and asked if I'd carry a suitcase from the railway station in Rome to St. Peter's. They must have believed I was an anticommunist because I was never a nazi."

"Are you sure it wasn't the Farfetched Foundation? The Congress for Cultural Freedom?"

"I don't know. But the truth is, I'll do anything once."

"I can't believe they just called you out of the blue, but maybe the standards were more relaxed in Italy. Most standards are, I guess. But here, when we started out in the United States, we couldn't be beat. And what's more, we were running the show. I mean, we were running the show abroad. We were the only team scoring against the communists."

Christopher rose and made it clear that he was going to continue the conversation on the way to The Bleakers. The men followed, loosely huddled around him to hear what he said. Katherine and Diana followed silently. Diana could see that her father was in his element, but it was one that made her feel furthest from him. He was always most attractive at these moments when he wielded a brilliant mood, his mind in royal working order, overflowing with ideas that rushed to power sweeping physical gestures. Chace and Herr Muehler were hanging on his words; Bucky was forced to take a back seat, walking to the left and right of the other men, but in recognition of his father's potent display of knowledge he attended. As his son, he might never be treated to the same passionate response as Christopher's guests, but he would be judged nonetheless by his father's achievements, by his standards of performance in the world. To succeed with him, it was crucial that Bucky understand his father's view of things.

As a matter of fact, Diana decided, if she wanted to succeed with her father she would also have to do as well as he had. He judged everyone by that standard. Everyone except his wife and his dog, Foster, who was moseying along behind the girls. (He was so sure of his place in Christopher's affections that he felt no need to study his master's speeches for clues to what would please him.) But she would probably never get into college, let alone understand the balance of payments, let alone be a senator. Hearing her father flame with passion for politics—the subject which was hottest to him and coldest to her—realizing she could never really interest him in the terms he found most interesting, she felt the world grew superficial around her. She began to suffer from a kind of visual aphasia. Objects—trees, the house, a fence—but people, too—her sister, her father—were all surface, so superficial they were meaningless.

Diana blinked and the darkness was harmonious, still composed of sensual memories of the night before. His lips were on her neck, his hands lightly roamed her body. His breath blew sweetly on her cheek. She opened her eyes again and saw her father and Herr Muehler and Chace, and she thought with the literalness of a Martian who'd only seen human beings in a textbook, *those are men*. A bright light went on in her mind, and underneath it hung a chart depicting the humanoid male without any clothes on. Between his legs were two eggs and a banana, or were those two eyes and a very funny nose? Or were they Ping-Pong balls and a night stick? She blinked and receded to enclose Nathan's tongue. She remembered this in her chest, accompanied by a sweet pang as she sucked the burly stranger's softness.

She opened her eyes, straining to hear what her father was saying. "We're just going to have to accept the fact that the President is the accident which crowns a system that somehow works. We don't know who the hell is going to end up on top or why. Next question. How much does it matter who's on the throne? Again the answer is going to have to be vague. We don't know. It's great if the guy is good. It may not really matter if he's bad. The economic system is bigger than the President in any case. It can go right on without a strong leader."

Listening to him made Diana feel lonelier and lonelier, frozen stiff under the Ice-O-Lation label. She would have pulled Katherine aside, into the nearest bathroom, but they had now reached The Bleakers. As they lined up behind their father to go in, Chace dropped back, putting his arm around Katherine's shoulder. Diana was glad they'd made up, sad there could only be two lovers to every love affair. Only two to a couple. Diana closed her eyes, recollecting his light, tickling touch that wrapped her up in warm arousal.

The group followed the leader into the living room, where Nathan was at work, knocking the last of the plaster out of the far wall. Rumpled insulating foil was visible between the studs, and the floor was covered with sawdust, painter's canvas and crushed cigarette boxes. The northeast corner was papered to catch the droppings of the family of swallows that had been allowed to linger under the eaves. Her father had taken pity on them though they had caused nothing but trouble, and he had delayed work in that corner while they raised their fledg-lings. In this partially completed state, the room looked more disheveled, less promising, certainly less useful than when its identity had clearly been that of an unkempt room in an old farmhouse. Seeing how their work seemed not to have gotten anywhere, that all they'd done so far was to violate what had been known and loved, Diana wished she hadn't come.

"Hey, Nathan, I've brought some tourists," Christopher hailed him. "I want to show off what a fantastic job you've done."

"Sure," said Nathan. "Let's go look around."

"Watchit!" Chace said, ducking as the swallow dove by his head, skimming Katherine's shoulder.

"Yeah, that reminds me, Mr. Nicholas," Nathan said. "We have really got to do something about these birds. We're going to be ready to work over there in the next week, but we can't do a thing until the nest is out."

"I was just waiting until she got her group out," said Christopher, darkening with embarrassment.

"One bunch has already graduated. I think she's laying again."

"OK, well, let's take the tour and then I'll do something about getting her out."

Christopher led the way, and Nathan lingered, bring-ing up the rear with Diana. "You look like you've seen the future and it doesn't work."

"I don't get it," she said glumly, unable to connect this strapping character with the sweetness she'd been nurs-ing in her memory.

"Lincoln Steffens said it. 'I have seen the future, and it works.' About Russia during the Revolution."

"Oh," she said, conscious that he was observing her with careful, intelligent interest. She couldn't imagine what he saw in her; if he saw anything, she was sure it was not what she wanted to be freed of. There was a dryness in him, an aridity which was impervious to her corruption, and without his having understood, without being able to deliver her corruption into another person's knowledge, she would remain locked in herself. It was as if she were a book written backward, as if she had to hold herself up to the mirror of another person to read herself right. And yet it had to be the right person, too, or else, as now, she just felt more jumbled than ever.

Nothing in his concerned eyes, nothing in the quaint, cocked angle of his big head, nothing in the thoughtful way he rolled his thumb around the nail of his third finger, nothing spoke of the rich mulch of rottenness fuming in her conscience.

"You want to take a walk afterward?" he asked.

She nodded mute acquiescence.

"Nathan," Christopher called. "I need you up here for some fine points about roofing."

Her father seemed on some prerevolutionary landowner high. When Nathan reached his side at the top of the stairs, Christopher whirled him into a detailed conversation about roofs and construction and costs. According to an accelerating logic of his own, her father flew from the problem of inflation to the necessity of the rich preserving what remained of American national resources. He sped from this spot to an unexpected place on the map, namely, Cuba, where he claimed the old regime had been the country's only hope for saving its real resources, particularly the sugar industry, which, having been nationalized, had been destroyed.

Nathan sailed his boat out of that safe harbor into the choppy seas of Marxist criticism of private property: how it created its own destruction in the form of the propertyless, who, finding themselves alienated, were forced to reclaim their humanity by destroying society. This is what the dispossessed in Cuba had done. They had liberated the true human essence, so long excluded from the social structure! When they turned the sugar industry over to the people, they put life back into the hands of the lifeless!

As Nathan steered his ship this way and that, the men descended to the first floor again. When Nathan was through, Herr Muehler tried to tell about his battle with the "For Sale" sign, his personal attempt to liberate the true human essence; but Christopher wouldn't let him get a word in edgewise.

"Look, Nathan, let's face a few facts. American know-how, American technology made the sugar industry what it was. These guys barge in, without any idea of what was what, and millions of dollars go down the drain. More jobs are lost than created. Is that what you mean by liberation?"

"As long as control is out of the hands of the people, they just aren't people. They're nothing as long as they don't share in the power. Capitalist society is a trial in which the people's experience is inadmissible evidence. They don't share in what's important, but they're not allowed to complain either. Or if they do, no one hears them."

Diana's father listened attentively, shaking his head slowly the whole time. Then he abruptly took up a broom and made his way back to the living room. He did this with a strange intensity and determination. It was as if all his talk about land and houses and Cuba had been a way of backing up for a running start on his real concern. Everyone followed like sheep, though he took no notice of his flock. He had successfully established himself as their

leader but now suddenly wanted to be alone. It couldn't
be done. His followers had all become his witnesses.

As he approached the corner with the nest, the lone female swallow left her perch to scold him, flapping her
shiny wings, bearing the rust and buff of her breast, flying
at him so furiously that he began to speak to her, pleading, "I know, I know, you think you own the place, but,
honestly, you aren't being fair. I admire a woman of
spirit! I do, really, I do! But there's only so much I can do
for you. You've got to meet me partway."

She dive-bombed, missing his head once and then missing him again so that it became clear she was bluffing. Almost involuntarily raising his arm as though to protect
himself, he flipped the nest out with a swift, hard jerk and
it flew through the air, hitting the floor, cracking and
spilling its four new eggs. It all happened so fast that the
muffled thud as the nest landed seemed to coincide with
the awful "splat" of the eggs breaking and the high
screech of the mother swallow whirling around the liquid,
half-formed brood, spreading in a shapeless mass on the
floor. In another second, the mother bird had quit the
room, gone forever, and Foster, skidding in from nowhere, pounced on the broken eggs and gobbled the bits
of bone and beak, swimming in transparent albumen.
When he finished, he looked up at Christopher, licking his
muzzle and frowning with muddled labrador bliss.

Christopher turned away in a daze, then he turned in a
full circle.

"Is everything all right, Mr. Nicholas?" Nathan asked.

Christopher gazed at Nathan blankly. He gave his
head a little shake. A forlorn smile curled the corners of
his mouth. Speaking from some faraway place to no one
in particular, he murmured, "We should have shot him
from a crowd."

In a rare, even a unique, gesture, Katherine came to her father's rescue by taking his wrist in both her hands and leading him away. There was a touch of daughterly possessiveness in the way she did this, and in her voice as she spoke to him, saying softly, "Let's go home so you can lie down."

"I guess you're right. I must have had too much coffee at breakfast," Christopher murmured, succumbing to Katherine's tenderness.

In her jealousy, Diana wondered why she hadn't thought of helping her father. She grouchily observed that he was limping as he left, and couldn't restrain the criticism that passed before her mind's eye: how could a cup of coffee get him in the leg? Where's your self-control, big boy? If you're so tough, how come you can't even take a little cup of coffee?

7

"Is he OK?" asked Nathan, coming to her side when they were alone.

"I'm sure he is."

And then, when this was cleared up, the silence was so terrible she asked in a panic, "How's the war?"

"Worse than ever," he said. "Shall we go out?"

She nodded.

"Come on down to the pinewoods. I'll show you the most beautiful spot on the whole property."

They left and walked past the Nicholases' to the hill beyond. The cropped grass was patchy with tuberous straw,

and spotted in places where the earth was exposed. Behind clouds, the sun at noon seemed to have reached a
place from which it would never move. It seemed hung
once and for all in its place in the sky, falling on everything with a thick, warming light.

"Don't tell me the war has begun to get you down," he
said, looking at her with new curiosity. A gentling process
was taking place in him as he observed her. The fragility
she'd felt buried in him now seemed to radiate through
his character, suffusing his attitude toward her with pro-
tectiveness. "Don't tell me the war has begun to get you
down?" he repeated softly.

"No more than anything else."

"Well, it should get you down more than anything. The
war is horrendous. And it's having horrendous effects on
the country. If you read the papers every day, normal existence is unreal, uninteresting—worse—anyone who can
lead a normal existence right now has got something
wrong with him."

She nodded, feeling a terrible lack of relation between
her real preoccupation and the evils of the Vietnam War.
The war's horrors threatened her now because they
existed; they seemed to dominate the world, and yet she
did not have a single emotion about the small Asian country. On TV news maps it looked a little like Florida. That
was all. That was the only feeling in her whole body
about Vietnam. But the thickness of its existence around
her—knowing a large part of Nathan's mind was completely involved in the Vietnam rice crop and weekly
death rate, knowing that he could actually make sense of
the war, feel deeply about it and also have his regular,
personal emotions: the thought of this exhausted her.
Without at all lightening her misery of self-centeredness,
her picture of how much Nathan incorporated made her

feel eccentric, unimportant, dumb. Though she'd dismissed him in the past as an emotional shrimp, now she questioned the importance she'd vested in knowing her emotions. Her real feelings were so queer and wrong, they were inadmissible. They were hopelessly snarled. She would never be able to live by them; they were too chaotic, yet she remained mired in emotion.

His foreignness, the foreignness of Vietnam, of the whole immense world outside her made her stomach ache, not with hunger but with a gnawing fear of her own nonexistence. She clung to the sun's warmth, feeling she was only real to the extent that she was hot and thus sensible to herself, though in this state the heat and her ache merged so that she was entirely diffuse, unspecific, pointless.

"Why are you so quiet? Are you depressed? Do you want to talk?"

The niceness in his voice and question was just what made her unable to answer. She was afraid his kindness would get her to take herself seriously, that she would cry and admit she knew nothing about the war or any of the things he was interested in. If she told him that the unbridgeable gulf between them depressed her, then that would be true of their relations, but her real emotions would still be beneath words, where he could not get at them. And if he started to comfort her about the unbridgeable gulf, the chasm would gape still wider without his knowing it or without her being able to say why.

He opened one of the rickety white wood gates and followed her through. When he came up alongside her, he laid his big, muscular arm around her waist.

"What's wrong?" he murmured sweetly.

"Oh, nothing, just very dark and very bleak. In the beginning, you know, there was nothing and no man made no one and saw that it was nothing." She had no idea where any of this came from, but he was charmed, she could tell, though it was still as if they were talking in code. She carried the joke along, making it more and more lugubrious until the notion was exhausted, and they had come to the path into the pine forest. He drew her in under the boughs, raised like twirled skirts, and led her over the thick blanket of rust-colored needles which pricked under her bare feet.

He took her to the far corner where the pines ended, though the needles extended smoothly in a corridor to where the regular wood began, full of vines and brush, hawthorn trees, spruce and oak whose brittle leaves gleamed wetly in the veiled light.

"Take that," he said and kissed her. "Take that and that and that," he repeated, kissing her repeatedly and pressing his hands into the small of her back, forcing her to tilt her head as she withdrew from his pursuing mouth.

"No," she moaned. "No," she said sadly.

"Yes, yes, yes," he muttered laughingly. "I'm going to break every taboo in your body."

He pressed his mouth to the base of her throat and gathered her up into his embrace. She felt him wrapped round her like a towel, as if he'd lifted her out of a bath and swaddled her in warm terry cloth. She yielded passively to the comforts of being held, letting herself be laid on the ground and caressed. The pleasure of his touch lapped at her awareness, and as he slowly moved his hand beneath her clothes, finding her breast, and then stroking her belly as he gently undid her pants, and finally strumming her between her legs, she responded mournfully, knowing in some dim way that this was inevitable, that she might stop him now but succumb another time. An awful sorrow heaved up in her, a feeling that the final physical act would be empty of her real presence, the way speech no longer embodied her spirit.

She shook with grief, with unbearable knowledge, with the ghostly elusiveness of life and of herself. She was shattered, shivering with disappointment, and suddenly trembling, ferocious, biting him wildly on the neck and shoulders, pulling at his clothes, the inside of her own chest flushed with something sweet and irresistible like melted chocolate. All her sensations seemed to vibrate tautly along inner wires, a network of silver threads stretching from his moving hand to the end of every limb. For one instant her body tore away from her and raced pell-mell toward dissolution. Then the tumble of her feelings fired her with panic and as quickly as she'd grown passionate, she leapt up, staggering as she tried to pull her clothes around her.

There in the forest, in the clear light, their nakedness seemed shocking to her, even sordid, particularly the way Nathan was knocked back on his elbow, his clothes in disarray, the undulating muscle of his chest and stomach exposed and white (his skin was the sort that never tanned), his pants half open, half pulled down, revealing his albino pubic hair and purple erection.

"What happened?" he cried, and his look of anguish and humiliation also seemed sordid to her, the repulsive reminder that this actually was happening, though the fact that it was seemed a blot on her confusion, the vision attending her own near climax.

For just as she'd woken from her trance, and found herself close to the edge, with her pulses quickening, her restraint flying by like banks beside a river as it surges toward a waterfall, just then, as she had despairingly thought she would give up and hurl herself into what she could not stop from happening anyway, just then she saw her virginity as the only fixed, changeless thing in a streaming world: the only part of her that the world had not touched. At the very lip of the falls, on the verge of letting go, she clung to the arbitrary perch of her virginity, knowing it was makeshift and temporary, a dilapidated shack in which she felt she could store the secrets of her secret self—a self she didn't know, or didn't want to know, a self that continually avoided being caught and yet must reside somewhere, presumably there where the world had never entered, in a safe place no one had ever seen. Without this security, she would be utterly defenseless. There would be nothing between her essence and the moving world, nothing between her and death.

"Sorry, sorry, sorry," she wept, but continued to dress. Wisecracks barked at the heels of her larger, inchoate swirling feelings and added to her inarticulateness, nipped painfully at her own misery. I wouldn't do it for a million dollars, she heard her own inner voice saying, followed by a chorus from her brother, yeah, then how about all the tea in China?

"Wait," said Nathan as she began to back away. "Wait," he said, pulling his own clothes around him. "Talk to me; don't go off like that."

Her tongue was snarled by a welter of tones and conflicting feelings. She waved her hands wildly, sobbing and shaking her head to rid herself of her tears, terrified by having gone to pieces, but almost proud that she could feel so strongly; ashamed, finally, for having been unkind to Nathan when he had only been kind to her, but also depressed by the thought that he could afford to be kind because the experience didn't involve half the complexity it involved for her; furious that she didn't dare lose her virginity, and appalled by the seriousness of what she was going through; aware of her predicament as one she'd mocked in prissy girls, and seeing herself both as a figure of fun and yet beyond help because she couldn't say what was wrong. Finally, she spat out bitterly through gritted teeth, in halting fragments, "Middle . . . class . . . sexual . . . guilt."

"I know, I know, OK, OK," he soothed. "You're not the only one. We all have it."

His niceness was exactly what was wrong, what she held against him. Niceness wasn't enough, could not carry her over the complexities that loomed here for her. The phrase "boy scout socialism" popped into her mind, followed by an old familiar voice saying, go on, give yourself a break. Turn on your heels and get going. He'll get over it. What the hell, he can't want you for yourself. We all know you're here today, gone tomorrow.

Hello, old pal, she thought, realizing she'd missed this private tone, and that while it was gone she'd been through *a lot*—she'd nearly been swallowed up by stuff hanging around out there in the universe. Now that the old devil was back in the saddle, she felt much better, and wondered if she hadn't imagined things which there was no need to account for.

"I'm sorry," she said, but she continued to button her shirt and tucked it into her pants.

He sighed unhappily, pulling his pants on while he still lay there on the ground. Then he stood up, drawing on the work shirt he'd shed at some point while they were necking. She noticed that he had a funny look on his face, as if he'd just eaten a bad clam. At the same time, he seemed to be struggling to keep the bad clam down. The last time she'd seen a look like this on his face—last night —they had sex ahead of them. Now it was behind them. What was she supposed to do? What could she do? She couldn't tell him all the compliments she'd told him already the night before. And she hadn't had any time to develop some new ones. Still, for reasons not yet clear to her, she felt called upon to buck him up a little. The fact was, she did feel sorry for him now, though in a way he might not have appreciated.

She didn't pity him because he seemed hurt. She pitied him because whenever he was hurt he acted like such a jerk. He got this incredibly dumb look on his face, as now, when he just looked terrible. Why so glum, chum? Don't you know, you gotta be tougher? Tough, as my dad says, is when you don't give a goddamn about all the people who don't give a goddamn about you.

"Nathan," she began, but it was a complete stab in the dark. She still had no idea what she could or should say.

He swiveled his head away from her and started off, limping slightly. Everything seemed to go to a man's leg. It must be some kind of phallic symbol. Too much coffee made her father limp. Hurt feelings made Nathan limp. Five minutes ago she had just about had a nervous breakdown, but did you see her limping?

Still, there must be some way to salvage the situation. Just because her feelings had been so complex, and his were now so hurt, it seemed humanly important to find a formula which would make them feel better with themselves and with each other. There was nothing in her feelings for Nathan that resembled the magical transformation out of herself into Chace, but on some sort of scales she and Nathan were equivalents. Morally and/or psychologically they weighed the same in her mind. Which was why she felt answerable to him at that moment. Seeing this, and feeling this was a discovery of a true bond between them, she was relieved. She honestly wanted to make peace, and she had something real which, in honesty, she felt she could give.

"Nathan, have you ever had the feeling you were turning into someone else?"

"Of course not."

"Well, in my experience I realize I have two ways of reacting to other people. One is that—wham—I just *am* the other person. It's actually an incredibly delicious experience, though it strikes in odd places. I might as well tell you I have been both my sister and her boyfriend in previous incarnations. Now my other way of reacting is the way I react to you. It means you're a stranger to me, and I have to think to know what you're thinking. I have to work to figure you out. I don't have a lot of natural feel for what's going on inside you."

"I'm glad to hear you admit it. You're very insensitive to other people's feelings, and I'm just amazed to find out that you know you are."

"Now, wait a minute. I'm not attacking you, I'm leveling with you. I'm telling you how my feelings actually work."

"Look," said Nathan. "If anybody knows how your feelings work, it's me. You don't think I've seen your feelings at work? How about when you blew my head off yesterday? How about the time you went to sleep in my face? That was weird. Your feelings are weird. And they're unpleasant, too."

"I didn't ask you for your opinion. I didn't even ask you to hang around me. And for a big fat left-winger, I think you're being completely unfair right now. I think you think your hurt feelings are more important than my hurt feelings, and just because I didn't pooch you up, and pet you to death back there, you're still having a fit. I'm offering you equality and honesty and all you want is compliments."

"And I'm telling you that you are the biggest bitch I

have ever met, the most unsympathetic person, let alone
woman, which you are far from really being, and I would
just like to add that you wouldn't know equality if it
punched you in the nose. Your idea of equality is that you
can treat me like dirt, but that is my idea of the slave
mentality turned upside down."

Lucky for them they had marched right up the hill to
the turn where he could go his way and she could go hers.
They separated with a violence, each one in a huff designed to offend the other, though both missed the other's
performance because neither deigned to turn back.

8

If Christopher had moved the swallow's nest when he first knew about it, everything would have been fine. But he didn't. It had not actually seemed necessary. Though the adult birds did fly through the living room from time to time, the work had not been affected until all the walls had been torn down. By then, four wet, featherless babies had been hatched, and the nest had been exposed, resting on a beam in the corner of the roof. Once the plaster was down, the parents' droppings fell in a wider and wider circumference, but it just seemed too brutal to remove the nest before the little birds were big enough to fly away.

Their pursuit of their task was so pure and poignant and irrelevant. How removed they were from the true life of the globe, the life of power, and yet these creatures went about their business as if it were important. They made him ache.

And then he did something he did not normally do. He did not bury the emotion the birds aroused in him. He let his feeling grow. First his tenderness about them seemed to swell in a perfectly understandable way. He felt toward them as he did toward Foster. He had always been a dog lover; well, now he'd become a bird lover too. As the baby swallows grew into svelte little fledglings—eager to try their wings, lining up behind their parents for flying lessons, always making a tremendous racket, but particularly if any human trespassed what they came to believe was their space—as the birds grew and prepared to depart, Christopher's tenderness toward them seemed to attract more tenderness.

He began to make a sort of fool of himself over these swallows, acting like a man hopelessly, pathetically in love. In one part of himself he didn't care what anyone thought, he was delirious with feeling. But the other part of himself, the civilized, socialized part, knew it couldn't go on. Still, the lover—the man with three days' growth of beard, bellowing in an alleyway, hammering the brick wall of the building in which she lived, shedding tears that burnt his cheeks—the lover had to be tricked. Christopher had to do the awful thing quickly, in public, so that the act was outside and visible where the mad lover could not prevent it. Unless he was really and truly crazy and was going to make a fool out of himself for a sparrow. Or was it a swallow? He'd never known the names of birds.

One swift stroke with the broom handle had done the

dirty trick. But how was he to know that she'd already filled the nest with eggs again? And what was Foster doing? It was awful! The old labrador looked up dizzily, his face a parody of the proud expression he used to have when he excelled in field trials. Christopher had stared back at Foster in a daze. In his dream, Cuba came to him as a beautiful brownish Latin woman; she wore a tight-fitting red dress, high-heeled, toeless shoes (amazing ankles), a black tasseled shawl to match the color of her sleek hair: a mistress of the mind. Passionate, trembling, southern, untrustworthy. She came to him out of a tropical landscape he had never visited. A land of parrots and gambling casinos. As if his life had led to 1961 step by step by understandable step, and then suddenly had rolled up like a window shade, leaving him stranded on a strange beach in the company of babbling foreigners, none of whom could keep a secret.

Christopher turned around, but, having nowhere to go, he turned around again.

"Is everything all right, Mr. Nicholas?" Nathan asked.

No, things were not all right, but could he hide how bad they were? And then he thought it was luck that put Nathan in front of him at this exact moment. As soon as this thought crossed his mind, Christopher doubted the reasoning. Had he imagined that there would be some salvation in making his point of view clear to Nathan? He had. Christopher took him by the shoulders and said in a burning whisper, "Do you realize how easy it would have been to have Castro shot from a crowd?"

But had he really said Castro? He didn't know. Christopher tried to read Nathan's face for what he'd done. Nathan looked like he was going to cry. Or was he going to laugh? Oh Lord, help me, Christopher prayed. Help me hold my tongue. Help me button my lip. And lo, con-

trary to His usual indifferent treatment, He sent an angel
to assist Christopher. A beautiful, innocent, trusting girl
came and took him away. More poignant, more humbling
that she should lead him off by his wrist and not by his
hand. As if he were so far out of line, the normal physical
symbolism did not apply. Though her firm grip was
sweet, they could not go out hand in hand. It was as if
he'd been handcuffed by an officer of the divine law.

Christopher gratefully succumbed, refreshed by her
mercy, by her *ignorant* mercy. Katherine forgave him,
though she did not know what it was she forgave. She
made him feel there was nothing he could have done
which was unforgivable, and this cured him of his inco-
herence, though now depression came in its place. Hadn't
he always known the invasion wasn't going to work? That
it had been a dreadful mistake from the start? There were
too many people involved. The Cubans in Miami were
too susceptible, too volatile, wouldn't hold together on
any issue. Going through with it, knowing the plan probably couldn't fly. Too late to admit it was wrong. Willing
the fantasy aloft. A poorly hatched plot, gobbled up before it had its chance to try its wings.

He was delivered to his own doorstep, an angel before
him, the mob at his back. Herr Muehler, Chace and
Bucky quietly awaited their signal. Would the angel give
them the sign to lynch him? Would she let him keep his
life? Did he want it? What was left of his glorious inherit-
ance? A poor little acre which he barely had the strength
to harvest. All he would reap was his failure and shame.

Once indoors, the angel called upstairs and his mortal
wife descended. She was the one person whose judgment
he could not bear. Katherine murmured something into
her mother's ear. "Well," said Joanne calmly, "it's almost
time for lunch. Why don't you all go wash up?" Her gaze

brushed kindly over Katherine and settled on her husband, who knew it was him she held in her arms. She was uncanny in her sensitivity to his moods, as responsive and musical as she was when they danced.

"Something awful has happened," Christopher blurted involuntarily.

"I know," Joanne answered quietly. "I know," she murmured, acting her part of the duet.

I know! I know! How did she know? What did she know? He wasn't even sure himself of how these plots and counterplots connected. Did she know there had been a direct order from Castro to Oswald? He didn't. No one did: at least no one he knew. Or did she know for a fact that the Mafia in the CIA's hire were so mixed up with the thugs in Castro's hire that they caught each other's crimes like germs? What did she know, exactly? That the country was wildly off course, up to its neck in bloody implications? Well, that wasn't news. Everybody knew that.

As the kids drifted to their rooms, Christopher drew unexpected strength from denying his wife's sympathy. He started up the stairs in front of her, turning back only to invite Herr Muehler to join him in a prelunch martini. This suggestion put new life in the old boy, and he trotted past Joanne to follow at Christopher's heels. As Christopher rounded the top of the stairs, he saw Joanne, leaning toward Chace, coming slowly after them.

His wife was wearing a loose pale purple shirt and rusty rose skirt. The colors of her clothes and the soft cotton fabrics were somehow the conductors of her voice, her being, confiding and receiving confidences from the handsome boy beside her. Christopher felt her lilac ocean subtly stir under his glare. He wondered if she contained more than he did, whether she had taken his thin dissemblance in with what was truly vulnerable about him. Clearly, she was finding out what she could from Chace, yet even if she were to learn every last fact, Christopher wasn't sure this would make her wiser than she already was. He was never sure if she understood the awful evidence of her senses. In any case, she did not resist it. Life washed in and out of her consciousness like tides washing in and out to sea, and if she didn't have a policy, or wasn't a teacher, she was the next best thing.

She was richly experienced, full of the awful confidences people pressed on her involuntarily: strangers on trains, confiding their adulteries and sorrows; all her own friends turning to her, unable to help themselves, responding to her fluent communion with passion both dark and light. Yet she remained untouched by stupidity or cheapness. She had the ocean's undertow and pulled the world down into herself, taking in the whole murderous order of creation, the myriad cruelties of love. She was related to the moon and, like the sea, she could cleanse herself, scraping the sordid grime from whatever evil she had known, rendering it into her own essential, natural force.

There were things in his life he would never be rid of. Blank checks of forgiveness from angels weren't enough. He needed his corruption recognized, known by the proper judge before he could feel acquitted. At his elbow, Herr Muehler was giving him home recipes for martinis.

"Do you know the song that Chace and his roommates taught me?"

Christopher shook his head.

> *"Heart full of joy, hearts full of youth,*
> *Nine parts gin to one part vermouth."*

"We'd be dead if we drank that. Maybe that's what people mean when they say 'dead drunk.'"

Herr Muehler patted his friend and gave him a gleaming, loving, touching look. Christopher's spirit rose hopefully, yearning toward the possibility of real, acceptable mercy. Was this old satyr his proper judge? Did he have the necessary grim knowledge? Hadn't Herr Muehler been forced, morally forced to become an adventurer just to survive? The history of Europe had driven him to extremes: the very place from which he might have the best view of Christopher's situation.

He put gin and vermouth—three parts to one—in the silver cocktail shaker, tossed in a handful of ice and began to play a Latin rhythm. Christopher shook it high; he shook it low. Cha-cha-cha. He filled two little wine glasses with the oily brew.

Herr Muehler raised his glass gleefully, his eyes like merry crescents.

"Where's Diana?" Joanne asked, coming into the kitchen as the two men were taking their first sips.

"With Nathan," Katherine said on her way to the living room.

"Kids, you can set the table. Herr Muehler, don't you want to wash?" Joanne asked with velvety command. She was, in fact, asking him to leave the room for a minute.

"Of course, of course," he complied, downing two gulps. "One for strength and one for good measure, right?"

"Right," chortled Christopher, in deep league with Herr Muehler.

As soon as they were alone, Joanne maneuvered closer to him, inquiring softly, "What's wrong, sweetie? What happened over there at The Bleakers?"

Her body was a born magician with an IQ off the charts in intuition. But to Christopher just then she was like a great natural athlete who'd never lost a game, and so had not the slightest idea that what she had was unusual, or that her act could have been astonishing if she'd developed it. There were some exams you couldn't pass with intuition and he was one of them. His problem could not be solved by uncritical extrasensory perception. She would need to know more, much more: she would need to study economics and history and the nature of justice. She would have to look out the window of the living room she'd made so beautiful, beyond the green and stony loveliness of the landscape, beyond the blue Narragansett Bay, beyond the still unravished borders of America to back roads in small foreign countries where scorched craters gaped and men were hastily executed with guns made in Massachusetts. And more, she would have to see and know in her bones, as he had come to feel in his bones, that her living room and the landscape were held in death's palm, not just the death that would naturally come to them all, but the death he himself had assigned with his signature. For years this had been the staff of life for him, this *shit*—yes, shit, there was no other word for it —and if he hadn't eaten it, the world would have been shittier than it already was. But even if all that sank in, she would have to know still more, she would have to know the dread, and the reasoning against dread, and the dreadful precautions had led them all into universal contamination.

Joanne clearly felt his silent assault on her. She began to move briskly back and forth from stove to sink, dumping the hard-boiled eggs into the copper colander with defensive quickness. She wanted a crumb from him, any little recognition that he saw them as in it together. When he wouldn't give it to her, she began to scold him for something completely unrelated. "While you were gone, I finally got into your study. It's a complete mess, but I hardly know how to start cleaning up. You've got papers everywhere! I don't know if I should look at them or not. But I can't very well clean with my eyes closed."

"Phooey. It's nowhere near that spooky. Do you think they'd send me into retirement with a whole lot of secret papers? If you want to find out what I've been doing at the office, just go read Tad Szulc in the New York *Times*."

Christopher assumed she was hinting at her own fears about his work, but he saw this from a hundred miles away, a distance which also forced him to see her body as the mechanical doll of her alarm. Gone the blinding grace, her subtle, fiery radiance which burned without scorching. This alienation was bitter to him, but no more bitter than everything else. It was all bitter, ashen, bereft. And when and if he finally taught her this lesson, maybe they would have something in common again.

The egg salad sandwiches and soup were put on the table. Christopher poured wine into the grown-ups' glasses. Herr Muehler returned in a clean shirt—as threadbare as the dirty one had been, but pressed. They got ready to sit down and the phone rang. Joanne answered it. Christopher could hear her voice, rising and falling with a gladness only he recognized as insincere. "El-lie! How *are* you?"

A long pause while Ellie told Joanne in detail about her latest disasters.

"You'll never guess who's turned up," said Joanne. "Chace Harsh, Frank's son? Yes, he's Katherine's beau."

"Those dumb, broken-down dames cost about two hundred dollars a day. Just to keep them in drink and telephones. There oughta be a law," Christopher grumbled, though he was also amused. For sheer awfulness, nothing was funnier—in a world struggling with ghastly, insoluble problems—nothing was funnier than Ellie Snow's nose

dive. If life were a play, her sob story would be trotted
out as comic relief to the true headaches of the cold war.
Hell, she was downright funny if you held her up to Vietnam. A man could split his sides thinking of her having
one or ten too many, her coherence slowly sinking as her
garbled tale of how she once slept with Kennedy began
to rise. Let's have a slide up there side by side with the
chiefs of staff discussing whether they can use the bombing of North Vietnam as a pretext for going in to wipe out
the Chinese arsenal of A-bombs. It was particularly awful
and therefore especially funny that this shipwrecked doll
and these pale, serious men were somehow related because they had both, so to speak, served under the same
leader.

Christopher's interior adventurer was piqued to bitter
humor by the goad of Ellie Snow and Kennedy. Her story
was probably true. She had once been extraordinary-look-
ing, a champagne blonde with legs like Ginger Rogers.
Kennedy was famous for sleeping with anything that
moved. To the degree that Christopher was depressed by
the thought of Kennedy's philandering (it was the least of
the world's worries), his own spirit was honed to a bright,
high finish. He began to hold forth with a sandwich in
one hand and a glass of wine in the other. Christopher
talked with his mouth full, and sometimes, after he swallowed a bite, he sucked his big front teeth. His earthiness
was lit by barbaric, ducal splendor; his confidence was
such that he dared present his own case to Herr Muehler,
this gypsy judge.

It was, however, only politic to take the long way
around, and recognizing this as the key to his own defense, Christopher began, "Of course, much depended on
Kennedy. True, he was willing to learn, and he was tough
the way you've got to be tough if you're going to govern.

I mean if you're going to make decisions in the only part of government which really makes any difference. I am talking about foreign policy and the decisions of government which pertain to weapons, our relations with our allies and our relations with our enemies. Basically, all questions of foreign policy boil down to who you can afford to kill and who you can't."

He could not avoid noticing that every word he said extended the pall he was mysteriously casting over his children. Was he repeating himself? Herr Muehler was giving him his characteristic attention—a mixture of concentration and inattentive, forgiving love. His son looked ill. Bucky slumped against the back of his chair. Despite a tan, the color of his face was shading into lobster tomalley. He had stopped eating, though his eyes were glued to his plate. Katherine had leveled a cold, inquiring glance in his direction, the only child to meet his effort part way, and yet in such a scientific way she made him feel like a bug.

Help, he cried silently to her. *Help!* But they were all filmed over by a thin layer of ice. His voice was a hot flame of will, gushing out of his glacial lips arching toward the moon to no avail. He did not thaw. His children retreated further from him. He began to tear off chunks of himself and hurl them onto the bonfire of logic. If the fire was allowed to die, if no one saw his signal, he'd be left to expire alone on this desert island of isolation. He might perish anyway, consumed piece by piece in the flames kept burning to show he was alive.

"I've had some experience, as you will perhaps recall, in carrying out our country's foreign policy. I've slugged it out in the arena, as a person has to if he's going to fight for his beliefs." Here he swung his hands in opposite circles and shoved his lower lip forward in a dinstinctly

Gaulish "*et alors*" look. When he continued, he pressed his fingers against his lapels, lifting his prominent nose and saying, "I would not for the world ask you to consider my experience." Though his gestures were the ones he used when he was confident, he realized he'd taken himself back into the vicinity of distress and dread, that he really wasn't sure what he was going to say, or if he should. But there was no turning back. He forged on, both afraid he would speak gobbledygook and afraid that he would be absolutely clear. "I mean merely that my experience in terms of its outcome was not all success, that is, in its likeness to a definition of failure I accept in some ways, but not in others, what could be called my experience provides a convenient test to illustrate my theories. There are dirty jobs to be done in a dirty world. Someone has to do them. Do you realize that the people who are keeping America safe are neurotics and criminals? When Hitler was the enemy, good men behaved heroically. Same for Stalin. But now only the sewer rats will do what has to be done. The good men can't because they've agreed to pretend nothing dirty's going on. You see, the good men have agreed that goodness itself is only a pretense, but a very important one, perhaps the most important one in a world without goodness. Power is the reality, goodness the illusion. Children, your father has been in the business of illusion."

Both of them were now turned toward him, their faces like subjects under hypnosis, as though they were all in a dream. Herr Muehler looked more attentive than ever and more surprised. Nothing like crime to liven up the party. For Christopher the worst was still to come. The fear was like the fear just before jumping. Wondering if your parachute was going to open. The British sergeant's voice in his ear, "Piss off, Yank."

Whang! He was out. His nose hit the far rim of the hole in the plane's belly. His head was knocked back so it smacked the rear metal edge. A transition of pure pain. Pure pain did not hurt. It was completely illuminating and obliterating at the same time.

"But did I make a go of it?" Christopher asked theatrically. "No, I failed, failed miserably. Somehow I was not only no good at contriving the necessary appearances, but also I couldn't escape contamination. Listen! you could probably find a run-of-the-mill Hollywood director able to do a better job than we did. We were lousy at deception, but we all got dragged down. It's so pathetic. Think of me, a good labrador with my Harvard Law School diploma in my mouth, wagging my tail, retrieving like a good boy for all the senior prefects. How did I end up in the same cell as Howard Hunt? You might just as well be really democratic, really fair and throw in Oswald, and once you've got something in common with him you're only a breath away from Goebbels. Once you've sunk low enough, you begin to rise on the ladder of monsters. You start out in the religious war against Hitler, and you end up in Stalin's shoes."

He was utterly spent. The fear of dying had given way to the bliss of dying. He was safe, limp in the arms of his harness as he softly fell in amniotic darkness. His legs trembled sweetly. This was his reward for straining his courage, for striving, for not giving up, for deliberately facing death though death was terrifying to him.

"I'm exhausted," said Joanne, hamming it up as she staggered out of the kitchen. "What that poor woman has been through!"

"Is she the one who's had three lobotomies?" asked Bucky, reviving a little.

"Don't make it more awful than it already is," groaned

Joanne, filling a plate for herself at the sideboard. "It's *so* terrible what's happened, *so* hard to understand. When I first met her, she was irresistible. She could still hold her liquor in those days, and she'd be OK right up to the end of the evening, then—whammo!—she'd be incoherent. But while she was still making sense, she was amazing. Needless to say, I can't remember a single punch line, but we were constantly passing her remarks around. Was she the one who said, 'How can they tell?' when she heard Calvin Coolidge was dead? I guess it was Dorothy Parker, but that's just the sort of joke Ellie might have cracked."

Christopher was still floating. He was empty. He felt no pity or fear, but said quietly, "It's hard to believe those people have survived, if you can call their lives survivals. They never changed, but how could they avoid it?"

"Ellie was a friend of your father's first wife," Joanne said knowingly to Bucky.

"Not the Wicked Witch of the North?" Bucky asked with mock horror; her son could always be counted on to team up with his mother against Christopher's childless first marriage. "No wonder she came to a bad end."

"The only thing separating them from the true horrors of existence was a thin curtain of money," Christopher said. "When that parted, even just slightly, when they started running short, or when they couldn't buy their way out of certain harsh realities—like Ellie's second husband, remember, who was impotent and wanted to do a whole lot of strange things in the bedroom? Well, when that happened, those girls went to pieces."

"But we were no different," objected Joanne. "You and I both loved a good time. The descriptions of you at college were incredible. As for me, I know when the war started, it gave me my chance to leave home. It was my chance to go find adventure."

"But I broke away," Christopher cried, tossing his head and roaring. "I tell you, I broke away from my family. My whole life has been devoted to breaking away and I won't have you casually lumping me in with a bunch of worthless old sillies who'd be sleeping it off in the Bowery if their divorce settlements hadn't been so goddamned handsome."

As though to demonstrate the central gesture of his life, he thrust himself out of his chair with a shove that sent it back against the wall. But, then, the energy he threw into rising carried him into a white-hot frame of mind. *I inherited my mother's social conscience* was written there in boiling silver. The idea seized him for a second, happened so fast he saw but did not understand the words, and yet they made his brain shriek. The sensation of the soundless howl was as bright and shrill as the alarm of an air raid.

He commanded himself to move, but a screw was being driven slowly through his chest. He was frozen first by the fear of the pain and then by the pain itself. He gazed at Joanne and Bucky and Katherine. He was drained of all intention save a commitment to endure. His face reddened and one cheek grimaced involuntarily. He was dead and in hell: condemned to suffer in front of the only person who could release him, but cut off from her because her standards were improper. He could not accept her uncritical warmth, could not yield to the comforts she offered. For her, home was where you went when you failed. For him, home was what you left.

And then the pain released him. He could breathe again and move. Joanne rose in her seat, saying, "Are you all right, Christopher? Are you all right?"

He snorted. "I've had it. I'm not worth throwing in the trash. But I'm still alive in case that's important."

"Did you have an attack?" Joanne asked. "What was it?"

"Did I have a heart attack? No. It's my angina. It's just a little worse than usual, that's all." He spoke coldly and started toward the library in a proud, angry way calculated to keep anyone from following him.

9

Joanne had welcomed Chace and Herr Muehler's arrival, and she was glad to see them go. They'd brought new life into the household, yet, as always seemed to be the case with life, what began as fun reached inexorably toward chaos. Another day of guests and the place would be a shambles. As it was, though they had been gone almost ten days, she was not entirely sure she could get the lid back on the pot, though it certainly helped to have the children rising and going to work every day. There was nothing else for them to do *except* go to work at The Bleakers. But this was the moment for precisely that. If

Joanne craved the pleasures of relation and intimacy, of knowing what was going on in the world, of being in on her share of the gossip, she was also exhausted by intense activity. She required deep draughts of solitude to support her addiction to social experience.

She loved the return of routine as much as she loved departing from it, particularly when her schedule was involved in planning its own overthrow. Such was now the case as she turned to the problem of organizing the party to celebrate the completed Bleakers at the end of August. She did this kind of thing well, and she did it right. Though the party was going to be on Saturday, clearly the whole weekend would be taken up. The children's friends were all going to be imports, drawn from the boarding-school network throughout New England. All these people were going to be drawn out of the world into the world unto itself of Nicholases in summer residence at the Saunderstown barn. Motel rooms would have to be reserved, many starting on Friday, because guests who came from far away would come then to justify taking a long trip for one party.

In her own youth, Joanne had gone far and wide to parties. She was embarrassed to admit that her mother had actually taken her out of school on a tour of debutante parties. There was, however, a great difference between the parties she had attended with her mother and the one she was now planning to give. With slight variations, the people at her debutante dances were always the same, a crowd who'd grown up in Providence and who, in differing percentages, went out of town to attend their cousins' parties in Boston or a roommate's coming out in Newport. Joanne's children had no hometown, though at school they frequently associated with the offspring of their parents' hometown circles. Still, her children did not really belong to any group except their family, and this, even on good days, was an uncomfortable nest.

No matter. She was an optimistic person. She coaxed a list of names from each child, discovering as she did that Diana had the fewest friends to invite and Bucky the most. But this could be turned to the party's advantage, despite the fact that he was one year younger than his youngest sister. A party never suffered from too many men! Even if his Groton classmates were younger than his sisters, they would creat a core of connection in the midst of a party of strangers. It would take away the curse of total unfamiliarity, and then, because it was going to be a house party, people would start to know each other on Friday and, as most of them were very young, they would have the quick capacity to turn events to private jokes, and to make the weekend a novel written by the guests themselves. They would have the self-conscious sense of the dance on Saturday as the high point of the drama. They would have the energy and art to shape the plot, the buildup on Saturday, as well as Sunday's denouement.

Katherine's friends were set apart from this younger group. They were older, and then, of course, there was the fact that Chace was the son of friends of theirs, and that Herr Muehler was older than Christopher. This had the effect of pulling Katherine into the grown-up world, though Joanne found she had mixed feelings about sharing the view from the top with her oldest daughter. If Christopher were a simpler character, it might have been different. If her marriage was easily translatable, she would have welcomed all her children into it. Because of its complexity she was not at all sure she wanted one of the children in the position of an equal, someone who could subject her relationship with her husband to frank scrutiny. And then there was the problem of whether it was even healthy for a girl of Katherine's age, a girl who would probably soon be a bride, whether it was healthy for her to poke around in her parents' marriage.

When she tried to discuss Katherine's changing relation to them, when, for that matter, she tried to discuss any subject with Christopher, he was extremely difficult. Yet he came and complained of hurt feelings when she left him alone for several days. The next morning, however, when she knocked on his study door to ask him about liquor for the party, he said it was a bad time for him to talk. He wanted to be informed of what was going on, but he did not want to be inconvenienced. All summer he had been in and out of this bad mood. One side of him tacitly commanded her to approach, while the other did nothing but strew the way with difficulty, changing the rules of approach as she drew near, and then punishing her for having been wrong. Still, in some genuine sense she wished him no ill, she wished no human being ill, providing she did not have to pay reparations for his broken career. But no matter how she strained to see him fairly, he wasn't *any* human being. He was her husband and she resented him for taking his suffering out on her without, at least, letting it be a subject they could discuss. Though her impulses were virtuous and selfless, her resentment taxed her charity, taking its warmth as the price for lack of satisfaction. She gave him the sympathy of a stone saint, but she had no other kind to give as long as he was so critical.

Fortunately, her other husband, Bucky, had been more frankly tender this summer than ever before. Perhaps this was so because he was at the right age for girls, but not yet sufficiently confident to approach them. He was practicing with his mother to see whether he was as good-looking and charming as he felt was necessary. Yet it also seemed that the availability of family life, after so long without it, put him in possession of a new toy. Or maybe it was a new toy without a wheel. Though he never directly said he wished he could know his father better, Bucky seemed to be suggesting something like it in his conversations with his mother about related subjects or, more to the point, characters. Coming home from work on The Bleakers, Bucky was often inclined to mention Nathan's name to Joanne. Almost regularly, after he'd taken a soda from the icebox and before he'd showered, he came to find her working in the garden or reading upstairs on the back porch.

He would report sketchily on the day's progress—it was all moving far quicker, the work was more rewarding than he'd thought possible—and then rather timidly Bucky would engage in descriptions and speculations about those he was working with. Character analysis was a kind of forbidden fruit in Nicholas family life, one which was vaguely taboo in the presence of their father and, of course, absolutely forbidden about him. This did not stop them from being keenly interested in one another's characters, or keep them from forming elaborate theories about one another which they shared in secret conferences such as the ones Diana and Katherine often held in locked bathrooms, or late at night, after a party with drink: then the barriers really fell, and the children would stay up all night, "eyeball to eyeball" (in Joanne's phrase), dissecting every last quirk in each other's characters, down to the finest shade of meaning, like the time in 1958 when Katherine threw Bucky's big fire engine out the window. It was well known to the children that their mother was drawn to this delicious apple of speculation, and that she could be tempted into eating it on occasions when her husband was out of earshot.

She knew they knew she could be seduced. Part of the pleasure of having Bucky come find her after work was the courtship involved. He had to master his timidity while wooing her participation, playing John Alden, in a sense, to her Priscilla by making Nathan seemingly the subject. In his attempts to bend Nathan to his ulterior motives, Bucky had to let his complaints shine through the loopholes in his admiration. This was tough. It was particularly tough because he had no quarrel with the way Nathan approached work. He was a light taskmaster, willing to do any job that he asked others to do, and also open to any suggestions. His leadership was naturally affirmed by the fact that he knew what needed to be done and the others didn't. Bucky's quarrel, which was inadmissible, had to do with the resentment he felt over his father's interest in Nathan. He showed, Joanne felt, great imagination in discussing this without really saying what he meant.

"I would say the only awkwardness in the work setup comes from Nathan and Diana."

"Really?" Joanne purred, taking a handful of weeds and pulling them out of the rosebed. "Do you think they're an item?"

"Well, he likes her, but she doesn't like him."

"That was my impression, too. But I still don't see why she's so hard on him. There's no other beau for her to enjoy this summer, why not Nathan?"

"It's odd to hear you call him beau," Bucky laughed. "He just doesn't fall into that category. No one in our generation does. And particularly not him. I mean, is there any such thing as a radical-Marxist beau?"

"I wonder why your father finds him so attractive?" Joanne asked, knowing she was supposed to. She wrapped her knees in her arms and looked at Bucky with false but earnest innocence.

"That's really a good question. Have you ever heard Dad's speech about the American appetite for idealism?"

Joanne shook her head, though she had heard the speech several times. It touched her to discover what a student Bucky was of his father's character, and she was happy to give him a chance to show how he'd done his homework.

"OK, well, Dad's idea is that the hallmark of Americanness, I guess you could say, is our appetite for idealism. In his father's generation it hungered for European culture. But now Europe is living off our crumbs, and we're looking for ways to satisfy our moral yearnings. In other words, we're still the same old new Adam."

"I like the way you put it," Joanne said, smiling and smoking. "Even if it is your father's idea, I think you've made it sing."

"Thanks. Hum a few bars, etcetera. Right? Anyway, I think he's drawn to Nathan because Nathan spouts Marxist ideology when you push the right button, and Daddy thinks this is the sign that he's a true American. You're going to say it's farfetched, but I really think Daddy thinks Nathan is the new new Adam. Even though Daddy doesn't agree with him."

Joanne thoughtfully tapped the long ash from her cigarette. Her son's elaborate insights made her want to weep. How carefully he'd pieced together the evidence about his father. She did not dare look at him lest she stroke his arm or leg. Her strongest impulse was to console him physically, but she knew it would represent the worst fraternizing if she did. She would be condoning the son's criticism of the father, admitting that Christopher had neglected Bucky. She puffed her cigarette, inhaled and ran her hand through her hair.

"Where does that leave us conservatives?" Bucky asked, making one of his father's gestures, shrugging his shoulders and touching both of them with his fingertips. "Aren't we moral, too? Basically, I think Daddy's a conservative just like me. He's sort of flirting with the left, not because he likes it. No, he thinks Nathan's Marxism may be the new necessary evil . . ."

"You've got to understand what a hard time your father has been through. He just knocked himself out for the government. But he feels he failed. And he's looking everywhere to see why."

Bucky drank from the gingerale, nodding. His eyes closed, so that his lashes lay babyishly on his cheek for an instant, and in that instant Joanne desired him. No sooner did the desire spring up than she squashed it, shocked. How could she be such a sewer? As a rebellious girl (a somewhat rebellious girl), it had been important to her not to be "nice"; she strove to be thought of as "naughty." But as a woman, the dark abundance of her own nature often frightened her.

The voices of her daughters reached her like refreshing breezes, clearing her murky interior atmosphere as they called her from the upstairs porch. "Hey, Mum, Bucky," Diana called, and Katherine echoed, "Hey, come up and see what Chace sent us."

Joanne stood, though as she did, she caught the worrying hollowness in Katherine's echoey voice. Joanne bristled slightly, almost cross with her oldest daughter for drawing on sympathies which were involved with her son. If there had been some way to avoid sharing Katherine's low, blue mood, Joanne would have. Just then she would have preferred to leave all feminine suffering under a rock, where she didn't have to deal with it. Hard enough to handle the sorrows, the complexities of men! But the process had begun; there was no stopping her own susceptibility.

Now, as always happened when she felt someone's misery, Joanne's sense of balance began to sink on one side until it was level with Katherine's depression, and then this space began to fill with equivalents from her own life, scenes or memories or ideas engendered by her feel of the other person's emotions. As she walked up to the porch, always with Katherine in view, Joanne flushed with partially realized recollections of her own father: waiting for him to come home from campaigning; playing cards in the kitchen with the cook, who told her the senator had been reelected; the whole house on alert; his itchy moustaches buried in her neck; sitting next to him at dinner, listening to his awful stories about poor people; his proper fear of God and socialism; later, saying her prayers while he watched and feeling akin to the poor people; feeling she, too, could be worthy of her father if she worked hard to pull herself up by her bootstraps and stood on her own two feet. Joanne's memories were drenched in the mood communicated to her by Katherine; she was remembering in her daughter's style, which made these old fragments of her life stick in her brain like pins.

Still, Joanne kept her eyes on Katherine, who did not move. She was standing beside an easel which Chace had left behind; it now supported the framed painting he'd been working on when he was visiting. It had just arrived by United Parcel and was what the girls wanted their mother and brother to see. Katherine's beauty, her rosy peach complexion, the curl of her freshly brushed hair as she stood beside the painting—all these, drenched as they were by gravity, suddenly became the image of a fact to

Joanne. By her own process of simultaneous translation, she had recognized the common experience referred to by the private language of memory.

She herself had been full of her father's face and love when, as a young woman, she had gathered her childhood together to give it away: when she lost her virginity to a boy who was later killed in the war. *Chace and Katherine are sleeping together.* She suddenly knew it without a doubt. What to do about it? How to think about it? What would she do if Christopher found out? She was scared of his knowing, as if he might be mad at her for having failed somehow. But how? Should she have told Katherine not to? What rules had she herself gone by? The rules of romance, of being swept away, of falling in love and giving herself out of wedlock as a blow against her mother's Victorian gentility. Not that she ever *told* her mother. Had her mother ever guessed? (*There* was a thought to make her dizzy with alarm.) But she'd been twenty-two the first time. Katherine was twenty. She'd trusted herself to handle the experience, but did she trust Katherine?

Joanne glanced from Katherine to Chace's canvas, which might, at that moment, have been a portrait of the atmospheric blurring between mother and daughter. It showed the pearl coalescence of sky and water, paying close attention to the difference in the surface of the bay and grayish clouds. Joanne admired the talent and intelligence in Chace's suggesting the abstract from the real, and felt a passing calm in seeing turmoil of emotion finished, refined and framed in place outside turmoil. Her still moment, however, was followed by new commotion, occasioned by Diana talking to Katherine about Chace in her imitation-Chace voice.

"Yeah, well, howdoya like the old masterpiece? This is

a guy with a fucha! And you've lucked in on the bottom story."

"Diana," Katherine protested feebly, inciting her sister to new terrier bursts of yapping appeal.

"I'm telling you, honey, the guy has got a real future. If he can do this well on paper, I'll bet you he can work miracles on walls. I think he's just about ready for housework."

At first Diana's patter was so askew and so unfunny, Joanne could not believe her ears. But finally there was no denying what an ass Diana was being. Joanne broke through her own paralysis, saying, "Diana, Diana, stop. What is wrong?"

"I'm glad you asked that question," she said in what appeared to be true confusion.

"I know you admire Chace," Joanne said softly. "But do you have to *be* him? Can't you live and let live?"

"Haven't you heard about Diana's weird condition?" Katherine asked. "If she likes you, she turns into you."

"Has she ever turned into you?" Joanne asked.

"Sure, many times," Katherine insisted. "She's great at it. Go ahead, Diana, show Mum what a good Katherine you can do."

"Is not man the animal who falls in love? Do you know why we say 'fall in love'? I mean, would not a truer description be 'I'm sunk' instead of 'I've fallen in love'? Would not 'I'm sunk' better describe what it feels like, which, as you perhaps know, is squishy, warm, and liquid? Like the sweetest drowning. And it's a hundred times better than being up against the wall, or death, as every Nicholas knows. Falling in love is that which occurs when the gulf between tradition and will gapes and we . . ."

So far the situation was strange, but it progressed still further toward unreality. Diana raised and lowered her eyebrows, looked hopeful and then despairing, tilted her head back in the attitude of a fainter, but then burst into tears. Instead of pity, Joanne felt horror. It was awful to see her own rich emotional nature gone to seed in her daughter's face. Diana threw herself into her mother's arms, saying, "Mummy, Mummy, why am I so weird?"

Joanne had to restrain an impulse to cuff her daughter. She felt like a cat whose kitten has been weaned but who comes back to try and nurse again. This was clinging after the day for clinging was done. Gently, exercising almost painful self-control, Joanne pushed Diana away, saying, "Come on, sweetie, you can pull yourself together. I know Chace is wonderful, but you don't have to walk like a sailor just because he does."

"I hate the way I act around him," Diana wailed. "I just can't help myself."

"Yes, you can," her mother insisted.

"I'd say that being in a family is the next best thing to being in an insane asylum," said Bucky.

"Well, is there any escape?" asked Katherine. "I mean, if you fall in love, does it mean you have to get locked up?"

"Well, not if you play your cards right," said Bucky, exchanging a glance with Katherine that was not missed by Joanne. It was a bawdy look they gave each other, suggesting realms of private jokes and knowledge about sex. Their summery youth made her jealous, filled her with awe, as though by being on the threshold of experience they suddenly knew more than she who had been through much. With this awe, a burst of real misery also rushed up.

The snake was coiled again in Eden. Katherine and Bucky, and even Diana, were ready now to lose their innocence, though Joanne had not yet finished losing hers.

To know temptation for the first time! It was the only time, the last time: and every other time was only a frayed variation on the first, more and more frayed as one aged, until, like her, all that one had was a remnant of sexual innocence, not even innocence—sexual ignorance, inexperience—until there was nothing one hadn't dreamt of doing upside down and backward, until one's remnant was overworked to the point of corruption, though she clung to it anyway, working it to threads in her dreams until she would have worked it to nothing and then she would be ready to die. Now that this dumb century had succeeded in bringing all this sex to the surface, what were they going to do with it?

Joanne felt an instant of panic, fearing that things were so different for her children growing up that even a parent of good will might miss the boat. One's upbringing went out of date so fast. Hers was of no use to her daughters, and her husband hadn't even heard that fathers were supposed to be friends to their sons. (Let me make this perfectly clear, she thought, I only slept with two men in my whole life—but was this one too many or three hundred too few?)

Christopher opened the screen door and beheld his wife with three of their children. The sight of him made Diana duck her head and turn her face so that he could not see she was crying. When he saw the painting, he stepped out and gave the canvas his serious attention.

"It's good," he said at last. "Is that what he's going to do? Be a painter?"

By referring to Chace as 'he,' Christopher managed to make him seem like a distant fiction. Whether he was going to be a painter or not was of no personal interest; it was only a question of objective fact.

"I guess so," said Katherine.

"Ah, well, I only hope he can make a living," said Christopher, turning around, his newspaper still in his hand. His physical presence, and the catlike (jungle cat-like) way he handled himself, made him a center of muscular grace while at the same time casting everyone else into awkwardness. Until it was clear where he was going to stand, people were thrown into confusion and kept colliding with each other as they tried to get out of his path.

As this drama passed before her eyes, Joanne became aware that she held her hand to her mouth in an attitude of horror. She stepped closer to her husband, focusing on the headlines whose meaning she had already absorbed. She forced herself to read the story of Richard Speck killing eight nurses, unable *not* to read but pierced by fear. What the last moments must have been like! Cooperating with the man, humoring his ghastly weirdness, hoping it would all pass, realizing there was no hope, feeling his fingers tighten on her throat!

"Awful, isn't it?" Christopher asked, noticing she'd been hypnotized by the front page.

"Horrible. Those poor girls. They must have been so terrified."

He closed the paper and saw she was speaking of the story under the big headlines. "Oh, you're right," he said, wrinkling his nose. "It's grisly. But, do you know, I think we have to be grateful for maniacs. At least they're isolated cases. But look at these," he said, shaking his head and tapping three smaller headlines about Hanoi calling up reserves, Ho Chi Minh's determination to fight for as long as it took, and ten young men smashing up a farmhouse where known pacifists were living. Then Christopher turned back to the editorial page and read a few lines from Reston's column, in which the analogy was drawn between the bombing of Vietnam and the use of power against blacks within the United States.

"Of course, what's funny about this is that Reston, Pillar of the Community, is mouthing left rhetoric. Nathan Baker's been getting after me about the war as an imperialist war fought by blacks, the 'oppressed class,' as he's fond of calling them. Now here's Reston saying approximately the same thing. It's all such a bloody mess," he cried, and rattled the papers with frustration; it was a mess he'd like to be involved in cleaning up.

Joanne wondered why she thought of her husband as detached. He was highly emotional, much more emotional than she was. He was going out of his mind with emotion over the world and his defeat in it. Still, she said nothing; her daughters said nothing.

Only Bucky rushed in with a word of comfort, and he got interrupted. "But the liberals . . ."

His father shook the papers at him, saying, as though waking in the middle of his own trial, "I *am* a liberal. I don't like what's going on in Cleveland and Chicago any more than Stokeley Carmichael. And I don't blame the blacks for getting their guns and shooting us down. I'm all for them." And then he sagged and said confusedly, "But, you know, if it comes to a shoot-out, I'll fight on our side. In the end, I'm on the side of the law. I just don't see any other way." He sat down in a chair and listlessly reopened the paper, withdrawing from their company back into the world of print which tortured him so.

She would never understand him, Joanne thought, watching him retreat. He was so different from her father. Maybe all men were. Her father had been distant, too, but so encouraging whenever she saw him. Her adorable papa! He was the big, burly man in a smoking jacket, standing by the fire before the guests arrived. He was the comforting, strong, protective eminence who watched you shyly approach with a wonderful twinkle in his eye. He was the kind, courtly, distant giant who leaned down and said, "Has someone been a good little girl today? Has she had her ballet lesson? Is she going to show her papa what she learned?"

It made her want to please him in whatever way she could. It made her like obeying him, want to do his will. She had rebelled against her mother, sure. What girl didn't? But she had always done what her father wanted. It made her sad that her husband wasn't at all like her father, as she had thought when she first met and fell in love with Christopher.

10

She could not believe her own ears. *Could not.* Diana cringed, writhed, shriveled inwardly when she heard her own voice doing the world's worst imitation of Chace Harsh. How could she? How could she go on to do such a lousy parody of Katherine? She must have askew loose. Ha, ha. Not funny, Diana. No, not funny, though maybe antic. Antics were what the daddy dear had on top of his head. Pins and needles were what were sticking into dear little Diana's brain. Her mind hurt, not that she minded, never having had much mind over matter to begin with.

Take the matter of her virginity, whacher might call a

sticky wicket, eh, mates? 'Ow could a giwrl in 'is day an aitch keep 'er 'ead up when she couldn't even fall? And oo is this bloke oo's doin' this fake cockney accent? She could hardly understand it when she read it in dialogue in Dickens, so how could she possibly expect to be able to ape it? What kind of monkey business was this? Ah well, she shouldn't be ashamed; there was plenty of absurdity in the theater of herself, and she had a million more second-rate actors where the half-cocked cockney came from. She had a skinny butler and a fat washerwoman in there, a tomcat and a tomboy, a shepherd and a shepherdess, a man and a woman, both of them weird, if not actually queer, in which case, thanks God, thanks a lot.

Much as she loved girls, she hated lesbians. Not that she'd ever met one. Not that she wanted to. She was bad enough without hanging around with a bunch of chunky, out-of-it fatsos with pimples and untidy buns. She even hated the word "lesbian." She'd rather think of herself as homosexual if she had to think about herself this way at all. Unfortunately, she hated to think this way about herself. The mere thought made her twitch, made her want to get out of there—as if she could jump her identity the way hoboes jumped trains.

Quite apart from the safety issue, the terrible problem of scraping her knees as she fell from her swiftly changing train of sarcasm, she had no place to jump to. The world moved by as quickly as she was flying along within, and she, at least, had the anchor, the security of always fleeing the same problem. She would have to give that up if she leapt into the aimlessly accelerated world. Even when her swiftly speeding nerves slowed, and she could see the exterior landscape more clearly, she saw no home for her turmoil.

During work, Nathan's presence inflamed her inner

roadrunner, sent her tearing inwardly, darting frantically along the zigzag track of query and counterquery. Why didn't I do it? Why did he want me to do it? Will I die if I do it? Will I die if I don't? Why is he so scary? Why am I so mean? Her galloping insecurities rode roughshod over her terror about the situation, terror of its unfamiliarity and strangeness, but a terror that remained unexpressed. Diana knew another person could have said to herself, "honey, take it easy, Nathan just wasn't the right guy." This more relaxed person was, unfortunately, one of the few characters Diana's character did not have at its beck and call. As long as she had to be around Nathan, Diana remained keenly aware of her tension, and this was aggravated by a shrinking, humiliated sense that he was mad at her and had a right to be. This was another problem she might have shrugged off if she hadn't had the problem of worrying about it all in the first place. It was also a problem with the comic distinction of taking place under the surface, where she was quarreling with Nathan about the very thing (sex) which, at a deeper level, was causing her grievous anxiety. This duplicity trapped her ambivalence, literally capped it, while her ambivalence generated painful doubts about things which had once been sure.

Diana could no longer read Katherine's meaning, could not enter into her sister as she had before. For every question Diana had about herself there was now a twin question about Katherine. Why didn't I do it? Why did she? Katherine's mysteriousness had never been an obstacle before, but now, when Diana distrusted herself, she could not trust her sister either. If her confusion had become so thorough, she couldn't throw the minimum together to get out the door.

And then the world beyond her own threshold seemed

to pull farther and farther away. It was not just that the surest feature in the landscape had come into question; it was also that Katherine seemed to have moved into the distance, where she was at home on the horizon which Diana viewed from miles away. In the evenings, after work, it was usual for the Nicholases and Bakers to eat in their separate establishments. The Bakers ate early, the Nicholases usually much later, after their baths and the cocktail hour. Concerning the latter, Mr. and Mrs. Nicholas were like British explorers who established elaborate camps in the midst of the unexplored African bush: without this central symbol of civilization all was lost. But it took an effort to maintain, particularly in a form that let the participants enjoy the fruits of the culture while paying tribute to it. Having waited for the last straggler to get upstairs, having brought whatever was being cooked to the point where it could wait an hour before it was heated and served, having set the table and otherwise cleared space in time, the Nicholases finally sat down to their drinks.

Diana thought it was a tiring way to celebrate the joys of civilized living. In particular, it involved a draining falsification of her real mood, though perhaps this is what the British Empire came to teach the savage in her heart: that higher thoughts and civilization meant speaking from an authority other than yourself, certainly not *her* self, who or which could have only spoken with authority about what it was like to be in total disarray. She might have been a wheel with a fractured hub, unable to support any line into the world outside her troubled center. She could not put aside her distress because it was her essence, but unless she did, she could not participate in the cocktail hour.

If Diana had drawn up a list of the topics which were

the real subjects of her emotions, it might read something like this: If I am brave enough, will I just get through this? What if it gets worse? Why am I so terrified? Am I the worst person alive? Who's worse than me? And why? Why do my emotions feel so awful?

If she were to draw up a list of topics which seemed to be proper subjects for civilized discourse, the list might read something like this: Is the two-party system a reality in America today? Did the Gulf of Tonkin resolution constitute a declaration of war or has Johnson exceeded his powers? Has modern art become so abstract that it has lost its audience?

Diana watched through her wrong-ended binoculars while marionettes, one for each member of her family, gesticulated woodenly, raising their hands as they made their points, bowing and bending, reciting editorials memorized by their invisible operators. As Diana watched and listened, the marionettes seemed to grow more and more alike, though physical differences remained. Bucky differed from his mother because he had a crew cut and his mother had soft brown curls. Katherine had a short, faceted nose. Diana's father was taller than the other dolls in his family circle, but he was still moving toward solid similarity with the rest. They sounded like parrots squawking or donkeys braying.

A new blond marionette came onstage. His name was Nathan. Hi, Nathan. Can you say "hi" to the kids, Nathan? Nathan flung up his arm in greeting. Diana pulled herself together. You do this by rolling yourself into as small a ball as possible. Given the situation this was difficult because she was sitting in an upholstered chair. She drew her feet up, embracing them and resting her chin on her knees.

"Diana!" her mother cried. "Please take your feet off the furniture."

There were a number of calming assumptions in her mother's reaction. First, that Diana was doing something well within the normal realm of badness. This was reassuring, just as the familiarity of the reprimand was reassuring. Her mother was always getting after her children to take their feet off sofas and chairs, though normally it was their bare feet flung up absentmindedly during the day. Never mind that this was the evening, that they were sitting around having drinks, that Diana had shoes on. She put her red Capezios back on the ground, feeling that the ground itself, the form and content of the chair as reliably stable objects, had all been restored by her mother's unquestioning belief in things and behavior having commonly understood meaning.

Diana was quick to make herself observe the situation outside her eyes and not the one within. Don't turn back; it will start all over again, the endless aggravation in the spiky darkness. And God won't turn *you* into a pillar of salt, no such luck. You'll have to feel every last spike as you twist and turn in the Iron Maiden of your soul. Diana devoted herself to Nathan's strangeness, the oddness of his wandering in out of the bush. Didn't he know this was the last outpost of civilization, that you had to be invited? The answer to that question was "no." Turned out her parents were happy to have him, especially her father, apparently because Nathan was the only one beside Christopher and Joanne who could really talk highfalutin, the shared dialect of their class and his education. The Nicholas children had fallen out of the first category and had not yet risen into the second, making them second-rate sparring partners in the realm of exercising their parents' total experience.

If Nathan's arrival was surprisingly well timed—just after the first highball, at the start of the second—his departure showed a keen sense of atmosphere as well. Without prompting, he started to melt away as the moment neared for the family's final move to the table. By then, however, it seemed to Diana that his presence had extended discussion for so long that she'd eaten a barrel of salted peanuts and could have cared less about eating a meal. Unfortunately, according to the unwritten rules of civilized life, you couldn't back out of dinner at the last minute. You had to graze with the herd, a convention that also applied to two people who had almost slept together and then had a quarrel after they hadn't. This convention kept Diana going to work. It was what kept her in the room when Nathan dropped by for cocktails (aside from the fact, which she saw as a blessing, that he came only to see her parents). If she'd had her real way, she would have moved to the next town and started all over. She assumed that he, too, would have liked to leave the mess behind. It was only his unique relation to her parents that kept him coming round, working out the negotiation between the best of the past and the best of the future.

But as he started to leave, Joanne urged Nathan to stay. He protested; she insisted. He gave Diana a hurt, but also an exploratory, look. It flew to her distress like a drill to a cavity. She flew to the telepath, signaling in every gesture—in the glass she brought to her mouth and the drink she emptied, in the involuntary shiver in her shoulder, in the sudden twisting of her face away from his scrutiny— don't stay on my account; don't leave on my account; don't do anything on my account. Nathan wired back his own message expressed in code. To an outsider, it probably sounded like he said, "Thank you, Mrs. Nicholas. But, honestly, I have already eaten, and I can't interfere with your meal." To Diana, the total insider, there were words within words, and he was really saying, "I've already had a taste of your daughter's bad temper, and I think I'll skip the main course."

She did not want his attentions, but giving him pain hurt her as well. Just as she blamed herself for his unmanning in the woods, so she felt guilty now for poisoning the atmosphere between Nathan and her parents. It was all part of her sinister influence on everything, her sinister but *unseen* influence. How could her parents know that they could never persuade Nathan to stay for dinner, not because of anything wrong in them but because there was everything wrong in her? Eagles of hysteria, hawks of self-hatred began to darken her inner sky, all ready to dive and alight on this perch. Her badness was infinite; she could descend and descend and descend, and find a specific horrible wrong at each new level, but there was always depths of wrongness below. Her troubled contents would continually influence her behavior. She would continue to offend, to horrify without ever being able to hope that she could really uproot the evil in her.

Her mother was yielding to Nathan's determination to go, but in return for his release she wanted assurance that he would be back, bringing his parents, the next night. "Why don't you all come to dinner? We live right next door and never see each other. Come, please come."

"Fine with me," said Nathan, his glance lowered to his feet. "I'll get my mother to call you."

"Do," said Christopher. "I want to tune in tomorrow to this same station. You say we drove Castro into the arms of the Soviets, and I say he was a communist from the start. His revolution was never a socialist revolution, not really. He was always talking to Moscow, if not actually taking orders."

"Well, we'll go on from where we left off. I think you're wearing cold war blinders, but there isn't time right now to tear them off. We'll have to leave it for the moment," said Nathan, brightening to the subject, darkening to Christopher's view.

His exit left Diana swelling with dread. As long as they lived in each other's vicinity, their relationship would not go away as she wished it would. Every failure between them increased her sense of involvement and some obscure feeling of responsibility. Her rage against the situation was totally stifling and thoroughly stifled. Though her mind whirled round and round her dilemma, she could not say what was on her mind. Her inexplicable sense of responsibility wrapped her in chains, forcing her to hold her tantrum in. Unexpressed and ungraspable, her anger was infecting, always growing in the presence of its cause, and yet having no outlet, soon growing greater than any cause, becoming finally baseless and universal. Everything added to it: the dinner conversation which she couldn't join, the TV program in which mules talked and nuns flew—in which every irrelevant improbability was explored, leaving her own painfully real improbability stuffed inside her aching brain.

Neither a talking mule nor a flying nun, she felt she was a lady fairy, feminine in her sympathies but masculine in her recalcitrance. She was feminine in her lively, restless intelligence; masculine in her moral will. She was feminine in her hammering the next day at work, feminine in missing nails and playing hooky in the bathroom so she wouldn't have to talk to Nathan, feminine in the wild, wordy hysteria that characterized her self-consciousness. She was masculine in her calm outward appearance, never betraying the frothing dogs of her feelings, the clatter of her mind as it dined upon its contents like false

teeth biting night. She was masculine in her bravery; if
the man in her had been famous, he would have been famous for being brave. Take that and that and that, cried
the homunculus within, beating back her terrors with his
sword. She was masculine in her character (which, until
you get used to it, is just another form of unhappiness);
she was feminine in her personality.

She was feminine in her desire to be consoled, masculine in proudly not asking for it. As her reward, the level
of her misery remained unchanged, and after work she
could look forward to its continuance in the dinner party
awaiting her in the evening. She was both feminine in
helping her mother without being asked to and masculine
in not doing more than was absolutely necessary. All on
her own she set the table; then, by ignoring the fact that
ice and glasses were needed for drinks, that all the food
had to be prepared, that the guests had to be made comfortable, Diana got out of doing anything about these
other tasks.

Yet if she was unaware of difficulty in the practical
realm, she was keenly tuned to it at the level of the irrelevant (that is, if the never mentioned is the irrelevant).
Nicholases and Bakers were sitting in a loose circle on
chairs and sofas. At one end, Christopher, Mr. Baker and
Nathan were in a clump, practically a huddle, developing
their strategy on how to save the world.

"See," said Nathan, "Dad says the current protest is
just part of the ebbing and flowing, but always ongoing,
left-wing critique. And I say it's something entirely new."

"But the liberals . . ." Bucky protested, having been
forced into the position on the sidelines because he was
sitting three seats away. He didn't make himself heard
and got up and went and sat on the arm of the sofa by his
father.

Joanne was doing the work of five, the number of people in her family (of whom four were living off her labor). Katherine had been called to the phone. Bucky was searching through the silver bowl of cocktail nuts for the pecans, the only kind he liked. Mrs. Baker was sitting beside Diana at one end of the sofa.

"There's something in between the left and right," insisted Bucky, and waved a nut in the air. His words went in one of Diana's ears and out the other, meeting Mrs. Baker's sentence going the other way: "Have you and Nathan quarreled?"

Diana stared at her feet, her mind strung out along the crosscurrents of the men's conversation coming from one side and Mrs. Baker's coming from the other.

"But I'd say the liberals—and I'm including FDR in this—have just served up a watered-down version of ideas originated on the left." Thus spake Mr. Baker.

"I'd say what's going on now is radically different from anything that's happened before." Thus spake Mrs. Baker, Big Chief Grouchy Ego to those who knew her well—like Diana, who worried that she had gotten to know Mrs. Baker much better than was good for her. Turned out Big Chief thought they'd hardly scratched the surface.

"I haven't had a chance to tell you much about myself, Diana. My family were South Dakota farmers. German stock. Strict as hell. Baptists, but really they belonged to a strange sect of their own. Milked the cows and read the Bible and went to church. My mother's fifth child, my only sister, was premature. Blinded by an overdose of oxygen in the hospital incubator. Parents thought this was a sign from God. Refused help. Never would let her be treated. Never took her to any of the special schools. They felt she was their punishment and she became that. She grew up savage—crazed with frustration. My parents never ever knew braille existed. Do you know what I'm saying, Diana? Do you know what I mean?"

"I do," she said tremulously. "I know what you're saying. I *am* what you're saying."

"Then you'll understand that I might as well have been raised in the Middle Ages. When I met Arnold, I was four hundred years behind the times."

Diana was Mrs. Baker's chuckle of self-appreciation and all her secret messages: her self-importance and her feeling that her life story was the key to the rest of the world. Mrs. Baker was politics; politics *were* her. She was power: the power to take power and the power to hold it. Diana was the subliminal message in Mrs. Baker's voice, saying, "Diana, you've scored the first point. My son is interested in you, and you've held him off. Well done. But you can't go further without my help. Let's join forces. Let's rule together. We're alike, Diana. We both take the world personally. But if you work with me, you can make the world obey you personally as well."

Diana looked around her. Thanks to a radical sharpening of mood, the woman she'd become seemed hilariously funny to her. Unfortunately, no sooner did it seem hilarious than she caught Bucky's eyes. Now he got on the telepath (dial I for Intuition) to say he saw she seemed to be having as hard a time in her conversation as he was having in his. Christopher and Mr. Baker had taken over, excluding both their sons in their heated exchange about the political mistakes of their parents' generation.

"My father was too extreme," said Christopher. "He was too much of a conservative."

"And my father wasn't radical enough."

While Diana watched, Bucky fingered the little hollow between his nose and upper lip in a subtle, self-deprecating, wicked gesture, "Hmmm," he seemed to suggest, "I see you and I are social flops." This brought Diana's laughter dangerously close to the surface. Miraculously, just as her chuckle reached the top of her throat, it was drowned by a wave of hilarity so intense it was as silent as the high-pitched whistle only dogs can hear.

Her mother came into the circle, waiting for her chance to announce dinner. Before she could, Bucky rose from his seat, saying, "Why, mother, you're just the person I've been meaning to speak to. I mean, I've been meaning to speak to someone . . ."

"OK, I'd love to hear what you have to say, but you'll have to wait until we're at the table. *Le dîner est servi.*"

"Curses, foiled again," piped Bucky, addressing himself through his index finger and raising his eyebrows in the style of Groucho Marx.

"We'll just have to continue this another time," said Mrs. Baker, at Diana's side, as they got to their feet.

Flames of laughter leapt up from her midriff, melting her head and driving her to prayer. Oh God, if you're up there, for Christ's sake don't let me laugh out loud. A stitch of suppressed laughter made Diana rock slightly. She glanced at Bucky to see if he was suffering too, fearing (hoping) that if she found one whit of support all was lost. She would howl and clutch her sides and roll on the ground. No need to be afraid. His back was to her, but in the absence of frontal evidence she took the cloth of his plaid shirt as proof that he was still in sympathy with her against the group in which they were misfits. Was theirs the lost love of a wayward girl and a bad boy? The thought had never crossed her mind before, but why not give it a whirl?

Outlaws by nature, related by birth. She knew him through and through, and in his dark moments, made darker by the darkest secret of their incest, he saw his redemption lay with her. She, meanwhile, knowing she was his only hope, carried his salvation—her love—in her heart, living without similar hope, fully conscious that the very flaws which she saw and forgave were the ones that made it impossible for him to truly understand her understanding of him.

Now that they were lovers, they were at one beneath their surface separateness. He might be waiting in line for his food, and she might be waiting two people behind him, but inside their life stories were being rewritten and re-entwined in the light of their merger. Looking back, she saw their fights as omens, auguring this fateful moment when she fell for him. As for their rather distant relations between fights, Diana saw these as strained by a taboo desire which, finally, had erupted. She began to be jealous, to feel all her own actions resonating with the awareness she imagined he had of her; she began to believe that everything he did he did in relation to this awareness of what her feelings would be about his doing it.

Once they had their plates, Joanne sent people to their places at the table, directing them according to the list she had in her hand. "OK, Nathan, you go down by Christopher, and Katherine, you sit on Nathan's other side . . ."

That roped him off. *Phew.*

"Amy, you sit on Christopher's other side, and Bucky, you're next to Mr. Baker."

That roped *her* off. Double phew. Diana was safe and could even hope that she'd find the true place of her heart's desire on Bucky's other side. She did! Her mother had Diana between her brother—well, let's face it, her lover—and Arnold Baker, who was on her mother's right. "There," Mrs. Nicholas exclaimed, and began to sit down.

But as she did, she remembered, "Christopher, I've forgotten the wine."

"What could be worse?" he asked with his peculiar brand of mock horror, peering over his glasses to see if the table was, in fact, lacking this most essential ingredient. "Hey!" he cried with sudden inspiration, "We'll drink up the Bolla."

"I think it would be great, but let me warn *my* children. Bucky," Joanne said, leaning down the table, her index finger didactically shaking, "don't forget how strong it is."

"While the rest of you were at work today," Christopher explained, taking hold of his lapels as he addressed the table—with his lids at half-mast, his expression both poignant and clowning, he resembled Pierrot—"my wife and I were brewing homemade liquor. We got talking about what to serve at the party, and we both remembered a punch we used to have in Germany. We weren't sure how it was done, and we decided to experiment. We didn't make that much, but we ended up with two pitchers' worth. One's a little different than the other."

"One's weighted in favor of brandy and the other is weighted in favor of white wine. And both are lethal, let me tell you," said Joanne. "Don't be misled by the fruit that's floating in it. You think you're drinking something innocent because there are strawberries in the glass. But go get it, Christopher. Dig in, boys and girls!"

Bucky did not seem as enthralled as Diana to find them placed together. Maybe he was jealous because Nathan got put beside their dad, but rejection, being satiric misfits together, was, after all, their main bond. As true lovers, they could celebrate the things that hurt them in their former lives. They *were* one another now, had no need to be lonely, jealous or afraid. Diana turned and

waved her lover's flag, saying, "Hey, Bucky, didja hear
the one about the czar and czarina?"

"Yeah, about six million times. Come on, shut up," he
said wearily, preferring jealousy and fear to what she had
to offer.

"I see," Diana observed, holding her hand over her
wineglass as her father started to fill it with punch. Dizzi-
ness was causing her intense nausea, though she tried to
get control of herself by pointing out that people were
often in different moods. Bucky was just in a different
mood than she was. That was her first approach, followed
by a deeper, truer, more bitter realization that they were
different in something more essential than mood. They
were different people. He was no more she than she was
he. So much for that affair. So much for all her romances.
They were all imaginary. But this shouldn't cause her any
worry. She could count on her crush generator to drag in
strangers off the street whenever she found her fantasy
loved ones had grown cold. Her emotions were a closed
(albeit crazy) system. She could flick the switch for anyone. Once the machinery was set in motion, it could convert anyone at all; even the most hateful character on
earth could become the most cherished to her.

Go ahead, she dared herself as her father sat down at
his seat at the head of the table. Why don't you fall in
love with Hitler while you're at it? She watched his handsome face, waiting for him to be bathed in a new, sugary
light. Of course, there would have to be a brief intermis-
sion between her love affair with her brother and her new
one with her father. But she could imagine it, believed it
was completely possible for what she regarded as her father's indifference to be sweetened in her deep-seated assembly line. And lo and behold, sure enough the machin-

ery began to crank out appreciation for his tyranny—just what she used to hate about him.

It was the humble but powerful love of a slave girl for the king. Though she knew his nosepick was superior to her brain's highest thought, still she was not afraid to bow down in her heart, to make him a place big enough for his bigness.

But as she gave herself over to this, it seemed depressing and even sordid that she could take up with her father's authoritarian flaws as easily as she had taken up with her brother's sense of humor. And she had taken up Bucky's sense of humor as easily as she once devoured Chace's tough-guy sensitivity. All were equal in her appetite. There was nothing preventing her from falling in love with someone she hated for reasons she despised. (As opposed to her father, whom she hated for reasons she actually respected.) She could love slime. She *was* slime.

A person could scream. But Diana didn't. A person could also be highly isolated from the information striking her senses. And Diana was, though the situation and people were dancing on her mind with high-heeled clarity. Her father was laughing loudly. Nathan was getting tough. Her father was filling up the glasses. Nathan was swilling punch. The salt was standing on the table. The food was leaping into people's mouths, going down their throats, plunging into the dark life of the gullet. Chairs were moving back. Things were going very fast. People were milling about, drinking coffee. Hundreds of feelings were stifled in the air, screaming in a silent language known only to Silencers. A tribe of funny little brown people who, without our knowing it, fill the atmosphere. Visible in the laboratory under a microscope.

Bucky's nose was very red. It was close to Nathan's nose. Nathan's nose was very big. Diana wondered what

kept their noses on. Why were everybody's arms and legs
hanging off their torsos? Why weren't they flying around
in the same constant rearrangement as everything else? It
began to get dark around the periphery of her vision. And
now Bucky's arm came off. (It must be awfully late: it
seemed so dark around her eyes.) Bucky had thrown his
arm at Nathan's big nose. Things were coming apart at
the seams! The truth was out. Now the house would fall.
Her head would fly into its puzzling pieces.

Whoops, not so fast, Diana. Her father had separated
the boys, but Nathan was a different person since things
had begun to fly apart. He raised his massive head and
roared, "You screwed the revolution. You killed Che. You
took Cuba and flushed it down the toilet of American foreign policy."

"I appreciate that, thanks. I hope I can do as much for
you someday," said Christopher.

"You took the first really possible socialist revolution
and you fucked it up the ass."

"It was your friend Castro who fucked it, Nathan. He
betrayed the socialist revolution you love so much to the
goddamned communists."

Then Nathan began to reel around like a great
uprooted oak, and said Castro looked into his heart and
played what he saw by ear, which was what all creative
heroes did, and that Castro had the purity of the true revolutionary type, but that there wasn't one pure person left
in America—the only one who came close was I. F.
Stone and—here Nathan paused briefly for breath, expelling it in a whoosh as he continued. "I'm not even sure
I. F. Stone is pure because I'm not even sure there's such a
thing as purity. But still it's the only important thing on
earth. The only thing, although we'll never get it, only see
it up there where we can't reach it. You've probably

heard of Einstein. Well, I'll tell you something. He said if we could see far enough we'd see the backs of our heads because light curves, in case you're interested. And that's why there's no purity. If you looked far enough to the left, you'd just wind up on the right. It's garbage," he cried. "We're garbage and there's no point trying to act above our station. We shouldn't even try to get out of our trash cans. We should nestle down into them and find out what the laws of garbage really are, and then if we can't be pure, maybe we can make sense. Garbage sense, of course, but sense."

Diana couldn't believe her ears. She hadn't any idea that Nathan was half as interesting or crazy as he revealed himself to be in his drunkenness. She hadn't realized how much they shared. But when she heard him going on about I. F. Stone and purity, it hit her how that was the only thing of importance to her, too. She watched him, listening with dreamy detachment. When his horrified parents finally ended his soapbox harangue, Diana saw the whole scene with a strange fondness. Good-bye, she thought sadly, as his parents took him off. Good-bye, she dreamed as though this were their final farewell. All hard feelings toward him seemed to lift up and disappear into the sky of her mind. All hard and all soft feeling toward him and everything else went up in smoke. She was completely afloat, pure air at last.

11

In the morning, Diana awoke in her body, but she still was not truly of it. Her real worry was whether or not her mind was back in place. She got out of bed carefully, like someone carrying a book on top of her head, and bore her brain carefully, carefully to the bathroom. She was in for a shock when she looked in the mirror. She had a face in fine health. If she were a stranger—and she was—looking at that face, she would never guess that it was like a Hollywood facade, covering nothing. And yet, by observing all this, she could sense her mind revving up, could feel it race and start to skid on its own awareness of itself.

She began to move, trying to keep ahead of her own mental speeding. Walked out the door, turned circles, moved. Was there no calm truth on earth? Was there no stable reality? Some things must be stable, some people who were extremely wonderful or lucky or good must be stable. Like Katherine, for instance. Diana watched her talking—short for fighting—with Chace, who apparently had just arrived.

Katherine was standing there in short shorts, curling her unique toes. Yet Katherine, for all her comedy, could never be absurd. Her beauty was incorruptible and could only be itself no matter how awkwardly Katherine moved or dressed. If she was awkward, she was beautifully so, as now, when she straightened up in her boy's white button-down shirt, tied just below her ribs. Her legs, with their full thighs and round calves, were a surprise in such a thin creature. And her kneecaps—which Diana noticed for the first time—Katherine's kneecaps were unlike anything else about her. They had a slow, uncomprehending, pudgy look, the look of someone very different from the slim, quick-witted creature with whom the alien kneecaps were hitching a ride. And yet these faceless faces, these pure expressions of another character in Katherine's repertoire, these, too, came under the governing principle of her beauty so that they made sense in the context of her whole body.

Katherine—who could govern her uncharacteristic kneecaps by the sheer force of her beauty—Katherine was stable. She was an exception to everything that ruled Diana. She was particularly untouched by the ugliness Diana could not exclude from her experience. And yet, without ever having been tainted either by ugliness or the greater contamination of not being able to distinguish what was sordid from what was pure, let alone what was male from female, without being broken or crazy, as Diana felt forced to admit she was, Katherine knew everything and had a perfect relationship with her boyfriend, Chace, himself a highly sympathetic, brilliant, talented and not at all sordid person. Therefore, it was not necessary to be the way Diana now discovered herself to be. Yet she could not imagine being different. Being obscenely indiscriminate wasn't necessary for being wise or smart or great. In fact, you couldn't be obscenely indiscriminate and be perfect, and seeing this, Diana was also forced to realize that she was a complete failure.

If Katherine could forgive or embrace her in her awfulness, then, Diana thought, maybe the day will come when I won't be so awful. She did not know exactly how to perform this errand, but went out, still in her nightgown, and stood behind Katherine, having her failure intensely in mind and trusting in the Western Union of mental telepathy to get her message across. Katherine's face was turned slightly away when Diana pulled up, and just as Diana was trying hardest to broadcast her inferiority for Katherine's blessing, Katherine's head whipped in her direction, spitting the word "idiot" with terrifying contempt.

Tears welled up in Diana's eyes at the same moment that Chace's head ballooned next to Katherine's. "Screw you, baby," he said for Katherine's ear. And then, in another instant, Katherine and Chace had flown to opposite sides of the driveway and were suddenly in deepest conversation: Katherine with Diana, who she'd pulled over to the front door, and Chace with Nathan, who had appeared at the end of the hedge.

"I can't get married," said Katherine to herself. Her green eyes were pale with introspection.

"Please don't leave me," Diana begged.

"I'm going to have to leave him if he won't let up. I'm going to have to make him leave me alone," whispered Katherine in despair.

"But if he leaves, I'm lost, too," Diana said in bewilderment.

"Wouldn't you choose me over him?"

"Oh, I would, if I were you, and I am, aren't I?"

"Diana," said Katherine, taking her shoulders in a tight grip. "Let's get something clear. There are two of us here, and one of them is me and one is you. I'm Katherine and you're Diana." She paused for an instant, looking thoughtfully askance. Then she added, "Or is it vice versa?"

Diana laughed with real merriment. Katherine's wit was like water splashed in her face at just the right moment. Diana was so cheered she actually laughed again when Nathan called to her, "Diana, Diana, I've come to apologize to your father."

"OK, Katherine, as long as you're me, you take him up to Daddy. And in the meantime I'll go to Mexico with Chace for you. Or as you."

"Fat chance," murmured Katherine, raising her voice to say, "Hey, Nathan, how areya feeling?"

Nathan's shoulders drooped; he let his arms hang and swing at his sides. "I feel horrible," he moaned.

"I bet your mother gave you hell," teased Katherine.

Nathan rolled his eyes. Yes she did. He leaned against the post under the roof, cupping his forehead with his hand. Diana was struck both by the beautiful fishy whiteness of his forearm and by the manly curve of his muscle.

"What are you still doing in your nightgown?" he asked Diana.

"Oh, we haven't been to bed," Katherine went on wickedly. "We stayed up all night talking about what a show you threw. Whether we would ever be able to receive you socially again."

"Don't rub it in!" cried Nathan, covering his face with his hands.

"I guess we'd better give him a break," sighed Katherine. "Go cover up, Diana, and take him into the throne room."

"Yes, master."

Nathan waited for her in the hall while she put on a rumpled trench coat and followed her upstairs. At the top, he held her by the arm, asking, "Are you mad at me?"

She was surprised that he asked this, as if they still had a relationship. Maybe he had her mixed up with another girl also named Diana. In case he was making an honest mistake, she tried to explain what she for some reason believed was already clear. "I thought you were brilliant last night, Nathan. I was really amazed when you said all that stuff about purity. You know, purity is probably the most important thing in the world to me—purity, not compromising."

It was his turn to look amazed. "You're not mad?"

She shook her head. No, she wasn't mad, but she was beginning to wonder if he realized she also saw their common interest in purity as the main reason for no longer regarding themselves as involved. They were off the hook at last. She started to mention this, but he was gripping her arm, ecstatically babbling, "Diana, Diana, you're too good. Too good to me. I'll make this up to you. I swear I will. From here on in, you call the shots. I'm yours!"

She blinked. Whose was he exactly? There was a terrible misunderstanding here, but the complexities defeated her. Normally, their nonrelation was a problem because he did not understand it as such. Now it was a worse problem because he seemed to believe it was the basis of a relationship. "I think Daddy's in the living room," she said, backing away.

Her father was sitting with his newspaper by the picture window. Outside a dry August light baked the green landscape. Inside it was cool and would stay that way until noon, when the sun beat down on the roof overhead.

"Hey, Nathan," said Mr. Nicholas, starting to struggle out of his chair.

"Please don't get up," said Nathan. "I'm here to apologize about last night."

"Oh that," said Mr. Nicholas, and relaxed in his seat. "That doesn't matter. Sit down, both of you, come on in. What the hell, you had a good time. It's all over with now."

Her father motioned them into chairs, and Diana took her place, feeling she was more a guest than Nathan was. He and her father had a real intimacy between them, beginning with their common interest in politics, which had apparently been enhanced by Nathan's drunken truancy. There was nothing like disobeying to bring you closer to the authority figures in your life. At school, Diana had found sinning to be a highly effective way to form relationships with teachers. Unfortunately, sinning—for all the temporary depths it imparted—was a dead end. You got closer and closer as you fell farther and farther, and then they sent you home. Needless to say, sinning did not work at all well at home, not for her, anyway, though Nathan was getting his money's worth out of *his* Narragansett Bay fiasco.

"I'm really sorry I laid all that on you about Che. Well, that was only bad manners, so I guess I have to apologize there for not being polite. The thing that really bothered me was all the garbage about garbage."

"It was only garbage," her father said sympathetically. He drew several deep breaths like a man who's surfaced after a long dive.

"Thanks," said Nathan, "but I didn't know how depressed I was until I started going on about how nothing made any sense. You know how Catholics treat despair as a sin? Well, I'm an atheist revolutionary, but I feel the same way. If I'm as unhappy as I said I was yesterday, I've had it."

"Even atheist revolutionaries get depressed," her father suggested. "Or maybe they get depressed more than anyone else. It's hell to care about politics. If you're a moral person, the world is going to drive you nuts. It's even occurred to me that the only answer to the mess is for everyone on earth to agree to commit suicide at the same moment. Then, presumably, if there is a God, and if He has any kind of a heart, then I hope He'd make Himself known."

"That sounds crazy to me," said Nathan. "I'm banking on history and reason to slowly but surely realize themselves."

"That's *really* crazy," her father protested. "History is all about winning and losing, we both know that, but you're not going to tell me that the people who win are moral. Or reasonable. The people who win are *powerful*. That's why they win."

"They're so strong they can inflict their rules on other people," said Diana.

"That's right," her father said with some amazement. He didn't know that her ignorant mind was fenced in by equipment that measured and analyzed the world outside her borders. Sort of like Soviet Russia, Dad. Keeping a weather eye out so nothing new will seep in.

"They couldn't care less what the other people are feeling," she said, challenged to show her father just how much she was not the stooge he imagined. "Not that it matters, mind you. It might as well be the strong over the weak and the crazy. I mean, my own feelings are so complicated I can barely understand them, and they're so weird they aren't like anybody else's."

"Typical capitalist-competitive-terminal individualism," snorted Nathan. "Dead-end, whining, antisocial, prepolitical consciousness . . ."

"This is serious," said Mr. Nicholas, joking uneasily. *The generations can't mix:* it was one of her father's favorite mottoes. Beside the one about character being another form of unhappiness until you got used to it. He wouldn't go for Nathan and Diana fighting in front of him. Diana bit her tongue to keep from telling Nathan to go shove it.

"It wouldn't be serious if her attitude weren't so rampant. It wouldn't matter if one prerevolutionary, unliberated adolescent regarded herself as hopelessly, unreachably unique. But we're all in danger of feeling that way. As soon as I got drunk, I showed my real colors," said Nathan. "I showed my secret despair!"

"It was probably the booze," said Mr. Nicholas. "A lot of times liquor brings on moods you wouldn't normally have. Many people are completely different when they drink."

"I hope that's the case," said Nathan, shaking his head. "I was really shaken up by how I reacted. I hadn't realized I was even capable of those feelings."

"You've never been drunk before?" Diana asked, implying anyone who was anything was drunk frequently.

"Not that drunk. Have you?"

"Have I what?"

"Been that drunk?"

"No," she admitted grudgingly.

"Tough guy talks tough, but underneath you're just as conventional as the next square."

"All is not well in paradise?" her father asked, uneasy again.

"He is not my boyfriend," Diana said emphatically.

"Certainly not," Nathan agreed, but his eyebrows reared up comically. "She's so beautiful when she gets angry, sir."

"I've always thought that was when she was most terrifying."

Amazed you ever noticed, she thought, blushing and angry with herself for coloring, in no mood to be teased. Oversensitive and overserious—she knew it, couldn't be different—she looked away, yearning for the right companion of her heart to help her through the fires of self-consciousness. Katherine's old place was empty. Didn't matter. Katherine had probably never been in there anyway. It might just as well have been a chair sitting in there listening to her thoughts. Her eyes fell on a plain straight-backed chair by the sideboard. Her hardened heart began mechanically to manufacture a new romance.

It was clear to her now that all the others had been a mistake. She saw that love could only be perfect when it was wooden, as now, when she was so completely taken by the chair. The old song was right (but then the old ones always were): some enchanted evening, you may see a chair across a crowded room. Well, this was that enchanted evening (never mind that it was the middle of the day).

"We've lost her," said Nathan.

"I'll leave you to find her," her father said stiffly, rising to his feet, ready to get out of there.

"Well, I'm here to give her the chance of her lifetime," Nathan said to Mr. Nicholas. "The Newport Folk Festival is on tonight, and I'm going to let her go with me if she's good."

"I would say that any young female, given the opportunity of which you speak, would be delighted to accompany you."

"Great, I'll take your word for it then," said Nathan, slapping his knee and standing. "You're a pal, Mr. Nicholas, and knowing you're a man of honor, I know your daughter will be as good as your word. This is a triumph, sir, for all that's wholesome in a young man's heart!"

Chair, do you believe what's going on here? Do you see how I've been trapped into this idiot date with big boy? Chair, do you see how they treat me as if I weren't here, as if I were a chair?

"Diana," said Nathan, going down on one knee before her, "be at The Bleakers at seven. We'll wine and dine you before we take you to the big city of Newport."

He then shook Mr. Nicholas' hand in what Diana guessed was a further failed attempt at self-parody. The only good thing about it was that once he'd finished making an ass of himself, he left the room, the house, but why not the whole area?

"That guy is really a jerk," she announced when she heard the screen door slam.

"Oh come on, he's not so bad," her father said. "Socially he may be gauche, but I've got to hand it to him. His heart's in the right place. I may not agree with his opinions, but at least he's deeply involved with the world. That's the important thing."

OK, Chair, there you have it. You see the hell in which

I'm doomed to live. My own father is trying to get rid of me by pawning me off on that burnout. This is really the last straw. There's such a thing as pushing a person over the edge, and Dad has just done it to me, his own daughter.

Well, I don't care, Chair, because now I've got you, and I don't have to take shit from anyone. This is a really intense, really pure, really stable relationship. The first in my whole life. In fact, I'd like to take time out now to tell you my whole life.

I was born in 1948. Pictures show a cheerful, charming, good-natured baby. Soon, of course, I grew into a child, subject to the cruel treatment of subtly unloving parents and siblings. I was a rare child, if I do say so myself. Perhaps a poet of a human race, a gifted child who did not yet know she was gifted, and though I could not be taken from my natural family, I met a chair, a kindred spirit, a conspirator. The chair tried to impart some part of its affection for me (the intensity of which surprised even the chair), and did this for deeply moving reasons. The chair had once been like the girl, and though the chair had made a life for itself in the world, it was not really of it, either. The chair knew what it was to be wounded. . . .

I seem to be running into a problem of time, Chair. If I were really going to do my background justice, I'd be here about sixty years, but there's a lot going on in the present and it's important to move on. Ever heard of Narration Hysteria? I think I've got it. Where things are only real to you because you are saying them to another person, place or thing with whom you are madly in love. I am going to my room now, Chair; I am lying on my bed, trying to read, though I can tell you it's hard to read and talk about the fact I'm reading at the same time. . . .

Chair, unfortunately I have to interrupt this broadcast to say that a subplot is developing. You know, I'm just lying here on my bed, looking around and noticing what's in my room and thinking, why, these are the members of Chair's family. These are my in-laws, so to speak. What I appreciate about you and your relatives is the fact that you do your jobs quietly, dependably, with none of the egotism which makes life so depressing among humans. You're all sturdy and stable and just plain good at what you do. But there's a reason why you haven't risen as a group. I'm not saying this to be mean, I'm saying it for your own good. Do you realize we've been thick as thieves for nearly two hours and you haven't said one interesting thing? No wonder you've got a bad stereotype. Ever heard of the phrase "stiff as a board" or "boring as a chair?" Well, these stereotypes are usually based on a partial truth. And the fact is you're a little too stiff and a little too boring. What you probably don't realize is that being stiff and boring is your way of being egotistical. You're probably protecting yourself from ever getting hurt, but let me point out something you may not have noticed. First of all, I am doing all the work in our relationship. But it's more than that. I'm doing all the work in the world. It's *my* voice that's keeping things alive. If I weren't saying, I'm getting off my bed and looking out my window—if I weren't telling you how time is passing; how I'm eating lunch and telling everyone I'm going to the folk festival; hearing Bucky, and Katherine and Chace say they want to come, too; hearing Dad rave some more about how the press won't let the CIA keep its secrets (I won't tell him ours!); and thinking at least I'll have some real company (that is, if Chair sits up and dies right); if I weren't telling you that I'm whiling away a boring afternoon, these events wouldn't be happening.

In case you're interested, which you're not, I'm getting dressed, being careful not to get too dressed up lest anyone think I'm trying to look nice. No, I'm not falling into that trap. I'm putting on my blue jeans and turtleneck and this coral necklace and earrings. I wouldn't try hard if I were me because then people would think I have something to show off. And I know damn well I don't. If your face takes after your father's feet, you don't advertise by wearing big, curly hairdos.

OK, I'm on my way, saying good night to mummy, telling her I'll be home by midnight. Now I'm walking along to Nathan's house, now I'm walking into it and here's the scene. They are all on the alert either because they never have people over for dinner or Nathan has never had a girl over, or, most likely, they think I represent public opinion and they're all still *très* distressed because Nathan threw a show.

Mr. Baker is the only vaguely calm one. Nathan and Mrs. Baker are flitting around like hummingbirds, even though he's about six feet seven inches and can't really be considered birdlike. But Mr. Baker asks me if I want a beer or coke, and I figure I'll give them a little scare. I am compelled to ask for a martini. After last night, they don't know whether to allow me to or not. They're so far down the hole in their behavior, they don't dare criticize mine. Well, if there's one thing I hate it's inequality. Guess I'll even the score and do unto Nathan what he did unto our house. Well, hee, hee, hee, Mr. Baker gives me my gin, though he looks a little shocked, I have to admit it. I sip my poison while they all drink their sodas—I guess Nathan's on the wagon now—and we carefully avoid any sensitive subjects. I happen to know we're avoiding sensitive subjects because my nose has been specially trained to sniff out falsity of every shade and kind. (Who said he had a built-in shit detector? I'm with him whoever he is. Here's to ya, pal. Can we help it if we're great?)

Whoops, even great people have problems. The sound of Mrs. Baker's voice attacks my nerves. Then, to my worse horror, Nathan and his father leave to set the table and prepare dinner. I am alone with this creature, who's going to swallow me if I'm not careful. I feel her getting nearer. I feel myself yield to her.

I feel her sexual attraction to my murder and I know I am helpless. When Mrs. Baker talks again, once more I become her and her urge to do me in. "I *was* a basket case, though Arnold gave me something to hang on to while I went through the worst of my collapse. I went down, Diana, down, down, down into myself and what I saw was terrifying and I thought I would never come back. I thought I was stuck forever at the bottom of a deep black well, and it made me very bitter, lying there in primal ooze like a slug. And while I lay there, I swelled up and I was sore afraid and I swelled until I couldn't even see the tiny bit of sky once visible to me at the far distant top of the well. And then one day I had a child, Diana, a big son and it was as if all the air had gone out of me, ff-ff-ff-ff-ft. Like a burst plastic beach ball. At first all I could see was my skin slopped to one side, but slowly, slowly I understood that I'd had a son and I saw that I'd been resurrected at last as a man, as someone real, and that this was a second chance! I was going to recover! I was going to have my revenge after all, through my new life as a little boy and through my mind. I saw that I could change the course of history, that nothing would ever be the same now that I'd shed my sex . . ."

Why do I keep coming round and round to this woman? I am my terror of closeness with this strangu-

lating seaweed of a monster woman. Her wet, gaping, vile
mouth! Her jagged teeth of glass.

"I want to tell you my secret," I blurt out involuntarily.

"Tell me, then," she says sweetly.

"I love you," I blubber. "I love you."

She pats my hand, says, "I love you, too, Diana. I think
it's very healthy for women to express their emotions for
one another, and I'm glad we've admitted we have a special understanding."

Though she has suddenly become a guidance counse-
lor, underneath it all is crazy murk. She sucks me in and
spits me out. Thank God, I'm not alone with her—the men
are back. I am helpless but temporarily safe. We're called
to dinner. When I hear the word "dinner" I become it. I
look, as though by seeing the speaker I will see the per-
sonification of the word I've personified. As though I can
push the outside world outside me again. But I *am* the
outside world. I am Mr. Baker saying grace. *I* am Mr.
Baker saying grace? I don't usually pray, but there I am,
the prayer itself. I am my fork and the potato salad and
the sausage on my plate. I am anything anyone says.

I begin to tell them about my deep interest in going to
law school and they are fascinated. They want to know
why and where and exclaim all over the place about how
they didn't know I had the slightest interest in the law.
But I can be darn cagey when I have to be and I tell
them how I think society is very legal, but that there
aren't enough laws to cover all the dangers. (This is kind
of a private joke, of course, because what I really mean is
that there should be a law against getting kidnapped by
robots, namely, the Bakers, who I now clearly realize are
robots.) And then this gets them going about whether
there should be more or fewer laws so I don't have to talk
at all for a while. I lean back and admire the workman-

ship on these robots. Gawd Almighty, they are cleverly constructed! Somehow they have built into them the ability to develop whatever turn the conversation takes and yet it's just as clear that they aren't thinking for themselves. All their thoughts are prerecorded. If I hadn't been extra smart, I might not have guessed what I've guessed or been able to plan how I'm going to get away. As long as they don't suspect, I'll be OK, I'm sure of it. I go on acting perfectly natural, smiling and laughing and being agreeable. I don't even faint when it turns out that Mr. and Mrs. Baker are coming to the folk festival with Nathan and me.

"Us old lefties can't pass up an opportunity to sing 'This Land Is Your Land,'" says Mr. Baker, but I doubt it even though I smile an understanding smile. My own true feeling is that the murder, my murder, will be executed in Newport, where they can easily get rid of the body. But I am an actress supreme, I do not betray the slightest quiver of fear. On the ferry going over to Newport I chat and charm and sympathize. I am the go-between for two unlikely groups: the Bakers and Bucky, Chace and Katherine. When Mr. and Mrs. Baker go back into the cabin, we pass Chace's flask of wine around. I drink merrily, though this may be my last drink ever if I do not succeed in outsmarting the robots. Still, I am confident, incredibly confident, breathing the sea through my snoutful of gin, toasting the pale evening sky.

After the boat docks, I wave good-bye to my brother and to my oldest pal, Katherine. I am moved by the incredible poignancy of the fact that this may be our final farewell, but I do not weep for fear of giving myself away, for fear that it is part of the plot: if I cry, my tears will wash my eyeballs out of their sockets.

And then the Bakers and I start along Thames Street

on foot. There is a raunchy sweetness here in the dark bars, their windows hung with Schlitz signs, their doors ajar, spilling sailors, music from the jukebox, the delicious smell of greasy fried food, which hovers in the humid air. Bars alternate with pawn shops and thrift stores, the contents of their windows almost lost behind a dim screen of dust; no one cares if they sell the junk they advertise. Down here by the docks it's a navy nighttown, an alleyway for sailors, bums and whores. It would be easy to get lost down here! All I have to do is get away!

I say I have to go use a bathroom, that I'd better go now before we go uptown and get inside the park. We all duck into the next bar/restaurant. For a moment I'm afraid Mrs. Baker will come with me, but she doesn't. They stay up front, ordering coffees to go. My heart is pounding, pounding; it's escaped its cage and is knocking on my throat. I go toward the back, following the arrow to the ladies room. Farther down the corridor are swinging doors to the kitchen. I look back toward the bar; I can't be seen. I go on into the blaring lights, stoves, swinging pots, people wrapped in smeared white aprons.

"How do I get out of here?"

A man with brown hair and a black beard points to a door at the back. Over the transom, a red exit sign. I go. I'm out. I'm free. I breathe deeply, inhaling the salt from the ocean and meat cooking inside on the charcoal grill. I run, turning and twisting whichever way the street urges me to go until I have circled back to the waterfront, below the ferry dock. I stop, leaning against a building, closing my eyes at last and gasping for breath. Slowly, the sharpness in my chest subsides. I can look around with a leisurely glance. There are boats in the harbor, great, beautiful sailboats with soaring masts. They rock slightly, towering above their wooden berths, monuments of order come to rest.

Once more I breathe deeply and smell the salt promise of the infinite sea. I am that fragrance and the boys washed ashore, wearing white pants and no shirts. I am their brown, bare backs, their hard breasts cupped to their bodies like massive quahog shells. They come to me; they return to me, having only gone out of me on the continuous filmstrip of my vision. We fall toward the open doorway of a crowded slum bar. People press in around us. The jukebox blares. Rock 'n' roll so loud it is like a form of heat. I feel the noise as warmth. The press of bodies defines my limits. I am surrounded and warm, drinking at the bar. A strange ecstasy begins to bubble up in me, generating a pure insight into the types I'm with. I see these people, I see these people, I see all of them for what they are: the Restless Wanderer, the Good-Hearted Bore, the Prig, the Poet, the Lost Sheep, the Conformist, the Loser, and on and on. I am a cornucopia of human types, reproducing the names of everyone around me. But I am always above them or below, always more or less, always unknowable to myself though I know others instantaneously, women as well as men: the Beehive Hairdo Meanie, the All-American Girl, the Brain Who Tries to Hide It, the Tart, the Golden Girl, the Glamor Girl, and so on. They are all here in the throbbing crowd. All of America is there: Mick, Spick, Finn, Swede! Pole, Wop, WASP and Puerto Rican!

I move from the bar, part of the pulse, the music itself. The Rolling Stones, down and dirty, singing "Satisfaction." Here's to you, boys! Here's to the whole great, green, grungy, greasy, grimy, gritty, grubby, groovy twentieth century! I am dancing. Everybody is dancing. I am pulling an imaginary rope and pumping my hips like a bellringer gone mad. I know the people around me. I am them, my mind starts up its proliferation of their types: the Hot Ticket, the Show-off, the Conceited Weakling, the Sweetheart Whose Luck Will Always Be Bad. I am no type. What type? Who? But death awaits me in any label I might choose. It's death to fit inside any previously lived life. As I name the others, I feel myself flying into fragments. Nothing governs me at bottom; at bottom I am chaos. My eyes feel this chaos welling up, spreading out: wet and violent and obliterating. My eyes are sinking fast. All this will be gone in a moment. All these others will drown when my eyes finally surrender.

And then my arm above the elbow begins to burn. I feel some hot, identifying pressure there. Then I see a hand gripping my arm, its thumb pressed deep into my flesh. Someone's put his finger on me after all. My sensations now gather under the thumb, taking their character from the rough character of the pressure being applied. I'm being pulled through the crowd, pulled toward a man I immediately recognize as the Beast, the mirror of my soul, come to claim me at last. Medium height, thick arms, sandy thatch of hair, lean face with a swaybacked nose. His eyes are shut. He shuffles to the music. His dungarees cling to his elongated thighs; his T-shirt conforms to his shoulders and chest. His fingernails are dirty. His knuckles are work worn with grime driven deep down into their gnarls. He wrenches me against his body. His grip tightens so that where I have gathered under his touch I squirm with sexual desire. This desire is real and universal, the only thing inside me that feels like gravity, that makes me feel specific and unfettered, particular and still extensive, alive but not banal. He grinds his teeth against my lips. I grind myself against him, feeling his belt buckle catch my skin, wanting it to catch, wanting to grind my skull into his skull, wanting, wanting and seeing in the darkness now that I've finally closed my eyes, seeing my own sensations flare in the diminishing space between the still mounting blackness and the different darkness of my conscious remnant. It's as though I were being lowered into a dark, padded cell, its walls cushioned, I now see, by milk-full breasts. I'm lost and lowered, yielding entirely to my mouth, to the hard press of our bodies, and as I yield to my desire, its consummation and loss are all one: I have it all, and have it all at once. I desire and my desire dies. I desire, I die. Desire, die; desire, I . . .

12

In her dream Joanne was serving drinks and dinner to Christopher and Ellie Snow in a dimly lit, shabby restaurant. Atmosphere of the forties. Joanne was wearing brown and white wing-tip shoes. Hems went below the knees. Her own hair in a droopy pageboy. Christopher and Ellie Snow just as they had seemed to her when she first met them: glamor boy and glamor girl—"girl" pronounced "g–earl," as if the speaker were presenting the word on a black velvet pillow. Ellie's precise, *Vogue*-ish beauty was at its noon perfection. She was lively and healthy and quick; she was incredibly admired, but she did not admire her admirers. She and Christopher were equals in detachment, the quality which made them feel superior to others.

Neither Christopher nor Ellie recognized Joanne, and when she rattled the china to make them take notice, they looked at her with annoyance. Waitresses should be seen and not heard! Joanne turned away, filled with forgiveness, knowing life had drawn the wool of easy success over their eyes, knowing they neglected to think of her feelings because they'd been so encouraged to think of their own, dreading for their sake the moment when life dropped its act and gave them a turn with the back of its hand: and life inevitably would, life being the ultimate democracy and distributing its unhappiness among the high and low, rich and poor, smart and dumb.

As she turned back to the kitchen, Joanne saw she had three other customers—Katherine, Herr Muehler and Arnie Jackson, Joanne's first boyfriend, the first person she'd slept with and the only other one beside Christopher. In the dream, Arnie was dressed as a soldier, apparently on leave from the war in which he'd later be killed. He was sitting by himself at a table between Herr Muehler and Katherine, both of whom were also sitting by themselves. Joanne wasn't sure how old she was, but she could see that Herr Muehler was his true age, sixty-fiveish, that Katherine was nineteen, and that Arnie was twenty-three—his age when he was shot in France.

Herr Muehler hailed Joanne as though to order, but when she got to the table he began to tell Joanne how much she stirred him, how much he wanted her. At the same time, Joanne noticed Arnie noticing Katherine. What if he picked her up? How could she get rid of Herr Muehler? She couldn't afford to be ungracious. If she had to compete with Katherine, then she'd have to excel in tact and guile because she wasn't sure she could physically hold her own against her daughter's beauty.

And yet Joanne was also furious at Arnie for not realizing who she was. It's me, Joanne, your first love! If she had to remind him of how well they understood each other, then the romance was flawed. But she had always felt he knew what she was going to say before she said it. And he had so often been moved to do the very thing she wanted without her having to ask. Yet here he was like any other callow, common soldier on leave, picking up the first pretty girl he saw.

She was withered by bitterness, though she blamed Christopher and Ellie more than she blamed Arnie. They didn't even know enough about her to know she'd loved and suffered—perhaps even more than they had with all their stupid marriages between them! Whereas she, *she'd* had a great love and now saw this great love tarnished before her very eyes. Well, she was sick of sacrificing herself for all these people who never noticed what she did for them. Though it made her feel rather cheapened to have to step in to save her so-called perfect love, Joanne had no other choice. It was more than she could bear to have her memories ruined.

"Herr Muehler," Joanne said kindly but firmly, "you've made me feel much more alive than I've felt in years. I appreciate this flirtation, but I'm a happily married woman. This can't go on. I need your help. I need you to take Katherine home. She's too young to be in this kind of place. Hurry!"

And then Joanne went to Christopher and Ellie's table and presented them with a bill for twenty-five hundred dollars. She was amazed by her own audacity. But he pulled out his wallet and paid without a word of complaint and then he seemed to evaporate, along with Ellie

and Katherine and Herr Muehler. Joanne was finally
alone with Arnie.

He stood up and, as he did, he seemed to follow his
face and his face followed his prominent brown eyes. He
was all sculpted head, all eyes and purity—hopeful, reverent, virile, bony, intense. He took Joanne's breath away.
She was pierced by emotion, the same touching, painful,
sharp emotion he'd evoked in her when she knew him,
but now tinged with relief because she'd missed him so all
these years.

Pounding on the door. The police? No, it was Christopher, awake, as always, before her. Getting up noisily—
his way of expressing disapproval of her sleeping late.
Hitting the floor with his feet, crashing against his bedside table. Her dream absorbed his noise as the distant
thunder of guns. Now there were candles, otherwise no
light. A small Negro band in a corner, dominated by the
saxophone, playing "Mood Indigo." Arnie took her waist
in his arms. She encircled his neck. Though her head
rested on his collarbone, there was a thin shaft of air between the rest of their bodies. As they danced, it was the
sense of being enclosed, of being gathered, that moved
and aroused her: the feel of his folded hands in the small
of her back, the actual sensation of the space between his
crooked elbows and the curve of her own waist, the pressure of his lean muscles against her upper arms.

The music changed. "April in Paris." She put her hand
on both his shoulders; he drew her waist toward him and
now her head fell on his throat. She moved her hand to
the bristly back of his neck, where the tendons strained in
what felt like anguish. Her lids half-closed; she gently
lapped his ear. Where his erection bobbed against her
through her skirt, she felt herself widening, as though her
sensations were being swung in fuller and fuller circles

from a narrowing, glittering, nervous pinpoint. Then, as she began to lie back in his arms, to yield to this ravishment, he pressed his sandpapery face against her neck. She felt herself rising, on the verge of flying free from an unbearable tautness. As he sobbingly burrowed, rooting in her neck with mole-blind urgency, her censor awoke with a start. She was splashed with consciousness, cut short without completely awakening.

"Foster," Christopher called softly. His voice sounded strange. Her lids opened slightly, slowly; she realized it was the middle of the night. The hands on the clock said eleven-thirty. They had both been exhausted. They had taken advantage of the children's absence to go to bed at nine. No wonder she couldn't wake up. She'd hardly finished the first phase of her nightly cycle; and she who passed through the stages of sleep as the moon rose and fell in the sky could not wake up now without feeling unnatural.

"Foster," Christopher repeated, almost as if he were moaning. Then she could vaguely hear the old dog's nails click-clacking on the rugless corridor as he came in from the dressing room, responding with his aged shuffle to his master's call.

Joanne rolled over, patching up the holes in her dream. A certain amount of bothersome reality had seeped through her wakefulness. In her dream she was Christopher's wife and Arnie was the young stranger he would have been if he'd come back from the dead and met her now, at forty-five. Yet she was stirred and could remember how aroused she'd been in her previous dream, and this recollection aroused her again, and she could tell that he also trembled with the same illicit longing. His eyes grew serious, tragic with desire, with the doomed beauty she'd seen gleaming in his look before. He was still a soldier, and there was a war, but it had to be a recent one, a war which could alter the normal routine to such an extent that the previous Arnie Jackson and Joanne Goddard would yield themselves freely to impulses usually buried miles below the social surface.

There had been a war in America. The East Coast had been bombed. Nuclear bombs had been dropped close enough so that most of the people they knew were dead. Someone was wounded, lying at the back of the night-club, groaning. Miraculously, Arnie and she had survived, but who knew for how long? They danced without music, shyly, tragically, the last people on earth. Mercifully, the groaning stopped. She was almost back to where she was before, spreading within to a far horizon from the diminishing dot of pleasure. Arnie was bent to her neck. He spread his hands over her haunches and rammed himself against her (there were suddenly no clothes); he was tunneling, tunneling and she thirstily received him. She strained for the final flick that would collapse the dense, distended point at her core and bring up the flood of relief, the boundlessness and imminence that would roll through her, shedding her even as it carried her beyond herself, even as she mushroomed into the palest hues of the spectrum and faded into the universe.

But her own straining cut into her sleep, roused her so that she had to intensify the theatricality of the dream. She heard a weak groan and, moments later, a louder one. She was way beyond soft music and candlelight. Her dream stage director now worked to shock, to take her by surprise—quickly before the censor could intervene—and assaulted her with new, brutal details: fires burned all round the house; the sky was terrifyingly red; Arnie's nails cut her flesh. Still, she could only bring herself to a certain point, and as she stalled there, inciting herself with the worst things she could think of—there's been a dreadful war, everyone's dead, you're alone on earth, you only have moments left, you can do anything you want—Arnie's face began to change, to become her son's, and when she realized it was Bucky in her arms, she woke instantly, repelled.

She sat up, and the horror she still felt about her dream seemed to surround her, as if the contents of her own imagination had tainted the atmosphere of the room. "Christopher?" she asked uneasily, sensing him at the foot of the bed.

"Christopher?" she asked again, reaching and turning on the light. He was sitting on the bed, the back of his pale blue pajamas to her. His back heaved and he groaned pathetically. Joanne was stunned, still under the influence of her dream, so powerfully affected by it that it was as if it were reality, as if reality had become the dream and the dream a nightmare. Christopher was groaning, wounded in the corner. He had probably seen her with Arnie, and she had danced on, letting the poor man lie there.

"Oh Christopher," she said, a sob in her throat, though her eyes were dry. "I didn't know. What happened?" She almost asked where Ellie was, but her realism was gaining the upper hand. This was *actually* happening. Her husband was in mortal pain, too ashamed or proud to wake her. Poor hurt boy sitting with his dog.

"Terrible pain," he whispered when she sat beside him, gently putting her arm around his shouder. "Like the time in Washington . . . at the ballet." Last May they had taken a party of people to the theater, Christopher had been bothered by angina all day, then had to rush to the men's room from his seat at the theater, and was violently ill. He was so sick and afterward so weak that he obeyed his wife and went to a doctor, who checked Christopher's heart, found no damage, but said this was something to watch. Nausea of that order could be a symptom of a heart attack.

"Do you feel like throwing up?" she asked.

He shook his head, letting his hands drop between his knees. "My mother died of a heart attack," he said.

"I know," she murmured, surprised to hear him telling her what was so well known.

"Be brave," he said. "Be brave." It was hard for Joanne to tell whom he was addressing. "Be brave until the worst evils have been solved. Wait until we've got these nuclear weapons out of the way. Wait until the racial horror had been improved. Be brave until then," he finished, holding his hands to his face and groaning loudly.

Again Joanne felt the barriers between dream and life disappearing. The presence of Christopher's mother was so strongly in the air that Joanne raised her face, as if she would see old Mrs. Nicholas there in the darkness. The night was alive with the woman's tough, challenging spirit, and Christopher's pain seemed to pass through Joanne, moving with her pulse into the breathing blackness. She was wholly transformed into a medium between the living and the dead, feeling her husband's buried boyhood beating its fragile wings. As if he could fly away, fly anywhere outside his mother's sphere of influence. Joanne remembered his memories, felt she'd fallen through illusion into a world where one saw in the dark as a blind person sees in the light: by sensing sensations, by interpreting the quality of the air around him, by putting forth emotions like hands and finding them clasped. Yet Christopher couldn't trust what he felt. It could all be done with mirrors. You could make anyone

believe anything you wanted them to believe. It hurt to
be afraid; it hurt him to feel.

There was an agonizing confusion of time and trust, of
suffering and feeling that women had betrayed him.
Joanne felt for him, felt as him, knowing how the pain re-
duced him—just as he had always feared would happen if
he were brainwashed. He could not survive with his
honor intact. At the instant of the greatest pressure,
Christopher was insane, and Joanne with him, holding
him as he rocked forward in desperate agony, talking to
angels, addressing his torturers, telling them with babyish
fervor that he'd done everything he could, but no matter
how much he'd achieved she'd never been satisfied. She'd
wanted a king, not a son. He was in an agony of rage, of
despair, of succumbing. His will swooned, hers collapsed
at last; pain washed their ancient struggle into outer
darkness.

When it was over, he was innocent again, shockingly
vulnerable. She stood and looked him over, touching his
hair, his face, his shoulders. He watched her watching
him the way a child would, utterly selfless in his self-
centered dependence. His wonder inspired her. She could
forget herself as she had with her babies—when she had
sacrificed much, feeling both she and the demanding
baby were swept away, as lovers might be, effaced by
their sensual communion. As with a baby with whom she
ceased to be a private personality, so now with Christopher there was a falling away of their particular struggle
and marriage. They were faceless, speaking out of eternal
forms in a wholly impersonal but completely moving
process. For once emotion's course ran smoothly through
the deep grooves cut in universal human experience.

"You look all right. Your color's good," she said.

"It always is," he answered simply, sweetly.

"But you're purplish there around your lobes," she said, and touched his ears.

"It was as if an elephant was standing on my chest. It was squeezing the life out of me. My mother was there at the end. I mean, she seemed to be."

Joanne nodded, urging him to lie down while she called the Rhode Island Rescue Squad. He had to go to the hospital, that was clear. She insisted on this with more force than was really necessary. He made no objections. He still seemed egoless in his attitude toward his health. When she had finished making her call to the rescue squad and to the hospital, she told him to lie down while she packed a few of his things. Christopher did what she suggested, stretching out on his bed, both cooperative and yet detached, as if he thoroughly shared her concern for some other third person.

Tom Williams, the man driving the ambulance, was also the owner of the garage the Nicholases used. When Joanne opened the door and saw him in this other role, her sense of the familiar world transformed into a passion play was confirmed. She drew courage from the feeling and went back upstairs to help her husband into his coat. She lifted the shoulders of the jacket with religious awe before the circumstances. His suffering was timeless, softening the sharp edges of pride the way the ceaseless days had worn away the features on carved medieval tombs. As she descended with Christopher's arm drawn through her own, she was struck with humility for the heroism thrust on them through no virtue of their own. A great calm attended her in this moment when she was asked to rise to an almost unbearable occasion.

In the ambulance, lying down quite comfortably, Christopher talked about his will. It was in order, with no surprises for Joanne, whose own will was identical save that Christopher was the recipient. Both wills had been drawn up by the same lawyer, an old friend who Christopher now asked Joanne to call in order to arrange a few changes in small amounts he was leaving to Groton and Yale. Though tears seeped from her eyes as he spoke, though her mind filled with a succession of images of her loneliness if he should die, her concern for herself was impersonal. She wept as though for another woman, for all women who love a man, who live for him and, when he's gone, who grieve for him. She felt no remorse for her particular resentments that summer, no longing for any particular period of happiness. She mourned the passing of this handsome man, this stranger whose poetic subtlety was more available to her in this transcendent hour than it often was in domestic routine.

Attendants carried Christopher into the hospital through the emergency room at South County, where they were met by Dr. Williams, the son of a friend of a friend. Joanne had telephoned him at home, having met him recently at her cousin's, and he had immediately arranged to get to the hospital as soon as they did. He had an unusual but completely winning manner for a doctor, a way of speaking calmly that grew out of a sensitive but unexpressed perceptiveness. Dr. Williams began his technical questions as soon as they found him; he listened to Christopher's heart, took his pulse, lifted the patient's eyelids. Yet all the while, through his unhurried attention, his humane touch, his tactful but observing glance, Dr. Williams searched them out as people with characters and a story to tell. There was almost too much dramatic aptness in finding themselves delivered to this witness. He seemed to see them with a sort of tenderness and concern meant only for private emotion. In his consoling presence Joanne felt herself growing weak, drained by the reality as she had not been before.

After they had taken Christopher to his room and settled him, Dr. Williams drew her aside, saying, "Your husband has had a bad heart attack, but you've handled it bravely." His kindness brought on the tears she had controlled in the ambulance, the tears for herself. Her knees began to tremble. "If you want, I can give you something to sleep. Have you got anybody at home?"

She shook her head, no, she did not want sleeping pills. She nodded, yes, she did have children at home, or should have by the time she got back. Dr. Williams explained that he was going to remain at the hospital with Christopher, but he had arranged for her to be driven home by Tom Williams. "I would drive you home myself, but there are certain tests I ought to run, and I'm going to arrange for Mr. Nicholas to be hooked up to a machine that's like a big TV. . . ."

Joanne kept nodding as if she were listening, but her attention had withdrawn from Christopher's predicament into her own. Having forgotten smoking entirely, she could now think of nothing else. She discovered she had her wallet but not her pocketbook. Still without paying attention to Dr. Williams' words, she followed his rhythm for an appropriate moment when she could ask him to loan her some change for the cigarette machine.

"Listen," she said in a rush during a pause in his kind flow. "I don't want a sleeping pill. But could I possibly borrow enough to get some cigarettes?"

His thoughtful glance turned bright and ironic, as if she had solved a mystery for him. "Ah, so that's where you've wandered off to. I shouldn't let you, but who am I to disapprove." He withdrew a rumpled pack of Marlboros from his own pocket. "But we're both going to have to give these up, you know that."

"Of course, I swear I'll never smoke again after tonight. Just this once," said Joanne, greedily seizing a brown filter and putting it to her lips. The doctor lit it for her and she inhaled, throwing back her head and releasing the smoke with a great sigh of relief.

"Thank you, Dr. Williams. You saved my life."

"Funny thing to say about a lousy cigarette, Mrs. Nicholas, but this is not the moment to lecture you. Or me. Mrs. Nicholas, I want you home and in bed by the time I count to, oh, four hundred thousand."

Joanne laughed girlishly, pleased to be treated like a child. The young doctor seemed confused to find himself cajoling her in this nearly flirtatious way and followed his light reprimand with careful, neutral instructions about when she could return to see her husband the next day.

On the way home, she felt the circumstances in all their bleakness once more weighing on her. If only Christopher had been more careful, hadn't been so ornery. He shouldn't have been playing tennis, working at The Bleakers, trying to save the world with or from Nathan. But, no, it was not his way to admit weakness, accept help. Had to fall down nearly dead before he admitted that he was in pain. What did he need a wife for? Not to confide in, that much was clear. Driving down the highway in the off-duty ambulance, Joanne felt homeless in her knowledge, orphaned by the truth. Her marriage was oppressively silent in the very places she had the most to say. She was ready to analyze the human heart into its last trembling quiver. He felt the heart had more to hide than any other part of the body. Yet he was all she had. Without him, without their marriage, she would not recognize herself. She would not know how to know herself.

But what was in her marriage if not her heart's desire? (The poor man lying in the hospital—what did he know of her real thoughts, and how would he feel if they were revealed to him?) Her marriage was her life's work, after all, and that, in the end, is all it was: work. It was the tables she had set, the silver she had polished, the beds she had made, the floors she had waxed, the meals she had cooked, the miles she had driven her children to their schools and lessons, the groceries she had bought, the phone calls she had taken. The phone was ringing when the ambulance pulled into the driveway. No doubt it was Ellie Snow, calling to recite her list of woes, the higher problems of the fallen woman. The phone rang and rang as she thanked Tom Williams for the lift; in fact, she was most grateful to him for not talking, but she did not think it was proper to express her gratitude for that. She was only sorry that she was going to have to break her own silence if she went inside and answered the phone, still ringing, ringing.

If they really wanted her, they could wait for her. In no particular hurry, Joanne walked through the screen door, sermonizing to herself on the phone as one of the great home wreckers of the twentieth century, as one of the most dangerous threats to peace of mind (along with sex), one of the most uprooting, illiterate forces of the times.

"Hello," she sighed, taking up the receiver at last.

"Mum?" Katherine asked timidly. Shades of a decade ago, when Katherine had tiptoed into Joanne's bedroom and said just as politely, "Mum? Mum? I thought I'd better tell you. I was backing out of the garage and, well, you know the garage door? It's sort of falling off where I hit it."

"What is it?" Joanne asked.

"Diana's disappeared."

"Where are you?" she cried, unable for a second to remember what her children were all doing while their father lay near death in her arms.

"We're in Newport. We were all at the folk festival. Remember? Diana went with Nathan and the Bakers. After they got off the ferry, they went to get coffee. Chace and I went ahead with Bucky, but then, apparently, Diana just ran off while they were ordering."

"You won't believe me, but your father's had a heart attack."

"We didn't know anything until the Bakers found us at Festival Field. They thought maybe she was with us . . . What?"

"Daddy's had a heart attack."

A grave silence while Joanne's bad news washed over Katherine's distress. Just as Joanne had found it difficult to accept new disaster, Katherine found it hard to feel properly horrified by this surprising new emergency. Both women were too involved in their own crisis to respond to the other's demand. In Joanne this had the effect of making her entirely sensible about what Katherine should do. "Have you been to look for her?"

"What about Daddy?" Katherine asked.

"He's fine. Well, he's survived. He's in the hospital. But let's take these emergencies one at a time. Have you looked for Diana?"

"We did. Chace and I went to some of the bars along the waterside, but we couldn't find her. When the festival got out, all of us—Nathan, his parents, us—we all stood at different gates watching for her in case we'd been separated."

"Has anyone called the police?"

"Not yet."

"OK, you come on home. I'll call the police. She could be anywhere if she got it into her head to run away. Are the Bakers upset?"

"They're being really nice, but I think they're worried. They couldn't figure out what was going on. I mean, it was a *crazy* thing for her to do."

After Joanne hung up the phone, she lifted it again and called the Newport police. She explained what had happened, described her daughter, accepted their reassurance. ("Don't worry, these kids like to seem wilder than they really are.") Actually, for the moment she was too exhausted to be afraid for Diana; and then she was also superstitious in a way which made her feel better if she flew after a terrible plane crash. Because her husband had had a heart attack that night, Joanne was sure her daughter would finally come home safe and sound. If her husband hadn't had a heart attack, she would have had the energy to consider Diana's physical safety as being perhaps the first but by no means the only cause for worry. Running away from the Bakers *was* a crazy thing to do. But was it only crazy/rude or also crazy/self-destructive? The former was conventionally punishable. She did not know what she would do about the latter.

Joanne really did not understand her daughters' problem. (Despite their differences, she thought of them as suffering from a similar dilemma.) The idea of having to deal with "it," whatever "it" was, added to her nervous chill. She went and huddled under her covers, having tossed a quilt on top of the skimpy summer blanket, trying to sleep, knowing she would not, certainly not until the children had come home. She thrashed about, worrying over Christopher in a grainy, inarticulate, headachy sensation, wondering about Diana in a more fully conscious way. Katherine acted strangely with Chace. Diana acted very strangely with Nathan. These girls had some mysterious problem with men. Joanne had felt them both yearning for a chance to swap miseries with her. Katherine wanted to make complaints about Chace, Diana about her father—the basis for a sad unity with their mother. If Joanne let them, Katherine and Diana would lay their lives sorrow to sorrow with their mother's. They wanted Joanne to embrace their dissatisfactions with men —or was it their fear? They wanted her to legitimize their objections, admit they had some right. Joanne preferred dancing cheek to cheek.

She tossed, wide awake, squeezing her eyes shut. The generation gap. That's what it was. The generation gap lay between her and her daughters. Hers was the "April in Paris" generation, she thought, and her overstimulated mind hurt itself by beating out the tune—da-dee-dee-da-da—and singing, "Where can I run to?" She began to speak inside her skull, saying, "We had our merry, wicked side, 'The Lady Is a Tramp,' 'Just One of Those Things,' 'Cheek to Cheek.' They're not romantic. That's the difference. They're not romantic at all. Its what glues a marriage together, but you have to be willing to be romantic at the right time. And they're not romantic a bit. They're sexy as hell, but sex breaks things up and romance glues them back together."

The clarity of her own voice inside her head had given her such a headache that she got out of bed. She took several aspirins and poured a drink of scotch. She had hardly begun to pace about the living room when noise in the downstairs hall announced the return of everyone who'd been in Newport. They flocked upstairs, approaching her with tact until her warmth, her relief in having company, made them warm, too. Everyone talked at once. Bucky was incoherent with excitement about the various emergencies. The Bakers were flabbergasted. Nathan was despondent. Then Joanne was in tears and Bucky was flabbergasted. Nathan was still despondent. Chace got drinks for everyone. Katherine had a turn at crying. Nathan remained despondent.

The phone rang and they all ran into the kitchen, crowding around Joanne while she took the call. "What?" she cried, trying to hush their impatient questions with her hand. "Who is it?" "Is Daddy OK?" "Have you found Diana?"

"We think we may have your daughter."

Joanne covered the phone with her hand and said, "They think they may have found Diana." Then she said into the receiver, "Well, where is she? Is she all right?"

She was in a hospital. Her arrival had been reported half an hour ago. Taken there after a car accident. Unconscious, badly broken leg, fractured skull. No wallet. Wearing white shorts, striped jersey and a thin gold chain around her neck.

"That's not Diana," Katherine said, rebelling against her own tearful urgency. "This is ridiculous! I'm wasting my good tears." She patted her eyes as though she were damming the water supply for when it would really be needed.

The anticlimax brought the hour to a farcical pitch. The gathering ceased to be distinguishable from any party that had lasted until three-thirty in the morning. People theorized openly about their father's character and sister's whereabouts. After the Bakers staggered home at four, there was another postmortem, more head shakings and forehead slappings about how despondent Nathan had seemed.

"He looked unhappy."

"He *was* unhappy."

"Boy, he was *really* unhappy in Newport."

"No, he was much more unhappy when he heard about Daddy."

"God, the poor guy."

"Yeah, he was really unhappy."

Gradually it became clear that the night was so old and they were all so exhausted that even people of their brilliance weren't going to solve any more problems until they'd had some sleep. There was a halfhearted movement to pile into Joanne's bed with her, but she put a stop to it. The moment might invite such whimsical togetherness, but it would be hard to explain the next day. Though their manic gaiety had come on them naturally enough, in the morning it would be hard to explain to the people whose misery had caused it. Even if she didn't tell Christopher, the next day her conscience would hurt because of how hurt he would be if he knew they'd had fun when he was near the brink of death.

13

Diana was still drunk when she woke up, but soberly so. Her mental hysteria had passed, but how many brain cells had gone with it? In the wake of her former intoxication she was sodden. She was also on a strange beach. She opened the eye on the down side of her nose and saw its triangular shadow looming out in front. She guessed it was very early morning; she hoped it was the next morning and not three days since she could remember dancing in the bar. She thrashed, rolling over as though to smother her prancing nerves. She opened both her eyes and saw a naked man asleep on his back beside her. Her horse balked, would not take a jump.

Her vigilant eyes coldly noted the stranger's face. He had a dip in his nose like the sagging back of a dude-ranch nag. Only the iciest control kept her from saddling up this observation and riding over the nearest cliff. But with rigid scientific frostiness she drew her nerves so tight she could hardly breathe, and studied his slightly parted mouth, its upper lip dotted with small, dry scales and one corner filled with a sandy crust. Her glance took in the little stubbled hill of his chin, toured the rolling platter of his chest and checked out his prick, flopped at the same angle as his unconscious head.

Seen through the binoculars of her self-control, the penis in its scraggly nest had a certain oafish charm, like a peasant sleeping it off in a haystack. His prick had the sweetness of all beasts. She couldn't hate Foster, particularly not when he was snoozing with his head on his paws. But her forgiving affection toward the stranger's pooch was severed by hatred for everything she saw in his master's face. She despised what was brute and blunt and sullen in the stranger's face. There was no word strong enough for the repulsion she felt when she connected the flaws buzzing round him like flies and the seepage between her own bare legs. It was as if an army of insects had entered her, as if she'd let him invade her with her hideousness, as if she'd spread herself wide and had her carcass cracked up the middle and now hung on display in the butcher's window like any other piece of tail.

She was alone in this mess, alone, alone, alone in the world. She had no magic coins to see her through her ordeal. Not even a silly hat just to keep them laughing. No, she was alone without a single myth to guide her. Who had ever warned her that being nuts was part of normal life? Who had ever helped her with her real problems? Well, she'd done it. She'd gotten rid of her virginity. Now maybe she would be more like other people, more one thing than another. It had been a bitter, bitter loss or victory—she did not know which. She stood, stepped across him and took a crap on his peacefully heaving chest. Bomb for mental health! I am alone, alone, alone. Kill for inner peace!

Then she took off his plaid cowboy shirt which she had on and threw it down beside his crumpled T-shirt, lying there like a joke-shop imitation of spilt milk. She pulled on her own black turtleneck, started down the beach. Ahead of her, reddish cliffs formed a point to the left, and rising up in the clear new day, in all their majestic nonsense, were the towers, spires, and gables of The Breakers, Château-sur-mer, etcetera. At her level, PEPSI dominated, stamped in large letters above the closed green shutters of the common house of hotdogs. Right beside it a crisscrossed wire wastebasket overflowed with candy wrappers, king-size popcorn tubs, old paper cups. Along the shore, the surf went on splashing gently, reaching for her bare feet where she stood to put on her blue jeans.

When she was finally dressed, she gave her lover (who shall have to remain nameless—were they ever even introduced?) a last, unfond look. We slugged it out in the arena and it was a draw, old buddy. Funny how doing your worst made you feel it was possible to start anew, maybe even to start out right. Yet, as she thought this, Diana had a vision of Katherine crying in her mother's embrace. In this fleeting picture, Mrs. Nicholas was saying, "There, there, it's all right. Go on, get it out. Get it all off your chest. You'll feel better when you've had a good cry."

There were certain things, one in particular, that Diana would never be able to get off her chest. It was sitting on Mr. X's chest right this very minute. She would have to go through life hiding her scarlet "S" (for shit, as opposed to Hester's "A" for adultery; Diana still had that to look forward to). She would never again be free to take off her clothes in front of her mother and sister, in front of anyone else, for that matter. So long, Mr. X, we're branded for good, outlaws to the death. She'd earned her letter at last. Too bad she couldn't wear it on a big white cableknit sweater the way Bucky wore his "G" for being on the Groton tennis team.

She began to trot toward the paved road. As she did, a police car drove into view. It came to a stop. She ran to the fender. The policeman emerged slowly on his side, wearing a state trooper's hard-brimmed hat. Handsome hat, ugly face. Fat and soft and pale. Overweight jowls, plump body in beautifully pressed, tailored blue shirt and dark uniform pants. Heavy leather belt and holster. Hooked his thumbs into his belt and stood and watched her.

Wisecracks began to flare up in her mind: ah, the law and order butler, come with a menu at last. My choice of systems, eh? With anarchy, you recommend the heaviest chains, and with greater self-government, you think just a side dish of restrictions will suffice. But as these wisecracks began to bounce around her mind, they began to unite with the jangling of a violent hangover. She had to suddenly lean against the fender for support.

"Where ya goin' girlie?"

"I'd like to go home. I live near Wickford," she mumbled, experiencing afresh what man has experienced all through history after a night of excess: nausea, sweating, and longing for a quick death.

"Is anybody looking for you?"

"I don't know."

"Get in. I'll radio the station. See if there have been any calls." As she got in, she saw that the concession stand blocked Mr. X from view. Just as well. A quick picture in the style of a TV police drama. One plainclothes law-and-order butler yells to another, "Hey, Smitty, quick! There's a guy here with shit on his chest!" God, it was enough to nearly make her puke. Actually, she did puke, rolling down the window in the nick of time. Blew lunch. Looked like dinner and breakfast, too. She'd never drink again. I swear to God, I'm turning over a new leaf, taking the pledge, and if you'll just cure this hangover (instantly), I'll start my new life as an angel.

They passed the Viking Arch, turning by the Art Association. She saw a tanned young man walking down the street and thought of how preferable it would be to be him, starting his day without her uproar of mind and nerves. Why couldn't she be him? Why did she have to be locked up in this dirty old jail of her own body?

"Hey, girlie, you're wanted in Newport, heh, heh. There's been a tracer out on you since midnight, sister. Whyn't you tell your parents you weren't coming home? Save them some worry."

Funny how doing your worst got you into a peck of trouble. She began to consider what and who she was going to have to face when she got back home. The Bakers, her parents. People were going to want explanations, and she didn't have any. She had no idea what happened after she started dancing with the Beast in the bar. Well, she had some idea, but that was unmentionable. She'd just have to tell them she'd been insane, on top of which she'd had too much to drink. It was the truth, after all.

Lie back, take your mind off the hook. Enjoy the view (being careful, of course, not to barf). They were among the first cars to pull onto the slick decks of the Jamestown Ferry, the first off on the other side, driving by the big, run-down resort hotels and the guest houses ("No Vacancy") beyond, the fields with feeding geese, and then the fields with graves. Up, up over the slippery top of the Jamestown Bridge. Long views both north and south, and right below them a single sailboat powered by a motor in the windless morning. They drove on past the Plum Beach Club on one side, the beach grasses on both. It was all more familiar than it had ever seemed to her, as if in the last twenty-four hours it had composed itself formally into a fixed past and a hometown. As they climbed to the traffic light and took the turn past the neighbor's stretch of stone wall, Diana felt the apprehension of a prodigal son or daughter. She could remember back in the old days when the neighbor's Champ-des-Corbeaux always drew a blank, though she knew it involved a literary joke, and therefore would have liked to "get" it. She just never had, perhaps because she'd constantly failed French and other languages, including her own. As a matter of fact, she still did not get Champ-des-Corbeaux, but that now seemed like the least of her worries. Mainly, she was worried about getting three days away from now.

"Bucky, Bucky," she cried when she saw him standing outside the front door. "Bucky!" she repeated, jumping out of the car. "I've had a nervous breakdown."

"You're goddamned right you have. Are you out of your mind? Where the hell did you go? Everybody's been going nuts trying to find you. Daddy's in the hospital. He had a heart attack."

Just then her mother came out in a nightgown and wrapper, her face pale beneath her summer tan. She looked exhausted, though as she approached Diana her eyes filled with tears and she suddenly looked Katherine's age. "Oh Jelly, Jelly," she murmured chidingly.

Ellie? Ellie? It's me, your daughter, Diana . . . Nonetheless, Diana looked down at herself to make sure she hadn't turned into her childhood symbol of the disorder potential in becoming an adult.

"Oh Jelly Bean," her mother said again, addressing Diana by the name she'd had in the nursery. "What a night for you to pick to disappear. Your father nearly died, and you take off in Newport. No one knows if you're with a murderer or where you are."

Diana gritted her teeth, grimacing as she watched her mother settle things with the policeman. Shake, shake of their heads, tsk, tsk of their tongues, nod, nod, point of her mother's finger, flourish of the policeman's pen, shrug, shrug, smile, smile, wave, wave. The policeman was dazzled as most grocers, druggists and servicemen were when they first experienced the rays of Mrs. Nicholas' charm gun. He drove off, looking like a happy man and shooting an inquiring farewell glance at Diana as he left: could that dustbin really be the daughter of the Queen?

The Queen herself seemed to be asking the same question as she approached her dustbin daughter. "We're all exhausted, Diana. We were up until six, worrying about you and your father. Now that I know you're safe I could kill you."

"How's Daddy?" Diana whispered.

"He's OK, I think. He had a good night. I just talked to the hospital. You'd better clean up. Go on, take a bath, change your clothes. I'll come talk to you when I've calmed down a little."

Diana welcomed her mother's anger on the theory that it had to spend itself, and that it might as well be now as later. In fact, if her own temper was anything to go by, her mother's eruption would soon clear the way to self-recrimination, apology and groveling. In the meantime Diana knew enough to retire. She shed her clothes and took a bath in such hot water it was like lying in a furnace. Afterward, she was as clean and pink as a young pig. She crawled between the fresh sheets and lay like a sacrifice waiting to be chopped into pieces for the gods.

A knock. Diana looked at the door and it opened. Katherine stuck her head in, pale and pretty and wide-eyed.

"Is Daddy going to be all right?" Diana asked.

"I think so. Mummy says he almost died last night, but I think *she* almost died from fear. I talked to the doctor this morning. He said we had every reason to believe Daddy would make a full recovery."

"*Phew.* I couldn't tell if he'd had a heart attack because they thought I was dead. But he didn't know I disappeared, did he?"

"No, I'm sure he didn't. He couldn't have. But where did you go? What did you do? Remember, I am your most trusted adviser and confidante."

Diana was speechless, though not for want of things to say. She longed to be in unison with the Katherine who saw the mountain in every molehill, who knew the meaning of life in all its complexity. Diana wanted Katherine to apply her genius to her tale of drunkenness, but she still wasn't quite sure how to tell the tale. "First you tell me what happened after I went off. How did you find out I'd run away?"

"We met the Bakers at Festival Field, and they wanted to know if you were with us. You weren't, so then everybody got a little worried. I said Chace and I could go look for you, figuring you'd rather see us than the Bakers if you were up to no good. But we looked around town in a few bars and you weren't to be seen. We gave up, and then the Bakers got upset, wanted to call the police."

"Was Nathan mad?" asked Diana, flinging her arms over her face as though to ward off an answer.

"Not really mad but hurt, I think. It was scary for him to have you disappear . . ."

"Don't rub it in, please don't rub it in. Go on, tell me the rest, but gently, gently."

"There's not much to tell. We restrained the Bakers from calling the police, but then I called Mummy to find out what we should do. That's when she told us about Daddy. And she was the one to call the police. In fact, I *know* you couldn't have had anything to do with Daddy's heart attack because when we phoned she had already taken him to the hospital."

"Oh God," groaned Diana. No matter what Katherine said, Diana felt her hatred had indirectly struck her father down. If she had not actually put a knife in his heart, she had added unnecessarily to the general worry pool. "Ardmelia," Diana asked, "do you think I'm Ellie Snow? Do you think I'm going to wreak havoc on myself and everybody else who gets involved with me?"

"First I need the facts. *What* did you do last night? Remember, there is no shame between two sisters such as we are."

"Got drunk and fucked a barfly."

"Nice play, Shakespeare."

"But aren't you going to reveal the hidden meaning in my story? Isn't there anything grandiose that I can say about myself?"

"Last time I tuned in," said Katherine, "I thought you

were going off to sleep with Nathan. What happened to that project?"

"I guess I knew him too well."

"That's the point, dummy. You're supposed to do it with people you know well."

"It was a little more complicated than that," Diana confessed. "Are you ready for the big bomb?"

"Try me."

"You see, I was sort of worried I might be a homo." (Her mind flashed a dreadful recollection of Mrs. Baker in her horrendous incarnation of the night before. O Chair, where were you in the hour of my need?) "As a matter of fact, there was a moment there when I thought I was going to have to commit homo adultery with his mother."

"Diana!" Katherine cried, laughing with outrage. "I do *not* believe you. You would never have done anything with his mother. Come off it. What are you talking about?"

"Well, I jumped her, but she wasn't having any."

"Diana!" Katherine yelled. "This is really too much. I knew you were crazy, but I didn't know you were *crazy*."

"But there's a happy ending. I did it, right? I'm not a homo."

"How many times do I have to tell you? Man is *not* an animal."

"I thought he was, but he fell in love."

"But that's the point," said Katherine primly. "Perhaps he is a beast, but he can rise above it by falling in love."

"Well, if you like being in love so much, why aren't you married, Ardmelia? Answer me that."

"Maybe I'm a homo, too," said Katherine, smiling. "I mean, it's all right to do it with a man, but I'd much rather live with my sister. As far as the important things go, like jokes, hopes, dreams and thoughts. I always carry you around in my heart and tell you things as they happen. If you weren't there, I'd be awfully lonely."

"Ditto."

"And yet," sighed Katherine, "I think we have to be ready to go it alone. Maybe man is the animal who walks alone when he falls in love. But that's why he has character. It's the only solution to life's problems. But until you get used to it, character is just another form of unhappiness."

"I guess you realize whose favorite phrase that is?"

"It's not my own?"

"No, it's Dad's. I guess you two just share some noble wavelength high, high above the rest of us."

"Diana, I'm going to tell you one of your worst qualities."

"For my own good?"

"For your own good, you little creep. You live in a glass house, but you love to throw stones. If I sometimes express myself in a rather profound yet flowery way, it's because life sometimes invites us to celebrate its amazing complexities. You'll notice that just now I've been making an effort to speak plainly to you, partially because you're quite simpleminded"—Katherine delivered this insult in a delicious tone and gazed innocently at the ceiling—"and partially because your problems are quite, quite simple. You have a severe tendency toward alcoholism compounded by advanced nymphomania."

"You really know how to make a person feel wonderful," Diana said, pleasantly enveloped by their shared tone. Somehow, knowing exactly what her sister meant and perfectly appreciating Katherine's mix of humor and irritation made Diana sleepy. It was totally relaxing to feel so at home, and once her nervous hung-over frizz was

soothed, her exhaustion caught up with her. The last bar-
rier between Diana and dozing was the gratitude she felt
for Katherine's accompaniment. Maybe it was just because they'd lived in the same house all these years, but
Diana felt it was true nobility—no other word would do—
yes, NOBILITY, that kept Katherine from putting Diana
in an incinerator with the rest of the garbage. Katherine
was such an *angel*. If there was only some way to pay her
back; one good turn deserved another. "Tell me your
troubles," Diana begged. "How's Chace? How's life?"

"Answer hazy. Ask again later."

Diana bowed to Katherine's right so as not to reveal
herself further. Diana was, after all, Katherine's creation,
the product of Katherine's intelligence and answers: why
would an author consult a book she'd finished writing? It
could only tell her what she knew already. The last bar-
rier was swept away. There was no reason to remain alert,
and Diana was asleep before she'd completely rolled over.

Katherine was still in the room when she faded. Her
mother was there when she awoke. Diana gazed at
Joanne out of a convalescent calm, conscious of her
mother's awe-inspiring beauty. Watching her while she
paced slowly beside the bed, Diana enjoyed her mother's
comforting height, the harmony of her features, the bold,
jutting nose, the warm, oak-colored texture of her skin.
Her familiar smell deliciously filled the air, bringing a pa-
rade of beloved memories, going back through all the
dressing rooms her mother had ever occupied. Her closets
had always been filled with fragrant dresses which, even
in their empty, hanging forms, suggested the smooth con-
solation of her waist when she took the child Diana in her
arms.

"I think it's best if you don't tell me what happened,"
her mother said, finally starting to speak in her voice of

fairness, a voice in which there was much sound reasoning and only partial satisfaction for Diana's craving. "It's not that you could do something which we would consider unforgivable, even if we were critical. It's just that there is only so much emotional energy to go round and your father needs our attention now."

"I hate him! I *hate* him!" Diana blurted, as much to her own surprise as to her mother's. But when she saw her mother's look of astonishment, Diana felt as she did when she had a bad case of flu. It was as if she'd thrown up and thrown up and thrown up until she couldn't believe she had anything left to vomit. And yet, after a pause it was clear that there was one final upheaval on its way, one last bit of poison to come up. "I hate him," she repeated.

"Don't say that. You don't mean it."

"I do. He's a fuck. He's an idiotassholefuckershithead," she said again, knowing her mother was right: it wasn't really what she meant. But whatever was coming up had to struggle against a crushing weight from outside, the rock of her own inferiority pressing down, down on her right to exist. This couldn't go on. Diana was tired of her Extraordinary Awfulness, bored to the roots of her teeth by the mammoth envelopment to which she was so drearily, hopelessly attached. If she was going to spend her life crushed in the arms of this monster calling her all the names she deserved to be called, if she agreed with everything she so gigantically held against herself, why couldn't she at least let her mother off the hook? Why couldn't Diana let go of the fine mortal pacing the floor beside her bed, this beautiful woman with her deep, romantic tie to her husband, with her voluptuous taste in furnishings and clothes, with her naïve, youthful niceness?

"I got drunk and lost my virginity. And that's not all, Mum."

"Oh, Diana, did you have to . . ."

"I said I got drunk and slept with a stranger. I'm a failure, Mummy. I'm awful, awful . . ."

"I heard you, Diana. I heard what you said the first time. I asked if it was necessary, that's all. Whether you really had to go and roll around in the gutter and then come tell me about it."

"You have never loved me, Mummy! Never! Never! You have never loved any of us as much as you've loved Daddy." It was amazing how full of crap she was. Next it would be coming out of her ears.

To her astonishment, her mother was silenced by this. "You can't really feel that way," she said.

"But I do," insisted Diana, ready to discount it if her mother did, feeling truly empty, as if she had been sick for the last time and was finally ready to cooperate.

"I'm sorry you do," her mother said, sitting beside her on the bed and brushing Diana's hair from her forehead. Joanne laid her hand mercifully alongside her daughter's face, gazing at her with such affection that Diana could feel it entering her body, could feel herself filled by a forgiveness as thick and nourishing as soup. She had lost all hope of this and thus was open to it with an innocence which heightened her sense that this was miraculous. Her mother said, "I love you, sweetheart. I always have, you must know that. Have you forgotten who I am? That I'm your mum? I couldn't not love you. But I think I was better at sharing myself with you all when you were babies. Having a little baby is like having a love affair. You can't imagine how delicious it feels to live in the embrace of a beautiful, plump little baby. Of course, I had nurses, too. I only knew the love-affair part of babies. And then, when you were bigger, I went back to being my selfish old self, more interested in other grown-ups than kids. And, of course, more interested in my love affair with my husband. I've never actually liked playing with children. But I never stopped loving you, Diana. I loved you then. I love you now. I'll never stop loving you."

The word "love" bathed Diana in light, cleansing sweetness. She knew this sweetness, this obliterating satisfaction, as a haunting memory long in danger of being dismissed as a cobweb or a fantasy. It gave rise to a motion of spirit which made Diana think of another word she'd heard of but never had occasion to use: "soul." For a moment she felt her own soul breathing the fresh air of love, and then, with the simplicity of an infant, Diana fell into a restful sleep.

14

Christopher shared his hospital room with an ancient bone of a man who, through no fault of his own, depressed Christopher by constantly reminding him of what the future might one day bring. His roommate was a good patient, but Christopher was a bad one. Once his initial weakness passed, Christopher insisted on moving unnecessarily, which set off alarms in the hall, where his heartbeat was appearing on a small TV screen, bringing nurses at a run to his bedside. He hated the hospital food, wouldn't touch it. He fought with one of the older nurses about using a bedpan. He simply refused. Finally, the doctor decided it would be better to let Christopher go home early, both for his sake and for the staff's. Perhaps he would submit to being quiet and getting the necessary rest in his own house.

Joanne brought him back to a master suite designed for their pleasure and now getting its full use as Christopher's infirmary. He felt as much like a guest as an invalid—as if he'd been sent away to a distant relative's castle to recuperate. Lying in bed, he appreciated the design and color and detail as a pure connoisseur of architectural accomplishments. Or perhaps he was more of an anthropologist as he surveyed the shape of their bedroom, admiring the airy, pale purple which was Joanne's trademark as a decorator.

Though it could not be found on any standard color card, every house they'd lived in had at least one room painted this elusive hue. It was a light, soothing color with what seemed like an inner life; this pale, pale purple suggested the limits of human perception, the last thing anyone could say before becoming spirit itself. The color pleased him in the same way as Greek pottery or feats of Aztec technology. He was moved by this bedroom the way he was moved by evidence of intelligence and order that had survived from the past. He was gladdened by signs of recurring human aspirations, and by the amazing variety of imaginative solutions. And yet he was also aware that the civilization which had produced him was on the wane. He was a type whose time was up. Part of him belonged in the American Museum of Rugged Individualism and Rigid Anticommunism. Part of him belonged with the suits of armor, the vast tapestries and chalices, the noble pomp, the fanfare and self-sacrifice of King Arthur's sort of courtly Christianity, all consigned to the Ripley's *Believe It or Not* of history.

To a degree that astonished him, his personal past had just fallen away. He ate and slept and survived as a being alone with eternal questions, as a traveler with a few assignments to complete while he rested in this particular inn. These assignments were vague, inchoate things—scrambled thoughts that rose up in his mind while he spent the morning sitting in a chair doing crossword puzzles. He often found himself wondering what it meant that he hadn't died when he was much more depressed, much more agonizingly confused than he was now. He was grateful he hadn't and wondered why. He was disturbed by thoughts of people dying when they weren't prepared to die—of people dying while their lives were unsolved or in terrible messes. This bothered him frequently, though he could neither figure out why nor lay it to rest.

Did people die as they had lived? What about the young men killed in wars? Was there any reason they had to die young? Did the agony of people who'd died unhappily live on? Could others live out the snarls of misery left behind by people who'd died before they'd understood whatever they were meant to understand? What was his real question? Was he really asking if there was a God? Or what this God was like? Had this God saved him from dying for some reason? But why had He let others die horribly?

Christopher didn't know, but he slowly ceased minding that he didn't know. His children were embarrassed by his new, childlike openness, and by his obliviousness to his role in their embarrassment. Like a child, he found his children strange and wondrous. He still lived apart. Though his nonparticipation was not new, its tone was. He was no longer proudly withdrawn, the ogre in exile in their midst. People left him alone, but they addressed him carefully, sweetly, as if he were handicapped. He didn't mind. It was all out of his hands. Others would have to take over the responsibility and do the work.

One day Nathan looked in on him to tell him that work on The Bleakers was completed. Christopher was struck, then upset, by Nathan's cold manner. He insisted on giving a factual account, but this amounted to unfriendliness in what was supposed to be a friendly visit. There was no appeal to any of the established areas of affection between them. There was even a punitive note in Nathan's refusal to relax. Christopher was at sea. What had he done? He tried to think back to the day of his heart attack and realized how little he remembered. While Nathan formally praised the Nicholases' kids for having worked hard, Christopher ransacked his recollection for some clue. Again Nathan referred to the children, drawing his lips tightly around the words "your children have really made an effort since your illness." The way the boy stressed the words convinced Christopher that they contained the secret of whatever was bothering him. But what was it?

Since his heart attack, Christopher's childhood had emerged with incredible clarity in his memory, but his recent past was dim. He could remember sitting with Nathan and Diana, but the only words that came to mind were "Clear Lake," and without knowing what they referred to, he was sure they had nothing to do with the conversation of that morning.

"Clear Lake. What about Clear Lake?" Christopher asked, making a stab in the dark.

"The convention?"

"Oh, is that what it is?" Christopher said with disappointment. He sighed like a frustrated lover.

Nathan the robot wouldn't take him up on the sigh. He pressed mechanically on. "You and I talked about it when

it was still in the organizing stages. It's all set now, and I
think it's going to be interesting. Since the blacks have
pulled out and want their own thing, complicity is emerging as the big issue. You know that I'd decided to go to
the University of Wisconsin over Harvard. Well, I hadn't
been entirely sure if I'd done the right thing. But now
I'm glad. I'm convinced that the level of political consciousness is so much higher among Wisconsin students,
and that this may have some effect on the administration
in the long run. Of course, both Wisconsin and Harvard
are pretty bad, but Harvard is clearly the worse of the
two. I mean Harvard *was* the Pentagon under Kennedy,
the Pentagon, the State Department, the Treasury.
There's something to the arguments that say the only way
this country is going to get a fresh start is to bomb Harvard."

"Nathan, *what* is wrong?"

"Nothing," he said prissily, like a person defending a lie.
Only his extreme social naïveté made it possible for Christopher to believe he hadn't planned the whole thing as an
act. Only a truly innocent person would go to such melodramatic extremes to hide what was really bothering him.

"If I've done anything to offend you, please accept my
apologies," Christopher said, making matters worse.

"If I've done anything to suggest you've offended me
or that any member of your family has offended me,
please accept my apologies."

And that was the end of that. But when Joanne came in
with lunch, Christopher described the bizarre interview
and asked her if she had any idea why Nathan had been
so huffy. And she answered him falsely, not by speaking
but by raising her eyebrows and tilting her head to the
side: it was a bad actress' parody of wonderment. What
was going on here? What was everybody keeping from
him? What wasn't he strong enough to know?

"Why don't you tell me the truth?" he cried. "Why are you keeping things from me?"

"Don't get overstimulated. There's nothing to really get excited about," Joanne said, motioning for him to calm down with her hands. "He and Diana have, as they say, broken up. He wants to keep his relationship with you separate, but he hasn't mastered the genre."

"When did all this happen?"

"I guess the night they went to the folk festival. The same night you had your heart attack. Well, they didn't break up that night, but that was the night Diana, Diana . . ."

"That was the night Diana what?"

"Well, I'm sorry it came up."

"But, having come up, is it your plan to pass on your information, to declassify it, so to speak, or are you still going to keep what you know to yourself?"

"You act as though I've enjoyed keeping a secret from you," she protested.

"Well, whether or not you've enjoyed it, are you going to share it? Or perhaps I'm being too direct. Maybe you'd like me to ask you questions, to help you express yourself. For instance, did Diana's misbehavior have anything to do with her wise lip? Did she hurt Nathan verbally or by her acts?"

"Christopher, don't. It was never that big a romance, but they ended the relationship they had. Leave it at that. Nathan clearly wanted it known that his quarrel with Diana didn't affect his respect for you."

"I'll tell you why I mind," he said, alarmed by his own candor but unable to veil it. "I'll tell you exactly why I mind. Because you prefer them to me. You love the children more than you love me."

"Christopher, wait. This is truly absurd. You can't mean what you're saying."

"Then tell me what Diana did."

"She ran off with a man she met in a bar and didn't come home until 7 A.M."

"Jeezus," he said and whistled. The implications loomed unpleasantly. He was forced to thread this fact through his recent convalescence. He spontaneously pictured (as a movie director filming a fictional situation) the moments of his heart attack, his trip to the hospital—all this unfolding side by side with Diana's escapade, her disappearance, her scruffy return. (A strand of curiosity began to unwind its questions. Where did she go? How did she get back? What did she do?) He now saw his hard-won, newly discovered innocence in terms of the conspiracy which made it possible. Every consoling gesture, word and attitude displayed by his family had been a mask; beneath it was what they all knew and weren't telling him. It wasn't that he wanted to have been involved. It was more that his state of mind, his philosophic mood, had been staged (Family Keeps Secrets From Ex-Spy!). Thanks to the others' deception, he'd imagined he was free to treat himself as a work of art, to ask eternal questions because he didn't know enough to ask the real ones. "I better know more about this. Is it as bad as it sounds?"

"Well, it's terribly complicated. We know she lost her virginity."

"We do? God, times have changed."

"They sure have," said Joanne. "For the worse."

"I never told my parents when I lost my virginity. You're not supposed to tell them, are you?" Christopher asked.

"I think she's gone to great lengths so that we'd know how unhappy she is. She was incredibly upset the morning after she'd been in Newport. Believe me, she was truly overwrought. The funny farm was not out of the question. It seemed important just to get her calmed down, and then to worry about whether she was pregnant."

"Wait a minute. I can only take one problem at a time. What are we supposed to do if our daughter's thrown herself away on a stranger? Has she broken a rule? Is there some punishment we can administer? Maybe we should see this as her initiation ceremony, though why I should know the date and hour of my daughter's deflowering . . . Anyway, maybe the point is to get it all over with in an impersonal situation."

"Well, that's fine if you want an impersonal grandchild. Until she'd had her period, there was no way to know if she was pregnant or not. I'd debated about when and if to tell you, and one of my plans was to tell you once I knew for sure if there were any consequences. But now she's had her period. So we don't have to worry about that. But now *you've* got to talk to her."

"About her period?" asked Christopher. "Are you kidding?"

"No, the fact that she stayed out all night and then had to tell me what she did is all of a piece with the trouble she's been in at school and the whole problem of what she's going to do next year. We've put off facing it, but the time has come. And, frankly, it won't do any good for me to do it alone. I know she wants your attention, too."

"I don't know why," he grumbled. "I'm a shadow of my former self. And I'm exhausted. I certainly can't talk to her today. And probably not tomorrow either."

He gave her a sweet, boyish, wounded look. "I don't know what to say to girls," he complained. He thrust his head deep into the pillows, pulled the covers up around his neck. "I'll do it, but not for a while. I just really need to get rested up first."

Joanne nodded sympathetically. She took his tray and

left him alone to sleep. In a dream she came back through
the door, informing him in a significant voice, "Diana's
going to the hospital for a period. They're putting her into
deep snow until this has all blown over. But you're allowed to see her. She asked specifically for you."

He went, bowed down by a terrible sense of obligation,
wishing he did not have to go, and ashamed that he
wished this. His daughter was in a special hospital, one
which had been created just for her, in fact. A stage-set
facade of institutional brick stood in front of a reception
room connected by a corridor to the wing where Diana
was staying. A single nurse staffed this pretense but took
her role seriously and performed it well. Acting as though
there were a labyrinth of hallways in which he might get
lost, she instructed him carefully in the twists and turns
he should take to get to his daughter's room. Long before
he reached Diana's door, he saw blood coming down the
corridor. The trickle in the hall intensified as he neared
her room, and when he opened the door, she was gushing
blood, spurting rivers of it like a hydrant. He slammed
the door and began to stuff towels in the cracks and to
wad them with sheets he found in stacks on a dolly. He
wanted to get all this back under control. He didn't want
to hide anything or to avoid disturbing knowledge; he
just wanted to get the mess so it was manageable, so men
of good will and common sense could discuss it. But no
matter how many towels he used—mopping up the mess
in the halls, spreading bandages everywhere, heaping
sheets on sheets on sheets—some pale, suggestive, sordid
taint always seemed to seep through, and always seemed
to be more than his standard of "manageable" could bear.

15

After the Newport beach fiasco, Diana had a week when she didn't have to face Nathan, but the whole time her mother watched her like a hawk. Joanne tried to veil her interest, but it was dreadfully clear that she thought keeping her daughter quiet would somehow hasten the arrival of her period. She finally said as much. It made Diana think of yesteryear, when she and Katherine read about "the onset of menstruation" in books about sexual development and how to do "it." She had always hated "onset" (even more than she hated the word "menstruation")—somehow so Martian, so creepy, so technical. But she had also hated the idea of the "curse," as it was known in the preppy circles she frequented. Thanks, Nature, thanks a lot. What if I don't want a bunch of yecchy gunk coming out of me? Talk about a stain on your purity. This was *really* disgusting. But typical. Nature was full of all sorts of shit.

She never kept track of her yecchy gunk, and had no idea when next to expect it. Fortunately, a mere week passed before the onset of this girl person's seventy-second period, and she supposed she should be glad when it came. But while she waited for it, and when she got her yecchy gunk, Diana was miserable. She hated having her period be the object of her mother's curiosity. She was offended by having science investigate that which was painfully private. Yet who, she asked, was *she* to be offended? Wasn't it rather bee-zarre for her to have these aesthetic niceties? Why should waiting to get her period, under her mother's scrutiny, present any problems to a girl who'd felt nothing about fucking a barfly and crapping on him afterward? The young lady herself was conscious of the excess of feeling on one side, and the absence of it on the other. Sometimes, when the present misery of being a dirty hosebag-in-waiting got to be too much, she played with her mind. (Yes, records also show she could not keep her hands off herself; she was like a boy at boarding school and developed dark circles under her eyes.) She played with her sense of the Newport beach fiasco, turning it around tonally, moving it from the height of tragedy to the depths of the ridiculous, and never minding whether her approach was high or low. She could conceive of it languidly, as if she were a southern belle entertaining her beaux on a hot summer afternoon, Ah do decleah! Li'l ole me is just the silliest li'l ole thing! Ah fucked a bahfly and crapped on him aftahwahd!

Her chameleon mind, with its restless impulse to cast her experience away from her, to turn things inside out, could as easily treat it all as a puritan nightmare. Without troubling her feelings, she could run her drunkenness through as an allegory of the stress in her spirit, incurable and infinitely negative. She had washed herself away with liquor, then forgotten it all in a demonstration of her nature as a series of zeroes—a mouth, a gullet, a stomach, a womb, a cunt—all zeroes, all empty, a single shaft leading nowhere, down which all her experience would disappear. And she could up the drama from there. The hours she'd lost while drunk contained a crucial missing link between her "before" and "after" selves. She had been most fully herself during her oblivion; she'd been forced to be by the falling away of all her restraints, and yet her act of finally *being* was lost to her, had been violently induced and then forcefully removed. It was as if she'd been pregnant and gone through a grueling labor and given birth to a monster—as if the monster had been taken away and disposed of while she was screaming and thrashing under a drug which made her forget everything except the feeling that something horrible had happened. It was as if everyone else knew the awful truth which she could now never know, even if people tried to tell her, because the truth had to be experienced to be known. Only eyewitnesses could discuss the truth, and then only among themselves.

Blah, blah. It was all words. Ya gotta lotta potential, kid, but let's stick to the facts. None of her mental gymnastics touched her to the quick the way her mother's daily darting glance of inquiry did. Diana shriveled every time her mother looked and found her wanting. And when she finally did get her period and went to her mother with the news, Diana's voice was a squeak; and she shed tears, as she had the first time, when her mother said, then as now, with the same misplaced inflection, "Oh, darling, *congratulations!*" (For what? For having a stain on her purity? Or for having one stain on her purity make up for another?)

And then, having shown herself to be a good woman, both healthy and not pregnant, she had to go apologize for being a bad girl. You'd think we were living at King Arthur's court, Diana thought, and held it in. (Remember how your fourth-grade teacher wrote on your report card: "Diana's sharp tongue often gets her into unexpected trouble." Too bad you didn't listen then. Too bad you had to wait until it was too late—until after your life of crime started instead of before, when it might have stopped you from starting.) But was it an apology, exactly, that she owed Nathan? She felt she owed him something, but she rebelled at her own conventional idea that what she owed was an apology. Throughout their brief relationship she'd felt answerable to his desire for her, though she had almost no natural affection for him. He had always seemed alien to her. She had never fallen for his first premise the way she had for Chace's (not to mention Katherine's), and yet here she was, going over to face the music when she hadn't even put her quarter in the jukebox.

"O feet," she said to her feet as they did their job of walking out the door, "O feet, keep up the good work." I recognize this asphalt and this turn around the arborvitae hedge. If I were a sentimental person, I might recall the first time I strolled along this dear Arcadian highway on my way to meet Mrs. Baker for the first time, on my way to the sweet cliff where lovers leap. Ah, yes, I jumped, but I jumped alone, Amy. Thanks, thanks a lot. Where were you as I soared over the side? Standing back up on the top, all safe and sound, watching while I fell

and tsk-tsking that I should be so extreme. Well, you led
me astray, lady. Remember when we first met? You
suggested much to me. And then the next thing I know,
you deny that we were ever members of the same communist brain cell.

And now Diana faced the door; now she studied the
problem of whether to knock or not. As knocking was
completely absent from the relationship between the barn
and The Bleakers, it would be very symbolic if she
rapped. It would symbolize how much trouble she was in.
On the other hand, knocking had no place in the scheme
of things because it was possible to knock your head off
without being heard; the inhabitants of the house might
have withdrawn out of earshot. Finally, it is important to
add that while the barn had a doorbell, The Bleakers did
not. Yet the barn's doorbell was rarely pressed, as if the
custom of that rural parish would not allow upstart technology to succeed where knocking still had made no head-
way. At the date of this writing, the custom was as it had
always been: to stick your head in the door and yell, "Anybody home?"

That is why it would have had a special meaning if
Diana chose to knock, which she did, but so softly not
even a machine designed to detect flutters in the strato-
sphere could have recorded her tap. Even if the machine
was placed on the other side of the door. When, as she
hoped, no one answered her light touch, she turned to go.
But what is this? Why does she stagger back in horror,
her hand involuntarily clapped across her mouth?

Mr. Baker has come up from behind, on his way in
from the car, carrying a bag of groceries.

"Oh my God," she nearly yelled. "You scared me."

"I'm sorry," he smiled ruefully.

"No, *I'm* sorry," she said. "That's why I'm here."

He nodded, as if in agreement with her feeling that she had something to regret. However, he bided his time about forgiving her. "Well, come on in," he said, apparently succumbing to unpleasant necessity. He gave a special twist to the way he pivoted toward the door, aggressively showing her his back as he reached for the knob. She saw real aversion in his movements as he opened the door and stepped away from her. Yet there were subtle gradations of his aversion which she struggled to identify. When she couldn't, her sense of his rejection opened her to new, generalized terror. She stood in the recently completed kitchen of The Bleakers, her whole body growing pasty with sweat.

"It looks nice," she said experimentally.

"I know. You should see the living room. Why don't you go in and I'll get Nathan."

Terse, polite, he'd washed his hands of her. She was frightened, seeing how she'd created a dead end in her life where there had once been an avenue of possibility.

"Mr. Baker," she said. "I'm really sorry I took off in Newport. I probably caused you a lot of worry. I wish I could do or say something to make it all up to you . . ."

"Don't apologize. You didn't do anything wrong," he said, making it clear that he didn't like her because he didn't like her. No special reason. Unless it was part of Quaker doctrine to hate Diana Nicholases, and it was certainly part of being Diana Nicholas to feel bad about having been born. "We should never have let you have all those drinks. You were drunk, that's all."

Didn't Quakers have a law against alcohol? They did. That was it. That was why he hated her.

"Of course," he said. "I felt for my son . . ." *That* was it. Nathan was the success in this family, the one they had their hopes pinned on. Different from her family, where the parents were the successful ones. Well, she sure couldn't blame him for loving his son. Did that mean she had to blame herself for not following suit?

"I'm glad your father's doing so well," Mr. Baker said. "That was quite a night for all of us."

"Is Mrs. Baker here?"

Mr. Baker called upstairs to his wife. When she came down, Diana felt somewhat relieved to see what she identified as a faintly guilty look, as if (however involuntarily) Mrs. Baker recognized some responsibility for the role she'd played in Diana's thoughts. It hadn't all been a figment of Diana's overheated imagination.

"I wanted to tell you that I was sorry for the trouble I caused the night we went to the folk festival."

"Well, it was a bad night all around," Mrs. Baker said, relinquishing her claim to the note of self-righteousness her husband had struck.

"That's what I said," he added. "The point is, everyone's survived in one piece. That's the important thing."

"Except that you and Nathan have to talk before we go."

"When are you leaving?" Diana asked, hoping it was going to be any minute. Or an hour ago.

"In a few days," Mr. Baker said. "The summer session's over tomorrow, and since your parents decided not to give the party and things are finished here, we thought we'd leave you all in peace as soon as we could."

The Bakers went upstairs and Diana went into the renovated living room. The change was complete and remarkable. The new plaster walls were a gleaming white; the trim around the windows had been painted dark green. The complexity of the work that went into the room had all disappeared behind its attractive, simple appearance. The furniture was back in place, the striped rug

returned to the floor. Wood was stacked neatly in the fireplace. Diana liked what had been done, but it was still too
new for her to feel at ease.

"Hi," said Nathan from the doorway.

She turned, though she averted her face as if she expected him to hit her. Nathan radiated veiled difficulty
which she sent her private detectives to investigate. In
the meantime, she could not speak.

"You've really been shitty," Nathan declared, folding
his arms in front of him like an Indian brave. She could
not help noticing once more what an amazing physical
specimen he was. He was again wearing track shorts,
which were filled by his watermelon-size thighs. The
longer she looked at them, the more she had to concede
what powerful tree trunks those thighs were; and yet how
charmingly his knee withdrew beneath the flap above it,
like a sightless eye beneath an arch.

"I'm sorry," she offered, hearing herself repeat these
words but feeling she was doomed to repeat them to no
avail.

"I guess it's hard to be a rich kid. Or maybe it's hard to
be a WASP. Or maybe the real difficulty is having a father who worked for the CIA."

"Why were you so nice to him if you didn't like him?"

"I never said I didn't like him."

"You still acted funny in front of him," she said. Then,
in a killer flash of insight she added, "You acted like you
wanted him to like you. You acted like he was a king and
you were trying to get a job dusting his throne."

"I don't approve of the things he did officially, but I
still think he's an amazing example of his class, his type.
How do you account for your own lack of WASP graces?"

"He was shitty to me," she cried, leaping to her own
defense. She deeply resented being attacked for not being

as good as her father when she felt her father was available to other people's children, but not his own. Her sense of injustice flared, lighting the situation with sudden, unexpected clarity.

"Do you realize that's the first real thing you've ever told me about yourself?" he said.

The fact that it was, and the fact that she had never said anything before, found their places quickly in the connections now appearing in her mind. Nathan's social sensitivity before his political enemy, her rawness about her father: twins. They both felt like victims of other people's power. Yet she had also secretly depended on the gold standard of her parent's position in the world. She'd been arrogant but powerless as well. She thought of her cycles of tantrums and passive obedience, of how she'd flip-flopped between absolute rebellion and complete submission. In the midst of her incoherent core, she realized that her father was a man of a certain class, from a certain period of history. If there was an explanation that could lead to forgiveness, it was along this road.

"I may be a Marxist," she breathed, dazed by having her personal raw materials transformed into products such as others she'd seen in the market. Could it be she had something in common with the people of this world? Like Don Juan, who had never been in love, she had known many theories and, until now, never truly been moved by one. Even now, her grasp on the connection was fading.

"Fat chance," said Nathan. "You're about as much of a Marxist as Santa Claus is."

"I wouldn't be so sure. I may be the leading Marxist of Saunderstown, Rhode Island. I may be ripe for full conversion, and you may have missed your chance."

"No, no and yes. There will be no opportunity for me

to persuade you to see there's a better way of doing things. Not because I don't want to see another convert to the cause, but because I don't want to see you anymore."

"Thank you, Nathan, I needed that."

They measured each other in silence. She guessed he was physically the type of man she'd always be attracted to: big and muscular like a lifeguard. She admired heft in a man's physique. She wondered if a man would ever love her. She wondered if she would ever love a man. She wondered what love was. And though she knew there was none lost between her and Nathan, she was grateful for having known him. Hadn't her mother and her friends always gone around saying, "Never marry the first man you fall in love with." Translating very loosely to make it fall in the vicinity of her own experience, Diana thought that perhaps the version of the motto for her own time should be: "There's no reason to suspect everyone who comes along."

"Do you like to write letters?" she asked, or, rather, heard her own voice inquire.

"I'm not going to write you," he answered. One wrong turn deserves another.

"I didn't ask you to. I was just asking a simple question, completely in the abstract. Do you like to write letters?"

"Sometimes."

"Same here," she said and left it at that. Skipping the totally hypocritical (not to mention improbable) kiss on the cheek, as well as the rather ridiculous manly handshake, Diana slipped past him in the double doorway and made an uninterrupted dash down the corridor and out the kitchen.

It was great to be out of prison! The air had never tasted so good. It was almost like drinking the purest water. But what was this? Not a hint of fall? Diana hated the seasons to change. She didn't even like the day to be done. She longed for some heavenly monotony, some ecstatic sameness that would tide her over the next few eons. But now that she was a Marxist, wasn't her job cut out for her? She could put on her blue jeans and go to demonstrations, help bring down the stinking old U.S. Government. The place where Dad used to work.

And yet, when she tried to remember what it had felt like to feel like a Marxist, she could not revive the vision with anything close to pristine clarity. She thought back to the moment when her cycle of tantrums and obedience had so vividly struck her as the reverses of a single fish. She rebelled as blindly as she obeyed; either way she was irresponsible, responding to her sense of oppression without really changing her powerless position. That was what she had seen in her Marxist moment: how power was behind the power on the throne; how power ruled by force, through class and sex. The only way to fight back was through morality!

But what was moral, she wondered now, reentering the barn. And what, exactly, was the connection among force, class and sex? She felt a squirming in different areas of her emotions, but no headline proclaiming the fixed, eternal score. And what about this beautiful green silk sofa here in the corridor? Her affections for it were in another world from the realm of feelings that had lined up on the barricades. She loved the beautiful things in her parents' house. And now a whole balloon was swelling in her heart, filled with arguments about the preservation of great works of art. Stop the revolution, I want to get off! It wasn't just that she cared for art (in fact, she wasn't even sure she liked the "Mona Lisa"), it was more that the sofa had always been in the front hall. Surely, some things must be stable. She loved this house and all the things in it. In the absence of a hometown, the barn was the only center she had for her tender feelings. Tender feelings? Don't tell me you're going to lay claim to tender feelings? Tut tut, Diana Nicholas, the ever-truthful, art thou going to lie and say you care about anything? But she did care! Enormously! Now that she had to carry a gun and join the revolution, strong, protective feelings for her parents rose in her breast. She discovered love of home, of the back forty, of friends and family. (Hadn't she even felt stirrings of her soul? Maybe she was a Christian, not a Marxist. Maybe she was both.)

She was confused. She could remember that she'd seen things line up politically, but she could not recapture the argument, particularly since whatever the argument was had given rise to emotions she had not known she had and certainly could not uproot at a moment's notice. The hell with it. Forget force. Forget morality. I'm going to settle back down to my usual pattern of fragmentation.

About 20 percent of the time she took on the characteristics of whoever she was talking to, and during this 20 percent she also felt herself to be more the gender of the person she was becoming—be it male or female. Another 20 percent of the time she forgot completely who she was, though in this phase she was more susceptible to sexual desire, and literally thought she would melt, dissolved by sheer, unspecified lust. Apparently, when she was most characterless she was sexually hungriest, and the next truth was that this 20 percent lust could stretch to 100 percent if she wasn't careful, and then it was like running a raging fever, and she could think of nothing else and, yes, you know what the records show. However, an intense 9 percent of embarrassment could swell to a 60 percent majority and punish her severely for being (a) so obsessed with sex, and (b) so masculine. Diana read about 10 percent of the time, slept about 33⅓ percent. Approximately 15 percent of her day was spent looking at herself psychoanalytically and seeing herself divided into a team of her father's qualities and a team of her mother's. It was easier to be an amateur psychoanalyst than it was to be an armchair Marxist. The middle-aged professor on the outskirts of her mind picked up more psychological jargon than revolutionary hype. She was finally compelled to admit she was a lapsed Marxist, and that she might never find her faith again. One problem was that she couldn't remember why the faith had been important. On the other hand, if she just stopped reading those trashy novels and devoted herself to the study of Marx . . .

16

"Hello? Hi, Ellie," Joanne said somewhat wearily. "No, it's not a bad time to call. No, really. If I sound a little flat, it's because things have been hectic . . . He's better, he's resting. Oh, you saw Frank Harsh. He told you his son and Katherine were getting married? Well, they may, but he's jumping the gun . . . No, Ellie, it's not a bad time to call, but what's on your mind, sweetie? How are things? Well, we *were* giving a party. Didn't you get an invitation?" Joanne wrote a note to herself to send Ellie Snow an invitation, then remembered, "I asked you at the very beginning of the summer. You've just forgotten. But the fact is we've called it off. I mean we've called the party off," she said, and knew from the quality of Ellie's silence that something else was required. "But why don't you come that weekend? We haven't seen you in ages, Ellie. Come, we'd love it," Joanne said, crossing out her reminder. "OK? Done? Great. We'll see you then. We can't wait."

Joanne returned the receiver softly to the kitchen phone. She should have been prepared for Ellie's call. Joanne had made the foolish mistake of forgetting that she was life's voodoo doll. A pin had been taken out when Diana assured her (*finally*) that she was not pregnant. Another pin had just been stuck in a fresh spot. Now they had to contend with Ellie Snow on top of everything else. With apologies to her guardian angel, Joanne unstoppered the scotch (all the while actually seeing her page for that day marred by a terrible black mark for drinking hard liquor at lunchtime). There was simply too much pressure in too many places to insist on keeping these little rules. It was right that Ellie should come, but tiring to contemplate her.

Joanne took her glass out to the back porch and leaned over the railing, taking in her favorite view of the fields. She hunched her shoulders, then lowered them to relax in the warm August sun. Fortified and reassured, Joanne gave herself to the lush, dreamy landscape. Every second was a gift. Summer was a miracle, rescued with her husband's survival. It was as though the whole planet were tied to him, as though by coming through his disaster Christopher had brought everything back to life. She was keenly attuned to the gift of the sky, her marigolds and the rugged pines randomly growing at the bottom of the lower meadow. She felt the wings of her own happiness beating against the forces of discouragement (the scotch helped), her feelings rising up through her, through the landscape, through the universe.

She sat down as though to anchor her flying spirit. The screen door slammed and an open newspaper appeared, followed by Diana, who was deep in the middle section. Joanne's eyes brushed the headlines about the Texas Tower, but she'd already heard the story on the radio in the car. She didn't want to read more about the perfect young man, a model son, with a record of straight A's, a quiet, cooperative, modest boy who'd gone up to the top of the tower in Austin and opened fire in the crowd milling around below. (Imagine: you are on your way to get groceries, thinking about your list—milk, butter, eggs, ap— BLAM!) Why?

Diana sat next to her mother in a chair by the table. She began reading aloud: "The horror is over. The grief has just begun. Experts are asking why a boy with an outstanding record of achievement would do such a thing." She peeked out quickly at her mother, then dove back behind the front pages.

Joanne knew what was coming. Tomorrow's headlines would no doubt announce "The Failure of the Boy's Mother; How His Father Undermined Him All His Life." Automatically, her heart began to churn with sympathy, to ache for the boy's parents, for the boy, for the people he'd killed, for all their sorrow.

And yet, though her system of self-laceration switched on, nothing could stop the train of her bliss. It was coming through, scattering her guilts like chickens in its path. But who am I to be ecstatic? Doesn't matter, you are. But this joy is just an insult to the miseries of others. Shut up, it is. On and on came the train, steaming through her resistance, bringing her into a brilliant unity with the lacy silhouette of apple boughs. She gladly died into the plain, dry rocks in the field, becoming their plainness, their beauty. She *was* the stone wall, its homeliness and its beauty. Her ecstasy was her private work of art, seizing on the works of art before her eyes. But now the work was done. The train was gone, leaving her empty, almost bereft.

"Authorities say that Whitman typifies a familiar pattern of success achieved at too great a price. He worked under a pressure which finally broke him." Diana peered over the newspapers again, saying, "Sound like someone you know? He had a nervous breakdown. He freaked out."

"I think the country's having a nervous breakdown."

"I think I'm having a nervous breakdown."

"You're out of your mind."

"That's the second time someone's told me I was crazy when I said I was crazy. It doesn't make sense. Why don't you feel sorry for me?"

"Well, I hope you aren't trying to tell me you freaked out under the pressure of succeeding. Because you haven't even *tried* to solve your problems yet. If I'd seen you struggle to change, even if you'd just tried to get a job, I'd feel for your setbacks. But I haven't seen you reach that point."

"Aren't you glad I wasn't the guy in the Texas Tower?"

"I certainly am," said Joanne. "But it's nothing for *you* to be proud of. It's no credit to you that you aren't a maniac. Well, that you aren't a dangerous maniac. You're pretty maniacal in your own right. But you can improve, I know you can. And you're going to start by talking to your father about what you're going to do next year."

"Why not just have an exterminator come over and spray me with something that will kill me instantly?"

"Don't be silly," Joanne said while rising. "Let me go see if he's awake." She went into their bedroom. Christopher was sitting up in bed in his bathrobe, doing a crossword puzzle. "Diana wants to come and talk about next year . . ."

"Wants?"

"Wants."

Joanne returned to the porch, where she confided to Diana, "Come on. He said he was just thinking of you when I went in to ask if we could come talk."

Then she crossed her fingers, knowing the diplomat's tricks could fail and leave negotiations more nakedly exposed and aggravated than if they'd never been sprinkled with illusions of sweetness. There was a moment of silence when she felt her groundwork had been for naught. As they came into the bedroom, Christopher wore a look of determined blankness and Joanne was afraid it meant he was going to treat their visit as a complete surprise, requiring Diana to ask him for his attention—the very thing Joanne had claimed was already given. But then Christopher started the discussion, and Joanne realized his assumed innocence related to his daughter's body. He was not going to mention it, though he referred to her "night on the town, so to speak."

Diana seated herself in the chair by the window; her mother sat at the desk, watching and smoking a cigarette which, for some reason, tasted and smelled deliciously like dry leaves burning on an autumn afternoon.

"Well," said Christopher, "I guess we have a turning point in our midst. I mean, we've both got a turning point," he added, throwing his hands up in twin stop signals. (Don't get me wrong, his palms cried; I'm not saying anything about you that I'm not also saying about myself.) "I gather we've both had our night on the town, so to speak, day of infamy, comeuppance, what have you. Just that I know while I was having my disaster you were having yours, which I only mention so we need never bring it up again. It being great that it's over, and that you've now found out where you draw the line." As he said this, he clapped his hands and lowered his eyes to his toes, which he wiggled under the blanket. "In my own case, I've done a lot of thinking about how I got involved to the degree I did in ventures which were perhaps, in the last analysis, not entirely wise. And, you know," he continued, giving his "*et alors*" look, hunching his shoulders and thrusting out his lower lip, "you know, it's funny. I saw a lot of a certain type of guy of which I would say that I am a pretty good example. It's basically a type schooled in religious idealism even though no one's religious anymore. We were out to serve the Christian Absolute, which is why we felt justified in our dirty tricks. But it also isn't that simple. I went to Groton, as we all know, and was supposedly taught to believe, or maybe I mean I was taught supposed belief. I imitated everything about faith, all the spiritual disciplines—self-denial, fidelity, dedication—but it was hollow. I wanted to believe. I pretended to myself that I did, but it was false. I think that slowly but surely the falseness began to shine through my acts and to make them false, too. The truth triumphed, but the truth was awful. . . ."

Christopher paused, frowning as if he were searching for what he was going to say next. Joanne, the Moderator, tested the atmosphere to see how much more of Christopher's confession it could bear. She didn't really like to talk about the hard truths or facts of her husband's career anymore than he liked to talk about his daughter's period. Equality depended on being equally in the dark about the work they didn't share. Hearing him talk critically about his career made her simultaneously aware of its importance to him and its failure in the world. She wanted his work to be invisible in private but publicly respected. She started to say she thought that religion was somewhat off the point of what Diana was going to do when they got back to Washington, but her daughter spoke for herself.

"I didn't think you were good, but I thought you were absolute."

"Come again?" asked Christopher.

"Well, just that men were like this absolute police force because we had to do what you told us to."

"I never told you to do anything," Christopher protested. "I thought *that* was the problem. The absentee-father problem."

"But you were always hanging over my head. Even if I didn't know exactly what you expected, I knew I had to live up to your expectations. Maybe it was worse because they were vague. There was no way of ever knowing if I had pleased you. Thanks, Dad, thanks a lot. I'd just like to mention that I stuck up for you when people criticized the CIA."

"Well, I've stuck up for you, too. When your headmistress wrote and said you were crazy, I wrote and told her you were a rebel who thought for yourself."

"You did?" asked Joanne. The last thing she remembered was a talk at the beginning of the summer; that was when he protested the headmistress' idea of sending Diana to a psychiatrist, but he hadn't mentioned writing the woman to tell her what he thought of her suggestion. It gave Joanne the vaguely unpleasant feeling of finding the tables turned, of having a glimpse of what it would be like if he were much closer to the children. She wasn't jealous, exactly, but she was something very close to it.

"About the only thing I have done this summer is to move a few of those papers off my desk."

"You mean you don't mind if I never marry, don't have children and become the first lady President?" Diana asked.

"I wouldn't want it for my mother or my wife," Christopher said. "But maybe it's OK for my daughter. Next, I suppose, you'll want to get into Skull and Bones."

"Are you kidding? I think all that stuff is the height of corn."

"Well, you're wrong," Christopher said. "It's a fine club, and only the very best get tapped. You'd be lucky to get asked."

"But then she'd be lucky to get into Yale," Joanne pointed out, and could have cut off her tongue. She had meant to bring the conversation back to the point, or had thought that was what she meant to do, but bitchiness had crept in and she knew it. She also knew why. It annoyed her to have Christopher indulge Diana's waywardness. The last thing Diana needed was to be congratulated for being a delinquent. It wasn't fair to people who struggled to maintain their self-control—people, well, people like Joanne herself, who had powerful urges but suppressed them for the sake of her marriage and children and, yes, society. Then generosity triumphed and Joanne said, "I think I'm jealous. I've gone through life pushing my problems down, trying not to cause trouble. But now Diana's going to do it all differently and get away with it. If she doesn't have to get married, she can be as selfish as she damn well pleases."

"You didn't *have* to get married," Christopher said in a hurt tone. "We wanted to get married."

"That's true. I haven't forgotten, sweetie, really I haven't."

"And even if she doesn't have to get married, she has to make a decision about next year. Seriously, Diana, what are you going to do about your higher education? You need training. You've got to face that fact one of these days."

"How about the school of hard knocks, the college of my compulsions?"

"Oh, please, Diana," Joanne sighed, not even faintly amused. "You don't need to know your compulsions any better than you already do."

Diana thumped her chest, saying, "My teachers are here, inside my soul. I go forth to learn their names!"

"Envy, sloth, lust, greed, pride and avarice," her father said. "I forget the seventh."

"Those may be the names of the teachers inside your chest," Diana persisted. "But mine are . . . mine are truth, beauty, slime and Harry."

"That's enough!" Christopher cried, driven to lay down the law. "If you want to live at home, you have to get a job or go back to school. Which is it?"

"I'll go back to school," Diana said wearily.

"Now comes the hard part," Christopher said. "Now we have to find a place that will take you. This may not be easy."

17

Any chump knew school was a whole lot cushier than a secretarial job—which was all that Diana could hope for in her state of unpreparedness. Actually, with her nonexistent skills, she'd be doing well to get a job as a secretary. She'd have to bank on becoming a World-Famous Dishwasher if she didn't take the postgraduate year her father recommended. (Recommended, my eye! Required! Commanded!) He was now working on where she was going to go, and kept her posted on his progress. He had a friend of a friend who ran a school for problem students in Pennsylvania. But he had also talked to the people at

Madeira. Though Diana realized she would have to take whatever she could get, she balked at the idea of going through senior year with kids who'd only been second graders when she was in third. Too bad, said Dad.

Well, at least she did not have a tantrum. As the family vacation neared its end, about a week after the Bakers had gone Diana began to feel irritated. She hated moving, though she'd done it a million times, and she hated the signs that they were moving. She despised the cardboard cartons that were piled in the garage, ready to be packed. Whenever she noticed some new object put away for the winter, Diana felt a hole had been torn in her side, revealing the bottomless instability in everything. One afternoon she went upstairs and found her mother happily washing champagne glasses, wrapping them in newspaper and stacking the bundles in a box.

"Guess what?" Joanne asked cheerfully.

"What?" Diana asked gloomily, knowing she was going to hear bad news; it would have to be if it was about moving, which she feared it definitely was.

"We've rented this house for the whole year. No more students. We decided to make some money, and we've found a nice wealthy doctor and his family to live here at great expense."

"Oh, no. Why did you tell me that? I don't like strangers to be in our house. I hate to think of them telling jokes I probably wouldn't laugh at. It makes me feel like I've died."

"Well, it means your father and I can travel for a while, and I know you're going to like your nice new winter coat."

"No I'm not," Diana groused, ready to cry. She felt the way she had years ago, just after they'd moved from Providence to Washington and her parents suddenly announced they'd *sold* the house in Providence. Can you imagine? SOLD!! She couldn't believe it. She'd cried for days. How could they betray a place like that? And here they were, betraying this house and her feelings for it all over again.

"Hey!" came a familiar thug greeting.

"Hey, Chace," Diana responded, livening up a little. "Whenja get here?"

"You mean, when-did-you-get-here," her mother corrected lightly, enunciating the words Diana had slurred.

"Just drove in. Hey, Mrs. Nicholas," he said, rolling toward her like a sailor on leave.

"Have you got Herr Muehler?" Joanne asked, tilting her cheek for a kiss.

"Yeah, and we got the bear suit, too. I know you called the party off, but we figured we'd have a good time anyway. Right?" he asked and laughed, showing Diana his bizarre canines. When he laughed, he looked like a lovable werewolf.

Diana found him irresistible. She had always been in love with him, with his high coloring and freckled skin, his strong but gracefully modeled limbs, his pleasing, delicately angled hands. He was her type, that was all there was to it. (Hey, wait a minute, I thought whosie, whatsisname, Nathan was your type. Well, many are called, but few are chosen.) And she was just going to have to be big enough, noble enough, to renounce her feelings. He was Katherine's; Katherine was his. She happened to know they were engaged to be engaged, as some cornballs would put it. They would probably make it official next spring. Some people had all the luck. She wasn't one of them.

Now she was really irritated.

"You've come to the right place on the right day,"

Joanne said with a delicious appreciative purr in her voice. She obviously found Chace irresistible, too, but she used her seductive arts to cultivate a platonic flirtation, a genre beyond Diana's ability. Not only that, but how come Chace had all the luck? Diana wouldn't have minded being the object of a few of her mother's velvety pats.

"Ellie Snow's coming today—you know her, Chace," Joanne continued. "She's an old friend of your parents, and the thing she loves best in the whole world is a party."

"How would you like to wear the costume, Diana? Ya wanna be a bear?" Chace asked sweetly, telling her he was aware of her doldrum.

Unfortunately, it was all or nothing for her. She couldn't be like her mother and channel her love into something delicious but reasonable. Either Diana was just going to let herself go and become Chace completely and be consumed by her love, or she was going to go sulk in her room, though she said as she went, "Yeah, well, I don't know if I wanna be a bear. Maybe. I'll see later, OK?"

She was completely cross, furious about having to be good in a way which couldn't be seen. Chace didn't know she'd selflessly renounced her love, and neither did Katherine. She wasn't getting anywhere being virtuous; she wasn't even going to change the world. All of this on top of moving! A person could become incensed over life's refusal to be clear-cut and her own inability to develop a few rules and regulations that might make her happier. Then, as though Diana's irritation came to her in person, one of the most terrifying people she had ever seen walked into her room.

To say this stringy woman with frizzy hair was a walking case of irritation was to put it mildly. So mildly, in fact, it was to lie, to willfully deny the concentration-camp thinness of this wretched creature, the bluish-red of her complexion—like the color of underdone steak. No, this was the spirit of electrocution come to walk the earth, here to give the remaining prisoners something to look forward to. This was a person who had been through hell, and who, having been crucified by the devil, had quite a sense of humor. She had been to the Revlon counter and bought makeup worthy of the most dilapidated bag lady in New York City. On top of the true underdone steak of her complexion, she had slapped on blotches of pancake makeup; a trembling hand had painted wavy lines of black around her eyes. Her lids were greasy blue. She had shoveled lipstick on her lips, which, in their looseness, reminded Diana of the sort of baggy bloomers women used to don as underwear.

"Who are you?" Diana asked.

"More to the point, who are you?" the woman cracked out of the side of her mouth. "I'd say you had your fa-ther's body and your mother's face, or is it your mother's body and your father's face. In any case, darling girl, you remind me of both of them. So where do I find *mein* host and hostess? Hear your dad's had quite a time. Of course, those buggers in Washington use people like Kleenex, and your father was just the sort of bright, idealistic golden boy who thought he was going to give the world what for without taking it in the ear. Lucky for him your mother's a gem. And after that first wife, Joanne was the right woman at the right time. Let me tell you, they don't make 'em like that anymore. But look, sweetie, I've got to take a wicked piss. Don't just sit there. Where the hell are your parents? Look a little lively, kid, and take me to your leaders."

Diana obeyed. She slipped between the hag and the door and led her upstairs, calling, "Mummy? Mum? There's someone here to see you."

"Jo-anne?" the hag called merrily. "Jo-anne, darling girl, I'm here."

Joanne came out of her bedroom with her arms extended (though she was careful to close the door behind her), saying Ellie's name and enfolding the old broom in a warm embrace. When she held the witch away from her, Diana saw how chastened Ellie was by this welcome. The woman's manner broke, revealing an orphan with melting eyes in a tragic mask. And then, in another instant, the manner was back. She began to squawk like a parrot, as demanding and wisecracking and vulgar as a bird trained by an old sea dog. "Joanne, darling girl, it's time for my bath. I have to have four hot ones a day. It's my doctor's newest technique for my back, not to mention my drinking problem. You know what they say. Four baths a day keep the DTs away."

"OK, sweetie, we've got you set up downstairs in the guest room, which has a bath all to itself. You can take as many baths as you want." Joanne started to sweep Ellie down, away from the bedroom, saying, "Christopher's been looking forward so to seeing you. And he's going to get up for dinner, so why don't we go down and get you unpacked and you can have your bath before we eat."

Again Ellie's manner broke and she said vulnerably, "How is he really, Joanne?"

Joanne put her arm around Ellie's shoulder. Within the embrace Ellie seemed pathetic and doll-like to Diana, hardly the incarnation of terror she had first appeared. "We're taking good care of him, Ellie. He's not as fit as I'd like him to be, but he's better."

Diana watched the two women descend, one survivor

and one victim, and she ran to the kitchen, where she thought she'd find Katherine and Chace. They were there, and Diana said pell-mell, "God Almighty, wait until you see Ellie Snow, who just got here. You won't believe it. I didn't recognize her. She's a hundred times scarier than the last time she was here."

Katherine looked up from the Triscuits she was buttering and asked, "Wasn't that the time she got drunk at lunch and threatened to slug mummy when she tried to take her out of the room?"

"Right. That was the time we made a pact never to grow up like any of the grown-ups we know."

"I remember that," said Katherine, slapping Diana's hand as she tried to filch a cracker. "But whatever happened to my childish dreams? Ai-yi-yi! I'm just a single girl headed down the garden path to marriage like any other grown-up. Chace, it's all over between us. I have to go invent radium."

"Yeah, well, uh, you'd really be doing well if you turned out like your mother," Chace said.

"Yeah, well, uh, I guess we all know why you like her so much," Diana grumbled.

"Yeah, I guess we do," Chace said dreamily, looking off into space, probably recalling Joanne's many velvety taps and pats.

"You just wait until the revolution's come," Diana said. "And Mum's been working in a factory for a while. I guess she won't be all smooches and lovey-dovey caresses then!"

"I guess not," Chace sighed.

Everyone slowly assembled before the meal, adults and children, but the real meeting was between Ellie and Christopher. Of these two, he was the first into the living room, dressed as he would have always dressed for sum-

mer dinner—in slacks and a shirt and jacket, but no tie.
Then Diana saw that he was also wearing leather
slippers, and she was conscious of how these changed him
from a vacationing man of the world into an invalid. His
step was subtly altered, too, and to a degree which made
his efforts to hide his slight infirmity more noticeable.
Diana would have said he was being incredibly brave if
she'd been accustomed to thinking he had anything to be
brave about. His frailty still came as a complete surprise
to her, and when she saw him pouring tomato juice as his
cocktail, she felt a quiver of fury—as if he was carrying
this all just a little too far. She could remember him having martinis before dinner, and throwing his coat in the
air, and jumping around the room clicking his heels. Sure
his career had come to a bad end, sure he'd had a heart
attack, but did that mean he had to act like other people
in the same position?

Diana's emotions soon changed to wariness. Ellie Snow
was tottering down the hall toward the living room, looking a little refreshed from her bath. She had on a fancy
flowered silk dress that at least drew attention away from
her short hair sticking up on end all over her head.
Diana's mother was rising from her chair to go and bring
the new guest into the circle, but there was another note
in the air. Her mother was presenting Ellie to Christopher, as if she were literally a gift (some gift!). But that
wasn't all. Diana strained to perceive what else was happening, feeling jealousy close on her detective's heels.
Was this an old girl friend of her father's? If so, why was
her mother sacrificing herself, giving the ex-bride away,
so to speak?

No, this was not an old romance, this was more surprising, more devastating. Christopher turned now, having
seen his wife leave, and having known, probably from the

click all heels made in the corridor, that someone was there, turned with the naked look of a robber caught opening a safe. It was not so much that he looked guilty but that he looked as if he knew the game was up. And then Diana saw that Ellie had a similar expression—the proud, vulnerable, hesitating face of one who had something bad to tell a person whose forgiveness she wanted. These two were old friends, Diana realized, old *friends* who'd known each other deeply along illusionless lines. They knew they'd become the kinds of wrecks they'd once pooh-poohed in their untarnished, impeccable youth. They both waited for the other to be the first to show the white flag.

You could have knocked Diana over with a feather. She was thrown for one big loop. Reading her impressions as they came in over the wires, she wondered if her senses had lost their minds. To begin with, grown-ups didn't have friends that counted. They went out to dinner a lot, but they didn't have friends the way, say, Diana had Katherine and Chace. Next, her father was the sort of busy man who had no interest in the opinion of women, except maybe his wife, and then only when she agreed with him. But the situation at the front was changing fast, and there was no time for the home office to quarrel with the eyewitnesses.

There was a second when Christopher and Ellie took each other in, another second while they registered the changes, and then, putting their hands on one another's shoulders, they bent over, closing a heart-shaped space and decorously kissing on the mouth. They held each other away for another searching glance, and again Diana couldn't believe what she was seeing. There was incredible power in the fact that these two had known each other for so long and were now hoisting in the latest installment of one another's lives. There was a special tang to their exchange, the clear, vinegary evaluation of equals held in balance on the seesaw of friendship.

Joanne closed their encounter by sweeping Ellie into the group and introducing her to Chace and Herr Muehler. The latter showed an immediate interest in this new addition and maneuvered openly so that he was sitting next to her.

"Drink?" he asked, raising his glass.

"No," she said. "It makes me gaga."

"Me also!" he exclaimed. Then he touched his finger to the side of his nose and said solemnly, "You have been through so much, darling. You have been through the wars."

"As a matter of fact, buster, you're right. I *have* been through the wars," she cackled appreciatively, giving him a sexy once over.

"Which ones?" he asked.

"You name it. Booze, pills, divorce, craziness, suicide. I won that last one by mistake. Bad aim with a razor blade." She held out a thin wrist with scars x-ing the top of the forearm. "Maybe I didn't really want to win. Missed on purpose, you could say."

"But no bombs or guns or torture chambers?"

"None of that, and if you're going to tell me that I shouldn't complain, honey, I agree with you. Compared to having your head blown off in a trench or going to prison for what you think—compared to those, getting shock treatments is probably a picnic. But I didn't bring the subject up, remember? You asked me. I didn't cry in my beer."

"Oh my darling," Herr Muehler said tenderly. "I have only kindness for your sorrows. I want to hear about them."

"You really want to hear about them? Well, where shall we start? Back five years ago, just about the last time I was here? I'll tell you everything I remember, which isn't much. I was with Höltz then, around the time that my mother died. She was from Colorado originally, so we rented a hearse and trucked her in and figured we'd go on to San Francisco after we dropped her off. We had her in the casket, along with a case of gin . . ."

On and on she went, sailing through the tale of the drunken trip across the country, her arrest and drying out, how awful Höltz seemed when she met him in the clear light of day, how she got addicted to uppers because being sober was such a downer. On and on, through her stay in institutions, her attempted suicide, her different doctors. Though she held everybody spellbound, Joanne began to go in and out of the kitchen, bringing in the clam chowder and the bowls and calling everyone to come to the table.

"I know, I know," Ellie said, getting up from the sofa. "I've gone on too long."

Actually, the picaresque tale had imparted a cockeyed gaiety to the little party. As they sat down to their soup, Ellie started to describe another scene and found she had inspired a whole chorus of helpers. "Christopher," she began. "Remember the old story you told me years ago? It's about two great men—two great New Englanders?"

"Maybe it was Bucky and Christopher Nicholas," chimed a voice.

"No, Emerson and Melville," chimed another.

"You know the story I mean?" Ellie asked. "One of the great men goes to jail for not paying his taxes."

"It was Stalin and Gandhi, I remember now," cried Diana.

"God, this really requires grace. I mean, this is pressure."

"Grathe under prethure, oh no," Bucky squeaked in the persona of his index finger. "Get her out quick. She'll be crushed!"

"That, my boy, is enough," Ellie said, encouraging him to the hilt.

"Back to the story," Christopher said. "Quick! While no one's listening."

"Reminds me of the time . . ."

"Anyway, there's a war on or something . . ."

"It's definitely Gandhi and Stalin."

"One great man goes to jail for not paying his taxes, and the other great man comes to visit him."

"That was nice."

"And the guy on the outside says to the guy on the inside, 'What are you doing in there, Mahatma?' But the guy on the inside turns it around and says, 'What are you doing out *there?*'"

"You remind me of the monastery," Herr Muehler said. "I was always looking out the window and wondering what I was doing inside."

Katherine and Diana took away plates, kibitzing and complaining and begging Ellie not to finish the story until the next course had been served.

"What story?" asked Ellie. "I'm so confused about who is telling what, I hardly know what's going on."

"Well, this all began because you wanted to remind Christopher of that story so you could tell him one like it," Joanne explained. "How something that happened to you was like Stalin and Gandhi."

The girls were now bringing in the plates with spaghetti combined with haddock and chutney. It was a dish Joanne had brought with her from her mother's kitchen.

Because of the chutney's rusty colors, and the contrast of hot and cool, it was a recipe which always reminded Diana of the autumn. Eating the fish and noodles and condiment somehow reassured her about the arrival of a new season, as if by finding an echo of it in the meal she had rediscovered the familiarity hidden in the strangeness all along.

Conversation, having wandered afield once again, came back to the point Ellie tried to make in the beginning. "All I wanted to say before I was so rudely interrupted— so rudely interrupted so many times—all I wanted to say, Christopher, was that I often had the feeling in the nut-house, when the keepers came along and shut me in for the night, I often wondered what they were doing out there. Most of them were ten times crazier than I was. Crazier and meaner. And I often thought of you, Christopher, and of how you and I would have laughed our heads off if we'd been in the nuthouse together. It would have been fun."

He chuckled, worldly and rueful, but touched by cynical relish, too. "We've all gone to pot, Ellie. You know what my big project is now. I'm doing a study on whether to let girls into Skull and Bones, my old secret society."

"Don't do us any favors, sweetie," Ellie said and looked at Joanne.

"He wouldn't, not on your life," was Joanne's reply.

"Do you realize I can't finally think of one good reason to keep women out? Equal rights are equal rights. But this is it, fellas. This is the end of civilization as we have known it."

"But aren't you glad?" asked Ellie.

"Maybe, but how is Skunk Armour going to feel when he finds out the girls have chased him all the way into the only place where he ever got any privacy?"

"SKUNK ARMOUR!!" hooted Ellie. "I haven't thought of him in years. Not since the last time I kissed him. Is he still alive?"

"Was he ever?" Joanne asked, and the three of them giggled like children.

Then Joanne said to Diana, "Where's that bear costume? Go put it on for Ellie."

Diana went down to the study where Chace and Herr Muehler would sleep. She took the beast off its hanger in the closet and struggled into it, finding it incredibly hot; but as she grew used to the heat, it was wonderful—like a sauna, purifying and intense. When she came back into the living room, Herr Muehler had put on a Beatles record and was waiting to dance with Diana. Despite the bulk of the costume, she felt light on her feet (all the while feeling 8.9 percent in love with Chace and wishing he loved her, the beast, instead of Katherine, the beauty). Herr Muehler twirled her with a deft comedy that brought gales of laughter from the little audience. The bear's head wobbled on her own, and Diana stretched out her furry arms, maneuvering beneath the heavy head like a seal trying to balance a bottle on its nose. More laughter, and she saw her father and Ellie pulled back in their chairs, sitting side by side.

How sad they seemed, but how gallant. Diana dipped, bending her knees, then finding Herr Muehler behind her, holding the paws as if she were a ballerina and keeping time to the music by tapping his worn, polished shoe on the floor beside her. Still gazing at her battered father and his battered old friend, Diana suddenly, cruelly felt a rush of confidence. They were old, done for, done in, but it didn't have to be that way. She reached out both paws to the company at the table, and slowly but surely one by one, they all came and filled the space with movement.

Her mother rose from her seat, looping one arm around Bucky's shoulder and taking his hand, laughing lightly as she always did when a man resisted her. She drew him out onto the floor, and all the while Bucky looked the way he did when she dragged him to art museums; but Diana also saw a barely defended tenderness in her brother's expression and it sparked her own mother worship. Live forever, Mum, goddess of fun and feeling! Taking Herr Muehler by the hand, Diana went and cut in on Joanne and Bucky, and they danced in a circle of four. Her brother shot her a silly, half-hostile look, but he was visible on another level to Diana behind the mask. The advantage of being in costume was seeing without being seen. The self within the bear she seemed to be could see the sweetheart within Bucky's momentary appearance as toughie.

She had doubled back again! By bringing her beastliness into the open, she turned it into another facade. There was no escape from duplicity. But there was having a good time and hero worship. In the end, the mind feels, the bones know. Chace and Katherine joined the dancers. Katherine held Diana's paw. Inside her hot bear head Diana dreamed high-mindedly, as Katherine would if Diana really was her sister, which she might just really be in the life beneath the life behind appearances. Who could say? Anything was possible.

Now her father and Ellie came into the circle, her father smiling in an exposed, sheepish way. The grin of a man who had once been a gifted athlete and now was wounded, fallen, so that he danced carefully, carefully for fear of hurting himself further. Ellie danced gently, stiffly, tentatively, like one who had never been energetic—as if she had never won the Charleston contest at the Stork Club in 1942. Watching her now, Diana noticed her poor, skinny legs all covered with small burns. They were scary and repellent, hard to explain. The shape of the cigarette burns. Deliberate? It was OK. Her father and Ellie were done for, done in. She would have taken them up in a bear hug, except that they were too fragile for such rough mercies. They had been harshly used by history; she was going to ride its back and take them with her, up over the hardships that had crushed them.

Stop the revolution, I want to get on again. O brothers and sisters in the human agony, Diana the Bear says, it's not against the law to hope. Try it, you'll like it. Diana the Bear says we're all in it together, that the dance has just begun.